THE
VIETNAM
GUIDEBOOK

The First Comprehensive Guide for
Tourists and Business Travelers

THE AUTHOR

BARBARA COHEN, M.D., served as a major with the US Army Medical Corps in Vietnam from 1970 to 1971 and was awarded the Bronze Star. Her service was as a psychiatrist at the 95th Evacuation Hospital in Danang ("China Beach"). Over the years she has traveled to Vietnam many times and currently is working on a novel that presents the Vietnam War from a Vietnamese point of view. She is, in addition, completing travel guides to Cambodia and Laos. Dr. Cohen lives and maintains a private practice of psychiatry in Northern California.

THE
VIETNAM
GUIDEBOOK

*The First Comprehensive New Guide
to Vietnam
with Angkor Wat*

Barbara Cohen
Foreword by Fredric M. Kaplan

HARPER & ROW, PUBLISHERS, INC.
New York

EURASIA PRESS
Teaneck, New Jersey

FIRST EDITION, 1990
First Printing

Typography by David E. Seham Associates, Inc. Vietnamese typography by Sunrise Printing, San Jose, California. Text set in Goudy Old Style.
Downtown city maps cartography by Dennis Wozniac, Burlingame, CA; Haiphong and administrative region maps cartography by Machiko Terada, Foster City, CA; and the remainder of maps cartography by Jan Brent.

Produced by Eurasia Press, 168 State Street, Teaneck, NJ 07666-3516

Library of Congress Cataloging-in-Publication Data

Cohen, Barbara
    The Vietnam guidebook : the first comprehensive new guide to Vietnam, with Angkor Wat / by Barbara Cohen ; foreword by Fredric M. Kaplan.
        p.   cm.
    Includes bibliographical references.
    ISBN 0-06-096464-2
    1. Vietnam—Description and travel—1975-   —Guide-books. 2. Angkor Wat—Description—Guide-books. I. Title.
DS556.25.C64 1990
915.9704′44—dc20
                                                                                    89-45790

90 91 92 93 10 9 8 7 6 5 4 3 2 1

CONTENTS

I ◼ VIETNAM AT A GLANCE

II ◼ MAKING THE DECISION TO TRAVEL TO VIETNAM

III ▣ TRAVELING IN VIETNAM

DE GUSTIBUS IN HANOI
By Fredric M. Kaplan / 196

IV ▣ THE VIETNAM TOUR: CITIES AND SITES

9
CONTENTS

10
CONTENTS

11
CONTENTS

FOREWORD

For most Americans, Vietnam remains a difficult, if not precarious, subject. The Vietnam War, as a topic of discussion, has been conspicuously avoided for much of the 14-year period since the war ended. Only in the past few years—beginning perhaps with the dedication of the Vietnam Memorial Monument in Washington, D.C.—have people begun to look back at the war and talk about it, often directly engaging US veterans of the conflict.

But despite the passage of 14 years (16 years from the official US troop withdrawal), important issues connected to the war remain unresolved. Unanswered questions about unaccounted-for US prisoners-of-war and soldiers missing in action continue to inflict needless anguish and suffering on affected families, friends, and countrymen. Vietnam's political and military posture within the region raises questions about that country's international strategies. And although it seems less traumatized by the conflict, America remains confused, angered, and still exhausted by the war's gnawing complexity and by painful memories of what happened there.

This book is a deliberate attempt to move past the war and its implications in the belief that the war does not speak sufficiently for the country of Vietnam and its people. In 1990, Vietnam is a country of realities that extend beyond the war. With a population of over 60 million, Vietnam represents a major part of Southeast Asia. Its land—with most of its physical wounds beginning to heal—gives the impression of a lush tropical pastorale, superficially peaceful, and its people, although poor—even in comparison with their regional neighbors—seem busy, accepting, and cordial.

Many of its ancient traditions—Buddhism, reverence for the past and scholarship, brillant handicrafts, and mixtures of strong ritualized belief systems—are surprisingly intact. The people appear to be more the products of an ancient enduring civilization than of the militancies and brutalities of recent decades. These people inhabit tropical forests, cool mountain ramparts, and exquisite beaches and coastal strands.

Admittedly, there are also terrible economic and financial problems. Even an official tour guide published in Hanoi in 1988 alludes to an "unstable infrastructure worsened by a long war." But these conditions have also led to the recent opening to tourism as a new source of foreign exchange. Whatever the underlying motives, the welcome to tourists "from all over the world" seems genuine and unabashedly friendly.

This book is offered to its readers in the belief that Vietnam is worth a visit. It is a country of great beauty, interest, and substance. Vietnam in 1990 is beginning to find its way back into the international community. That progress, for many people, should be worth watching.

Fredric M. Kaplan

INTRODUCTION

*"I used to see Vietnam as a war rather than
a country."*

—John Pilger, Do You Remember
Vietnam?

ATV Network Production, October 3,
1978

About the size of New Mexico, the diminutive land of Vietnam is 12 hours' flying time from San Francisco. Most Westerners, especially an entire generation of Americans, know Vietnam through the one-dimensional and unavoidably distorted lens of a televised war. Although postwar Vietnam had been inaccessible to Westerners for some time, the government of the Socialist Republic of Vietnam approved general tourism in 1987. This official open-door policy invites each of us to experience personally all of the dimensions of Vietnam—its people and its rich, ancient culture.

I first visited Vietnam with the United States Army Medical Corps in Danang, where I treated psychiatric casualties. I say "visited," but "visited" does not accurately express the essence of my year's tour of duty. Like many other women and men who served with the military in Vietnam during the later years of the conflict, I rarely left the confines of the barbed wire boundaries of the compound. Outside, road mines and sudden attacks by seemingly friendly people forced commanders to restrict our free-time travel. Consequently, our interaction with the local people was limited.

Upon my return to America, it struck me that I had not spent the year in an Asian country. For all practical purposes I had been a resident of a miniature, bizarrely distorted, and isolated piece of the States. I decided to address my ignorance about the Vietnam beyond the barbed wire. I began reading about the people, culture, and history. I discovered ample material on Vietnam, the war, but little concerning Vietnam, the country.

In 1987, I was invited to speak at an International Scientific Conference being held in Hanoi. In preparing for the trip, I discovered a conspicuous lack of resource material in English about that historic city halfway around the world. Then, in the latter part of 1988, I joined one of the first US tour groups to visit Vietnam under the country's new tourism program. On both visits, I kept notes about my frustrations, as well as the delightful surprises, hoping future travelers might profit from them. This is the book about Vietnam—the country, not the war—that I wished had been available to me before I embarked on those trips.

With over a thousand miles of pristine coastline and lush verdant mountains, Vietnam's main attraction remains its people's stubborn will to survive, which is so painfully entwined with that of the United States.

Readers interested in Asian history, in particular, will find information on historical sites helpful in planning their itinerary, while the armchair traveler can go globe-trotting in the imagination and enjoy the descriptions of life in present-day Vietnam. Veterans of the military may also find this book useful in discovering the fate of their former bases and hangouts.

Travel to Vietnam is recommended to the hardy and adventuresome, or for those who have previously encountered Asia. Although power outages and water turnoffs may occur occasionally, the opportunity to observe, firsthand, the determined struggle of postwar reconstruction is worth a few inconveniences.

Tourist accommodations are equivalent to economy hotels in the US. Travelers are made to feel welcome and safe by the enthusiasm of guides assigned by Vietnamtourism, the official tourist agency of the country. Expect to encounter differing points of view on history, but little "propagandizing" on the merits of socialism. In all likelihood, you will not be dragged through tours of cooperative farms and factories—although spending an afternoon at a cooperative would certainly be educational.

In addition to organized sightseeing, tourists are permitted to explore the cities freely, and alone—an ideal way to get a feel for the people and their way of life. Visitors to any foreign country are likely to see what they are prepared to see. As perception has a major bearing on the experience of reality, it's a good idea to keep an open mind and try to leave one's preconceptions at home.

Travel to Vietnam is neither illegal nor unpatriotic. I am aware of the controversial and sometimes painful feelings aroused by the word *Vietnam* and the lingering suffering experienced by many as a result of the tumultuous political events of recent decades. I do not attempt to address the policies, inefficiencies, or shortcomings of the Socialist Republic of Vietnam, nor its future relations to other countries. On balance, this book does not deny evidence that the socialist state has work to accomplish regarding tolerance of dissention and individual freedoms. It is my hope this guidebook will provide a starting place to understand Vietnam—a country, not a war.

Although every effort has been made to ensure the timeliness of the information contained here, some details may be already out of date. I would appreciate hearing from readers who have suggestions, additions, or corrections that will enhance the usefulness of this guide. I will gladly incorporate appropriate updates in future editions.

Many thanks to my friends Jade Le, Thanh Mougeot, and Luyen Truong. Each of them has added to the depth of my knowledge about their homeland. I acknowledge Terry H. Anderson of Texas A & M and John Boyle of Chico State University for their helpful suggestions and for pointing out inaccuracies in early drafts. Joanna Williams of the University of California, Berkeley, and Nancy Volk of the University of Wisconsin, Madison, reviewed and substantially enhanced chapters in their fields. Special recognition goes to Jeffrey Barlow of Lewis and Clark College who, in addition to enhancing my knowledge, has "field tested" a draft on a lecture tour.

I also thank Beatrice and William Eisman, Jerry Di Giacomo, James Do, Joe Connors, and Betty Johnson. I acknowledge the assistance of Kathy Johnson and Don Cantor of the San Mateo Veterans' Readjustment Center, James Mayock, immigration attorney, and Ted Engleman of Multicultural Educational Exchange. I wish to express gratitude to Marie Therese Maramrie and Jacqueline O'Mahony of UNESCO.

I would like to acknowledge the enthusiastic contributions of the editors and writers provided by Eurasia Press. Their patience enabled the transformation of my scribbled notes into a readable text. Maxwell Eden and Debra Dunn deserve special mention.

The bulk of the maps were rendered by Jan Brent. Downtown city maps were drawn by Dennis Wozniac; the Haiphong and the administrative region maps by Machiko Terada.

I

VIETNAM AT
A GLANCE

VIETNAM'S PEOPLE

POPULATION

Despite long years of war, famine, emigration, and strong birth control efforts, Vietnam is one of the world's most densely populated countries. The first scientifically conducted nationwide census, taken in 1979 with the help of the United Nations Fund for Population Activities, calculated the population at 53 million.

In 1982, the government set a goal of a 1.7% national birth rate by 1986. The birth rate in 1988, however, was closer to 3%—nearly double the stated objective. Hanoi, the capital city of Vietnam, for example, contains 3,640 persons per square mile (1,400/sq. km.). Since Vietnam's vital registration system is still incomplete, all birth and death rates are approximate. The April 21, 1989, issue of *Asiaweek* estimated the population of Vietnam at 67.4 million as of January 1989.

Substantially more than half of the people live in lowland provinces of the Red River and the Mekong deltas. These provinces combined make up 24% of the country's area, the flat Red River delta being more heavily populated than the Mekong. Massive ongoing national public instructional efforts continue to encourage population shifts to less populated areas designated as "New Economic Zones."

URBAN LIFESTYLES

Twenty percent of the population live in cities. The country's three major cities, Hanoi, Haiphong, and Ho Chi Minh City (formerly Saigon), are large metropolitan urban centers organized into self-administrating units called municipalities.

Apartment Life. Most city-dwelling families live in apartments with two or three rooms attached to a small kitchen and toilet. On average, this space is shared by four or more persons: parents, two children, and often grandparents. Since rooms are multipurpose, furniture is kept to a minimum. In Southeast Asian fashion, a family will sit on the floor around a low table for meals. Shopping for fresh fish and vegetables is a daily affair—although small refrigerators are found in many private homes. Toilets in city homes are generally Western style with some locations still requiring that water be poured manually into the bowl for flushing.

Old market, Cholon

The central section of a traditional home is devoted to the ancestor's altar. Candlesticks, incense, decorative scrolls, and the ancestor tablets surround the in-house family memorial. The revered tablets are inscribed with the names of up to four generations of ancestors who look down from heaven upon the affairs of the household. Today's urban apartment is more likely to reserve a place of respect for a likeness of Ho Chi Minh rather than for an ancestor's altar. In the countryside, however, perpetuating a family shrine continues to persist.

Street scene, Hanoi commercial sector

Child Care. Working parents with children living in the city face the same economic difficulties as do their Western counterparts. Child-care centers for working mothers are increasingly available since few Vietnamese women can afford the luxury of working exclusively as housewives. After school, many urban children attend classes sponsored by the Young Pioneers (a scouting type organization fostering patriotism and socialist values) held at a Children's Palace, institutions specifically created to provide after-school enrichment programs for children of government workers. In the evening, adults may attend literacy courses, or work at a second trade, usually in the "free market," to supplement the family's income.

Urban Dress. Southern Vietnam has been heavily influenced by the earlier presence of the French and Americans. Consequently, the people of the South are more Western in their manners and style of dress than those of the North. Men and youth of both sexes now prefer jeans or trousers; few mature women wear skirts or dresses, preferring loose-fitting trousers. Thongs and sandals are commonplace, even in cities. Baseball caps inscribed with the logos of foreign businesses and sports clubs are favorite items among men. On a special occasion, a Vietnamese woman might wear the traditional costume, the *ao dai* (pronounced "ow zai"), a full-length, high-necked tunic slit to the waist and worn over white or black satin pants. Feminine high-heeled sandals called *quoc* (pronounced "kwook") complete the *ao dai* ensemble.

In spite of hot, humid weather (year-round in the South), it is not culturally acceptable for women to wear shorts (which presents no problem for rural men). From the Vietnamese point of view, especially in the eyes of the older generation, shorts on Caucasians are associated with the tropical clothing worn by the French, a vivid reminder of foreign occupation. On the practical side, children are permitted to wear shorts because they require less fabric and are therefore less expensive to manufacture than long pants. Since Hanoi and the North experience cold winters, scarves, hats, and sweaters are popular.

Street Life. Storefront doors along a typical busy boulevard are kept wide open to encourage shopping by the steady stream of passersby. Street vendors, especially numerous in the warmer South, routinely set up their businesses on the sidewalks. While traffic in Ho Chi Minh City is dominated by bicycles and motorized scooters, it is common to see oxen pulling loads on the streets of the capital city of Hanoi.

Dawn throughout the country brings out groups of older citizens who assemble quietly on empty streets to practice graceful Tai Chi exercises. Later, the tranquility of early morning shifts into a higher gear. Peaceful avenues in the south are taken over by people riding to work on bicycles and scooters, while commuters in Hanoi rush to make their bus and trolley car connections.

City Pastimes. The Vietnamese people love to gamble. Tickets for the state-sponsored lottery called Xo So are sold at local street stalls. A 25-cent ticket can win the equivalent of US$15,000, a veritable fortune in Vietnam. Clandestine betting—the So De or

Tram car, Hanoi

"People's Lottery,"—works off the state lottery and has the advantage of offering a wider range of bets.

Cafés are often the casual setting for men engrossed in a card game called *tam cuc*. A deck consists of 36 elongated cards, each featuring a Chinese word and picture, and contains two kings, ten soldiers, four generals, and four each of deer, horses, elephants, wagons, and cannons. Young adults also enjoy a night out at a café conversing and drinking strong coffee or eating *che*, a sweet pudding dessert. Recreation for children frequently takes place on the sidewalk where they play simple card games, jump rope, and toss coins. Watching television, not yet commonplace, is considered a special treat when available. A family that has acquired a television set will often invite neighbors to view programs for a small fee.

Lottery ticket seller

RURAL LIFESTYLES

Village Life. The overwhelming majority, 85%, of Vietnamese people live in rural villages. Consisting of several hamlets often surrounded by a thick hedge of protective bamboo, the village has always been the basic unit of Vietnamese society. The *dinh*, a combined temple and community center, occupies the center of a typical village. In addition to its established functions, a present-day *dinh* may be utilized as a hamlet (also called a Production Brigade by the government) administrative office, cooperative headquarters, public information center, or clinic.

Rush mats drying, Nhatrang

Country life is simple and follows a rhythm based on natural cycles such as sowing the seeds in spring, transplanting after the first rains, and harvesting in the fall. Many rural areas are still without electricity, and bedtime comes early because even oil and candles are expensive. For the most part, the socialization of the economy in the north has most northern farmers working on communes. The south, however, still harbors privately owned farms. Southerners engage in "free enterprise" by selling or bartering products such as vegetables, peanuts, or eggs at centrally located outdoor markets.

Country Homes. It is customary for several generations to share the same living quarters. The houses, usually three to five rooms, are built of local materials—mainly bamboo, wood, straw, and, more recently, bricks or baked clay taken from surrounding fields. Roofs are covered with palm-leaf thatch. Beds are spartan, elevated wooden structures covered with rush mats. Toilet facilities are located outside, sometimes built over a pond, and far from the main house. Near the house is the family's vegetable garden, which often includes some medicinal plants and perhaps a small fish pond. Fresh water is obtained from a nearby stream, town, or private well.

Rural Fare. The farmer's diet is simple, consisting primarily of a rice base combined with other grains, sweet potato, and manioc. Fresh vegetables and fish are also staples. On many days, the fare of the day consists entirely of rice and vegetables flavored with fish sauce.

Country Dress. Men and women wear loose-fitting cotton tops and dark pants. Shoes, even thongs, have little use in the muddy fields and are considered a luxury by some rural dwellers. Both sexes wear a wide, conical-shaped hat that offers protection from the sun and rain.

Leisure. Government policy urges that festive occasions such as weddings and the Lunar New Year be celebrated in a sober and non-extravagant manner. Condoned diversions include conversations with neighbors, playing cards, and other games. Although not gastronomically lavish by Western standards, a chicken or pig is slaughtered for a feast commemorating a special holiday.

Following a long day's labor in the field, a man might settle back with a familiar after-dinner habit such as a pipe or cigarette, while a woman might delight in chewing a quid of betel. A betel chew is made up of several ingredients: betel leaf, slivers of the areca palm nut, and a lime paste. The pieces of nut covered with lime paste are wrapped in a leaf, making a tiny package that fits neatly into the cheek pouch. The quid, as the entire package is called, contains a mild stimulant and an anesthetic that relieves toothaches while simultaneously suppressing the appetite.

NORTHERN FOLK TRADITIONS

Tooth Blackening. For centuries, upper-class Vietnamese in the North considered the display of natural white teeth by women to be shocking and uncivilized. To accommodate this cultural taste, girls reaching puberty underwent ritualistic blackening of their front teeth. Although betel chewing does stain the mouth and teeth, blackening the front teeth involved a more effective process that called for mixing the sap of the Lac tree with lemon. Spread evenly over the teeth before bedtime, the mixture was allowed to set overnight. By morning, the mouth would swell up to the extent that no food could be taken for days. The first application turned the teeth red and a second application left them permanently black. In addition to the desired darkened appearance, the black coating provided protection against loss from decay. When exposed to the French distaste for blackened teeth, many Vietnamese families stopped the practice. Today, the wide smiles of many older women are indelible reminders of this exotic but discontinued practice.

Water Puppetry. First surfacing in the water-rich areas of Hanoi as early as the tenth century, the *roi nuoc,* or water puppetry, is a uniquely northern Vietnamese art-form especially designed for depicting scenes from rural life and many episodes of national history. Later, interest in water puppetry expanded under the explosion of arts encouraged by the Tran Dynasty. Although considered an art-form of the "village pond" (or, of the common people), water puppetry shows were performed at royal celebrations such as the crowning of a queen or the birthday of a king. Two historic water puppetry stages, the Giong and the Thay, built during the 15th century in Hanoi, are preserved today.

Water puppetry is performed in the open air using a pond as the stage. The audience sits in front of the stage on the water's edge. Standing waist deep in the water, the puppeteers, or manipulators, deftly control the wooden puppets from the concealed manipulators' room with rods, wires, and strings hidden under the surface of the water.

The pond is a not only a natural setting for blending illusion with reality, the water also amplifies stage sounds for a natural ste-

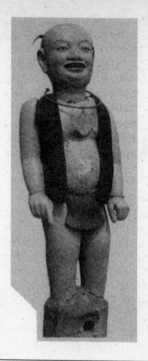

Water puppet Teu, the clown, introduces puppet shows with satirical humor

reophonic effect. Nearby trees, the blue sky, and the occasional passing cloud are reflected in the water, adding enchantment to the liquid stage. In the hands of master manipulators, stiff, lacquered wooden puppets, about 18 to 36 inches high, are magically transformed into graceful characters that walk on the water. Puppets appear unexpectedly from the aquatic stage and then, just as suddenly, disappear in a flash to the delight of the audience.

Harvesting of the Ruoi. The *ruoi* is a flat, bristly annelid (segmented worm), narrower in width than a chopstick and up to a yard (more than a meter) long. It thrives in the mud at junctions of fresh river water and salty seawater found in northern Vietnam. Harvesting the worms is possible only on two days of the year—on the 20th day of the eighth moon (September) and the fifth day of the 10th moon (November)—when they come to the surface to reproduce.

The worms are quickly scooped up in nets (Vietnam's version of the "grunion running" of Southern California) and later boiled so the bristles fall off.

Ruoi is a delicacy when sauteed with pickled onions and mandarin orange peel. If part of the harvest cannot be eaten immediately, the remainder is made into a sauce using a process similar to preparing *Nuoc Mam*, a fish sauce widely used throughout Vietnam. The desirable worm inspired a saying in the North: "Some must put up with the storm, others can eat *ruoi*." A close translation is advice couched in the phrase "If life gives you lemons, make lemonade."

The Quan Ho Ritual. Ritual peasant folk songs called *Quan Ho* are popular in villages throughout the Northern Highlands, especially in Ha Bac province during the spring. *Quan Ho* is an opportunity for young men and women from neighboring villages to meet one another. The boys of one village will be invited to sing "against" the girls of another. Typically, the boy's team will start singing (*a cappella*) a theme, usually earthy and having to do with courting. The girls are expected to respond quickly with lyrically witty double entendres and puns.

An example of a typical exchange of verses invented during the courting ritual:

"Let us enjoy ourselves before we grow old.
The young bamboo blooms for only a brief time.
Human beings are young once only.
Let us take advantage of that springtime blooming before age approaches with grim footsteps."

Sexual meanings are thinly disguised when the singer refers to flowers and bees. A boy might ask if a girl is available for courting by singing:

"Let me ask the apricot flower:
Is there a path leading to the garden where you are growing?"

The girl in question may respond positively by singing:

"The path to the apricot blossoms is marked with bamboo hedges so bees can easily find their way."

Or she may respond to the advance teasingly:

Men, how much are they worth? Just three pennies a dozen. One puts them in a cage and plays with them."

The words can get quite explicit and everyone in the audience, including grandmothers, let their hair down by shouting bawdy responses. The song continues by alternating—that is, one boy sings, then one girl—each responding to the previous singer's lead, and so on. Marriage engagements frequently follow the ritual of *Quan Ho*.

ETHNIC GROUPS

The Viet, or Kinh (Kinh is also the name for the Vietnamese language), account for 88% of the country's population and are concentrated mainly in the delta of the Red River, the central coastal plains, and the Mekong delta. In addition to the Kinh, the remaining 12% (in excess of five million) of the people include 53 distinct nationalities. These minority groups live mostly in the mountainous areas, stretching from the north to the south of Vietnam, which covers two-thirds of the country.

Highlander groups are distinguishable by their language, dress, and by physical features. The Hoa, the largest minority group of Vietnam, includes ethnic Chinese, who tend to live in the cities, and a subgroup called the Meo. Exact numbers of the Hoa population, many of whom left after Vietnam's break with China in 1979, are unavailable.

ETHNIC MINORITIES OF THE NORTH

Most of the ethnic minority groups of North Vietnam are descendants of emigrants from southern China. They still live in mountainous areas and retain the distinctive physical features of their forebears. These minorities fall into several distinct groups defined by their language.

Tai-Kadai Speakers. The largest minority group of the far North speak Tai-Kadai and include the Red, White, and Black Tai (also called Zao or Dao, but not "Tho" as they were once named, which is considered pejorative) who had settled along the broad river valleys to cultivate rice. The Zao population of 200,000 is divided into 30 groups. A typical Tai village consists of 20 to 50 families. In addition to farming, the Tai work as traders and caravan organizers.

---

*For a list of ethnic minorities of the Socialist Republic of Vietnam, see the Appendix Section.

Young women of Tonkin with gold beads, turn of the century

Among the three groups, the Red Tai (who live in the mountains of Thanh Hoa Province) women have the brightest costumes, with bright red turbans and tight bodices decorated with images of fish, birds, monkeys, and tiny silver beads that twinkle with every movement. Red Tai men's clothing is less distinctively colored. White and Black Tai (who live between the Black and the Red rivers) women wear long skirts and tight-fitting jackets buttoned in the front; a white jacket is worn among the former and black among the latter. The Tai people delight in a vigorous and lively form of dance music.

Tai-Kadai, or Zao, parents tell their children the legend of their canine ancestor, Ban Ho, the marvelous, powerful, five-colored dog who killed an enemy general. For his bravery, the dog was rewarded by a marriage to a princess who later gave birth to the 12 Zao families or tribes. To remind them of their heritage, the Tai-Kadai women will weave the five colors of the sacred dog into the fabric of skirts and bodices. In some instances, a special article of clothing will feature an embroidered likeness of the remarkable Ban Ho.

The Nung are another Tai-speaking group who live near the Chinese border, about 100 miles (160 km.) north and northeast of Hanoi, between Cao Bang and Lang Son. The Nung and the Tai minority have similar social organizations, strongly influenced by Chinese traditions such as inheritance going from the father to eldest son, who lives in his father's house after marriage. After the father's death, the eldest son takes the father's position of authority. In spite of laws against polygamy, the practice still exists among the Nung—primarily among the wealthy.

In their attempt to forge a formidable military counter-balance against the communist Viet Minh during the Second World War, the French sponsored the Tai Federation (a coalition of several northern Tai clans whose men served the French as local militia and border guards), knowing they could exploit the Nung's tribal sense of freedom from lowlander rule. The American involvement in Vietnam once again enlisted the Nung into military duty as guards and guides for the US Special Forces.

The Tay are a Tai minority group who live in the north and northeast of the Red River delta along the Lo River. Their special form of writing, in use in lowland Vietnam until the 16th century, suggests the Tay descended from a clan exiled from the capital city to the highlands at that time.

The Austro-Asiatic Speakers. The second largest ethnic minority after the Tai speakers is the Muong who live to the west and south of Hanoi around Hoa Binh and Thanh Hoa. They reside in long houses set upon stilts. Their dialect is similar to Kinh, the majority language of Vietnam. Despite an official government policy toward the "collectivization" of all lands, the Muong, who are expert farmers, still maintain private ownership of their traditional lands.

The Sino-Tibetan Speakers. Most of the minority groups of North Vietnam are descendants of migrants from China (some groups came to Vietnam hundreds of years ago and others in the

19th century), who now live in the mountainous areas of the country.

At one time, all the hill people in Vietnam from China were called Man. Today, the many names applied to subdivisions of this umbrella group make isolating and identifying them difficult. Living primarily in the western section of the far north of Vietnam, the Man (they resemble southern Chinese) also inhabit areas of Laos and northern Thailand. The men dress like the Chinese of southern China and the women wear large silver necklaces of chains and tubes; in some Man tribes, the women wear skirts that are embroidered at the hem.

Relative newcomers who arrived from China in the 19th century, the nomadic Meo tribe are found along the Chinese border at high altitudes where they raise cows, pigs, and horses. They also cultivate beans, vegetables, fruits, and medicinal plants, including opium. The opium crop is rotated with maize, a process which seems to improve the quality of the opium subsequently planted. The raw opium, in the form of black gummy balls, is sold for processing into heroin for international sale. Although the Socialist Republic of Vietnam acknowledges the existence of a small opium crop for medicinal uses, the true extent of the opium culture in Vietnam is unknown. (The price of opium in Vietnam in 1988 was about US $105 per pound or $225 per kg.).

Meo women wear white skirts and distinctive short jackets with tight sleeves and large embroidered collars.

The Giay (Nhang) live in Haong Lien Son and Ha Tuyen provinces where they still practice ritualized bride kidnapping, a rigorous form of "giving the bride away." The groom's family dashes to the bride's house on horseback on the wedding day and "steals" the bride away from her family.

ETHNIC MINORITIES OF THE SOUTH

Most of the 33 minority groups in the South are descendants of peoples who lived in the area before the Kinh moved down from the North. Since many of the ethnic minority groups are nomadic, there is some overlapping of tribal boundaries between the north and south. Mon-Khmer and Malayo-Polynesian are the two main southern linguistic families.

The Malayo-Polynesian Speakers. Present-day Chams, numbering about 100,000, can be traced to the Malay race from the Kingdom of Champa that once occupied the coastal areas of the

Young women of the Giay ethnic minority in the northern highlands

south. Although the Cham people were overrun by the northern Viet (Kinh) expansionist forces in the 16th century, they continue to this day to maintain their Hindu and Islam derived customs; they have a written language that is similar to Sanskrit (India's ancient classical language) and a matriarchal social system where the women choose their husbands and distribute their property to their daughters. Because of linguistic similarities and physical resemblances to peoples of Indonesia and islands in the Pacific, the Chams and other Malayo-Polynesian-speaking people are believed to be descendants of settlers from those areas.

The Mon-Khmer Speakers. The more prevalent Mon-Khmer tongue is related to the language of Cambodia. The Khmer people, numbering 700,000 in Vietnam, are descendants of the ancient mighty Khmer empire (9th to 15th centuries) that once stretched from the coast of the South China Sea to the Indian Ocean, with its capital at Angkor (now in Cambodia).

The Highland Tribes. Tribal peoples of the southern highland regions live in scattered villages on the majestic high plateau near Dalat and Ban Me Thout. The people in the surrounding area of Dalat are Koho-speaking, a Mon-Khmer group that includes the Ma, Cil, Lat, Sre and Mnong ethnic clans. Spiritually, these people are animists, with some following kinship systems dominated by the father's family and others according to the mother's lineage.

Among the Koho, traditional dress for men included loincloths, necklaces, and pierced earlobes fitted with ivory plugs. Women wore long sarong skirts made from their own handwoven fabrics. Today, the men rarely wear loincloths, nor do the young people file down their teeth to make themselves more attractive to the opposite sex. Although the women still wear sarong skirts, they use ready-made cloth instead of weaving it themselves. Highlanders traditionally live in extended family groups in long houses of bamboo and thatch; over the years these dwellings have been replaced by more substantial wood structures with tin or tile roofs.

The Malayo-Polynesian speaking tribes called the Rhade, Gia Ria, and Munggar of the Kontum area in the southern highlands are considered the most ancient of the cultures inhabiting the Indochinese peninsula.

Of the 2.2 million nomadic farmers in Vietnam, many of the highland minority groups grow dry rice using a farming method called "slash and burn." This form of cultivation calls for cutting down and burning all the vegetation in a chosen field prior to planting the crop. When the fields begin to lose their fertility after a few years, they are abandoned and the tribe moves on to find new areas of the jungle to cultivate.

Since "slash and burn" agriculture by itinerant farmers has proven destructive to the forest, the government has begun to encourage highland minority groups to settle in fixed locations. Once resettled, tribal people are encouraged and aided by the government through education and projects such as irrigation to cultivate paddy rice and other commercial crops such as tea, coffee, or medicinal plants.

In addition to halting serious deforestation, restricting former nomadic clans into sedentary farming communities promotes increased educational levels, access to health facilities, and the integration of the highland people into the country's social and political structure. In attempting to initiate these changes within ingrained social patterns, the government has encountered resistance from the nonconformist highlanders, partly due to their traditional distrust of the lowlander Vietnamese majority.

VIETNAM'S GEOGRAPHY AND CLIMATE

Vietnam lies between the Tropic of Cancer and the Equator. It is bounded on the west by Kampuchea (named once again as Cambodia in May 1989) and Laos, and on the north by China. Its more than 1,400 miles (2,254 km.) of pristine coastline are bathed by the warm, placid waters of the Gulf of Thailand to the south, the Pacific Ocean to the east, and the Gulf of Tonkin in the north. Vietnam is over 1,000 miles (1,600 km.) long and has an area of 128,000 square miles (332,800 sq. km.), making it a third smaller than California.

The country is elongated and narrow, vaguely tracing the shape of the letter S, with the population concentrated in the widened upper and lower regions of the Red and Mekong deltas. The narrowest point, the central "waist of the S," is less than 40 miles (64 km.) wide.

Hanoi lies at roughly the same latitude as Mexico City, with Ho Chi Minh City at the same level above the equator as Costa Rica. The 1,000 miles (1,750 km.) distance from Hanoi to Ho Chi Minh City is about the same as from Boston, Massachusetts, to Charleston, South Carolina.

PHYSICAL FEATURES

Stretching from north to south along the western section of the country, like the curvature of a spine, is the 750-mile-long (1,207-km.) Truong Son mountain range (formerly called the Annamite

Schoolchildren, Nhatrang Beach

Cordilla, or Chaine Annamitique). Its slopes are the source of many rivers that flow into the South China Sea. In some places, the mountains plummet directly into the sea, as in the majestically beautiful section between Hue and Danang called the Hai Van Pass, or "Pass of the Clouds." From this pass, the mountain range forms a large plateau (the High Plateau) 3,500 feet (1,068 m.) above sea level.

Most of the northern part of Vietnam, except for the Red River delta, is mountainous. The highest mountain in the country, Phan Si Pan, at 10,300 feet (3,000 m.), is in the north, west of the Red River at the Chinese border.

RIVERS AND ISLANDS

Rivers. Two great river systems cross Vietnam, the Red River in the north and the Mekong in the south.

One hundred years ago the course of the Mekong River was unknown to Westerners. In 1866, six Frenchman, led by Francis Garnier, formed an expedition to explore the Mekong. Although they were able to map over 4,000 miles (6,436 km.) of previously uncharted terrain, the river route did not lead to the heart of China as they had hoped.

Originating in eastern Tibet, the 2,800-mile-long (4,500-km.) Mekong River forms part of the border between Laos and Thailand, then crosses Laos, Cambodia, and Vietnam before emptying into the South China Sea. Several of its tributaries—for example, the Tien Giang River and the larger Hau Giang (Bassac) River—branch and flow through the Mekong delta. As it flows toward the sea, the Mekong branches off many times, giving rise to a local myth that called the river Cuu Long, or "nine dragons." The rich soil brought by these branches from the mountains during the annual floods makes the Mekong delta exceptionally well-suited for agriculture, especially for growing rice.

Because of Ton Le Sap, Cambodia's great natural reservoir, the Mekong plain never gets as dry as the northern Red River delta. Dikes, the main form of water control in the north, are unknown in the south, where the ebb and flow of the water levels has been achieved through a system of canals since ancient times.

Extending 250 miles (400 km.) into Vietnam, the Red River originates in the high plateau of Yunnan province where it flows to form a 30-mile (48-km.) stretch of border with China before descending into a narrow gorge just west of Hanoi. Later, the Lo (Clear) River and the Black River merge with the Red River that

Valley of Love, Dalat

wanders and branches through the Red River delta before finally
emptying into the Gulf of Tonkin. The Thai Binh River parallels
the Red River and joins the delta network 35 miles (56 km.) northwest of Haiphong. When the river systems in this area swell during
the heavy rains of the wet season, Haiphong and Hanoi are often
flooded.

Island Holdings. Vietnam has many islands. In the South China
Sea, Con Dao (formerly called Poulo Condor), was the once infamous Devil's Island of the French. Some islands are the focus of a
territorial dispute with China: the Paracels, 250 miles (400 km.) off
Danang, and the Spratley Islands, 400 miles (644 km.) off Vungtau
between Vietnam, the Philippines, and Malaysia. The dispute of

ownership is especially keen since it is believed these islands sit on valuable oil deposits.

Although there are no active volcanoes in Vietnam, there is some undersea offshore volcanic activity. Earthquakes are rare.

CLIMATE

Vietnam has a tropical monsoon climate. It follows an equatorial monsoon rainfall pattern of one wet and one dry season.

The north is battered by storms earlier and more fiercely than the south; from August to December, the coastal areas of the north are lashed by tropical storms. Because of its proximity to cold air swooping southward from China, Hanoi experiences a clearly defined winter (about 62° F (16.5° C) in January), contrasted with 100°F (38°C) temperatures during the hot and humid wet season from mid-May to mid-September.

Temperatures are less extreme in the south, on average remaining within the range of 78° to 84° F (26° to 29° C). The rainy season lasts from May to November. Weather patterns along the central highlands of the south include violent summer winds blowing eastward from Laos.

VIETNAM'S CLIMATE

Hanoi 53 ft (16 m) 21°02′N 105°52

	Temperature °F				Temperature °C				Relative humidity		Precipitation			
	Highest recorded	Average daily		Lowest recorded	Highest recorded	Average daily		Lowest recorded	1000 hours	1600 hours	Average monthly		Average no. days with 0.04 in +	
		max.	min.			max.	min.		%	%	in	mm	(1 mm +)	
J	92	68	56	42	33	20	13	6	78	68	0.7	18	7	J
F	94	69	58	43	34	21	14	6	82	70	1.1	28	13	F
M	98	74	63	53	37	23	17	12	83	76	1.5	38	15	M
A	103	82	69	50	39	28	20	10	83	75	3.2	81	14	A
M	109	90	74	60	43	32	23	16	77	69	7.7	196	15	M
J	104	92	78	69	40	33	26	21	78	71	9.4	239	14	J
J	104	91	78	71	40	33	26	22	79	72	12.7	323	15	J
A	101	90	78	70	38	32	26	21	82	75	13.5	343	16	A
S	99	88	76	63	37	31	24	17	79	73	10.0	254	14	S
O	96	84	71	57	36	29	22	14	75	69	3.9	99	9	O
N	97	78	64	44	36	26	18	7	74	68	1.7	43	7	N
D	98	72	59	44	37	22	15	7	75	67	0.8	20	7	D

VIETNAM'S GEOGRAPHY AND CLIMATE

Ho Chi Minh City (Saigon) 30 ft (9 m) 10°47′ N 106°42°

	Temperature °F				Temperature °C				Relative humidity		Precipitation			
	Highest recorded	Average daily		Lowest recorded	Highest recorded	Average daily		Lowest recorded	1000 hours	1600 hours	Average monthly		Average no. days with 0.04 in + (1 mm +)	
		max.	min.			max.	min.		%	%	in	mm		
J	98	89	70	57	37	32	21	14	69	61	0.6	15	2	J
F	102	91	71	61	39	33	22	16	66	56	0.1	3	1	F
M	103	93	74	64	39	34	23	18	63	58	0.5	13	2	M
A	104	95	76	68	40	35	24	20	63	60	1.7	43	4	A
M	102	92	76	70	39	33	24	21	71	71	8.7	221	16	M
J	100	89	75	69	38	32	24	21	77	78	13.0	330	21	J
J	94	88	75	67	34	31	24	19	79	80	12.4	315	23	J
A	95	88	75	68	35	31	24	20	77	78	10.6	269	21	A
S	96	88	74	69	36	31	23	21	78	80	13.2	335	21	S
O	94	88	74	68	34	31	23	20	77	80	10.6	269	20	O
N	95	87	73	64	35	31	23	18	74	75	4.5	114	11	N
D	97	87	71	57	36	31	22	14	72	68	2.2	56	7	D

Danang 10 ft (3 m) 16°05′ N 108°13′

	Temperature °F				Temperature °C				Relative humidity		Precipitation			
	Highest recorded	Average daily		Lowest recorded	Highest recorded	Average daily		Lowest recorded	1000 hours	1600 hours	Average monthly		Average no. days with 0.04 in + (1 mm +)	
		max.	min.			max.	min.		%	%	in	mm		
J	87	75	66	52	31	24	19	11	86		4.0	102	15	J
F	98	78	68	58	37	26	20	14	86		1.2	31	7	F
M	97	81	69	60	36	27	21	15	86		0.5	12	4	M
A	104	86	73	64	40	30	23	18	85		0.7	18	4	A
M	102	91	76	71	39	33	24	22	81		1.9	47	8	M
J	104	94	77	73	40	34	25	23	77		1.7	42	7	J
J	100	92	77	71	38	34	25	22	78		3.9	99	11	J
A	102	93	76	71	39	34	25	21	77		4.6	117	12	A
S	97	88	75	70	37	31	24	21	84		17.6	447	17	S
O	92	83	73	63	34	28	23	17	85		20.1	530	21	O
N	88	80	71	59	31	27	22	15	86		8.7	221	21	N
D	87	77	68	56	31	25	20	13	86		8.2	209	20	D

Source: Times Books world weather guide. Pearce, E. A. Times Books, New York, 1984.

HANOI'S CLIMATE — ELEVATION: 20

	TEMPERATURE					
	DAILY AVERAGE		MONTHLY EXTREME		REL. HUM.	PRECIPITATION (INCHES)
	MAX.	MIN.	MAX.	MIN.	10:00 A.M.	AVERAGE
J	68	58	92	42	78	0.8
F	69	58	94	43	82	1.2
M	74	63	98	53	83	2.5
A	82	69	103	50	83	3.6
M	90	74	109	60	77	4.1
J	92	78	104	69	78	11.2
J	91	78	104	71	79	11.9
A	90	78	101	70	82	15.2
S	88	76	99	63	79	10.0
O	84	71	96	57	75	3.5
N	78	64	97	44	74	2.6
D	72	59	98	44	75	2.8
Y	82	69	108	41	79	69.4

SAIGON'S CLIMATE — ELEVATION: 33

	TEMPERATURE					
	DAILY AVERAGE		MONTHLY EXTREME		REL. HUM.	PRECIPITATION (INCHES)
	MAX.	MIN.	MAX.	MIN.	10:00 A.M.	AVERAGE
J	89	70	98	57	69	0.6
F	91	71	102	61	66	0.1
M	93	74	103	64	63	0.5
A	95	76	104	68	63	1.7
M	92	76	102	70	71	8.7
J	89	75	100	69	77	13.0
J	88	75	95	67	79	12.4
A	88	75	95	68	77	10.6
S	88	74	96	69	78	13.2
O	88	74	94	68	77	10.6
N	87	73	95	64	74	4.5
D	87	71	97	57	72	2.2
Y	90	74	104	57	72	78.1

Source: The Weather Handbook

HISTORY OF VIETNAM

FROM ANCIENT TIMES TO 1954

THE AU LAC KINGDOM

Epic tales from a timeless past reveal that the genesis of the Vietnamese people began with a fantastic union between the powerful sea god, Lac Long Quan, and the lovely mountain goddess, Au Co. Of their 100 sons, half followed their father to his sea domain and the other 50 sons joined their mother in the mountains. These mountains were home to the legendary Hung kings who, according to the myth, descended from the mountain goddess, Au Co, and reigned over the Van Lang Kingdom (the area of present-day Hanoi), later named Au Lac.

To the southwest of Hanoi lies the Ma River valley, an ancient site where man appeared as early as the Paleolithic Age (300,000-500,000 BC). Recent archaeological finds have confirmed the existence of the Hung kings to the extent that they established a highly developed civilization called Phung Nguyen.

By the third millennium BC, the people of the valley, the Lac Viets (the Dong Son culture), had developed a highly complex and sophisticated society. The casting of a single Dong Son bronze drum by Lac Viet artisans, for example, required a knowledge of mining, metallurgy, and a technological proficiency capable of smelting large quantities of copper ore.

Toward the end of the Bronze Age, the Lac Viets, under the rule of King An Duong, lived and prospered on the plains at Co Loa, 10 miles (16 km.) north of Hanoi. The Vietnamese people recognize the ancient Lac Viets as their direct ancestors. Today, visitors can view remains of their ancient citadel at Co Loa.

Rugged mountain peaks, sheer limestone cliffs, and narrow gorges form natural obstacles along the northern and western borders of Vietnam. Added to these geological barriers, dense vegetation, tigers, panthers, fierce warrior tribesmen, and deadly malarial mosquitoes comprised a formidable array of deterrents to invasion. Despite these obstacles, foreigners streamed into Vietnam by carving out passable mountainous routes and hacking pathways that deepened over several thousand years. Eventually, the Yueh Chinese from southern China migrated to and settled in Vietnam's Red River delta area. Unable to resist the tide of emigration, the Auc Lac Kingdom was overtaken by the Chinese who later mingled with the indigenous Lac Viets.

HAN RULE

With the way already paved by the Yueh, Han Chinese military expeditions invaded the land of the Lac Viets where they set up regional administrative centers. These outposts were situated on hilltop fortifications surrounded by walls and moats with Chinese garrisons deployed to defend them. In 207 BC, the Chinese general Chao T'o reorganized the Red River area and portions of southeastern China into a single country called Nam Viet.

In 111 BC, the Han Dynasty completely annexed Nam Viet as a Chinese province called Giao Chi or Chiao Chih. The town of Luy Lau, southeast of present-day Hanoi, was the ancient capital of Giao Chi. Although subjugation meant having to pay taxes to the Han, the local citizens were also introduced to new forms of schooling, Chinese script, and Confucian administrative methods. The Chinese also showed their new subjects effective methods of cultivating rice and land development through dike construction.

TRUNG SISTERS' REVOLT

The grip of Chinese influence over Nam Viet weakened in the second century BC with sporadic rebellions resulting in brief periods of independence. Two well-known uprisings include the Trung Sisters who incited the people to revolt (AD 40-43) against the Chinese aggressors, and the moderately successful insurrection led by Ly Nam De (AD 544-602).

BACH DANG VICTORY

After Ly Nam De's brief reign, the Chinese once again regained control of Nam Viet, this time for several hundred years. In AD 939, a Vietnamese military genius, Ngo Quyen, altered history by defeating the occupying Tang Dynasty at the "Battle of the Bach Dang River." Ngo Quyen secretly riddled the river bed with spikes that, at high tide, lay undetected just beneath the water. As the Chinese fleet sailed confidently into the river to reinforce the troops in Hanoi, its ships were impaled on the hidden spikes. Immobilized, the Chinese warships, now easy targets for an ambush by Ngo Quyen's waiting army, were quickly defeated. The decisive engagement at Bach Dang River laid the foundation for the independent state of Vietnam. The first capital of Dai Co Viet, as the newly formed self-governing country was called, stood at Hoa Lu, southeast of present-day Hanoi.

Legacy for Today. A thousand years of Vietnamese independence lasted well into the 19th century. The long period of Chinese political and cultural domination in the northern part of Vietnam would not be erased by time. As a result, the North still retains many social characteristics in common with China such as Confucianism's legacy of administrative efficiency, which remained the model for the Vietnamese government until the French formed the country into colonial protectorates. The people also had a unique relationship with their emperor, who was not only a respected head-of-state but the father of the nation-family, and its high priest. This powerful love and awe toward an admired ruler remained characteristic of Northerners' feelings well into modern times, which explains why the revered Vietnamese patriot Ho Chi Minh was called "Uncle Ho."

INDEPENDENCE AND EARLY LE DYNASTY (AD 980-1009)

The early time of independence in the Red River valley is referred to as "the period of the twelve lords." This was an era of dissension, with autonomous clan leaders vying for ultimate control. Finally, one leader called Le rose to power. During the Early Le Dynasty, Buddhism flourished and was instrumental in unifying the government and improving education and the quality of daily life among the people.

LY DYNASTY (AD 1009-1225)

The Ly Dynasty offered its citizens the opportunity to rise in social station by founding a college in Hanoi (for civil servants called mandarins) based largely on the ability to pass required examinations; patronage and bribes for positions could not be eliminated entirely. Utilizing water management technology learned from their former Chinese oppressors, Vietnamese workers constructed irrigation projects that opened up vast areas for agriculture. Despite attacks from Chinese Sung Dynasty troops in the north and from the Champa empire at its southern border, the country experienced a period of internal stability. Under the rule of the Ly emperors, the Dynasty eventually expanded southward into the Kingdom of Champa.

TRAN DYNASTY (AD 1225-1400)

With the Mongol forces of conqueror Kubla Khan at their doorstep in the 13th century, Dai Viet (the state of Vietnam at the time) and Champa put aside differences and joined forces to resist their common enemy. Tran Hung Dao successfully defended Vietnam's capital city of Thang Long (present-day Hanoi) against Mongol attacks. The ingrained Vietnamese tenacity of will once again saved their homeland as the Tran reign withstood three invasions by several hundred thousand Mongols, the most feared guerrilla soldiers of their time.

CHINESE RETURN

In the late 14th century, Vietnam underwent a period of internal political disunity. Taking advantage of the discord, the opportunistic Ming emperors of China invaded Vietnam and re-established direct rule from AD 1407-1427. Again, the Vietnamese put aside political differences and joined forces under their leader, Le Loi, who, with the aid of the scholar and military genius Nguyen Trai, raised the banner of national resistance and forced the Chinese to withdraw after a ten-year struggle. The noble hero Le Loi founded the Later Le Dynasty, opening a new era of prosperity.

LATER LE DYNASTY (AD 1427-1789)

Although the Le Dynasty encouraged the arts, education, and especially land and social reform, its best known gift to the people was the creation of the most advanced legal code known in Southeast Asia at the time. With a growing cohesiveness, the Vietnamese once again pressed southward into the rich lands of Champa. Heavily influenced by Hinduism from India and later Islam, the Cham people (a race of Malay origin) were seafaring traders who lived in the south on the coastal strip of land between the mountains and the sea. The lush Kingdom of Champa once spread from above Hue in the north to the Mekong delta in the south.

The unremitting southern expansion or "drive south" into the land of the Chams was called *nam tien*, a form of Manifest Destiny. In 1471, the Cham people had been pushed back by the Vietnamese under Le Thanh Ton to a reduced kingdom, with its capital at Vijaya on the seacoast near present-day Nhatrang. By the mid-18th century, the Vietnamese kingdom had reached the Gulf of Thailand. Expansionism, however, did not eradicate the cultural differences between northern and southern Vietnam. To this day, people of the south, influenced by Hindu and Polynesian cultures, seem generally more easygoing and flexible, while northerners (as mentioned earlier) are more bound by Chinese-influenced Confucian thinking and ritualistic deference to authority.

RIVALRY BETWEEN THE TRINH AND NGUYEN CLANS

As the kingdom of Vietnam expanded southward in the 17th century, it became increasingly difficult for the Le Imperial government in the northern capital to exert direct control over its distant administrative centers in the south. With the Le emperor clearly in a weakened position of authority, the Trinh clan rose to power in the north (although still paying superficial homage to the now puppet emperor), seized land, and competed for leadership with another powerful aristocratic family, the Nguyen in the south.

WESTERN INFLUENCE IN VIETNAM

Portuguese Catholic missionaries, operating from Jesuit headquarters in Macao, had been teaching Christianity near Danang as early as 1550. Lured by the potential of riches in the spice trade, speculators formed the French East India Company to promote commerce with Southeast Asia. Trade began with Siam (Thailand), using the already established missionaries as go-betweens and translators. During the 16th century, European sea powers established trade with Indonesia, India, and China. Vietnam, however, remained closed to the West.

By the 17th century, French missionaries were converting entire Vietnamese villages, especially along the seacoast. In the main, the missionaries were welcomed by the emperors for their language skills, for their modern technical knowledge in such fields as medicine and astronomy, and, in some cases, for their access to arms. The new religion from the West, however, eroded the Confucian "Emperor-as-Deity" system and opened the country to subversive ideas from the "outside." Before long, the emperors feared Christianity might be the forerunner of foreign domination. Although they were not explicitly forbidden to preach, the priests were under constant surveillance, and conversion (by Vietnamese) to Christianity was considered an act of sedition by the suspicious imperial government.

THE TAY SON REVOLT

During this early time of European involvement in Asian affairs, the powerful Nguyen clan negotiated with the French and Portuguese for aid in their struggle with the Trinh, who, in turn, received arms and supplies from the Dutch. Under the reign of a powerless emperor, rivalry between the two feuding families exposed a scandalous, inept government, which in turn began a process that slowly eroded the social fiber of the country.

In early 1770, three brothers in central Vietnam led a revolt against the Nguyen family. The brothers called themselves the Tay Son, after their home village in Binh Dinh province. Their rebel movement gained in popularity among the restless, land-hungry peasants who were angry about corruption and land grabbing by wealthy mandarins. The Three Tay Son Brothers Movement spread decisively southward. When the revolutionary army finally captured Saigon, the defeated Nguyen survivors fled and were given protection by a French missionary, Pierre Georges Pigneau de Béhaine, Bishop of Adran. Restoring the surviving prince of the family, Nguyen Anh, to power became a personal mission for the Bishop.

The Tay Son rebels pressed north to take Hue. Nguyen Nhac, the oldest Tay Son brother, became ruler of the southern and central portions of the country. No sooner did the youngest Tay Son brother offer the emperor his services and loyalty, than Chinese troops arrived in Hanoi—either at the request of the disgruntled emperor or on their own—hoping to exploit the country's political unrest. Nguyen Van Hue, the youngest Tay Son brother, rushed his troops north to intercept the Chinese army. In a surprise attack on the eve of the Lunar New Year, he successfully routed the Chinese and became the new emperor, taking the imperial name of Quang Trung. His victory in the north ended the Trinh rule and united the country. He married the daughter of the emperor who had ruled the old dynasty from Hanoi. As emperor, Quang Trung set about reforming conditions for the peasants and liquidated the regimes of the feudal lords. But the rule of Quang Trung was short. After his death in 1792, the dynasty began to fall apart.

While Quang Trung (Nguyen Hue) was still emperor, the Bishop of Adran lobbied in France for military intervention in Cochinchina (southern Vietnam). When it became clear that official aid was not coming, the Bishop raised his own mercenary troops to place his protege, Nguyen Anh, on the throne in Hue.

After the death of Nguyen Hue, the Bishop's army helped Nguyen Anh take control of the southern part of the country. Then, in 1802, unification was complete when Nguyen Anh's forces seized Hanoi in the north. As emperor, with the kingdom's new capital in Hue, Nguyen Anh adopted the imperial name of Gia Long (from the cities of Gia Dinh and Thang Long). His monarchy was recognized by the Qing Dynasty of China, to which he paid tribute. In exchange for aiding Nguyen Anh's claim to the throne, commercial concessions were ceded to French merchants.

French Involvement. The French enjoyed their trade rights within Vietnam, but at the same time jeopardized their exclusive position. The missionaries, who had helped open up Vietnam to commerce, became increasingly aggressive and politically active. Emperor Minh Mang, Gia Long's successor, suspecting a foreign hand in the revolts that plagued his reign, repressed and arrested both native and French Catholic priests. When news of executions of French priests reached France, outraged protests reached Napoleon III, who finally approved official military intervention in Vietnam.

Around this time, the British were opening up Burma and China to colonial exploitation. Faced with competition by the English, the French became eager to find a quick way to the riches that lay deep in China. Although French explorers hoped that either the Mekong or Red rivers would provide such a water route, later expeditions proved the river route through Vietnam to China unnavigable.

FRENCH COLONIZATION

As the result of the French naval attack on Danang in 1858, Cochinchina, the southernmost part of Vietnam, became the first section of Vietnam to fall under French rule. Other attacks on Danang and Saigon followed. Seeing what befell China with the coming of Western Imperialism in the Opium Wars (1841), many Vietnamese, through ongoing guerrilla warfare, resisted French efforts to set up fortified trading posts. Because of continued resistance, France's acquisition of Vietnam occurred in three distinct stages—which explains why the country was divided into three parts (Annam, Tonkin, and Cochinchina) under the French.

In 1867, Cochinchina became a French colony. Since South Vietnam had the longest and most direct exposure to French (and later American) influence, it was and still remains the most "Westernized" region of the country. Cambodia to the southwest became a French protectorate ruled through a local puppet monarchy.

More treaties handed over more privileges and Vietnamese territory to the French. Annam and Tonkin were proclaimed French protectorates in 1883. The Nguyen Dynasty emperors, weakened by internal difficulties caused by their repressive regime, were powerless against the French erosion of their power. As puppet rulers, the emperors maintained their thrones while the French pulled the strings.

Using Cochinchina as their power base, the French, lured by the rich coal mines and the Red River as a possible route to China, proceeded to conquer the north. In 1887, French Indochina was formed of the protectorates of Annam, Tonkin, Cambodia, Laos, and the colony of Cochinchina. By 1893, the French Navy had secured the entire Indochina peninsula.

FRENCH RULE

Admiral Louis-Adolphe Bonard had the distinction of being the first in a line of French admirals who served as governors of Vietnam. The rule of admirals continued until 1879, when Charles-Marie Le Myre de Vilers was appointed the first civilian governor-general. Regional assistants to the governor-general located in each colony or protectorate were known as Senior Residents. Although the French retained the administrative mandarin system in the protectorates of Tonkin and Annam, a Senior Resident (technically an advisor to the mandarins), one in Hanoi (capital of Tonkin) and one in Hue (capital of Annam), actually controlled the protectorates.

Economic Development. With improved communications and transportation systems being built throughout the country, the French began economic development in earnest. The Bank of Indochina, founded in 1875, backed French companies in commercial ventures such as mining at Hongay and the enormous rubber plantation run by the Michelin company outside Saigon. Rice became the most lucrative export; rubber, the second.

The French worked largely through Chinese intermediaries who, in turn, made loans at usurious rates to Vietnamese farmers. The system was colonial exploitation, not in the interest of the Vietnamese people. Chinese merchants obtained rice cheaply and furnished it to French monopolies for export. Although much unused and swampy land in the Mekong delta was cleared and opened up for rice cultivation, the new rice supply was exported to Europe instead of being used to relieve desperate food shortages within Vietnam.

Industrialization in France demanded markets for its manufactured products. Paul Doumer, the French governor-general from 1897 to 1902, created French monopolies that manufactured and distributed alcohol, tobacco, salt, and opium. These captive markets provided 50-60% of the tax revenues taken from Indochina at the start of World War I.

Salt and alcohol monopolies were especially harmful to the common people. The salt tax tripled the cost of this essential nutrient and adversely affected the health of the peasants, particularly growing children. By French-imposed law, towns were allotted an amount of alcohol based on the adult population. Regulations further stipulated that each town was required to purchase the rationed alcohol from French distilleries. The growing tax burden created restless and landless peasants—a ripe source of cheap labor for French businesses. After experiencing the degrading conditions of coolie labor, many Vietnamese were easily recruited by rebel and nationalist groups.

EARLY AMERICAN CONTACTS WITH VIETNAM

The US began efforts to open trade with East Asia early in the 19th century. The first American known to visit Vietnam was Captain John White, a merchant sailor from Salem, Massachusetts. Previous attempts at commercial relations by other Americans were thwarted because the merchants were not prepared to trade in Portuguese currency, nor were they familiar with the numerous forms and regulations imposed on foreign traders.

In 1820, White arrived at Vungtau, where he requested permission from Vietnamese customs officials to proceed up the Dong Nai River to Saigon on his ship, the *Franklin*. After presenting gifts to the officials, White was asked to complete lengthy paperwork on the ship's complement and the nature of his cargo. After a month of waiting, the mandarin customs officials reported that since the emperor was in Hue, White would have to go to Danang (the port nearest to Hue) to get entry permission.

In Danang, White communicated with the officials in Latin and, after filling out 13 copies of crew and inventory information, finally received authorization to proceed on his journey. On the trip upriver to Saigon, White was impressed with the number of crocodiles and the skillful manner in which Vietnamese sailors maneuvered their boats using well-proportioned oars.

Upon reaching Saigon, White dined with the French governor of Cochinchina, whose residence was inside the walled citadel. After taking on a load of sugar, the *Franklin* returned home. White recorded his observations about his visit in his book, *History of a Voyage to the China Sea*. Although White did not describe any formal trade agreements reached while he was there, in all likelihood his visit opened the way for future official relations between the US and Vietnam that were to come 12 years later.

First US Diplomatic Mission. In 1832, Edmund Roberts arrived in Vietnam aboard the US Navy ship *Peacock*. Sent by President

Andrew Jackson to negotiate a trade treaty, Roberts headed the first official US diplomatic mission to Vietnam. He followed protocol and presented his credentials to the Vietnamese maritime authorities, who forwarded the papers to Emperor Minh Mang. Although the emperor's representatives attended a goodwill banquet aboard the *Peacock,* the request to enter the country was later rejected because of so-called irregularities: Roberts' name, which included a number of titles and places in America, was longer than that of the governor of the province. In addition, Roberts' letter of introduction from President Jackson had neglected to mention the emperor's full name and the proper name of the country.

Roberts returned to Vietnam in 1836 to pick up where he had left off. During negotiations regarding a commercial contracts treaty, he became ill and left the country in haste to seek medical help before finalizing the agreement. Vietnamese officials considered his sudden departure most uncivil. He died in Macao 20 days later.

Diplomatic relations between the US and Vietnam began in 1842. Things did not get off to a good start, however. In 1845, the *USS Constitution* ("Old Ironsides"), part of the East India squadron of the US Navy under the command of Captain John Percival, docked off the coast of Danang. The *Constitution* had been on its way from Canton to Manila Bay. Percival, called "Mad Jack," kept a coffin filled with high quality tea from China in his cabin, and reportedly had the habit of addressing the box during diplomatic dinners.

With Vietnamese mandarins onboard the *Constitution,* a plea came for help to free a French missionary imprisoned in Hue by Emperor Thieu Tri. Percival held the visiting mandarins hostage to negotiate the release of the missionary. When Emperor Thieu Tri refused to exchange the missionary for the mandarins, Percival freed his hostages, fired off a few shots of his ship's cannon, and sailed away. What impression, if any, "Mad Jack's" bold behavior may have had upon the the Emperor's view of Americans is uncertain. In any event, the missionary was later released to a French delegation.

Four years later, President Zachary Taylor apologized for Percival's unauthorized actions. The President's letter, dated August 1849, was delivered to "His majesty the magnificent King of Anam" [sic] by Joseph Balestier, envoy and minister to Southeastern Asia. The president wrote that he was sending the letter ". . . in order that you may understand how greatly I have grieved to hear it said, four years ago (which I have only heard of lately, for the first time, because your country is so far from mine) Captain Percival by landing men from his ship in Toorong Bay and firing on your people, and killing and wounding some . . . ."

In a polite but clear warning to the Vietnamese against taking reprisals, Taylor added that the matter ". . . ought to be forgotten and forgiven after my letter has come into your hands."

The first Vietnamese to visit America remains a matter of uncertainty. In all likelihood, it was Bui Vien, the first Vietnamese ambassador to the US. In 1873, when Vietnam was losing her lands to the French, Emperor Tu Duc sent Bui Vien (he came from a family of scholars in North Vietnam who served at the court of the emperor) to appeal to the US for assistance. The ambassador arrived in Washington and was eventually received formally by President Ulysses S. Grant, who seemed receptive to the idea of aid. Congress, however, rejected the plan.

MODERN REVOLUTIONARY MOVEMENTS IN VIETNAM

The central theme in the history of Vietnam is the people's ability to overcome foreign domination by defeating superior forces. From the Trung Sisters' uprising to oust the Chinese in AD 40–43 to, in more recent times, guerrilla groups which formed to resist the colonial French, feuding factions of Vietnamese have consistently put aside differences to expel foreigners from their homeland.

French Domination. Although Vietnamese resistance groups fought the French for many years, they lacked sufficient organization to prevent their country from being overrun. Under a policy of "collective responsibility," French security, in suppressing subversive activities, punished entire villages for sheltering rebels. Despite brutal reprisals by the French, elusive Vietnamese guerrillas continued their war of independence. When the French demanded more territory, Emperor Ham Nghi mustered an unsuccessful insurrection and was captured by the French, who exiled him to Algeria, where he later died. At the end of the 19th century, Phan Dinh Phung led a popular armed uprising against the French in Annam, a rebellion that became a model for future insurrections.

After Japan defeated Russia in 1905, the possibility of an Asian victory against foreign domination aroused Phan Boi Chau, a Vietnamese scholar regarded as the initiator of the Vietnamese nationalist movement, to seek Japanese support for Vietnamese independence. A patriot and contemporary of Phan Boi Chau, Phan Chu Trinh had similar goals but frowned on an alliance with Japan. Phan Chu Trinh broke ideological ranks with Phan Boi Chau to start his own movement, best known for founding a progressive college in Hanoi that espoused modern subjects and an enlightened philosophy. The French considered the school dangerous and ordered it closed. Phan Chu Trinh's followers were arrested and he was sentenced to serve a harsh prison term on Poulo Condor (now Con Dao)—France's notorious Devil's Island in the South China Sea.

From 1900 onward, although French colonial rule in Vietnam was firmly entrenched, ethnic minorities in the mountain regions continued to stage raids in an attempt to reclaim national independence. In 1916, Emperor Duy Tan supported a large-scale rebellion that resulted in hundreds of supporters being executed and the emperor exiled.

HO CHI MINH AND THE
VIETNAMESE COMMUNIST MOVEMENT

On the eve of the First World War, 100,000 Vietnamese youths were recruited by the French as laborers to support the war effort. During this time a Vietnamese nationalist called Nguyen Tat Thanh (as Ho Chi Minh was known then) lived in Paris, where he began his political career. Ho Chi Minh used several pseudonyms, but settled on Nguyen Ai Quoc, meaning "Nguyen the Patriot," which is how he was known in the 1920s and 1930s. He adopted the name Ho Chi Minh in the 1940s (see the Appendix Section).

The Vietnamese communist movement originated in Paris in 1920 when Ho Chi Minh became a member of the French Communist party. At that time, the only source for gaining support for nationalist causes among French political parties came from socialists and the newly formed Communist party.

In 1924, after a period of indoctrination in Moscow, Ho went to Canton (then the seat of the Chinese nationalist government) to form the Revolutionary Youth League among Vietnamese exiles living there. The enthusiastic support for the League from the Vietnamese expatriates in China and patriots living inside Vietnam foreshadowed the pivotal role Ho was to play later.

The struggle for independence was nonpartisan in nature and encompassed a variety of groups. Religious sects armed themselves for the precise purpose of getting rid of the French. Secret labor unions and other revolutionary groups were organized, among them the Trotskyite group and the Vietnam Nationalist Party.

Modeled after the Chinese Nationalist Party (the Kuomintang [KMT] founded by Dr. Sun Yat-sen in 1912), the Vietnam Nationalist party (VNQDD) instigated the first significant uprising against

French rule. The incident involved a Vietnamese military auxiliary that had been drafted to serve the French and was stationed at Yen Bay, north of Hanoi. The auxiliary rebelled against its officers, the insurgents were caught, and ten VNQDD leaders were summarily guillotined. Subsequently, relentless French repression of all nationalist movements forced anti-colonial groups underground.

As in the rest of the world, the depression years of the 1930s ushered in hard economic times in Vietnam. Prices of goods produced in Vietnam fell and factories closed. People were out of work and families went hungry. Unrest and rioting spread and the focus of the country's ills was directed against the French. Those insurgency groups capable of effectively transforming discontent into support grew steadily in number.

The Vietnamese Revolutionary Youth League formed by Ho Chi Minh in Canton in 1925 was succeeded in 1930 by the Communist Party of Indochina, organized by Ho in Hong Kong. The Indochina Communist party, uniting the Youth League and several smaller Marxist groups, modified traditional Marxist theory to accommodate the fact that 90% of Vietnam's population were peasants and farmers, not industrial workers. In 1930, the Indochinese Communist Party led a movement to set up "Soviets" in the provinces of Nghe An and Ha Tinh (now the unified province of Nghe Tinh).

The Communists were adept and thorough organizers. Party workers researched the local economic, political, and social structure of the villages in which they worked. They listened to grievances and gave people a broader picture of their problems by drawing a direct correlation between their complaints and the French occupation. After holding out hope for change, Communist operatives attempted to motivate, organize, and channel stirred-up emotions into activities such as strikes against French plantation owners and mass protest marches. To instill feelings of cooperation, party members helped farmers with their crops, conducted literacy classes, and distributed propaganda materials to reinforce the message of solidarity. In return, citizens aided the Communists with shelter and information.

In many ways, the organizing and propagandizing tactics of the Communists were similar to those of the US civic action programs in South Vietnam in the 1960s, which aimed to win the "hearts and minds" of the villagers.

FRENCH INDOCHINA WAR

Germany overran France early in World War II. In September 1940, Japan, an ally of Germany, began its occupation of Vietnam. Ho Chi Minh founded the Viet Minh to oppose the Japanese occupation (Vietnamese historians put the founding of the Viet Minh in the Cao Bang province of Vietnam, not in China). In June 1941, Ho Chi Minh returned home, after being abroad for thirty years, to expand the League for Independence of Vietnam (Viet Nam Doc Lap Dong Minh) or Viet Minh.

The Viet Minh Resist Japan. The Viet Minh were a coalition of communists and nationalists who shared the common vision for independence. Ho Chi Minh and like-minded nationalists, who had previously evaded French security forces by setting up their bases in China, turned their anti-colonial ideologies against the Japanese imperialists. The Viet Minh, employing the best underground activity and organizational techniques of the nationalist movements, managed to not only survive French repression, but to grow rapidly in membership.

The French colonial government collaborated with the Japanese and continued to rule the country for almost the entire war. Only in March 1945, six months before the war ended, did the Japanese take actual control and declare Vietnam "independent." Although a few French garrisons fought the Japanese for a brief time, most garrisons surrendered quickly, with a handful of French troops escaping across the border into China. In the end, the French offered little resistance to the Japanese takeover.

Japanese Domination. Japan, pursuing the concept of "greater East Asia co-prosperity," used Indochina as a source of forced native labor and as a base of operations for its war in the Pacific. Important minerals such as tungsten and tin, plus agricultural products such as rice, were exported to Japan to supply its war machine.

The Viet Minh organized guerrilla bands to attack both the French and Japanese. In April 1945, representatives of the American OSS (Office of Strategic Services) met with Ho Chi Minh in his underground headquarters. The Americans sought cooperation in their common aim to thwart Japanese efforts in Indochina. Ho agreed to provide intelligence networks and contacts, plus escape routes for American fliers downed in the area. In return, the Viet Minh were trained and armed with American weapons to harass the Japanese.

FOUNDATIONS OF THE
DEMOCRATIC REPUBLIC OF VIETNAM

Following Japan's surrender in August 1945, as agreed at the Potsdam Conference of Allied leaders, British troops occupied south and central Vietnam below the 16th parallel while Chinese troops were allowed to enter the north. Acting quickly from their jungle bases in the north, the Viet Minh liberated Hanoi before the Chinese arrived (this action became known as the "August Revolution"). In Hue, Bao Dai, the puppet emperor under the Japanese, surrendered the imperial symbols of his office to the forces of Ho Chi Minh.

On September 2, 1945, the Democratic Republic of Vietnam was proclaimed with Ho Chi Minh as president. Although independence had been won, Ho's regime had to deal with a devastating famine in which millions died. Initially, Ho, in an attempt toward political harmony, made efforts to give his government a broad base by inviting moderates and Catholics to join in positions of authority. Ho also sought international recognition and moral support from the US for his newly formed government, but global geopolitical factors prevented the positive response for which he had hoped.

The French in the south, after being released from Japanese military prisons by the British, were allowed to reinstate their previous colonial system. In September 1945, the French dislodged the Viet Minh, who had briefly attained power in Saigon, from South Vietnam.

China's Incursions. Under the conditions of the Potsdam agreement, 200,000 Chinese troops entered North Vietnam. Recalling that the last time the Chinese came to Vietnam they stayed for a thousand years, Ho Chi Minh permitted 25,000 French military troops to enter the North and establish order, hoping that the Chinese would withdraw. In negotiatons with the French, the Chinese agreed to withdraw from Tonkin while permitting French troops to land in Haiphong. In return, the Chinese would receive favorable trade arrangements with the French and safe access to the Vietnamese rail system that connected the southwestern provinces of China with the South China Sea.

In addition to wanting the Chinese out, Ho agreed to a new foothold by the French because he believed colonialism was dying. He also hoped for a more sympathetic French government (after France held her national elections in November 1946) that he could negotiate with in order to establish an independent nation.

Negotiations with France. In March 1946, after the French forces re-entered northern Vietnam, an agreement between Ho and the French recognized Vietnam as "a free state within the Indochinese Federation and the French Union" (these terms had not yet been defined, and their ambiguity ultimately led to the Second Indochina War). While the Democratic Republic of Vietnam continued to press for full independence, the fate of Cochinchina to the south remained unresolved.

In November 1946, full-scale war erupted between the Viet Minh and the French over disagreements concerning which government had the legal right to collect customs duty at Haiphong harbor. In the face of superior French troops, the Viet Minh retreated to the safety of their former jungle base camps. From these strongholds they gradually strengthened themselves through training and recruitment to wage yet another guerrilla struggle, the first Indochina War.

After the Chinese Communists came to power in 1949, they were able to aid Ho's military commander, Vo Nguyen Giap, with weapons, training, and sanctuaries. It seemed that for the first time the Viet Minh had the edge over the French. Then, in late 1949, the US responded to French requests for military help. The war in Indochina had been interpreted by Western leaders to symbolize Communist expansion toward the free world and, at the same time, containment of Communist China's millions (the "Domino Theory").

Ho vs. Bao Dai. In January 1950, China and the Soviet Union officially recognized Ho's jungle government. In June of that year, Communist North Korean forces captured Seoul. In the US, the Communist military victory in Korea caused a sweeping anti-Communist purge within the government and private sector led by Senator Joseph McCarthy, who also aroused fear with alarming rhetoric of an international Communist conspiracy abroad.

When the French attempted to reassert control by restoring Emperor Bao Dai to "power" as head of the French-supported Associated States of Vietnam in 1950, a sequence of events took place that would eventually draw America into a ground war with Vietnam, beginning in the 1960s. The US recognized the Saigon-based Bao Dai government, established an economic mission in Saigon to channel aid to the French through the Bao Dai regime, and called for the formation of a Vietnamese national army in the south to fight alongside the French. By 1953, the US was paying 80% of the cost of the French military effort in Indochina.

GUERRILLA WAR

"The Viet Minh fighters moved among the people as easily as fish moved in water." This popular expression summed up the activities of the Viet Minh, who posed a double threat to foreign invaders.

Viet Minh operatives could not only blend in and disappear within the Vietnamese civilian population, they were also organized. Carefully structured control and the inculcation of intense motivation and grass-roots discipline in recruits were important factors in waging the Vietnamese guerrilla war against the French and, later, the Americans. This process, called *dau tranh*, is often translated as "struggle movement." Douglas Pike, authority on Communist organizing techniques, describes the concept: "Summons to consecration, the call to heroic duty, the trumpet of the apocalypse." In addition, the party incited primal emotions such as hate, grievance, ambition, and revenge.

The Viet Minh, and later the National Liberation Front, organized the common people such as youth, Buddhists, women, students, and farmers into paramilitary support units. Adept at using the terrain as camouflage, guerrillas would attack and quickly disappear, to the frustration of the French, who controlled only the cities. By 1953, France had 250,000 men in Vietnam.

General Vo Nguyen Giap, commander of the Viet Minh forces, launched commando attacks and major offensives on isolated French forts in the North and eventually overwhelmed them. As a result, the Viet Minh had unimpeded access to supply routes to and from China. The French Expeditionary forces (its Foreign Legion), made up, in part, of German prisoners of war and Senegalese recruits, landed in Saigon in December 1945 and managed to penetrate provinces where the elusive revolutionary forces had maintained the resistance. Despite early victories, the Foreign Legion lacked the mobility of the guerrillas who spread the resistance throughout Vietnam.

THE BATTLE FOR DIEN BIEN PHU

By 1954, the world was ready for peace in Korea; international opinion had also turned against the war in French Indochina. A meeting to negotiate an accord in Korea was to convene in Geneva on April 26, 1954. Although the US, the Soviet Union, France, and Great Britain had agreed to this meeting for the express purpose of completing a peace treaty for the Korean Conflict, world leaders also hoped the conference could be used to negotiate a cease-fire in Indochina.

To bolster their position at the peace conference, the French needed a decisive victory against the Viet Minh. The assignment went to the French commander Henri-Eugene Navarre, who, hoping to maneuver General Giap into a direct confrontation, devised a strategy in which French infantry forces could finally use their experience in conventional set-piece warfare. Navarre chose to make his stand at Dien Bien Phu—a valley near the Laotian border in the extreme northwest of Vietnam surrounded by five low hills and 170 miles (274 km.) from Hanoi. He also hoped to block a Viet Minh takeover of Laos by cutting the supply route linking China to Laos.

Giap was willing to take risks and mobilized a massive fighting force. Since the Korean conflict had ended the previous summer, Chinese supplies previously earmarked for their North Korean allies could now assist the Vietnamese in their anticolonial struggle. Giap was able to assemble four divisions instead of the two expected by the French. In addition to a three-to-one superiority in favor of the Viet Minh, Giap's forces managed another surprise advantage by transporting heavy artillery pieces and positioning them on the near slope of the surrounding hills, instead of the expected far slope—an operation that went completely undetected by French reconnaissance planes.

The French Surrender. On March 12, the Viet Minh artillery barrage began. The French relied on air support from Hanoi, but C-47 transport aircraft fell prey to gunfire from the well-hidden artillery. Even the winds favored the revolution: many parachutes laden with French supplies dropped into Viet Minh territory. In keeping with Giap's plan to maintain an offensive position, Viet Minh were soon digging trenches that led into the heart of the enemy encampment. With the French now on the defensive, US president Dwight D. Eisenhower considered sending in Allied air power and perhaps even ground troops, but was unable to secure international support. The massacre continued for 55 days before the French finally put down their weapons. Today, a plaque on the surviving command post at Dien Bien Phu states the essence of Vietnam's landmark victory—the exact time and date of the French surrender: 17:30 (5:30 PM), May 7, 1954. The French Indochina War that began in 1946 had finally come to an end.

AFTERMATH OF FRENCH DEFEAT

The Cessation of Hostilities in Vietnam was worked out at the Geneva Conference and signed in July 1954 by France and the Viet Minh. Vietnam was provisionally divided, pending nationwide free elections, into Communist North Vietnam and South Vietnam. The temporary partition of the country was drawn on "a provisional military demarcation line" called the Demilitarized (cease-fire line) Zone (DMZ) at 17° latitude. At the time of the cease-fire, the Viet Minh controlled most of Vietnam's countryside. Major towns and communication routes, up to the 13° parallel and large areas below, were still under French influence.

The Cease-fire Accords guaranteed 300 days of free movement between zones. This grace period would allow the French and the Associated States of Vietnam military forces to withdraw from the North and similarly, the Viet Minh to withdraw from the South. The agreement also called for the creation of an International Control Commission to supervise the truce and, since the division was to be a provisional one, free elections would be held in two years (in 1956) "to bring about unification."

Bao Dai Flees. On June 4, 1954, six weeks before the Geneva Accords, the French had ironed out yet another treaty with Emperor Bao Dai that granted full independence to the Associated States of Vietnam—the puppet organization created by the French four years previously. After naming Ngo Dinh Diem prime minister, Bao Dai left for France and never returned to Vietnam. Neither the new government in Saigon, no longer considering itself provisional and primed for asserting its autonomy, nor the US ever signed the Geneva Cease-fire Accords.

YEARS OF TURMOIL:

VIETNAM 1954–1988

© *Arnold R. Isaacs*

A chill monsoon rain was falling on Hanoi as day broke on October 9, 1954. At dawn, green-clad troops of the Viet Minh 308th Division were already on the march, heading in from the outskirts toward the center of the city. Some rode in Soviet-built trucks and jeeps; most were on foot, plodding in long, order-

Arnold R. Isaacs covered Indochina as a war correspondent for the *Baltimore Sun* from 1972 to 1975, leaving Vietnam in the final helicopter evacuation just before Saigon fell to the Communists. He is the author of *Without Honor: Defeat in Vietnam and Cambodia*, an account of the final years of the war, and co-author of *Pawns of War*, a history of the conflicts in Cambodia and Laos. Now a freelance writer and a faculty member at Towson State University, Mr. Isaacs lives in Lutherville, Md.

FAMOUS BATTLES IN VIETNAMESE HISTORY

DATE (AD)	BATTLE	AGAINST	COMMANDER
40	Luy Lau near Me Linh	Chinese General To Dinh	Trung Trac Trung Nhi
938	Bach Dang River near Hanoi	Chinese Navy under Hoang Thao	Ngo Quyen
1077	Cau River North and East of Hanoi	Chinese Sung Dynasty forces	Ly Thuong Keit
1285	3 battles Thanh Hoa and Red River	Mongols of Kubla Khan's son, To-Gan	Tran Hung Dao
1288	Bach Dang River between Haiphong and Hanoi	Mongols under To-Gan	Tran Hung Dao
1427	Chi Lang Pass in Lang Son area	2 columns of Ming Dynasty troops	Le Loi
1785	Rach Gai-Xoai Mut near My Tho	Siamese Navy and Infantry	Nguyen Hue Emperor Quang Trung
1789 (New Year)	Dong Da around Hanoi	Thanh Dynasty in four columns	Nguyen Hue
1954	Dien Bien Phu near Laotion border	French forces under General Navarre	Vo Nguyen Giap

ly columns under the gray, sodden sky. Despite the rain and an all-day curfew order issued by the departing French military command, large crowds of civilians turned out to welcome the Viet Minh troops who were taking over the city, as agreed between French and

Viet Minh negotiators, exactly 80 days after the Geneva cease-fire. Banners and posters appeared along the route, hailing the arrival of peace and independence. Most numerous were the signs proclaiming "Long Live President Ho Chi Minh."

As Ho's forces marched into the city, the last French soldiers, many of them colonial troops from Senegal, Morocco, and Algeria, marched out, crossing the Doumer Bridge to the far bank of the Red River. The last man on the bridge was a Colonel d'Argence, carrying a French flag that had been lowered for the last time, in a pouring rain, at the French military headquarters at the Mangin Stadium.

SYMBOL OF VICTORY

Street by street, Viet Minh guards took over government buildings and other installations. At exactly 11 AM, their flag was raised over the Palais du Gouvernement, formerly the French colonial governor's headquarters. The new flag was red, with a yellow star in the middle. As the emblem of Ho Chi Minh's Democratic Republic of Vietnam, it was now to fly as the official national banner over the northern half of the country. Ho's representatives at Geneva had reluctantly accepted the temporary partition of the country—on the basis, however, that the line between the two zones was temporary and, in the words of the peace conference's final declaration, did not represent "a political or territorial boundary." Unification, Ho and his associates contended, would be achieved through national elections to be held, as agreed in Geneva, by 1956. Thus, even if their revolution was not yet complete, taking power in Hanoi was still a major success, and the red flags rising over government buildings were a symbol of victory.

THE SOUTHERN REGIME

In Saigon, 700 miles to the south, the flags were different, and so was the official view of the Geneva accords. Ruling in the southern zone was a government nominally headed by the ineffectual Emperor Bao Dai, who, after years of subservience to the French, had finally been granted full independence shortly before the Geneva ceasefire agreement. The Saigon regime had adopted a national flag with colors similar to the North's but with a different design: a yellow field with three horizontal red stripes symbolizing the traditional regions of northern, central, and southern Vietnam.

Unlike Ho's government, the southern regime refused to recognize the Geneva agreement—an "inequity," the newly named Prime Minister, Ngo Dinh Diem, called it, ". . . which hands over to the

Communists the entire north of the country." The day of the agreement, Diem ordered flags flown at half-mast throughout the country, in dramatic contrast to the Viet Minh's triumphant flag-raising when they entered Hanoi.

The different flags in the two Vietnamese capitals symbolized broader differences that were, at bottom, irreconcilable.

The Geneva accords were doomed by the fact that only one side accepted them as legal and binding while the other did not. It was as if a sales contract were signed by the buyer but not by the seller, or, more precisely, by a seller who was no longer able to deliver the goods. France, which had negotiated the agreement, no longer ruled in the South; Prime Minister Diem did. And Diem accepted no obligation to honor the agreement's terms; why should he, when he had never accepted them in the first place?

With the backing of the US, which also refused to be bound by the accords, Diem cancelled the planned national election. Moreover, by rejecting the Geneva pact, Saigon and Washington were left free to maintain that South Vietnam was a sovereign country, separate from the North. This meant that North Vietnam's subsequent support for a southern liberation movement represented "foreign aggression," justifying US intervention in defense of the South. To Hanoi, however, the existence of a separate southern government violated a binding agreement. The foreign aggressors, in the Communists' eyes, were those who sent arms, bombers, and troops to Vietnam to support an illegal regime in Saigon.

THE SEEDS OF WAR

These were not just legal technicalities, but fundamental disputes that fatally undermined the chance of peace. The end of the eight-year war with France, rather than settling Vietnam's future, had instead planted the seeds of a second Indochina war, more destructive and tragic than the first.

Although the Geneva agreement ultimately failed, it did bring five years of relative peace—the only such interval Vietnam would experience in the middle decades of the century. Even in that period, however, neither half of the divided country was wholly free of violence.

DIEM'S RETURN

Ngo Dinh Diem, the new leader of South Vietnam, faced such formidable obstacles that few, even among his supporters, predicted his regime would last. When he returned from a four-year exile in the US and Europe to assume the prime ministership in June 1954, the 53-year old Diem's credentials lay chiefly in his past opposition to both the Communists and the French.

But Diem had been secluded from his country's political drama for many years. "He impresses one as a mystic who has just emerged from a religious retreat into the cold world," a US diplomat commented after meeting with Diem on his way back from exile. The image was literal, not metaphorical; Diem, a devout Roman Catholic, had spent much of his time abroad living reclusively in Catholic monasteries. The same diplomat added that Diem seemed "too unworldly and unsophisticated to be able to cope with the grave problems and unscrupulous people he will find in Saigon."

To call Diem's problems grave was, if anything, to understate them. He had no political party nor any other organization through which to mobilize support for himself or his policies. Neither his senior military commanders nor the civilian administrators he inherited from the French owed him their loyalty. Diem's government did not even exercise authority in its own capital, which was effectively controlled by armed gangs belonging to a Mafia-like criminal syndicate called the Binh Xuyen. In the countryside, large areas were under the control of militias loyal to two religious sects, the Cao Dai and Hoa Hao. Against all these opponents Diem seemed to have only two allies that could be counted on: his family (chiefly his brother, Ngo Dinh Nhu) and the Americans.

Diem, however, proved unexpectedly resilient. With US help he thwarted intrigues mounted by disloyal army commanders. His forces defeated the private Binh Xuyen criminal army in Saigon and subsequently managed to subdue the Hoa Hao and Cao Dai militias. By October 1955, Diem felt secure enough to hold a referendum to confirm his leadership. With the suspiciously one-sided approval of more than 98% of the voters, the referendum deposed the nominal ruler, Bao Dai, and abolished the monarchy. The Republic of Vietnam, with Ngo Dinh Diem as its first president, was created in its place.

DIEM MOVES AGAINST THE COMMUNISTS

Having established his power, Diem was now ready to turn it against his old enemies, the Communists. Although about 100,000 southern Viet Minh had gone to North Vietnam following the Geneva accords, others had remained behind to prepare for the expected election. That network now became the target of Diem's police and military security agencies. Thousands of suspected Communist agents were arrested, held without trial, and frequently tortured while under interrogation. Many prisoners were never seen again and were assumed to have been secretly executed.

Like other repressive regimes before and since, the Diem government often failed to distinguish between real and imagined enemies: anyone who had fought against the French was in danger of being imprisoned and tortured, and so was anyone who complained about corruption or abuses of power by Diem's officials or police. Ultimately, the indiscriminate arrests and cruelty may have generated more enemies than were arrested or killed. In the short run, though, the anti-Communist campaign was quite successful. By 1958, southern Communist leaders were complaining to Hanoi that the movement might be destroyed unless the party shifted to a more active resistance.

PROBLEMS IN THE NORTH

In the Communist North, Ho and his associates had inherited a country already devastated by war and further disrupted by the vindictive departing French, who dismantled factories, government installations, communications facilities, and even libraries and hospitals, removing all movable machinery and other equipment. (At the Bacmai airfield outside Hanoi, the French even pulled up and took with them the linked metal strips used to surface the parking ramps and secondary runways.)

While coping with their crippled economy, the Communist leadership also launched a land reform program, intended not only to redistribute land but also to break the traditional authority of "landlords and former officials" in the countryside. Tens of thousands of landowners were convicted and many were shot after being denounced for acts of oppression. In the process, thousands of innocent people were wrongly persecuted. "Grave mistakes" were made, the party leadership acknowledged in the fall of 1956. The admission did not prevent an uprising by alarmed and resentful peasants in Nghe An province, Ho's birthplace. The uprising was crushed, with overwhelming force, by a full army division.

COMMUNIST POLICY IN THE SOUTH

The leaders in Hanoi, meanwhile, also had to respond to the changing situation in South Vietnam. Initially, the Communists who had remained in the South in 1954 were instructed to engage in "political struggle," not armed resistance. After Diem cancelled the elec-

tions and began his campaign of repression, the party approved selective acts of violence, chiefly assassinations of government
officials. During 1957 there were several hundred such murders, intended to intimidate government supporters and to win popular approval by eliminating corrupt or abusive officials. The party, however, still did not favor a full-scale revolution against Diem. The
southern Communist apparatus was not strong enough, Ho and his
associates felt, and in any case their priority was on consolidating
their own regime.

That remained Hanoi's view for several more years. But as
Diem's repression grew more severe, southern party officials pressed
for a more forceful policy before their movement was wiped out altogether. Finally, in May 1959, the party Central Committee adopted
a resolution calling for armed struggle in the South. Under the new
policy, units of up to 100 guerrillas were formed to begin the resistance war, which slowly intensified during the following months.
To assist the uprising, North Vietnam began sending back into the
South several thousand experienced agents and guerrillas from
among the southern Viet Minh who had come north in 1954.

In December 1960, a year and a half after approving the start of
armed struggle, the Communist leadership decided the time had
come to broaden the political base of the resistance. For that purpose a new front organization was formed, with the goal of bringing
together all potential opponents of the Diem regime. Like the Viet
Minh two decades earlier, the new movement, although directed
by the Communist party from behind the scenes, did not promote
Communist ideology or policy but appealed to patriotism and to
hatred of oppression. The new organization was called the National
Liberation Front of South Vietnam. Under that name, the Vietnamese revolutionaries would march into the most violent years of
their long struggle.

US INTERVENTION

On December 22, 1961, near a village called Duc Hoa, a few miles
west of Saigon, a US soldier was killed when the South Vietnamese
unit he was accompanying drove into a guerrilla ambush. The death
of Specialist 4th Class James T. Davis gave grim confirmation to a
new aspect of Vietnam's war: it was now becoming America's war
too. *

---

*Davis wasn't actually the first US soldier killed in Vietnam. Two Americans died
in a 1959 guerrilla attack on a South Vietnamese division headquarters in Bien Hoa,
near Saigon. In that incident, however, the Americans were not accompanying Viet-

Abandoned US-made tank, west of Saigon

US involvement, consistent with President John F. Kennedy's inaugural promise to "bear any burden" to defend freedom around the world, had deepened during 1961 as the Diem regime and its military forces appeared unable to cope with the growing rural insurgency. During his first year in office, although he cautiously sidestepped Diem's request for a formal defense treaty and turned down a proposal to send up to 8,000 American troops, Kennedy expanded the small force of US military advisors in Vietnam from 685 to slightly over 3,000. In 1962, US strength rose again to about 11,000. By now, Americans were facing combat regularly. US heli-

---

namese troops on combat operations, as Davis did. His death is officially considered the first during the period of active US military involvement.

copters ferried South Vietnamese troops into action, advisors accompanied them on the ground, and US aircraft regularly carried out bombing missions (albeit under the guise of training Vietnamese pilots).

American Involvement Intensifies. US bombing and artillery destroyed whole villages. Thousands of civilians were killed, wounded, or made homeless in the fighting. Thousands of others were forcibly moved out of their villages into what the Diem regime called "strategic hamlets"—guarded settlements where, theoretically, peasants could be kept under better government control.

The guerrillas, after being temporarily thrown off balance, rather quickly began developing new tactics to cope with helicopters, armored vehicles, and the other new weaponry appearing on the battlefields. Meanwhile, as they became more heavily involved in the war, the Americans discovered that supplying arms and tactical advice was easier than supplying competence, dedication, and effectiveness to the South Vietnamese leadership. Compared to the guerrilla leaders, Saigon's officers seemed lacking in aggressiveness and skill, while their corruption and abuses of power were alienating the population from the regime.

Victory, Not Compromise. US disenchantment with Diem and his government—and particularly with Diem's brother Nhu—grew sharply when, in the spring of 1963, a crisis arose between the regime and Buddhist leaders in South Vietnam's major cities. After government troops fired into a Buddhist demonstration in Hue, protests spread to Saigon, including the shocking public suicide by fire of an elderly monk. In response, special military units under Nhu's command carried out violent raids on pagodas throughout South Vietnam, confirming an image of Diem and Nhu as autocrats whose unpopularity was undermining the war against the Viet Cong.* Within the Kennedy administration, key officials began to conclude that Diem had to be removed. What concerned the Americans was not just the undemocratic nature of the regime or even that Diem's lack of popularity was hurting the war effort, but also the suspicion (which more than 25 years later has never been either verified or disproven) that Diem and Nhu might seek to cut a deal with the

---

*"Viet Cong"—a slang phrase for Vietnamese Communists—was the term commonly used in the 1960s by Americans and pro-Saigon Vietnamese to describe the National Liberation Front guerrillas. Particularly in the early years of the conflict, villagers still frequently used the term Viet Minh, which had been used during the war against the French. The revolutionaries themselves referred to their soldiers as *Giai Phong Quan*—Liberation Army.

Communists. To Washington, no deal was acceptable. After committing American military forces and prestige to Vietnam, the Kennedy administration required a victory, not a compromise.

Assassinations Bring Change. In Saigon, disaffected South Vietnamese generals were discreetly assured that the US would not try to block a coup d'etat and would continue aid and military support to a new government. The message gave a green light to a group of conspirators headed by Gen. Duong Van Minh, nicknamed "Big Minh." On November 1, rebel troops attacked the presidential palace. Diem and Nhu escaped, but surrendered the next day, after receiving assurances that they would not be harmed. Instead of being taken to safety, however, they were murdered—almost certainly by Big Minh's bodyguards, acting on his orders.

Exactly three weeks later, John Kennedy himself was assassinated in Dallas. The trauma of that violent death drove the Diem affair out of most Americans' minds, but in fact, Diem's murder may have been equally fateful, fundamentally changing the US commitment in Vietnam. Washington's role in Diem's overthrow and death bequeathed an inescapable American responsibility for what followed, making it more difficult for Kennedy's successors to avoid a deepening involvement in the war. Nor could any of the generals who followed Diem ever escape a crippling dependency on their allies. They and their successors were, as Kennedy himself once said about South Vietnam in a different context, "our offspring," for whom the US, in the eyes of both Vietnamese and Americans, was held responsible.

Aftermath of Diem's Fall. Anticipating a growing US intervention after Diem's fall, the leaders of North Vietnam realized that the southern guerrillas could not face American forces alone. But war with the US might be avoided, they calculated, if the Saigon regime collapsed quickly enough. Accordingly, Hanoi increased its support for the revolution in the South. During 1964, for the first time, units of regular North Vietnamese infantry were sent south. Other troops were assigned to improve and enlarge the infiltration route, a network of roads and paths snaking through dense jungles in the mountainous terrain of eastern Laos. Americans nicknamed the route the Ho Chi Minh Trail.

South Vietnam, meanwhile, was beset by instability. General Minh, who took power after Diem's fall, was himself overthrown in another coup three months later, which was followed by more than a year of plots, coup attempts, and power struggles within the military leadership. Not surprisingly, the war went badly, leaving American officials with a growing belief that a greater commitment of US military force would be needed to prevent South Vietnam's defeat. Meanwhile, US participation in the war expanded covertly. In June 1964, US jets began bombing the Ho Chi Minh Trail in missions that were officially called "armed reconnaissance." Along the North Vietnamese coast, American-controlled teams of Vietnamese commandos were put ashore to carry out sabotage and intelligence-gathering operations. (The program, called OPLAN 34-A, had little success. Few of the raiders succeeded in carrying out their missions, and almost all of them were captured by the North Vietnamese.)

Attack on the Maddox. Off the coast, US ships patrolled the Gulf of Tonkin, monitoring Communist military communications ashore. On August 2, 1964, one of those ships, the destroyer USS *Maddox*, was attacked by North Vietnamese gunboats. When the *Maddox* and another ship, the USS *Turner Joy*, reported they were under attack again on the night of August 4, President Lyndon B. Johnson ordered carrier-based US jets to bomb North Vietnamese installations on shore. The very next day, Johnson asked Congress for a resolution authorizing the use of military force to repel attacks against US forces and "to prevent further aggression." It was quickly and overwhelmingly approved.

As the first direct and publicly acknowledged clash between American and North Vietnamese forces, the Tonkin Gulf incident took the US across still another threshold on the path toward war. But Johnson and his advisors had acted on grounds that were, if not false, at least ambiguous. The initial attack on the *Maddox*, described in Washington as unprovoked, actually came on the heels of an OPLAN 34-A raid very close to where the *Maddox* was operating; Hanoi had ample reason to suspect the ship was supporting the raid. As for the second attack, subsequent investigations showed it almost certainly never happened at all and that the reports of enemy activity arose from faulty or misinterpreted radar and sonar signals.

Retaliation Escalates. Following the Tonkin Gulf bombing, the US did not immediately carry out additional attacks, but the precedent of retaliation had been set. Six months later, on February 7, 1965, following attacks on US installations in South Vietnam, a reelected President Johnson again ordered US bombers over the North. This time the bombing did not end with a single retaliatory raid; more strikes followed a few days later, opening an air campaign that would intensify until a single year's raids dumped more bombs on North Vietnam than had been dropped on Japan throughout World War II.

War Symbol: Vietnam MIG set atop wreckage of US B-52, Military Museum, Hanoi

The start of the air war led directly to the arrival of the first major US ground units in South Vietnam. Concerned that US air bases in the South might be attacked in reprisal for the bombing of the North, Gen. William C. Westmoreland, the US commander in Vietnam, asked for two Marine battalions to protect the huge airfield at Danang. The Marines arrived on March 8. (The landing, incidentally, showed how completely the US had come to dominate the "alliance" with South Vietnam. Though it was officially announced that the deployment had been agreed to by both governments, in fact, the South Vietnamese prime minister did not even learn about the landing until after it began.)

Meanwhile, the political chaos in Saigon was finally coming to an end. In June 1965, a military junta headed by Generals Nguyen Van Thieu and Nguyen Cao Ky took power and succeeded in ending the cycle of coups. Two years later Thieu would be chosen president in the only relatively free election in South Vietnam's history.

"A Sledgehammer on a Floating Cork." The initial Marine battalions were quickly followed by more troops. By the end of 1965, nearly 200,000 US servicemen were stationed in Vietnam; a year later there were almost 400,000. But the war they were called on to fight proved frustrating. American technology and the enormous destructive force of American firepower somehow were not able to decisively overcome a tenacious and elusive enemy. One journalist, Malcolm W. Browne, used a striking metaphor to describe the US effort: it was, Browne wrote, like using "a sledgehammer on a floating cork. Somehow the cork refused to stay down." Despite their heavy losses on the battlefield and the daily rain of bombs on their own territory, the North Vietnamese proved able to match the US escalation, sending increasing quantities of arms and troops down the Ho Chi Minh Trail to join the war in the South.

As the war escalated, so did civilian suffering. In South Vietnam, an estimated 25,000 civilians were being killed and another 50,000 wounded every year. Hundreds of thousands more were uprooted from their homes. Thousands of villages were turned into blackened heaps of ashes—in some provinces nearly three-quarters of all the villages were destroyed. In North Vietnam, the civilian population endured constant bombing and the heartbreak of hundreds of thousands of soldiers killed or wounded in the fighting in the South.

THE 1968 TET OFFENSIVE

Early on the morning of January 31, 1968, Communist guerrillas attacked cities and towns throughout the country, breaking a truce that had been in effect for the Tet, or Lunar New Year, holiday. In Saigon, a small squad of guerrillas stormed onto the grounds of the US embassy in the heart of the capital. Another Viet Cong unit seized the radio station, although they were unable to broadcast revolutionary messages because the link between the station and the transmitter was broken during the attack.

The Tet Offensive, which the revolutionaries called "the general offensive and uprising," was, in the immediate sense, a failure. The guerrillas were driven out of all major towns within a few days, with the single exception of Hue, where they held out for three-and-a-half weeks. Their losses were devastating, not only among ordinary soldiers but also among experienced party agents and guerrilla leaders. Nowhere did the population rise up to join the revolution.

Yet in the long run, Tet also achieved a major Communist goal:

halting the US escalation of the war. The American public was stunned by the attacks, which seemed to contradict all the optimistic forecasts issued by US commanders in the past. The embassy assault, even though no guerrillas got inside the building itself, appeared to suggest that no place in South Vietnam was truly secure. The public was also troubled by the unprecedented US casualties— 2,000 Americans killed in the first month of the offensive.

Changing America's War Policy. Within the Johnson administration, a number of officials who had already begun to doubt his Vietnam policy now saw a chance to change it. Joining the doubters was Clark Clifford, who took over as Secretary of Defense shortly after the offensive began. Key members of the "Wise Men," a group of prestigious informal advisors to President Johnson, also began expressing skepticism. "We can no longer do the job we set out to do in the time we have left," former Secretary of State Dean Acheson told the president bluntly, "and we must take steps to disengage."

A troubled President Johnson, reluctant to face failure in Vietnam but recognizing that his policies no longer commanded support, ruled out further escalation when he turned down a military proposal to authorize an additional 206,000 more troops for the war. Then, on March 31, Johnson announced in a nationally televised speech that he would halt the bombing over most of North Vietnam in an effort to get peace negotiations started. In an unexpected postscript, he declared that he would withdraw as a candidate for reelection.

After months of diplomatic sparring between Washington and Hanoi, all remaining bombing of North Vietnam was halted on the last day of October 1968. After several more weeks of delay caused by objections from President Thieu in Saigon, formal peace negotiations began in Paris shortly before the new US president, Richard Nixon, was sworn into office.

Along with the war, Nixon inherited a public that was clearly impatient for an end to the conflict. Early in his administration, Nixon ordered his chief foreign-policy aide, Henry Kissinger, to open secret contacts with North Vietnamese representatives. Nixon also adopted a program of "Vietnamization," gradually pulling out US troops while increasing arms and training for the South Vietnamese.

THE CAMBODIAN CONNECTION

One more new policy was adopted during Nixon's first months as president: secret strikes by heavy B-52 bombers on Communist bases in neutral Cambodia. The Vietnamese guerrillas had been using the

Downed American airplane

Cambodian sanctuaries since the mid-1960s with the acquiescence of Cambodia's ruler, Prince Norodom Sihanouk, who had no love for the Vietnamese Communists but hoped that making concessions in a distant, lightly populated part of his country might influence them to leave the rest of Cambodia alone. American military commanders, who had long wanted to attack the Cambodian sanctuaries, were enthusiastic about the secret bombing campaign. The raids, not alone but in conjunction with other events, helped upset the precarious balance which had preserved peace in Cambodia.

Cambodian Hostility Mounts. The weak army of the Cambodian government, seemingly encouraged by the change in US policy, began sporadic attacks on the sanctuaries; in response, the Vietnamese began arming and training an insurgent movement among the hill-tribe people who inhabited the border region. As armed clashes mounted, so did Cambodian hostility toward the Vietnamese—an ancient, deep-seated hatred that was further inflamed, for their own purposes, by Sihanouk's domestic enemies. Following violent anti-Vietnamese demonstrations in Phnom Penh, the prince was overthrown on March 18, 1970, a year to the day after the secret US bombing began.

With Sihanouk's fall, the war in Cambodia quickly spread. Beginning on March 27, South Vietnamese forces launched attacks into Cambodian territory. Two days later the Vietnamese Communists began assaulting Cambodian army positions throughout the border region. US B-52 strikes, still kept secret, were quickly redirected to provide direct support to Cambodian troops. In early April, U.S. aid shipments began flowing, also secretly, to the Cambodian army.

Neither the ousted Sihanouk nor the new Cambodian leader, Gen. Lon Nol, showed any interest in restoring Cambodia's lost neutrality. Instead, both quickly lined up with opposing sides in the regional war. In Beijing, Sihanouk called for a Cambodian liberation army to fight, in alliance with the other Indochinese revolutionaries, against his usurpers; Lon Nol and his associates, naively disregarding their military weakness and expecting unstinting US support, began mobilizing to drive the Vietnamese from Cambodian territory.

US Intervention in Cambodia. On April 30, the US openly intervened in Cambodia for the first time, sending 32,000 US troops across the border to attack the Vietnamese base camps. After a storm of US antiwar protests, including one in which four protesters were killed by US National Guard gunfire at Kent State University in Ohio, President Nixon announced that all US forces would be withdrawn from Vietnam by June 30, 1973.

When the deadline was reached, US officials proclaimed the campaign a success. But that was true, if at all, only from the viewpoint of US forces on the Vietnamese side of the border. In Cambodia, the departure of American troops left the new government in a dangerous position. Its army, badly outmatched by the Vietnamese, quickly lost control of much of the countryside, including the entire region east of the Mekong river. Those early defeats set a trend that would never be reversed. During the years that followed, Lon Nol's army gradually but steadily lost ground, while Cambodia's economy disintegrated and an agony of defeat, hunger, and despair overcame its seven million people.

Between 1970 and 1973, a Cambodian resistance force replaced the Vietnamese Communists on the battlefields. The insurgency in-

Underground living quarters for Communist guerillas, Cu Chi

cluded a number of factions, of which the most radical and violent was a group of Cambodian Communists known as the Khmer Rouge, or Red Khmer. Their leadership, which had already spent years in the jungle, was headed by a former engineering student named Saloth Sar, who would become known to history under another name: Pol Pot.

THE 1972 EASTER OFFENSIVE

In South Vietnam, American forces continued to withdraw during 1970 and 1971. From a peak of nearly 540,000, US strength had dropped to only about 70,000 when, on the last day of March 1972, North Vietnam launched what became known as the Easter Offensive.

Unlike Tet, which was carried out mainly by guerrillas who infiltrated cities and towns, the 1972 offensive was a largely conventional attack by North Vietnamese infantry, tanks, and artillery. The Communists seized one provincial capital, Quang Tri, and threatened two others before their assault faltered—largely due to extremely heavy US bombing in support of the South Vietnamese defenders. In response to the attack, President Nixon resumed full-scale bombing of North Vietnam for the first time since 1968.

The 1972 fighting reached levels of bloodshed and destruction never approached before in all the previous years of the war. Casualties on both sides were unprecedented. Over a million South Vietnamese became refugees. As the battle lines stabilized, it became evident that neither side had been able to gain a clear advantage. Instead, they had simply reestablished the stalemate of the past, but at a higher level of violence than ever.

A DRAMATIC NEW OFFER

Hanoi, meanwhile, was increasingly isolated from its principal allies, China and the Soviet Union, both of which welcomed President Nixon on official visits during 1972. The state of mutual exhaustion on the battlefields and the changed international environment prompted North Vietnam to make a dramatic new offer in the long-stalled peace negotiations. On October 8, Hanoi's chief negotiator, Le Duc Tho, handed Henry Kissinger a draft peace agreement which, for the first time, did not demand the resignation of President Thieu and the disarming of the South Vietnamese army *before* a truce. Instead, Tho's plan accepted the principle that both sides would remain in place during a ceasefire, while US troops were withdrawn and a permanent political settlement was negotiated.

Kissinger was elated. "We have done it," he exulted to an aide after reading Tho's draft. Over the next several days he and Tho agreed on all but a few details of a treaty. In a final exchange of messages, after Kissinger flew to Saigon to present the agreement to President Thieu, he and the North Vietnamese not only resolved all remaining issues but set a time and place for signing the agreement: the last day of October 1972, in Hanoi.

Thieu, however, balked. The most violent of his many objections was that the draft treaty allowed North Vietnamese troops to remain in South Vietnam. Unable to convince their ally, Kissinger and Nixon had no choice but to renege on their commitment to the North Vietnamese. Instead of traveling on to Hanoi for the signing, Kissinger returned to Washington, declaring that despite the temporary setback, "peace is at hand." During November, in an atmosphere of mutual recriminations, negotiations resumed in Paris.

The talks ended, without result, on December 12. Six days later,

at 7:43 PM Hanoi time, US bombs began falling on North Vietnamese airfields, opening the eleven-day campaign that came to be
known as the "Christmas bombing." The raids killed more than
1,600 civilians in Hanoi and the port city of Haiphong, according
to official North Vietnamese reports, while the US lost 26 planes,
including 15 B-52 bombers. Nearly 100 American airmen were
killed, missing, or captured before the bombing ended on December
30. On January 8, peace talks resumed in Paris, where the agreement was rapidly renegotiated. US officials later claimed that the
bombing of Hanoi forced the settlement; the North Vietnamese,
however, pointed out that the January agreement, in all but a few
minor details, was identical to the one negotiated in October, before
the bombing.

Under intense pressure from Washington, Thieu capitulated.
On January 27, 1973, the agreement was formally signed in Paris;
the guns were to stop at eight the next morning, Saigon time.

Cease-fire Violations. Instead, as one American official report
put it, the cease-fire "initiated a new war, more intense and more
brutal than the last." In the 48 hours before the deadline, the Communists attacked hundreds of villages and other government-held
positions; despite the cease-fire, South Vietnamese troops were ordered to keep fighting until they had recaptured what was commonly
considered to be Saigon-controlled territory. By the second week of
February, the Communists had been driven out of nearly all the
positions they had seized in their 11th-hour attacks. But government forces remained on the offensive, pushing farther into Com-
munist-occupied zones. Thereafter, both sides took the position that
in "self-defense" they were entitled to retaliate for cease-fire violations by attacking the other's troops and bases wherever they could
reach. Under those policies, except in a few scattered places, fighting continued at the same or higher levels as before the truce.

As provided in the agreement, the last US troops left South
Vietnam during a 60-day period after the cease-fire, while the Communists freed 595 US prisoners. But no other provisions of the
agreement were ever carried out. By fall, it had become an irrelevant
piece of paper, "like a dictionary," one observer commented, "for a
language that nobody speaks."

The Paris agreement contained no settlement for the conflicts
in Vietnam's weaker neighbors, Laos and Cambodia. In Laos, the
US-supported Vientiane government and the Communist Pathet
Lao concluded a separate ceasefire agreement on February 21, 1973,
which, unlike the Vietnam truce, did significantly reduce the level

of fighting. In Cambodia, where the insurgent movement in early 1973 was rapidly falling under the control of the fanatical Khmer Rouge, there were no negotiations at all. Despite heavy US bombing, the rebels steadily drove back the weak government army until, by early summer, they were threatening Phnom Penh itself. Their siege finally faltered just before the bombing halted, by Congressional order, on August 15.

AFTERMATH OF THE PEACE AGREEMENT

At the time of the peace agreement, despite Thieu's misgivings, South Vietnam seemed to be in a relatively strong position. During the rest of 1973, that impression persisted. But during the second year of the failed truce, the Saigon regime began to weaken militarily, politically, and economically. Acute inflation and the loss of jobs resulting from the US withdrawal combined to devastate the economy. A million workers, about one-fifth of the civilian labor force, were unemployed. Soldiers' and civil servants' salaries were no longer enough to buy food for their families. More and more men deserted from the armed forces, further weakening units that were already understrength from the unprecedented casualties since 1972.

In mid-1974, after the US Congress approved only $700 million in military aid instead of the proposed $1.4 billion, the army command suddenly imposed restrictions on artillery and air support, further demoralizing an army that had grown used to a US-style war of lavish firepower and air mobility.

The South's Growing Weaknesses. The deteriorating economy and the increasingly unfavorable military situation undermined President Thieu's political support. The South Vietnamese leader was further weakened when President Nixon, who was seen by most Vietnamese as Thieu's patron, resigned as a result of the Watergate scandal in August 1974. Within weeks of Nixon's exit, the first significant opposition movement in South Vietnam in many years launched a campaign of protests against Thieu, centering on the issue of corruption. In Saigon, antigovernment demonstrations continued for several weeks, until a violent police crackdown halted the marches at the end of October.

South Vietnam's growing weaknesses did not escape the attention of Hanoi. Beginning in October, party and military leaders held a series of meetings in the North Vietnamese capital to consider their strategy for 1975. Even before those meetings concluded, Communist forces opened an offensive in mid-December in Phuoc

Display at the National Military Museum, Hanoi

Long, a sparsely populated province at the southern end of the Truong Son mountains. In only three weeks, they captured the entire province, including the capital, Phuoc Binh. Encouraged by the Phuoc Long battle, the Hanoi leadership in early January approved military plans for "large surprise attacks" in 1975.

The offensive opened on March 10 with a powerful attack on Ban Me Thuot, in South Vietnam's Central Highlands. Instead of the seven to ten days anticipated in their battle plans, Communist forces overran the city in only a little more than 24 hours. After a government counterattack failed, President Thieu flew to the former US logistic base at Cam Ranh Bay on March 14 to meet with the commander of the highlands region, Maj. Gen. Pham Van Phu. His orders were stunning: in order to conserve soldiers and supplies, Phu was to pull back his forces to the coast, yielding the entire highlands to the Communists.

A Disastrous Retreat. The next night, government troops began withdrawing from Pleiku, Phu's headquarters. But the retreat
turned into a disaster. Instead of carefully organizing the withdrawal, Phu and most of his senior commanders packed up and flew to
the coast, leaving their soldiers to get out anyway they could. Along
the 135-mile route to the coast the leaderless, panicking South Vietnamese troops, accompanied by tens of thousands of civilian refugees, were lashed in repeated ambushes. Few ever reached the coast;
most were killed, wounded, or captured along the way. Mountains
of weapons and supplies were abandoned to the North Vietnamese.

Within a few days, government units in South Vietnam's five
northern provinces also disintegrated. Quang Tri province was
abandoned on March 19 ("Quang Tri does not a forest make,"
quipped the pro-Saigon press); a week later the North Vietnamese
occupied Hue. Danang, the country's second largest city, dissolved
in panic as soldiers and civilians fought to escape by air or on ships
and small boats. With almost no resistance, Communist troops took
over the city on Easter Sunday, March 30. After Danang, provinces
along a 300-mile stretch of the coast fell, as one writer put it, "like
a row of porcelain vases sliding off a shelf." Out of the abandoned
provinces, on foot and in desperately overcrowded boats off the
coast, flowed retreating soldiers and great rivers of refugees, amid
scenes of terror and suffering that would forever sear the memories
of those who were there.

PHNOM PENH FALLS

While South Vietnam's army collapsed, the war in neighboring
Cambodia was also coming to a close. Khmer Rouge ambushes along
the Mekong river had shut off all supply convoys to Phnom Penh
since January, leaving a US airlift as the only source of rice, fuel,
and ammunition for the besieged capital. Hunger, misery, fear, and
disease ravaged the city's population, swollen by more than a million
refugees camped in flimsy shelters at schools, pagodas, and parks.
Hospitals overflowed with the wounded and sick. On April 1, President Lon Nol left the country; twelve days later, helicopters from
the USS *Okinawa* and USS *Hancock* swooped into Phnom Penh to
evacuate US Ambassador John Gunther Dean and his staff. On
April 17, as white flags fluttered from windows and among the flow-
ering trees lining the broad boulevards, the black-clad teen-aged
soldiers of the Khmer Rouge marched grimly into the city.

In their relief that the war was finally over, people welcomed
the arriving rebels with smiles and cheers. But within hours, they

were stunned by an order as fantastic as it was cruel: the entire city was to be evacuated, at once and with no exceptions. Even sick and wounded patients were turned out of hospitals and forced to join the dazed, terrified crowds of people being marched away from their homes toward the city's outskirts. With that bizarre act of brutality, the Khmer Rouge revolution began—a revolution, as one analyst wrote, propelled by a fanatical belief that "everything that had preceded it was anathema and must be destroyed." Instead of the peace everyone hoped for, Cambodia was about to enter the worst years of its history.

PRESIDENT THIEU RESIGNS

By the time Phnom Penh fell to the Khmer Rouge, the Vietnamese Communists were a bare two weeks away from their own victory. On the evening of April 21, President Thieu tearfully announced his resignation. During the next week, as Saigon waited in a mesmerized, dreamlike daze, North Vietnamese forces closed in on the city from three directions. On April 28, while a late-afternoon thunderstorm rattled the windows of the Independence Palace, Duong Van Minh, who had last headed the government more than eleven years earlier after leading the 1963 coup against Ngo Dinh Diem, was sworn in as South Vietnam's last president.

Raid on Saigon. Minh, who in recent years had become identified with a "third force" movement aligned neither with the Communists nor with the Thieu regime, was convinced by some of his associates that if he took power the Communists would pause and negotiate rather than storm the city. But if there was ever a time for negotiations, it had long since passed. No more than ten minutes after Minh's inauguration, North Vietnamese pilots in captured US-built jets carried out the war's first and last enemy air raid on Saigon, striking Tansonnhut air base on the edge of the capital. Before dawn the next day, Tansonnhut was hit by an intense artillery barrage. At six minutes past three that afternoon, US helicopters from a naval task force off the Vietnamese coast began landing to carry out "Operation Frequent Wind"—the evacuation of Saigon.

During the next 16 hours, flying in hazardous conditions through darkness and severe thunderstorms, American helicopter crews were in the air almost continuously, shuttling nearly 7,000 evacuees from Saigon to the waiting ships. About 1,400 were American; the rest were mostly Vietnamese who feared reprisals if they remained in Saigon. Eleven of the embassy's Marine guards were the last to leave; the final flight plucked them off the embassy roof at 7:53 AM on April 30.

Four hours later, a dozen North Vietnamese tanks roared past the deserted embassy, heading for the presidential palace a few blocks away. The high steel gates in front of the palace were closed, but the lead tank, with No. 843 painted on its turret, easily smashed through the gate and raced the remaining few hundred feet to the palace's front steps.

As the rest of the tanks swarmed onto the lawn, a soldier leaped down and sprinted up the steps, waving a Liberation flag over his head. A moment later he reappeared on a balcony just above the entrance, still holding the flag. With both hands he flung it violently from side to side, signaling victory to the tanks and soldiers on the lawn below. More than 30 years after beginning their struggle, and at a cost in blood and suffering no one could have imagined when they began, Ho Chi Minh's successors had finally reached their goal: a unified Vietnam under the flag of their revolution.

THE AFTERMATH IN LAOS AND CAMBODIA

After the revolutionaries' successes in Cambodia and Vietnam, the Communists in Laos, the third of the Indochinese states, took power easily and with almost no fighting. In town after town, following public demonstrations adroitly staged by the Pathet Lao, demoralized government officials handed over power. In August, the revolutionaries took control in the royal capital of Luang Prabang and then in the administrative capital, Vientiane, completing their peaceful conquest. Three and a half months later, despite having declared throughout the war that they respected the 600-year-old Lao monarchy, the Pathet Lao abolished it and proclaimed the Lao People's Democratic Republic. King Savang Vatthana, who had predicted many years before that he would be the last king of Laos, abdicated with a final message wishing "happiness and prosperity to the whole of my beloved Lao people."

Instead of happiness and prosperity, however, violence continued to afflict the peoples of Indochina after the 1975 Communist victories.

Deadly Paranoia. Cambodians suffered the most. Under Saloth Sar, who assumed the name Pol Pot after the revolution, the Khmer Rouge emptied the towns and herded millions of people into forced-labor camps. Tens of thousands of former soldiers and officials in the Lon Nol government were executed, frequently along with their

Wild flowers surround a child's grave site, Dalat

families. In a deadly paranoia that seemed to grow with the number of their victims, the Khmer Rouge also slaughtered members of religious minorities, suspected "intellectuals," Buddhist monks, and others assumed to be "class enemies" or traitors. Altogether, it was estimated that between one and two million Cambodians, of a total population of only seven million, were murdered or died of starvation, exhaustion, or disease.

Pol Pot and his associates directed their most fanatical hostility toward their neighbors and former partners, the Vietnamese Communists. Repeated Cambodian raids across the border in 1977 led to a series of escalating retaliations by the Vietnamese. On the last day of the year, Cambodia publicly denounced Vietnam for "aggression" and broke diplomatic relations. China, the Khmer Rouge government's only ally, supported Cambodia; the Soviet Union backed Vietnam.

During 1978, the conflict worsened until, on Christmas Day, 100,000 Vietnamese troops smashed across the border in a full-scale invasion. Two weeks later, they occupied an all-but-deserted Phnom Penh. The next day a new government was proclaimed, headed by Heng Samrin, a former senior Khmer Rouge commander who had defected to the Vietnamese several months earlier. The country, which the Khmer Rouge had called Democratic Kampuchea, was renamed the People's Republic of Kampuchea. *

Despite their rapid capture of Phnom Penh, the Vietnamese did not win the quick, decisive victory they had hoped for. Instead, they found themselves facing a formidable resistance from scattered, but not defeated, Khmer Rouge forces. Eventually, the Khmer Rouge concentrated in bases in western Cambodia along the Thai border, where, with the discreet cooperation of the Thai authorities, they were able to receive arms shipments from their Chinese allies.

In 1982, the Khmer Rouge—claiming to have abandoned its violent revolutionary ideology but still under the same leaders—joined with two smaller non-Communist resistance movements, one loyal to Prince Sihanouk and the other led by a veteran Cambodian politician named Son Sann. The alliance, using the Khmer Rouge name for the country, called itself the Coalition Government of Democratic Kampuchea. Despite the fact that the murderous Khmer Rouge played a major role in the coalition, it was diplomatically supported by the non-Communist countries of Southeast Asia, the US, and most other Western governments.

Cambodia's Uncertain Future. By January 7, 1989, a full decade since the Vietnamese invasion, Cambodia's future remained unsettled. A Vietnamese pledge to withdraw by 1990 aroused an ambivalent reaction: it would end foreign occupation, but might also open

---

* As of May 1989, the Vietnamese-backed government in Kampuchea declared that their country had officially changed its name to the State of Cambodia.

the way for a Khmer Rouge attempt to regain power. Meanwhile, as fighting continued, some 300,000 Cambodians remained in refugee camps in Thailand, which was also the reluctant host to about 100,000 other refugees from Laos.

VIETNAM IN THE 1980s

In Vietnam, the 1980s saw the gradual retirement of the old revolutionaries and their replacement by a new generation of leaders. The major task facing the new leadership was reviving an economy which, officials freely admitted, had sunk into a disastrous state as the result of poor policies and blundering management. Under Nguyen Van Linh, who became General Secretary of the Communist Party in 1986, Vietnam embarked on a program of economic reforms similar to those taking place in other Communist nations, aimed at raising living standards by improving management, relaxing rigid government controls, and encouraging private enterprise.

"Forget the Past." More than a decade and a half after the last American troops flew out of the country, Vietnam's leaders were also openly seeking reconciliation with the US. "Vietnam wants to forget the past," General Secretary Linh told foreign reporters in early 1988. The US government refused to end its economic embargo or establish official relations while Vietnamese troops remained in Cambodia. But unofficial US-Vietnamese contacts gradually increased. Growing numbers of journalists, relief-agency workers, scholars, former soldiers, and curious tourists traveled to Vietnam, while a smaller trickle of Vietnamese students, artists, and other visitors were quietly welcomed in the US. Through such exchanges, both Americans and Vietnamese could begin to escape, at last, from the tragic burden of their past.

Author's Note: April 5, 1989—Vietnam announced that it planned to withdraw its remaining troops from Cambodia by the end of September 1989, leaving behind a pro-Hanoi regime. After the Vietnamese pullout, the Khmer Rouge can hardly be expected to participate in a peaceful democracy. Another civil war in Cambodia seems inevitable.

VIETNAM'S CULTURE:
THE SOCIAL ORDER

An understanding of Vietnam's cultural characteristics is important as a basis for understanding and appreciating the people.

SOCIAL CUSTOMS

The Vietnamese have a tradition of strong ties to the family and village. Politeness, sensitivity, modesty, and humility are Vietnamese traits. Although tourists may perceive a sense of reserve in the Vietnamese people, this behavior may be due to several factors such as cultural modesty, historic caution around foreigners, or the fact that for many years of political upheaval ordinary citizens were not allowed to speak casually to outsiders.

Talking involves a specific set of rules worth understanding. When speaking, a standard gesture of modesty may include covering the mouth with a hand, notebook, or napkin. While boasting is avoided, there is a tendency to swing to the other end of the spectrum by expressing oneself in a self-deprecating fashion—a manner of conduct some Westerners find cloying. The Vietnamese often imply meanings, preferring to talk around a sensitive subject before coming to the point. Although making direct eye contact is avoided, cosmopolitan Saigonese will understand this "look at me when I'm talking to you" trait as accepted Western practice. Villagers or Northerners, however, may consider such aspects of Western visitors' behavior excessively bold or rude.

Confucian love of knowledge reveals itself in the people's penchant for quoting poetry or the sayings of a wise scholar. Northerners especially display their patriotism and learning by reciting the sayings of Ho Chi Minh.

Time concepts held by Vietnamese and Westerners are strikingly different. The Judeo-Christian culture conceptualizes time as linear, or as an extended line along which progress may be made as milestones are reached. The Vietnamese, as other Asians with Buddhist or Hindu influences, conceive of time as cyclic and recurrent—there will always be another day, another season, another life in which to achieve one's goals. Consequently, there is less pressure to accomplish things quickly, or on the spot.

Gift Exchanges. The point of view regarding gift-giving and receiving among Vietnamese differs significantly from the Western expectation of "thank you very much" from the recipient. Vietnamese perceive good deeds as actions specifically carried out by the giver to accumulate merit for the next life. The giver, in fact, is indebted to the receiver for allowing the good deed to occur. Given this scenario, Vietnamese are sometimes not as effusive (although not necessarily any less thankful) in their gratitude as some Westerners might expect.

Maintaining Harmony. Placing great value on harmonious relationships and perpetuating pleasant relations, Vietnamese may prefer "little white lies" to offending someone with the blunt truth. However, Vietnamese who have been exposed to Westerners feel comfortable being frank with foreigners. Another method for maintaining harmony is the reluctance to express a personal opinion, or to give a negative response. When a Vietnamese nods and utters the Vietnamese "yes" (da) while listening, the meaning does not express approval. Whereas the English "yes" means agreement, the *da* is non-committal and conveys only that what the speaker has said has been understood.

While members of the opposite sex do not touch each other in public, this social restriction is relaxed a bit among the younger generation in a disco environment. With no stigma attached to members of the same sex touching, it would not be unusual to see two young men or two women holding hands as they walk along the street. It would be best to avoid touching any Vietnamese. Even patting a child on the head or back-slapping your friendly guide after a hearty joke is unwelcome.

The typical Western hand motion requesting another to come over (one finger or palm of the hand held upright) may be taken as an insult by some Vietnamese, as this hand movement happens to be their gesture for summoning animals. Beckoning a person Vietnamese-style requires holding the palm down and the hand slightly cupped, while simultaneously wiggling all four fingers back and forth as in the familiar American gesture made with one finger. Foot posture while sitting is another formality worth noting. Crossing one's legs and pointing the sole of the shoe toward another is considered rude.

In Vietnam, the smile (usually associated with amusement or approval in the West) can also mean anxiety, anger, fear, embarrassment, and even disagreement, given that a Vietnamese listener, not wishing to offend the speaker, will often smile—but doesn't really agree.

Despite differences in customs and matters of etiquette you may encounter, the Vietnamese people will appreciate that you are a guest in their country. As long as you are calm and polite, it is unlikely that you'll make a serious error. Should you have doubts about appropriate behavior in a given situation, observe the actions of the eldest person of your sex, and do as he or she does.

RELIGION

Most Vietnamese are Buddhists. The venerable pagoda (a building honoring Buddha) continues its role as the center for many village activities, although less actively now than in the past. While the socialist government discourages all religious activities in Vietnam, the Constitution of 1976 officially provides policies regarding religious activity (all are carefully monitored), including:

1. Freedom of religion and of atheism
2. Motivation of religious groups to implement socialist ideals (religious leaders are urged to mobilize followers to carry out the policies of the state)
3. Efforts to free the churches from the "shackles of imperialism" and return them to work for the masses
4. No misuse of religion to violate state laws
5. Requirement of a permit for some religious activities which are attended by many people from different areas
6. Prospective priests obliged to prove their socialist commitment before permission is granted for religious training

Animism. Underlying and co-existing with the more formally structured religions in Vietnam is animism, the belief that a governing spirit dwells in living and nonliving things. Thus, spirits dwell in trees, in rocks, and in the wind and rain. Since these spirits have powers, they must be appeased and coaxed by gifts of food, flowers, incense, and prayers to use those powers for good.

Buddhism. Buddha was an Indian prince who rejected the claims of the high-born Brahmans that they were spiritually superior to other people and that one's soul could secure salvation through the observation of social class duties. He preached that existence is a cycle of death and rebirth, and that anyone could achieve salvation through self-discipline. A person's well-being in this life was determined by actions in the previous life. Buddha taught the Four Noble Truths: (1) pain and suffering were a part of the continuing cycle of birth and rebirth; (2) suffering is the result of attachment to the things of this world; (3) suffering could end by eliminating attachments; and (4) following the "Eightfold Path" leads to the ridding of attachment and to the achievement of a state of peace called *Nirvana*. The "Eightfold Path" consists of right belief, the renunciation of sensual pleasure and cruelty to any creature, the practice of moderation in speech, conduct, occupation, and effort, and cultivating a life based on meditation and contemplation.

Buddhism reached Vietnam through contacts with the Kushana Empire of India in the second and third centuries. The Vietnamese people practice two forms of Buddhism: Theravada, for whom the ideal man is a saintly man, called *arhat*, and Mahayana (or the Greater Vehicle), which incorporates the existence of many Buddhas.

The Mahayana, the more popular of the two, teaches that each human has the potential to become a *bodhisattva*, a person who has achieved Nirvana but remains in the world to perform good works for his fellow man.

To a lesser extent, Zen Buddhism is practiced in Vietnam. Originating in China, Zen Buddhism is based on meditation rather than adherence to scriptural doctrine; it also holds only consciousness as real, not objects. The characteristic Zen teaching of *satori*, or sudden enlightenment, defines enlightenment as the direct seeing of one's own "original Nature." Vinitaruci, a Brahman from India, worked and studied in China before coming to Vietnam in AD 580. He lived in the temple of Buddha of the Clouds near Lu Lau (near Hanoi) and practiced a form of Zen Buddhism. Although Zen was established in Vietnam before his arrival, he attracted more followers to the tradition. His disciple, Phap Hien, continued his work.

It is common for temples in Vietnam to feature images of Quan Am, the female embodiment of supreme empathy. Like her Madonna counterpart in Western religions, Quan Am represents universal compassion. She is ready to reach out and comfort the suffering, without stopping to judge. For this reason, Quan Am is often depicted with a vase of blessed water and a willow branch. She uses the willow branch to sprinkle the water of compassion onto mankind.

The government has converted some pagodas in Vietnam to a variety of nonspiritual uses; monks and nuns are expected to perform productive labor with faith relegated to after-work hours.

Confucianism. Confucius lived in China from 551 BC to 479 BC. His teaching focused on rules to achieve an orderly and honest government. Whereas Buddhism crossed all social classes by dealing with individual introspection, Confucianism's emphasis on social

Buddha, Nhatrang

order in an authoritarian society appealed to aristocrats and those in power who wished to maintain the status quo. In a family setting, according to Confucian principles, the father deserved the greatest respect with the eldest son second in line. A woman was urged to obey her father first, then her husband, and when her husband died, her oldest son. The family system of duty and respect extended to friends, to the community, to representatives of the government, and to its ruler. In Vietnam, as in China, Confucianism and Buddhism exist side by side with animism.

Hoa Hao and Cao Dai. Hoa Hao is basically a modified Buddhist sect founded in the Mekong delta in 1939 by Huynh Phu So from the Chau Doc area of An Giang province where the sect has its headquarters. Followers, who live in the western part of southern Vietnam, have simplified their communication with the Supreme Being by eliminating temples and intermediaries in their worship.

Cao Dai is a synthesis of Christianity, Confucianism, Mohammedanism, and Buddhism. Its members (less than 2,000,000 in the 1960s) are concentrated in the south near Tay Ninh, Long An, and Ben Tre. The Holy See at Tay Ninh (at the foot of Black Lady Mountain) is the center of the sect's authority; the building also contains offices of high-ranking monks. Founded in the early 1920s, Caodaoism favored the Japanese presence in Vietnam as a means to free the country from French colonialism.

Hinduism. A form of Hinduism is practiced among the Cham people on the southern seacoast of Vietnam.

Taoism. Taoism is based on the Tao-te-ching ("Book of the Way of Life"), traditionally ascribed to the Chinese philosopher Lao Tze, but probably written earlier in the third century BC. Rejecting Confucian demand for obligations and social orders, Taoism focused belief in the mystical harmony of humans with the natural world. By the fifth century AD, Taoism had adopted many features of Mahayana Buddhism and offered a fully developed religious system for those who found the largely ethical system of Confucianism inadequate. The small Taoist population in Vietnam worships in a pagoda-like structure called a *quan.*

Catholicism. Catholicism was introduced to Vietnam in the 16th century by Portuguese missionaries operating from their Jesuit headquarters based in Macao (southeast China), the oldest permanent European settlement and trading post in Asia. By the 17th century, French missionaries were converting entire Vietnamese villages to Catholicism.

Today, Vietnamese Catholic citizens still carry the stigma of having foreign connections—a religious affiliation that makes them suspiciously unpatriotic in the eyes of the current administration. The anti-Catholic attitude of the present government has deep historical roots. Beginning in the 19th century, the Catholic Church developed considerable influence under French-colonial rule. Many Vietnamese, hoping to advance under the French-dominated society, converted to Catholicism. In 1954, when the Communists came to power in Hanoi, 700,000 northern Catholics, fearing religious persecution, fled south to support the anti-communist Diem regime that was later backed by the Americans who, as a rule, trusted Vietnamese Catholics. The Church posed another threat to the Communist regime. As the parish is the Catholic community, the priest is often consulted as an authority in matters other than religion. This meant that Catholics might follow the dictates of the Vatican, even in political matters—potentially undermining state control.

After 1975, Church-owned lands and schools were turned over to the state. In spite of the state's contempt concerning religious practices, Catholic masses are attended by young and old worship-

Funeral, Cholon

ers. Vietnam has 22 dioceses and three archdioceses: Hanoi, Hue, and Ho Chi Minh City. The Church in the north was isolated during the period when the reforms of Vatican Council II, held in 1965, were taking place in Catholic countries in other parts of the globe, including the southern part of Vietnam. One of the council's decrees, the Constitution of Sacred Liturgy, permitted the popularization of the mass in the vernacular, or local tongue of the people. While churches in the rest of the world were incorporating the council's reforms, Northern Vietnamese Catholics continued to observe their daily Mass in Latin—as they still do—beginning in Hanoi at 5 AM so as not to interfere with work schedules. St. Joseph Seminary in Ho Chi Minh City, closed since 1975 (when the Communists took over Saigon), reopened in 1987.

Today, Vietnam has the highest percentage (7 to 10%) of Catholics in Southeast Asia, after the Philippines. Because of the mass migration of northern Catholics to the south in 1954, the number of Catholics in the south is double that of the north. There are about two million Catholics in Vietnam today.

Protestantism. Though not a major religion in Vietnam, Protestantism is practiced by some 200,000 in the cities of the south and 100,000 in the north. Protestant churches are called Tin Lanh (Good News) churches.

HEALTH CARE

PRINCIPAL HEALTH INDICATORS IN 1984

Life Expectancy at Birth	56.7 (males)	61.1 (females)
Infant Mortality	35 per 1,000 live births (Vietnamese estimates)	72 per 1,000 live births (UN estimates)

Although recent wars have had a devastating effect on the health of the people, the health care delivery system provided by the Socialist Republic of Vietnam has generally improved conditions in the past 30 years. The centrally controlled state health care network has the potential of providing care to every person. The Ministry of Health oversees all health-related projects, produces and distributes herbal medicines and pharmaceuticals, trains health care workers, controls hospitals, and coordinates research. Health issues are a priority in Vietnam (the Ministry of Health was allotted 11% of the government's budget in 1984) and, unlike some other Asian countries, the Minister of Health is a respected cabinet figure.

Levels of Care. The socialized health care system in Vietnam offers primary, secondary, and tertiary levels of medical care.

Basic or primary health care is provided at the hamlet and village level. In almost every village, there is a public health/maternity center staffed by one or more assistant doctors, nurses, and midwives. In addition, there are part-time health workers called "hygiene activists," also known as "barefoot doctors."

Secondary care is provided at the province and district level. A physician medical director oversees the 500 districts within a typical province.

Tertiary care is provided at urban specialized institutes. In addition, these referral and consultant centers conduct research, plan and implement national health programs, and serve as training centers for medical students and residents.

Health care in Vietnam is free to everyone. Like the state educational program, the health system assures priority to government workers and employees of large state enterprises. When patients are hospitalized, their families are expected to provide meals. Although physicians number about one per 4,000 population, a good proportion for a developing country, lack of usable medical equipment, supplies, and even common medications frustrates the efforts of the country's skilled doctors. The chronic shortage of medicines supports a thriving black market where these drugs can be purchased privately.

Prevention. Health care in Vietnam emphasizes sanitation, immunization, and preventive measures at the local level. UNICEF assists in the immunization programs. Control of diseases such as tuberculosis, bubonic plague, cholera, and leprosy continues to challenge the evolving public health system. In 1975, the Socialist Republic of Vietnam extended its health care system into the south. While two-thirds of the southern provinces have socialized medical facilities, a few private doctors still practice, mainly in Ho Chi Minh City.

The Ministry of Health claims victory over four main social diseases—malaria, trachoma (eye infection), tuberculosis, and leprosy. Malaria, which used to affect some five million people in the mountainous and swampy regions, is no longer endemic but has not been completely eliminated, even in the cities, and has proven itself resistant to the usual anti-malarial medications. The malaria-carrying mosquito (the female anopheles) has also become resistant to the toxic effect of the pesticide DDT. Once affecting as many as ten million people and blinding 100,000, trachoma is gradually disappearing due to education and simple procedures employed to prevent the disease. Tuberculosis and leprosy are also on the decline.

Other National Health Concerns. Malnutrition and its resultant debilitation increase susceptibility to other diseases. Infants are especially at risk. Traditionally, mothers would breast-feed their babies for 10 to 12 months. Half the infants in Vietnam today are breast-fed for three months because working mothers receive only three months' maternity leave. After the infants are weaned, they receive a thin rice soup that falls short of providing all the nutrients necessary for optimal growth.

Dioxin is a toxic by-product of Agent Orange, one of the herbicides used by the US military in Vietnam, under the code name Operation Ranch Hand, to defoliate the leafy jungle and expose guerrilla hiding places. The Ministry of Health conducts research on the medical effects of dioxin toxicity with particular emphasis on the incidence of birth defects in sprayed areas.

The most common methods of birth control in Vietnam are the intrauterine device (IUD) and condoms. To curb population growth, government-sponsored educational efforts encourage two-child families, late marriages, postponing the first child until the age of 25, and not having the second child until 5 years after the first. Since the maternity leave benefit can be used only twice, salaried workers paid by the government who decide to have more than two children might have to give up their jobs.

Drug addiction (mainly opiates) and venereal diseases are health issues that concern the Vietnamese. Treatment programs have been set up for detoxification and for the rehabilitation of prostitutes. AIDS has not yet become a problem.

Traditional Medicine in Vietnam. Traditional Vietnamese medicine, in addition to its native therapies, includes medical practices absorbed from other cultures—most notably ancient remedies from the Chinese, who introduced their medical science during their thousand years' occupation of Vietnam.

The underlying concept of Chinese medicine is that health is attained by balancing sets of opposing natural elements. One set is the *yin* (male principle) and *yang* (female principle). In Vietnamese, these elements are *am* and *duong*—*am* being the male and *duong*

Herbal medicine instructor, Hanoi

the female principle. The male force *yin* is associated with foods characterized by their sour taste, beans, the seasons of winter and autumn, the hours between noon and midnight, cold and coolness, and internal organs such as the liver, heart, and spleen. Illness is classified as too much or too little of *yin* or *yang*. If too much *yin* is thought to be the cause of the symptom (as in stomach upset), the patient might be advised to consume foods characterized by *yang*, such as sweets, pineapple, mango, and tangerines. Hot and cold represent another set of elements which must be in balance for good health.

In the 14th century, traditional medical practices of Vietnam were formalized by Tue Tinh into a book called *Medical Precepts*— a collection of essays still studied by medical students specializing in traditional medicine. The Giam pagoda outside of Hanoi commemorates this notable Vietnamese healer.

During the French occupation, an elite sector of the urban population was introduced to Western medical concepts; rural areas, however, relied on trusted ancient remedies. Even while taking a Western antibiotic, the Vietnamese will often take a traditional "tonic" to improve their general strength and well-being.

The practice of medicine took on a political cast when the

French closed the Hue indigenous school of traditional medicine, whose practitioners were called *curers*. Closing down the school devalued the integrity of the *curers* and the accumulated medical knowledge of the native Vietnamese healing arts that had evolved over a 1,000-year period.

A traditional medicine department now exists at the level of the Ministry of Health, and there is also a national commission for the alliance of traditional and modern medicine. Each provincial public health service has an office of traditional medicine that coexists harmoniously with the practice of Western medicine. Both schools of medicine are equally respected.

There are two main traditional medicine schools in Vietnam: in Hanoi, the Central Institute of Traditional Medicine, and one in Ho Chi Minh City, called Tue Tinh, after the 14th-century traditional physician. These schools offer a training program no less rigorous than that undertaken by a medical student in the West. Disciplines include acupuncture, therapeutic massage, respiratory exercises, and classical and popular herbal recipes. These centers, with the assistance of the Institute of Materia Medica in Hanoi, delineate specific properties of herbs, quantify their potencies, and study how herbal recipes exert their effects, and contribute to the development of a national pharmacopoeia. Acupuncture is practiced in Vietnam for the specific treatment of 23 disorders. The Association of Acupuncture was founded in 1968, and the Institute of Acupuncture was established in 1982. There are 17 hospitals in Vietnam dedicated to traditional treatment.

The people are encouraged to grow medicinal plants in gardens (called the "family green pharmacy") adjacent to their homes.

Common Remedies. *Dau con ho* or *dau con cop,* a mentholated ointment similar to Chinese Tiger Balm, is a common remedy for a variety of aches and pains. Some common herbs in the Vietnamese traditional herbal formulary are eucalyptus, cinnamon, camphor, anise seed, roots of elephant grass, licorice, ginger, tangerine peel, citronella, and chrysanthemum. In addition, animal products such as snake oils, toad skin, and powdered deer horns are used. Dermal techniques include the vigorous pinching of the bridge of the nose, coin rubbing, cupping, and moxibustion.

Moxibustion has been in use in Vietnam since the time of King An Duong in the third century BC. Consisting of forcefully rubbing the skin with a spoon or a coin to produce bruises, the moxibustion procedure is used to relieve colds, flu, and chest pains and does not cause permanent damage to the skin. Cupping is the practice of treating a troubled area by heating a small glass cup and placing it on the skin with the open end downward. The high temperature creates a temporary vacuum that sucks the skin into the cup. Cupping causes small vessels in the skin to break and leaves a circular bruise as evidence that it was performed properly in drawing out the "bad wind" from the afflicted area. Sometimes individuals will attempt to treat themselves by burning an area of pain with a cigarette in an attempt to remove the "bad wind."

EDUCATION

History. After Ngo Quyen drove the Chinese out of Vietnam in the 11th century, the new independent state of Dai Co Viet (as Vietnam was called at the time) established its first school for sons of the royal family. The school evolved into a college mandated to train future civil servants, called mandarins. In order to make the college accessible to all citizens, the system provided for provincial, regional, national, and court examinations.

Because passing even the lowest examination required three to four years of intensive study, a boy had to be supported by his family or a wealthy sponsor. Technically, any boy could take the examinations to become a mandarin. In practice, mandarins came from well-to-do homes. Few peasant parents could afford the luxury of having a son spend years away without contributing to the needs of the family. Although formally excluded from the mandarin tradition, there are stories of ambitious young girls who dressed as boys in order to attend preparatory classes.

From feudal times up to the early 20th century, primary education was the responsibilty of the village schoolmaster, who taught the students several hundred Chinese characters, history, and poetry. The fundamentals of Confucian thinking (introduced during the Chinese rule), advocating the "middle way" for the worthy man's behavior, ceremonial ritual, and rules of propriety, were also stressed. Candidates eager for higher education had to pass qualifying provincial exams (offered twice yearly) before going on to meet the regional requirements, and finally, the all-important national competitions.

Preparations for the national examinations involved proficiency in Confucian doctrine and memorizing a list of forbidden words that the would-be mandarin had to avoid writing during his examination essay. In Hanoi, national examinations went on for days and were given in open-air camps, secured by guards to prevent cheating. Testing started early in the morning. Each hopeful candidate was given paper and writing implements and locked in a tent or make-shift booth. The student then wrote on the assigned topic until midnight. Papers were judged on poetic style, command of the Four Classics of Confucius and other revered texts, plus the careful avoidance of forbidden or taboo words. If a word from the taboo list appeared on his paper, a candidate was immediately rejected; the poetic and philosophically correct nature of the composition was ignored. After the papers were graded, only the top three students were awarded the degree of Doctor First Class, a credential that qualified them to become provincial judges.

During the Tran Dynasty (1225–1400), mandarinal exams were held every seven, and later every three, years, conferring the equivalent of master's and doctor's degrees on its ranks of civil servants.

By the 20th century, the French had done away with the traditional mandarin system of education. In its place, they had established libraries, research centers, and technical schools designed to stress the French language (which was used exclusively) and French culture. The district elementary schools started by the French were available to a mere two percent of the population. Although secondary schools had been established by 1919, there were only five such institutions serving the entire country. The goal of French-sponsored education was to turn out low-level civil servants who could help administer the colonial form of government. The French dissemination of the romanized form of the Vietnamese language did increase literacy among the people. In 1930 (the same year Ho Chi Minh founded the Communist Party of Indochina), at the height of their rule in Vietnam, the French established the University of Hanoi.

The US influence that permeated the south in the 1960s introduced an American-style educational system that resulted in a substantial increase in the literacy rate. After the Communist regime took over in 1975, the educational system of the south was restructured along socialist educational ideals.

Education Today. Broadening the opportunities for education was a major goal of the revolution, whose campaign for literacy began in 1945 under the stresses of war, blackouts, bombings, and the hardships of jungle life for the guerrillas. The aim of the curriculum reforms of 1979 included changes to shape education more appropriately to the country's current level of development. To create a class

Vietnamese girl studying a textbook, Cholon

of industrial wage earners, the Communist government had to modify the former system's philosophical orientation that used education as an entrée into an elite class.

Recent reforms have strengthened the socialist moral content and upgraded the practical sciences, technology, and vocational aspects of higher education. Lesson content has been standardized throughout the entire country, bringing the Westernized school system of the pre-1975 South into line with the conventions of the North. In recent years, more than 1,000 former private schools in the South have been turned over to the government. In 1989, a private university (Thanghong) was founded in Ho Chi Minh City specializing in Computer Sciences. The school uses classrooms in the Medical School. New upper-level schools established since 1975 include the Danang Polytechnical College, Nhatrang Marine Products College, and the Tay Nguyen College.

Primary education is now universal in the northern part of the country, with almost all children attending school at least to the third grade in the South. In 1985, the literacy rate for the Kinh majority group was between 85% and 95% (one of the highest in Asia). School attendance among some ethnic minorities in highland areas has been understandably irregular as these groups find formal education of little relevance in their agrarian society.

Education in Vietnam is compulsory and free. Daycare nurseries and kindergartens are set up as an all-important complement to Vietnam's educational and social system. Primary general schooling (the first level) is a five-year program that begins when a child reaches the age of six. Second-level schooling goes through grade nine and is completed at about age fifteen. In theory, these nine years are compulsory. The third level of schooling (or secondary education), grades ten to 12, leads to either college courses through special schools or to vocational and trade schools. "Special schools" (pre-college) for gifted students are available mainly to children of government workers.

Total secondary school enrollment in Vietnam in 1985 was 43% of the children in that age group. This figure is well ahead of its wealthier neighbor, Thailand, with 29% in 1986. National school enrollment is 16 million. Programs for the educationally handicapped are being developed.

Secondary students engage in work several times a week. In some cases, the school day is divided into two sessions, with half the day spent on classwork and the other half in learning useful labor skills, either in the classroom or on site in the field of endeavor. The grading system is from one to ten (ten representing the highest grade).

Vietnam has three universities and 90 colleges of higher education (excluding military schools), with a total national enrollment of 115,000 post-high-school students.

While recent efforts have created great numbers of literate citizens, the quality of education has not kept up with the quantity. Maintaining a high level of literacy has exhausted the country's capacity to support it. Classrooms are generally overcrowded—sometimes 60 students to a class with some areas on a three-shift rotating scheduled in the same classroom. As textbooks are chronically in short supply, students are often obliged to form study groups of ten to share the same book. Because teachers receive poor wages, they seek private tutoring positions (outside school hours) with families who pay a fee for their children's education. The government accepts aid from UNICEF in the form of writing materials and exercise books for the school children.

Countering the historically ingrained Confucian separation of education from the world of work and the feeling that it is demeaning to work with one's hands has been a major issue facing the Communist government. Lack of relevance in courses studied had reached a point where one-third of the students leaving school could not find jobs. Colleges and advanced schools emphasize both knowledge and the development of a socialist attitude. The aim of scientific studies is not theoretical or abstract study of natural phenomena. Of primary interest is the betterment of life through, for example, the development of improved medical and agricultural techniques, or the development of new methods of breeding fish.

Note: Archaeologists have a high status in Vietnam and currently publish a journal which includes contents in Vietnamese, English, and French. Fieldwork is conducted by the Institute of Ar-

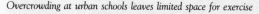

Overcrowding at urban schools leaves limited space for exercise

chaeology in Hanoi, where Ha Van Tan is senior archaeologist. Training in archaeology is conducted by the University of Hanoi. The Folklore Institute under chairman Dinh Gia Khanh conducts ethnographic research.

(For a list of institutes of higher education in Vietnam, see the Appendix Section.)

High school students, Dalat

THE ARTS IN VIETNAM

LANGUAGE AND LITERATURE

After winning its independence from the Chinese in the 11th century, Vietnam retained Chinese writing for formal and official documents until the 20th century. For less formal transcriptions such as stories, tales, and poems popularly inspired, the Vietnamese adapted the Chinese characters into their own form of writing called *chu nom*, commonly called *nom*. In *nom*, writers used Chinese characters to indicate the sound (phonetics) of the Vietnamese word rather than the original Chinese meaning—a system of characters as ideographs, or symbols that represented an idea or object.

The earliest forms of Vietnamese literature were written in traditional Chinese. Many Vietnamese classics such as the *Romance of the Three Kingdoms* were based on Chinese themes. *Nom* became the form for expressing popular modern literature, and true Chinese was maintained for academic documents. The students at the Van Mieu or Temple of Literature, the mandarin school at old Hanoi, used an ideographic writing system called *chu nho*, or scholar's language.

Development of Romanized Script. Although the Portuguese missionaries began the process of converting the Vietnamese language into a form that used roman letters, it was a French missionary, Alexander de Rhodes, who contributed most to the development of the romanized script called *quoc ngu*. Rhodes' innovation of tonal and diacritical markings proved essential for the understanding of the Vietnamese language. His Portuguese-Latin Vietnamese dictionary, published in 1651, helped other missionaries translate prayer books and catechisms into a written language accessible to the common citizen.

Quoc ngu was not popularized until early in the 20th century when the French closed the mandarin civil service schools in Vietnam. Thereafter, French and *quoc ngu*, which better lent itself to printing by Western printing presses, were used in French-Vietnamese communications. Some mandarins rebelled against this assault on their cherished, ancient hard-earned knowledge. Their unwillingness to convert to the new written language in Latin letters caused some mandarins to commit suicide, and still others chose exile.

Poetic Expression. Because the phonetic quality of the Vietnamese language lends itself well to poetry, the people pride them-

Preparing a New Year poster

selves on their ability to compose beautiful, properly stressed lines capable of eliciting a variety of subtle interpretations. The great national poet-statesman of Vietnam, Nguyen Trai (1380–1442), was also advisor and chief strategist to Le Loi, who drove the Chinese from Vietnam. After the Chinese were routed, Nguyen Trai wrote the *Proclamation of Victory Over the Wu* (Binh Ngo Dai Cao) in the first person as if it had been penned by Le Loi himself. A major significance of the Proclamation is that it can viewed as the solidification of a separate (from the Chinese) national identity for Vietnam. Nguyen Trai's *Collected Poems in National Language*, written in the *chu nom* form, denounces the superficiality of court life and praises the joys of the quiet contemplation of nature.

The 16th-century poet Nguyen Binh Khiem, author of a hundred or so surviving *nom* poems, is considered the outstanding writer of his time. In addition, there are two *nom* masterpieces adapted from Chinese poems: *The Lament of the Warrior's Wife* and the *Com-*

plaint of the Royal Concubine. The *Lament of the Warrior's Wife* is best known by its *nom* adapters, the woman poet, Doan Thi Diem (born 1705) and Phan Huy Ich (born 1750). The wife recalls the sad parting when her husband goes off to war:

> "When all through the earth and heaven rise dust storms.
> How hard and rough, the road a woman walks.
> Born to a race of heroes, you, my love,
> discard brush and ink for tools of war.
> I saw you off and sorrowed-Oh to be your horse on land,
> your boat upon the stream."

The *Complaint of the Royal Concubine* by Nguyen Gia Thieu (born circa. 1741) is a sensitive rendition of the inner feelings of the deserted concubine, a common theme in Chinese poetry. The concubine looks back upon her past beauty:

> "The bloom of my complexion made all women jealous;
> A glance from my eyes, iridescent as autumn pools,
> stirred up waves of passion that would overthrow fortresses.
> The moon strained to catch sight of me through my window blinds,
> Not even the trees and plants could stay indifferent to my beauty."

In the 18th and 19th centuries, the six-eight syllable verse called *luc-bat* rose in popularity. The first line of a *luc-bat* verse requires six syllables and the second line eight syllables. *Hoa Tien* and the *Kim Van Kieu* are outstanding examples of this verse form. The *Kim Van Kieu*, written by Nguyen Du (1765–1820), is the most popular masterpiece of Vietnamese literature. The title is taken from the names of the three main characters; the storyline is about Kieu, a beautiful and gifted young girl who suffers countless tribulations. The essence of the story is universal—young lovers are separated and finally reunited.

Every Vietnamese citizen, whether literate or not, knows at least some portion of the more than 3,000 verses in Nguyen Du's epic poem. Many can quote entire sections from memory. The following excerpt, in which the two lovers part after having vowed their love, expresses the bittersweet and melancholic tone that the Vietnamese love so much in their poetry and music.

"He climbed his horse, she let go of his gown—
autumn was tinging maple woods with gloom.
And off he rode as clouds of dust swirled up,
to vanish past all those green mulberry groves.
She walked back home to face the night alone,
and by himself he fared the long, long way.
Who split the lovers' moon? Half stayed and slept
by her lone pillow, half lit his far road."

Vietnamese are known to consult the poem for advice by reading a verse chosen at random—hoping to gain insight from the verse that will help them with their current problems. Marxists interpret the *Kim Van Kieu* as commentary on a corrupt feudal social system, while orthodox Confucians frown on the character Kieu's lack of moral responsibility and her negative effect on maintaining a stable society. But those who admire the work's characterizations stress the virtues of Kieu and her basic goodness of heart. Whatever the interpretation of content, the writing is appealing and charming. As a tone poem that must be chanted, every word takes on shades of meaning. Some parts of the poem are sung with a gasping breathy tone, while other parts are sung with a melancholic lilting.

A form of poetry evolved from the Chinese called *phu* also increased in popularity during the 18th century. A master of this form was Le Qui Don (1726–1783), the encyclopedist and historian.

The poetess Ho Xuan Huong (late 18th-early 19th century) has a special niche in Vietnamese literature. Her poems generally have two meanings, a literal one and a hidden, pornographic one. The poems—which deride pompous officials, extol free love and the equality of women, and express sympathy for unmarried mothers—are boldly simple and charming. Although details of Ho Xuan Huong's life remain a mystery, her outspoken themes suggest she was an early feminist.

Prose Literature. During the French colonial period, Vietnamese literature took on Western and political protest aspects with the nationalist movement reflected in drama, novels, and essays. The short story form with themes of satire and sexual romanticism, hitherto unknown in Vietnam, also grew in popularity. Since *chu nom* was expressed only in verse, Vietnamese literature had no prose until after the French introduced the concept. The evolution of the novel, which was well-developed throughout the Western world, is a 20th-century phenomenon in Vietnam.

Folk Tales. In addition to formally penned literature, Vietnam has a rich legacy of orally transmitted folk tales. Although folk tales have been written down in recent years, the preferred mode remains the oral tradition. Some folk tales are adaptations of ancient Chinese fables and still others are founded on the *Jatakas* (stories of Buddha's former incarnations). But not all folk tales are based on foreign influence. There are stories that recount the adventures of Vietnamese heroes as well. Folk tales also explain natural phenomena, such as the origins of Marble Mountain, the origins of the trio of ingredients in the betel chew, or the reason the water buffalo has wrinkled skin and horns. A striking feature of the Vietnamese folktale, noted by Westerners, is the ease with which human beings, animals, and even inanimate objects transform from one form to the other.

Ca Dao is a short, popular folk ballad sung without musical accompaniment. Sung by "traveling newscasters," *ve* are orally transmitted news stories and editorials spoken in rhyme that often glorified the actions of the rebels during the revolution. The word-of-mouth form of *ve* took the place of newspapers and TV in an illiterate society.

With the introduction of *quoc ngu* script and mass literacy among the people, oral traditions, although still maintained to a minor degree, are dying out as an art form. The first major volume printed in *quoc ngu* was published in 1925. The literary undertaking was a stilted prose version of the *The Red Melon*, a folk tale (originally in verse) that explained how the watermelon was introduced into the country. Since then, however, original works such as novels, short stories, narratives, and essays have contributed to a literary renaissance in Vietnam.

About 400 writers belong to the National Writer's Union (three-fourths of whom are Northerners), an organization formed to encourage writings of socially "correct" inspiration. The current poet laureate of Vietnam is To Huu, a Northerner best-known for his militant poetry that describes the struggle for independence.

RIDDLES

Vietnamese love riddles and guessing games. Here are two:

Five boys use two poles.
They chase a herd of white water buffalo into a dark cave.
What is this?

Answer: A hand using chopsticks to eat rice.

or

My heart is full of bitterness.
However, men still love me
and long for me when I'm away.
Pungent as I am,
I fill them with passion.
Who am I?

Answer: An opium pipe.

MUSIC

Songs. Since the Vietnamese language is lyrical, the voice can easily transform a poem into a song. Vietnamese music of the north follows the Chinese tradition of a five-tone scale in contrast to the eight-tone scale of Western musical notation. Southern Vietnamese music, influenced by India through the heritage of the Kingdom of Champa which occupied the south of Vietnam from the first to the 15th centuries, evolved four additional tones.

The nine-tone scale of southern Vietnamese music is a modification of the five tones of the Chinese scale plus four new tones. Southern tunes are characterized by a melancholic nostalgia with more decorative notes and half-tones than in the North.

Northern Vietnamese tunes express patriotism. Songs of determination and national spirit were morale builders, sung by the People's Army on their march south toward war, and by Youth Brigades working to repair bomb damage to military supply routes. In the mountainous regions of the country, highlanders enjoy a lively and vigorous form of music. Sampan drivers on the Perfume River in Central Vietnam sing Hue boat songs that glorify the deeds of the country's heroes.

In addition to the folk songs popular on the river, there is also a distinct classical form of music. Luong Dang, a mandarin of the Le Dynasty (1428-1788), established a type of music (based on the five-tone system which was popular in the court of the Chinese Ming Dynasty) that was performed at ceremonies held at the Imperial Court of Hue.

There were several categories of court music, depending upon the occasion. For example, there was the lofty music of the Nam Gio, a ceremonial sacrifice to the spirit of Heaven and Earth performed every year (every three years after 1888) at the altar called the Esplanade of Heaven. The Emperor presided over the sacrifice of hundreds of specially raised animals. Historically still shrouded in mystery (women and common folk were forbidden from attending), the ritual sacrifice for Heaven and Earth was perhaps the most important religious ceremony performed by the Vietnamese emperors. The Esplanade of Heaven ritual altar is less than two miles (under 3 km.) directly south of the Imperial Palace.

Court music also accompanied such occasions as the anniversary of the death of an Emperor, formal audiences and ordinary audiences with the monarch, and royal banquets. The sound of music enhanced services in Confucian temples and helped the sun and moon to return during an eclipse. Musical notations in Vietnam were written in Chinese characters until 1914. When the last emperor of Vietnam abdicated after 1945, court music faded away, as did the Imperial Court.

Vietnamese Instruments. Vietnamese instruments include five classic instruments: the *nhi, tranh, nguyet, ty* and *tam.* Together they make up an instrumental ensemble called, collectively, the five perfects (or excellences). Although remarkably simple in construction, these instruments are capable of expressing an exceptionally wide and powerful range of emotions.

A violin or mandolin-like instrument which can intone with great authority and clarity, the *nhi* consists of two strings stretched over a long sounding box. Classically, the strings were silk and the sounding box made of reptile skin. Today, the strings of Vietnamese instruments are wire and the boxes are made of wood. When the *nhi* is played, the box rests on the knee of the seated musician.

The *dan tranh* is a 16-stringed zither roughly 40 inches (100 cm.) long and comparable to the Japanese *koto.* Sixteen movable bridges raise the strings and separate them into sections. A plectrum is worn on the thumb and sometimes on the middle finger of the right hand. With the instrument positioned in front of the musician, the plectrum plucks the strings near the tail to produce the notes, while the left hand places pressure on the string between the bridges and the pegs for "ornamental" regulation of pitch and timbre. The *dan tranh* was once the the instrument of choice for educated young Vietnamese women to learn.

Better known by its common name, *kim,* the *dan nguyet* resembles a guitar with a long neck. Held like a guitar, the *kim* has two strings capable of producing soft, yet expressive music. The *ty* or *ty*

Classical musician, Nguyen Huu, plays the ty ba; his daughter, Dieu Quang, plays the 16-string zyther

ba, descended from the ancient lute, is a pear-shaped, four-stringed guitar with a sounding case that narrows toward the upper end. The *dan tam* is a three-stringed guitar. On occasion, an oboe joins the orchestra of the five perfects.

There are several additional instruments indigenous to Vietnam. The *dan bau,* a single-stringed lute (also called a monochord), features a brass string stretched across a trapezoidal wooden resounding case. One end of the string is attached to a peg, the other end to a gourd-shaped structure made of a buffalo horn called the *bau*. The *bau* has a thin, flexible plate projecting from it which the left hand controls to produce inflections and subtle expressions nearly as compelling as the human voice. Music of the *dan bau* is so alluring, young women are warned not to listen to a man playing it because they will fall hopelessly in love with the musician.

The bamboo transverse flute, or *sao truc*, is one of the country's oldest instruments. *Sao truc* lutes of terra cotta have been found in ancient burial sites. A wide variety of bamboo flutes are played by the ethnic minorities in the highlands. Lo Lo women, for example, play a tiny flute less than six inches (15 cm.) long at wedding ceremonies. Some flutes have ten holes, others eight, and one type used by the Thai minority group has a single hole. The *to rung*, a bamboo xylophone, is also played by tribes in the highlands.

A ball-shaped wooden instrument called the *mo gia tri* is used by monks during recitation of their litanies.

Classical Western orchestral music has not been neglected in Vietnam; a visitor can look forward to enjoying a symphony at the Hanoi Conservatory of Music.

TRADITIONAL ART FORMS

There are three prominent Vietnamese traditional art forms: lacquerwork, painting on silk, and wood-block printing. The Vietnamese also render simple ink drawings and watercolors in the Chinese tradition.

Lacquerwork. Lacquerwork evolved as a decorative application and eventually into an artistic medium in its own right. Song Be, a province southwest of Saigon, is known for its centuries-old art of lacquerware. In the north, near Hanoi, is a forest of *son* trees that produce a sticky resin, or sap, which is extracted for use in formulating lacquer. Depending on how it is treated, the sap will take on a black or brown color. For years, Vietnam exported the raw lacquer material to China and Japan. Today's Vietnamese lacquerware owes its brilliant sheen to a synthetic finish. In addition to its aesthetic appeal, a special form of lacquerwork was once used for waterproofing the small boats that provided transportation across the swamps around Hanoi.

The lacquer process: The first step involves sanding the wood until the surface is smooth. To prevent warping, the wood is sometimes covered with a canvas fabric. Next, a design is drawn on the wood, most often in gold. The gold motif is entirely covered with the black paint. When the paint has thoroughly dried, the artisan will begin pummicing the object with an abrasive to remove the paint until the gold design underneath emerges.

The surface of the object is repainted and polished many times. Egg-shell and gold dust are used to soften and shade colors to create an illusion of a dimensional relief. As each coat must dry thoroughly for a week, each article takes about three months to complete. A variety of techniques are employed to enhance the work, including varnish, mother-of-pearl, and cracked egg-shell inlay.

In the 1930s, Japanese lacquer specialists introduced stylistic modifications and new methods of production at the Fine Arts School in Hanoi. Traditional Japanese lacquerwork is found on practical objects such as boxes, trays, and screens.

Paintings and Other Artworks. Painting on silk is a centuries-old Vietnamese art form. Colors applied to a silk canvas evoke a soft sensibility. The Vietnamese excel in creating block prints of everyday scenes. Artist Vo Dinh has said that Vietnamese woodcut block prints are ". . . simple and direct in their charm. Matisse would have been delighted by their vegetable and mineral colorings. Rouault would have loved their bold designs, strongly defined forms, heavy black lines. Picasso would have appreciated their free and unconventional spirit, their dashing and playful air."

Ceramics. After winning independence from China's rule in the 11th century, Vietnam experienced a building boom that created a demand for ceramic tiles and a variety of glazework applications, including glazed bricks. Although Vietnamese ceramic work parallels the Chinese Han style and form, it demonstrates a distinctive cultural identity with uniquely Vietnamese motifs. Early earthenware of the Ly Dynasty was characterized by incised and painted decorations with a brown design on a white body. A typical vessel was first covered with a clear glaze, then a design was etched onto the surface using a sharp implement. The etching process removed the glaze along the design route. A brown glaze was then applied to the object. Since the previous coat of clear glaze had been removed, the brown glaze "took" along the etched lines to form a distinctive motif. (A collection of early ceramics from the Ly and Tranh dynasties are on display in the Hanoi Historical Museum.)

Glazed monochrome wares with white, green, and brown glazes were popular during the Tran Dynasty (1225–1400). A distinctive

Ceramic factory, Bien Hoa

apple-green copper glaze, used especially on small cups and jars, is especially characteristic of this period. During the mid to late 1300s, cobalt, which yields a deep blue (called Hue blue), began to appear in ceramic decoration. In the 14th century, ceramic jars, in both iron oxide brown and delicate blue and white, were exported to Japan.

The lime container used to store shell lime paste, an essential ingredient in the betel chew, is a uniquely Vietnamese ceramic product. Lime pots are squat and have a small opening on the shoul-

der. With the addition of a pedestal or a handle, the little pots
became quite elaborate.

ARCHITECTURE

Vietnamese architecture combines the superstitious practices of geomancy (consulting the spirits of the land for the most auspicious
site) with the practice of constructing buildings to face south, there-
by utilizing solar energy.

South-facing Homes. A Vietnamese expression says, "Marry a
kind wife; build a house that faces south." Traditional buildings
were rectangular with the entrance located on the longest side, or
the south-facing wall. In the winter, when the sun is low on the
southern horizon, the long southern wall collects solar energy to
heat the home. In the summer, when the sun is high over the house,
a low curved roof reduces heat buildup by keeping the sun out. The
end wall of the traditional Vietnamese house is gabled and smaller
in total area than the south-facing entrance wall. Although the end
walls of the rectangular building face the sun in the morning and
evenings, they do not collect much heat due to their smaller size.

Houses are divided into several compartments, with heat-pro-
ducing activities, such as cooking, performed in the cooler sections
of the house. With summer winds blowing from the south, the
south-facing entrance and windows are ideally located to catch
breezes necessary to ventilate and cool the inside of the house. During the cool season (especially in the north and the highlands),
northwest winds blow against the closed north side of the house.

Roof Styles. The traditional curved roof appeared in Vietnam
thousands of years ago during the Hoa Binh culture. The roof slopes
down slightly from its peak and comes to rest on eaves, where it
curves upward. Roofs in other Asian countries show an inward curve
along the ridge. The low (sometimes only five feet to six and one
half feet from the ground (a meter and a half or two meters)) but
upturned eaves of Vietnamese roofs allow more light to enter, facilitate ventilation of the interior, and provide support in heavy rains
and winds.

During the Tran Dynasty, the palaces of the former Ly Dynasty
underwent considerable renovations. Architectural complexes consisting of different buildings were enclosed by one wall, or enclosure.
Tran-style buildings, usually made of wood frames, were covered
with a four-slope roof with curved corners. The roofs were supported
by columns erected inside the rooms below, rather than hidden be-

hind the walls as in Western architecture. An excellent example of these support columns can be seen at the buildings of the Imperial Palace at Hue.

The roof was covered with tiles in a double layer. Thin but large "mat" tiles were topped by thicker but smaller curved tiles. Doors made during the Tran period were decorated with carved dragon figures for pagodas and flower and leaf designs for residences. A typical Tran house had several steps that led from a courtyard into the building. These houses stood on square plots of land and were open on three sides; houses of a later period were opened only at the front and stood on a rectangular plot. Many pagodas built during the Tran Dynasty incorporated towers as part of the overall complex. Built in 1305, the slender, lotus-like, 14-story stone and brick Pho Minh tower in the My Loc district of Ha Nam Ninh province is a good example of this type of structure.

Four Mythical Animals. While viewing older Vietnamese buildings, look for the four mythical animals. The dragon, symbol of nobility and power, is sometimes depicted with snake-like characteristics. The unicorn, usually pictured smiling, represents kindness and wisdom. The turtle represents long life and often carries a stone tablet on its back upon which are written the good deeds of mankind, or whomever is being honored by that particular work of art. The phoenix symbolizes peace and is depicted as a long-legged animal with five different feather colors and five tones in its song. The *tu linh* dance, which is performed at folk festivals, honors the four sacred animals of Vietnam.

Common Forms of Vietnamese Architecture. Examples of monuments and buildings follow.

Am is a small, out-of-the-way building (a wayside shrine) honoring Buddha.

Dinh. Of the different types of buildings in Vietnam, perhaps the *dinh* or communal house best symbolizes village life. In ancient Vietnam, the daily facets of religious and civilian activities were inseparable, with the center of village life revolving around the *dinh.* Used for public gatherings where important village decisions were made, for trials, for handicraft displays, and for theater groups, the *dinh* was also the place where one worshiped the village guardian spirit. The guardian (or tutelary spirit) could be a former national hero, the founder of the town's handicraft, or even a totemic animal.

The grounds around the *dinh* had a wall and a triple gate. Three porches (tam quan), four roofs and columns, called "generals," gave the dinh an imposing presence. A dinh was constructed to face south and contain five to nine semi-partitioned compartments. Rites and village meetings were held in the antechamber of the communal house. The room behind the antechamber served as a preparation area and a place for women to sit during meetings. Dinh structures are now used as public information and education halls, party or brigade headquarters, and maternity and public health clinics. There are ancient dinh buildings in the north open to tourists.

Mausoleum (lang mo) is a tomb of a king, high-ranking mandarin, or nobility.

Pagoda (chua) is a building erected to honor Buddha. Typically, two sacred ponds flank the main entrance. Another characteristic is the presence of four terraces. The ponds are on the first level, the bell tower on the second. The third level has a front hall and the main altar. The top level contains stone and brick stupas, tombs of former head monks.

Quan is a place of Taoist worship.

Stele (bia) is a slab of stone with an inscription recording details of a construction (for example, the number of men who worked on the project, how much wood was used, and who designed the structure), names of honored scholars, or the contributions of a deceased emperor.

Stupa or tower (thap) is a part of a pagoda complex, sometimes standing separately from the main pagoda.

Temple or shrine is a place of worship for various deities. The name (den, mieu, dien, phu, nghe) indicates the size of the structure and the character of the cult.

Van mieu or Temple of Literature is a place honoring the cult of Confucius and his disciples. These temples were built in the capitals of Hue and old Hanoi (Thang Long).

Van tu or **Van chi** houses the cult of Confucius and outstanding scholars native to a village. The building is called a van tu when it has a roof and van chi when it is an open-air shrine.

DRAMA

Unquestionably influenced by the Chinese, Vietnamese theater has managed to produce three uniquely traditional artforms of the stage: the Hat Boi (or Hat Tuong), the Cheo, and the Cai Luong or the Kich.

The Tuong (Hat Tuong, Hat Boi or Court Opera), more developed in central Vietnam, has a classic and formally stylized character. The content is most often epic in scope, portraying legends of superhuman heroes. In the true traditional Vietnamese theater, set design and production elements are kept as simple as possible; there is no stage scenery, no curtain or lighting effects. Actors must adhere to precise rules concerning their characters. Should an actor deviate from the expected characterization, an experienced audience (well versed in the rules) may demand that the actor repeat a recitation. Makeup and costuming are also determined by convention. From the first moment a character steps upon the stage, the audience knows whether he is a dishonest mandarin, a Chinese governor of occupation, or the hero. "Quan Am Thi Kinh" is a favorite play in this classic genre.

The *Cheo* or *Cheo Co* is the popular opera (more comedy than tragedy) that combines singing with gesturing. According to legend, a Chinese actor, Ly Nguyen Cat, introduced the popular form of theater when he settled in Vietnam during Emperor Tran Du Ton's reign (1341–1369). Ly Nguyen Cat's first troupe, called a *Phuong Cheo,* included 12 performers. Another variation says it was the Chinese Taoist and acting teacher, Tong Dao Si, who brought *Cheo* to Vietnam. Actors subscribe to yet another version concerning the origin of *Cheo* theater. According to them, *Cheo* and the acting profession was first established by Dong Phuong Soc, a dignitary in the court of the Chinese king Han Vu De in the years 140–86 BC.

Cheo theater has been preserved in the north. Khuoc village, near Hanoi, has a *Cheo* theater troupe of repute that also promotes the art of classic Vietnamese theater. The entire village participates in the productions, in teaching theater arts, performing, providing music, and staging.

The *Cai Luong* or *Kich,* or "Renovated Opera," came out of South Vietnam in the 1920s. This relatively modern form combines drama, modeled after French comedy, and singing. Scenes are elaborate and are changed frequently throughout the play. *Cai Luong* is similar to the Western operettas and more easily depicts the inner feelings of the characters. Songs of the *Cai Luong* are based on variations of a limited number, perhaps 20, of tunes with different tempos for particular emotions—this convention permits a composer to choose among 20 variations to express anger, and as many to portray joy. Upon hearing the first bars of the well-loved sad tune, the *vong co,* the audience reacts with gasps of recognition and applause.

FILM

Film studios are located in the Tu Liem section of Hanoi Municipality. Due to limited resources and access to processing equipment, Vietnamese films are produced in black and white. About one third of the films produced in Vietnam, even in the late 1980s, deal with the war that involved the US. Here are a few examples of Vietnamese films and their themes:

Deserted Field, a gold medal winner in Moscow, depicts how a Mekong delta farm family survives helicopter attacks. When the heroine's husband, a guerrilla, is killed by a helicopter, she assists in shooting down another. As she approaches the body of the enemy pilot, she sees a photo, dropped from his wallet, of his wife and young son.

Girl on the River contains a nude scene and criticism of the actions of a party official. During the war, a prostitute had saved the official's life. After the war, she asks for his help in obtaining an honest job. He refuses to recognize her. Yet later, when a news article exposing the woman as a former prostitute is about to be published, the official blocks its release.

Fairy Tale for 17-Year-Olds concerns a sensitive young woman in Hanoi at the end of the war. She loves and dreams about a soldier fighting in the south. Just as the war ends, she learns that he has died.

Facing the Sea, adapted from a contemporary novel by the same name, tackles socio-economic problems facing a fishing enterprise at the end of the war. The heroes battle corrupt bureaucrats in order to set up an efficient management system.

ECONOMY

In 1982, Vietnam's Foreign Minister, Nguyen Co Thach, summed up the economic condition of his country: "Very bad but not worse." Since then, Vietnam's economy has perhaps gotten "worse." Inflation in 1989 exceeded 700%. For a combination of reasons (poor management, low investment, population explosion, and natural disasters) the rice available for consumption dropped from 669 pounds (304 kg.) per capita in 1985 to 616 pounds (280 kg.) per capita in 1986. To make up for severe food shortages in 1988, the government appealed to the United Nations for emergency food aid.

After 1975, the US government discontinued aid to the south and placed a trade embargo on Vietnam. Some American allies supported the embargo by not trading with Vietnam. The Socialist Republic of Vietnam assumed the defunct Republic of South Vietnam's membership in the International Monetary Fund (IMF) and joined the World Bank in September 1976. Although Vietnam managed to obtain a $90 million credit for a small irrigation project from the World Bank, the bank denied further aid in 1980—a precedent that influenced the IMF into cutting off economic support as well. Diversion of considerable resources to maintain an enormous military (primarily as a direct result of the Kampuchea incursion) has worsened Vietnam's economic situation.

ECONOMIC STATISTICS

POPULATION OF VIETNAM	65.4 MILLION (JUNE 1989)
KEY ECONOMIC INDICATORS FORECAST FOR 1989:	IN US$
Gross National Product	$18.1 billion
Gross National Product Per Capita	$130
Gross Domestic Product Growth	5.4%
Twelve Months of Exports	$0.7 billion
Foreign Debt	$7.9 billion
Price Inflation	800%
Imports	negligible
Surplus/Deficit (minus)	−$8,000 million

Source: *Asiaweek*, July 7, 1989

Vendor, Nhatrang

Rice shipments from China to Vietnam stopped after Vietnam's military incursion into Kampuchea in 1979. In that same year, the massive exodus of Vietnam's Chinese population caused a severe and sudden shortage of the skilled manpower that had kept the economy rolling. Many of the Chinese who had left were experienced businessmen, miners, fishermen, and manufacturers. Unemployment is high today and the situation would be even worse if it were not for the military and the new economic zone plan that provides work for about two million people.

The wage system in Vietnam favors the "blue collar" worker. On a monthly basis, factory workers earn about 120,000 to 150,000 *dong* (about US$24–30) while professionals such as teachers, doctors, and military officers earn less than half that much, about 40,000 to 60,000 *dong*. A family of four can get by on 60,000 to 70,000 *dong* per month. Households are encouraged to cultivate their own vegetables, breed fish in family ponds, and raise chickens or pigs. The ambitious can supplement their income by moonlighting. In November 1988 the *dong* was devalued at 5,000 to the dollar.

MARXIST-LENINIST THEORY

The government of Vietnam is based on the economic and political philosophy originated by Karl Marx (1818–1883), who believed the primary determinant of history is economics. Marx rigorously maintained that human beings labor not merely for themselves as individuals, but for the collective enjoyment and improvement of the entire species. The basis of his theory is that socialism is inevitable because the weaknesses of capitalism will cause increasingly severe economic crises and deepening impoverishment of the working class, which will ultimately lead to revolution.

Under capitalism, the working class of individuals (the proletariat) invests its labor while the capitalists, or middle class (the bourgeoisie), profit from the fruits of that labor. It was clear to Marx that capitalism led to the excessive accumulation of riches by the bourgeoisie at the expense and exploitation of the working class. Marxism maintains that workers must engage in a class struggle to seize control over production and achieve a classless society. Following the abolition of class differences by proletarian revolution, the state—which Marx believed existed primarily to enforce the exploitation of the propertyless class—would wither away. The revolution would occur in stages from socialism to communism. A state would evolve in which the entire system of monetary rewards would vanish and "society can inscribe on its banners, from each according to his ability, to each according to his needs."

Marxism considered "Imperialism"—the inherent need to exploit backward nations—the inevitable result of capitalism. Russian revolutionist and the major force behind the founding of the USSR, Vladimir Lenin (1870–1924) modified Marx's thinking to allow for the possibility of revolution in a nonindustrialized society. Present-day communist regimes, while claiming Marxist ideology, often veer sharply from it. Labor unions and improved working conditions for workers in industrialized capitalist societies have, to some extent, discredited Marx's economic predictions.

In Vietnam, the application of Marxist-Leninist theory is realized in the form of state-owned factories, farms, communication resources, and transportation systems. Although the state provides schooling and medical care for all its citizens, employees of the government reap the best benefits.

REFORMS

The North has been working toward socializing the economy since 1955. As a result, all sectors of labor and management, including farms, factories, and businesses, were centrally controlled and almost all workers (at all levels) were employed by the government in some way. Citizens directly employed by the state were able to buy (at highly subsidized prices) food, fuel, and other commodities at state-operated stores. Economic reforms introduced in 1985 abolished the state ration system that had previously subsidized the purchased of basic commodities for state employees. To compensate workers for this change in policy, salaries were linked to a cost-of-living index. Losing state price subsidization meant factories had to introduce cost-accounting as a management tool to improve overall operations and production.

The economic reform of 1985 also provided an increase in incentives for individual productivity—a distinctly capitalistic carrot.

A government parade to encourage the public to buy savings bonds

Farmers in the north were allowed to till fallow or unused cooperative land without paying taxes; a contract system was introduced that allowed families to retain a greater proportion of their harvest; permission was granted for private marketing of agricultural products. The government's new policies were designed to encourage small-scale and family businesses in urban areas as well. Hanoi City has eliminated taxes on small-business enterprises. As a result, many restaurants, closed because of high taxes, have now reopened.

In 1987, despite ideological flag-waving and Communist rhetoric, a commercial bank in Ho Chi Minh City opened its doors and began doing business in a manner typically Western in concept. The unique feature of this bank is that it is not totally state-owned. Although controlling interest (51%) of the bank's shares is owned by the city government, the remaining 49% is distributed among nongovernmental institutions and private individuals. (For a list of banks in Vietnam see the Appendix Section.)

There are other models of free enterprise that have managed to succeed within the cracks of the Communist government, especially in South Vietnam. For example, in 1988, *The New York Times* reported on how capitalistic initiative helped create the Hoang Anh Cooperative, a small, privately owned art-handicraft business located in a suburb of northeastern Saigon. With no bureaucratic intermediaries to stifle the self-sufficiency project, the art export business has grown and is thriving with over 450 employees. The cooperative furnishes pleasant working conditions, pays taxes, and provides services that the state reserves for government employees only: good medical care, housing, kindergartens, and an unofficial social security system.

COMMUNICATIONS AND FOREIGN TRADE

Foreign trade and investments depend on a good communications system. Vietnam currently has such a system and is trying to improve on it. Most of the airports, except those in the North, were built by the US military to handle massive jet traffic that had been generated by the war. As a result, much of the tarmac is still intact, providing good facilities for air traffic, including Vietnam's own airline. Ground travel includes a national rail network that connects all major cities over the length of the country. The main port of Haiphong handles ships of up to 10,000 tons. Other commercial ports are located at Danang, Ho Chi Minh City, and Quinhon. In addition to the existing Intersputnik satellite earth station, the completion of a newly installed (1988) communication system (using an Australian telecommunications earth station) has markedly improved communications on an international scale.

Nguyen Xuan Oanh, an economist who received some of his training in the US, heads Vietnam's Bureau of Economic Research and is the principal author of the early 1988 Foreign Investment Law designed to attract Western investors. The Council of State in August 1988 established a State Commission for Cooperation and Investment charged with setting up favorable conditions for the new foreign investment law—one that allows full foreign-owned enterprises, protects the investors' right to repatriate their profits, guarantees against nationalization, and permits foreign companies to station foreign managers in Vietnam. This progressive legislation is considered by some business people to be the most liberal in all of Asia.

Vietnam's main trading partners are the USSR and Japan and, to a lesser extent, Singapore and Hong Kong—a Hong Kong-based company has formed a joint venture car rental service for tourists. Japan is the country's largest non-communist trading partner, especially for Vietnamese oil and seafood. Other foreign partnership agreements include neighboring Thais who have negotiated joint fishing enterprises; the VIBA company of West Berlin, which has set up a factory for electronic telephone parts; those British companies which have opened tourist businesses in the major cities of Vietnam and have set up a window frame factory in Vungtau; and Club Med, which has begun negotiations for a beachfront resort. Although the number of foreign businesses negotiating with Hanoi has increased, inefficiency and red tape still exist.

A majority of the consumer goods in Vietnam, estimated to be worth more than US$150 million a year, come in the form of gift packages from friends and relatives abroad. Other consumer goods are smuggled in from Thailand. More than 75% of legal imports include technical equipment, medical supplies, and foodstuffs that come from the Soviet-centered trade group COMECON. Vietnam sends raw materials to the Soviet Union to repay accumulated aid debts. As a rule, however, Vietnam has been limiting its imports to obtain a favorable balance of trade.

AGRICULTURE

Engaging more than 80% of the work force, agriculture is the basis of Vietnam's economy. Although rice is the primary crop, corn, cassava, and sweet potatoes are also grown for subsistence. The Red River delta in the North produces an abundance of rice (sometimes three crops a year), but it does not produce enough to feed the tremendous population of the area. To supplement this food shortage, grains from the rich Mekong delta in the South (the South has the advantage of a warm year-round climate and river geography advantageous to agriculture) are routinely shipped north.

Other food products include tropical fruits, such as pineapples, bananas, watermelons, seven types of mangoes, litchi, and rambutan, which are exported to the East bloc. Although many private fruit orchards were converted to rice fields (attempting to build reserves toward self-sufficiency) after the reunification of the North and South in 1975, today's agricultural agenda calls for diversification. Cash crops such as rubber, coffee, and tea thrive in the decomposed basalt soil found in the high plateau regions.

Collectivization in the North, in effect since 1955, has developed into a workable and accepted way of life. Attempts to collectivize the South have been met with resistance (via passive revolt) by private land owners. As a result, the government has introduced a different methodology to increase production in the South. The contract system is one approach that has already proven itself a worthwhile departure from strict party-line dogma. This incentive works by having cooperatives subcontract agricultural production to farmers who are permitted to sell crops raised over the contracted amount on the free market.

Rice Cultivation. The labor-intensive process of rice cultivation in Vietnam has gone unchanged for centuries. No modern machinery is used; water buffalos still pull wooden harrows to plow seedbeds. After a seedbed is plowed and harrowed, it is allowed a two-day rest to "air" the soil. The earth is plowed once again with most of the irrigated water allowed to run off; the seeds are then sown on a smooth, muddy surface.

After several days, when the plants have established themselves, the seedbeds are refilled with water. The young seedlings must be uprooted and transplanted when they reach a certain stage. If they remain close together too long, they will develop root rot; transplanting must be done quickly.

Twenty or 30 plants are gently uprooted from the nursery bed and, while being held in one hand, a careful slap against a leg or foot loosens the mud from their roots. The clean seedlings are placed in piles and distributed throughout the new field. Transplanting is done mostly by women, who grasp the seedling roots just at the root top and, using their thumbs, poke holes into the mud and guide the seedlings into the slots.

Transplanting rice, Hanoi

Irrigation also relies on age-old methods which may seem simple, yet require much practice. Two workers, up to their thighs in water, use one common basket to transfer water from an irrigation canal into the field. The team works in rhythmic, seemingly effortlessly smooth and nearly dance-like unison to manipulate these simple, water-proof woven baskets by means of ropes attached to the tops and bottoms of the baskets.

During harvest time, caravans of wooden wheelbarrows full of rice plants are pushed or pulled by seasoned, strong workers from the fields to central distribution areas.

FISHING

Vietnam's extensive access to rivers and the sea supports a vital freshwater and saltwater fishing industry. The Fishery College at Nhatrang was established to improved fish breeding methods. Most of the shrimp and lobsters farmed in the Mekong delta are exported to Japan and Thailand.

Fishing at dawn, Nhatrang

FORESTATION

"Forests are gold," said Ho Chi Minh, prophetically urging the wise use of natural resources. In addition to a variety of native timber, other forest products include bamboo, cinnamon, lacquer, resins, and quinine. By absorbing rain water into root systems of trees, forests also act as a natural barrier in protecting the lowlands from flooding during the rainy season. In 1943, 44% of Vietnam was forest. Today, forest acreage covers less than 25% of the country. Deforestation, or the loss of forest cover, is a serious problem for both wild animals and man. As the forests dwindle, wild animals lose their natural jungle habitat. The tapir and the Sumatran rhinoceros, for example, are already extinct; the *koupry* (a wild cow) is nearing extinction.

The rapid loss of Vietnam's forests has several causes: semi-nomadic agricultural (slash and burn) methods, fires, residual effects of wartime herbicide (Agent Orange) use, plus unrestricted cutting of timber for construction and fuel demands of a rapidly growing population. In 1985, a National Conservation Strategy introduced an educational campaign for ecological reconstruction designed to facilitate reforestation, more selective harvesting methods, resettling of the nomadic mountain minorities, and setting aside of protected parklands.

MINERAL RESOURCES

The majority of Vietnam's mineral assets are located in the North, with oil reserves in the South. Anthracite (coal), Vietnam's principal mineral resource, is mined in Hon Gai (near Haiphong) in the North. Coal provides 91% of the country's energy. Steel and iron plants are located in Thai Nguyen (North of Hanoi). Tin, lead, tungsten, zinc, phosphates, bauxite, chromium, and copper are extracted from northern mines. Offshore oil had been discovered in the South by American oil companies before the US exodus from Saigon in 1975. A major source of oil is a joint Vietnamese and Soviet venture off the coast of Vungtau. France has a small oil refinery in Ho Chi Minh City that produces diesel fuel. Vietnam also has a production-sharing agreement with the Indian petroleum company, Hydrocarbon India Ltd., for oil exploration. As technology develops within Vietnam, oil will become an increasingly significant source of energy to fuel a growing industrial power base.

INDUSTRY

Vietnam's heavy industries—cement and steel production, food processing and canning, and textile manufacturing—are concentrated in the North. These industrial enterprises are working at less than half their capacity for a variety of reasons, principally energy problems. To remedy chronic power shortages, the government has invested heavily in dams and hydroelectric projects. The Soviet-built Pha Lai thermal power station and the Black River project, both in the North, are nearing completion. Although the Dong Nai River project (the Tri An dam) in the South was completed in 1987, it was still not fully operational in early 1990. The Swedish-financed Bai Bang paper plant in Bac Thai province has encountered problems in obtaining raw material.

While many small industries remain in private family-owned hands, all industry, shops, and factories above the family level were nationalized in 1978. Since then, however, relaxed economic reform efforts have encouraged more small private industries to prosper, such as the manufacture of bicycle and farm tools. About 75% of the handicrafts and small industrial products manufactured for export go to socialist countries; the remainder is shipped to Japan, Singapore, Hong Kong, and Western Europe.

GOVERNMENT AND POLITICS

I mmediately after the fall of Saigon in 1975, the Communists set up a Provisional Revolutionary Government in the South. A National Assembly was elected in April 1976, and in July it ratified the unification of the country, establishing the Socialist Republic of Vietnam. In December 1980, after Vietnam adopted a new constitution along the lines of a proletarian dictatorship, the Communist Party began its goals of transition toward a fully socialist state.

The highest legislative body of the state is the National Assembly, whose 496 members are elected for five-year terms by universal suffarage of citizens over 18 years of age. The National Assembly elects a Council of State, or Presidium, which functions as the "collective Presidency"—the standing organ of the National Assembly that meets only twice yearly. A Council of Ministers, which serve as Vietnam's executive branch of government (its cabinet), consists of the prime minister, vice premiers, ministers, and others of equivalent status responsible to the National Assembly.

Government Building, Hanoi

GOVERNMENT AND POLITICS

PROVINCES OF
VIETNAM
★ = Municipalities

© 1988 Barbara Cohen

LOCAL GOVERNMENT

In 1976, the administrative regions of Vietnam were restructured, establishing three self-governing municipalities: Hanoi, Ho Chi Minh City, and Haiphong. In addition, province boundaries have been shifted to form 36 provinces and one "special zone": Vung Tau-Con Dao.

NATIONAL GOVERNMENT

The National Assembly Chairperson is Le Quang Dao

Council of Ministers in January 1988

Prime Minister	Do Muoi
Agriculture and Food Bach Thao	Nguyen Cong Tan
Building 37 Le Dai Hanh	Phan Ngoc Tuong
Communications/Transport 80 Tran Hung Dao	Bui Danh Luu
Culture 53 Ngo Quyen	Vu Khac Kien
Defense 42 Tran Phu	Le Duc Anh
Education 21 Le Thanh Tong	Pham Minh Hac
Energy 54 Hai Ba Trung	Vu Ngoc Hai
Engineering/Metallurgy 54 Hai Ba Trung	Phan Thanh Liem
Finance 8 Pham Huy Chu	Hoang Quy
Foreign Affairs Dien Bien Phu	Nguyen Co Thach
Forestry 123 Lo Duc	Phan Xuan Dot
Foreign Trade 21 Ngo Quyen	Doan Duy Thanh
Justice 5 Ong Ich Khiem	Phan Hien
Information	Tran Hoan
Interior Tran Binh Hoang	Mai Chi Tho

Internal Trade 91 Dinh Tien Hoang	Hoang Minh Thang
Light Industry 7 Trang Thi	Vu Tuan
Marine Products Bach Thao	Nguyen Tan Trinh
Planning 6B Hoang Dieu	Dau Ngoc Xuan
Public Health 138 A Giang Vo	Pham Song
Science and Technology 39 Tran Hung Dao	Dan Huu
Social Welfare/Labor 12 Ngo Quyen	Nguyen Ky Cam
State Bank Directorate	Lu Minh Chau
State Inspection 28 Tang Bat Ho	Huynh Cong To
Supply 37 Nguyen Binh Khiem	Hoang Duc Nghi
Price Commission 3 Mai Xuan Thuong	Phan Van Tiem
Vocational Education 9 Hai Ba Trung	Tran Hong Quan
Water Resources 164 Tran Quang Khai	Nguyen Canh Dinh

Each province is divided into four to twelve districts of 100,000 to 200,000 persons. Each district (called wards in municipalities), in turn, is divided into 16 to 25 communes, or villages. A commune consists of eight to ten hamlets of 800 to 1,000 persons each.

Vietnam is governed "by committee." Every two years, districts, towns, and villages elect delegates to people's councils. The council, in turn, selects an executive arm called the administrative committee. Headed by a chairperson, the people's administrative committee makes important day-to-day decisions.

THE COMMUNIST PARTY

The ruling party of the Socialist Republic of Vietnam is the Communist Party. Vietnamese have a saying: "The party leads, the state manages, and the people are masters." In 1980, Article 4 of the new constitution described the Communist Party as "the only force leading the state and society." It is, therefore, important in discussing the functioning of the government of Vietnam to better understand the core-role played by the Communists.

Members of the Party play roles of importance equal to that of elected officials on all levels. The Communist Party of the Socialist Republic of Vietnam, which in 1989 had about two million members, influences every aspect of life, from health care services to the military. The Party reaches people in the workplace through party chapters—organizations that provide both leadership at meetings and education, and ensure that the party's goals are carried out in schools, factories, and cooperatives. The Communist Party implements party decisions through the Central Committee (which elects

Party Headquarters in Ho Chi Minh City (formerly housed the French City Hall)

the Politburo, the highest policy making body of the Party) and a secretariat. In addition to directing the work of the ministries, the Politburo initiates and directs the legislative decisions of the National Assembly.

National party congresses are held every five years (the most recent was the 6th, held in December 1986) to discuss and eventually ratify decisions made by the Politburo and Central Committee. The National Party Congress also drafts a Political Report and elects the Party Central Committee which, in turn, elects the Party Central Executive Committee (or Plenum Committee: 116 full members and 36 alternates in 1988) and the Political bureau.

In July 1989, the Politburo's 13 full members were:

POLITBURO'S FULL MEMBERS

Party General Secretary: Nguyen Van Linh

Dao Duy Tung	Nguyen Duc Tam
Doan Khue	Nguyen Thanh Binh
Do Muoi	Nguyen Van Linh
Dong Sy Nguyen (General)	Tran Xuan Bach
Le Duc Anh (General)	Vo Chi Cong
Mai Chi Tho	Vo Van Kiet
Nguyen Co Thach	

OTHER POLITICAL ORGANIZATIONS

Mass organizations such as the Vietnam Confederation of Trade Unions, the Vietnam Women's Federation, and the Vietnam Youth Federation have considerable influence in the following areas: implementing party policy, educating the opposition, and providing information for the National Assembly to consider. The Fatherland Front, the most boadly based and politically influencial of the mass organizations (including specialized trade unions, women's union, and religious bodies), puts up the lists of candidates for election to district congresses. All Vietnamese are eligible to join the Fatherland Front and it is considered "patriotic" to do so.

The Socialist Party and the Vietnam Democratic Party were disbanded in 1988.

JUDICIAL SYSTEM

The People's Supreme Court, which supervises all local courts, is the highest court of the Socialist Republic of Vietnam. Its members are elected to five-year terms by the National Assembly. Judges of the people's courts, located in each province and city, are elected for three-year terms by local administrative committees. Elected people's assessors function somewhat as jurors do in the US. A defendant has access to assistance by a member of the jurists' association, who insures that formalities are followed and explains the proceedings to the accused, but has no obligation to act as the defendant's advocate. Minor disputes and crimes on the grass-roots level are handled by local courts called reconciliation organizations. The new penal code that went into effect in 1989 made some legal reforms but retained the death penalty.

FOREIGN RELATIONS

Vietnam is a member of the United Nations, Non-aligned Movement, Comecon (Council for Mutual Economic Assistance), IMF (International Monetary Fund), World Bank, and Asian Development Bank.

Foreign policy hinges on friendship and cooperation with the Soviet Union and other socialist nations, and a "special relationship" with Cambodia and Laos.

Relations with the Soviet Union. The loss of aid from the West and China forced Vietnam into a closer alliance with the Soviet Union. There are about 6,000 Soviet advisors in Vietnam who have worked on over 250 economic aid projects (as of 1988), including building power plants, reconstructing the rail system, building the Hanoi Cultural Palace, and completing the Thang Long Bridge, a project that had been abandoned by the Chinese. Vietnam, in turn, ships canned shrimp and fruits, textiles, and raw materials to the Soviet Union. Unemployed Vietnamese provide labor in the Soviet Union through the "guest worker" program. The Russian language is taught in Vietnam's grade schools; bright Vietnamese students compete to attend advanced schooling in Moscow.

Relations with China. Strained relations with China came about as a result of several factors over a period of time. In the 1960s and early 1970s, Vietnam tried to balance its friendships with the Soviet Union and China. Both countries had aided Vietnam during its fight against the American-backed southern regime. An easing of relations with the West led to mainland Communist China's admission to the UN in 1971 and to a visit by President Richard Nixon in 1972. During this time, China had also been distancing itself from the Soviet Union. In 1975, Beijing backed (with arms and Chinese advisors) the Democratic Republic of Kampuchea (Cambodia) under Pol Pot whose "communist" forces (the Khmer Rouge) attacked Vietnam's southwestern border. In 1978-79, Vietnam invaded Cambodia, overthrowing the regime of Pol Pot and provoking a brief invasion by China. Vietnam had nationalized all Chinese businesses in May 1978, forcing a mass exodus of Chinese from the country. In February 1989, China and Vietnam agreed to bridge their differences: China agreed to withhold military aid to rebel forces who oppose the Vietnam-backed government in Cambodia.

Relations with Thailand. In April 1989 Thailand reoccupied its former embassy building in Ho Chi Minh City. The Thai mission, which had been taken over following the fall of the South Vietnamese government, will be converted to a consulate office. The Thais anticipate that Ho Chi Minh City will become an important trade center. Its current embassy is located in Hanoi.

Relations with the US. In the late 1980s, two highly charged, emotional issues stood in the way of establishing improved relations with the US—Vietnam's military occupation of Cambodia and its cooperation in locating US soldiers who were either missing-in-action (MIA) or still prisoners-of-war (POWs) in Vietnam. By fall 1989, Vietnam had pulled out its troops from Cambodia and was actively cooperating with US officials in accounting for American MIAs and POWs. In 1988, the Vietnamese government made changes in the wording of their 1980 constitution which eliminated any hostile references to the US and China.

Relations with Laos. About 30,000 Vietnamese troops still maintain security in Laos against armed resistance by anti-Communist Lao (Lao-the lowlander majority group in Laos) and other ethnic minority groups of the highlands who are opposed to any government intrusion in their nomadic life-style and what they are permitted to grow—the present government is trying to encourage the highlanders to settle down in permanent villages and to raise food crops rather than opium.

Other Relations. Relations between Vietnam and its ASEAN (Association of South-East Asian Nations) neighbors are improving. India has especially close ties with Vietnam and has aided the government in building agricultural projects.

MILITARY FORCES

Vietnam has the world's fourth-largest standing military force, the largest in Asia outside of China (which is followed by the Soviet Union and the US) and the highest military-to-civilian ratio in the world. The military siphons off more than 50% of Vietnam's budget. A three-year military tour of duty is compulsory for men over 18. There are three elements of the national defense: the regular (main) force, the paramilitary forces, and the reserve forces.

MAIN FORCES

People's Army	980,000–1,000,000
Navy	12,500–40,000
Air Force	15,700–20,000

After the Americans withdrew from the South in 1975, the government had to deal with border confrontations with Cambodia and, in 1979, the incursion by China. Some military experts believed Hanoi had mobilized as many as 600,000 troops against the China threat. Although the Vietnamese Air Force had acquired a vast amount of military hardware abandoned on the airfields by departing US forces in April 1975, most of it is unusable due to the lack of spare parts. The Air Force has 270 fixed-wing combat aircraft and 36 armed helicopters. The Navy has also substantially increased the number of its combat fleet.

During the 1960s, the US military developed the deep-water piers at Cam Ranh Bay, which is also important to the Soviets who now hold a lease on the strategic port that docks more than 30 Russian naval vessels, surface combat ships, and submarines. (This was not, however, the first time in history that Russian ships were

MILITARY INSIGNIA OF THE PEOPLE'S ARMY OF VIETNAM

LAPEL PATCHES

Infantry	bright red
Air force	sky blue
Navy	purple
Border defense	green
Technical specialist	light gray

Ranks and Insignia of People's Armed Forces of Vietnam, 1988

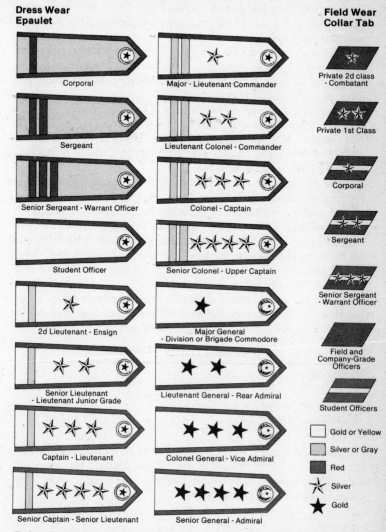

Dress Wear Epaulet

Corporal

Sergeant

Senior Sergeant - Warrant Officer

Student Officer

2d Lieutenant - Ensign

Senior Lieutenant - Lieutenant Junior Grade

Captain - Lieutenant

Senior Captain - Senior Lieutenant

Major - Lieutenant Commander

Lieutenant Colonel - Commander

Colonel - Captain

Senior Colonel - Upper Captain

Major General - Division or Brigade Commodore

Lieutenant General - Rear Admiral

Colonel General - Vice Admiral

Senior General - Admiral

Field Wear Collar Tab

Private 2d class - Combatant

Private 1st Class

Corporal

Sergeant

Senior Sergeant - Warrant Officer

Field and Company-Grade Officers

Student Officers

☐ Gold or Yellow

☐ Silver or Gray

■ Red

✴ Silver

★ Gold

*The first rank given applies to the army and air force; the second, to the navy. Where only one rank is given, it applies to all three services.

GOVERNMENT AND POLITICS

in Vietnam. In 1905, before their defeat by the Japanese in the Russo-Japanese War, the Russian Baltic fleet docked, with French permission, in Cam Ranh Bay to refuel for their trip to the Sea of Japan where they had hoped to block the Japanese Naval supply line. After a two-day battle, the Japanese defeated the Russians, winning the Russo-Japanese War.)

Vietnam bases provide the only Russian air strike forces deployed beyond Soviet borders. Tu-95 Strategic bombers and T-16 Badger medium-range fighters utilize Danang, Tan Son Nhut, and other airbases around Hanoi.

There are no weapons factories in Vietnam. Ninety-nine percent of its arms come from the Soviets, who have also installed six main radar centers throughout Vietnam. These Soviet-run centers control a total of 50 smaller sites nationwide, capable of tracking aircraft within a 100-mile radius.

The Reeducation Camp program and the New Economic Zone program are administered by the Army. Active-duty soldiers are employed in the construction of factories, public buildings, and housing. Army units widen the Ho Chi Minh Trail (now called the Truong Son Highway), work in coal mines, maintain petroleum and oil lines, build and repair bridges, and operate factories and rubber plantations, as well as harvest rice. A naval unit near Cantho produces *nuoc mam* (a fish sauce staple).

Vietnam's second line of defense is the paramilitary force. Totaling three million people, the paramilitary forces consist of border defense, regional forces, and armed youth assault forces.

PARAMILITARY FORCES

People's Regional Force—Provincial Level	—	500,000
People's Self Defense Force—Urban and People's Militia Rural at the District Level	—	1.1 million
Armed Youth Assault Force	—	1.5 million

The third element of the Armed Forces of Vietnam (semimobilized reserve force of 500,000), called the Tactical (or Strategic) Rear Force, consists of veterans, disabled, and overage men. This group is reserved for emergencies.

II

MAKING THE
DECISION TO
TRAVEL TO
VIETNAM

US GOVERNMENT POLICY ON
TRAVEL TO VIETNAM

The US has not yet established diplomatic relations with the Socialist Republic of Vietnam. This means there is no American embassy to provide the usual consular and protective services for US citizens traveling in Vietnam. Great Britain and Australia have embassies in Hanoi.

A US Treasury Department—Foreign Assets division—ruling of February 1988 permits American citizens to visit Vietnam with some restrictions. American tourists can engage in financial transactions related only to their travel, that is, paying for meals, hotel rooms, and travel between cities in the country by bus or plane. In other words, they can purchase, without limit, items used and consumed in Vietnam. US citizens cannot, however, return to the US with merchandise worth more than US$100, and this dollar limit on purchases can be used only once every six months. Items brought back from Vietnam must have been purchased for personal use (not for resale) and must return in the traveler's accompanying baggage. The use of credit cards for payments within Vietnam is forbidden by the Treasury Department (a moot point since credit cards are not yet generally accepted within Vietnam).

Researchers and news media personnel can bring back publications (books, magazines, newspapers, films, posters) for reference and research. Research materials do not have to be included in the $100 purchase limitation, and some items in this category can be shipped to the US, but must not be for resale.

HEALTH CONSIDERATIONS

While the government is working to improve its public health and sanitation problems, Vietnam is not recommended for persons who tire easily or are susceptible to infectious diseases. It is almost universal, even for people in excellent health, to experience flu-like upper respiratory symptoms— probably due to an unfamiliar virus to which Westerners have not yet developed an immunity. Another common ailment involves stomach problems, which often can be debilitating. Health facilities are staffed by diligent and trained personnel, but equipment is outdated. Persons with unstable diabetes, severe asthma, cardiac irregularities, or other conditions that might need immediate and sophisticated medical attention are advised to limit their travels to countries where Western medical care is readily available.

CONSIDERATIONS FOR THE RETURNING VIETNAM VETERAN

It is a common desire among former US military personnel to return to the foreign countries in which they served. This is especially true of Vietnam veterans who wish to return for a variety of reasons.

TYING UP LOOSE ENDS

Many veterans wonder what has happened to old Vietnamese friends, girlfriends, a wife, or a child. A return trip might mean getting in touch with them after a long separation that has been compounded by many powerful social changes. Still other veterans desire to "re-experience" or re-think an emotional and eventful time in their lives. As one veteran put it: ". . . tying up loose ends, resolving something left hanging in emotional limbo years ago." Some are simply curious and want to find out what happened to their former bases, hootches (small living quarters), bars, and "hangouts."

In an *Atlantic Monthly* (December 1988) article, "No Hard Feelings?", James Fallows wrote: "The fundamental surprise (in Vietnam) was how few signs there are of America's presence. If you didn't know that the United States had put so much time, money, hope, and despair into Vietnam, you'd never guess it from the looks of the country today."

While the former US military firebases (that functioned primarily as artillery installations) have been demolished, the major airfields are still in use, and some hangars house rusting aircraft. A few bases have been taken over by the People's Army of Vietnam and are off limits to tourists. Some Bachelor Officer Quarters (BOQ) have been converted to guest houses for Soviet and Eastern European advisors, such as the guest house in the former MAC-V (Military Assistance Command-Vietnam) compound in Hue, or converted to hotels for tourists—as is the fate of the former South Vietnamese BOQ on the Perfume River in Hue.

Veterans who may want to look up old friends need to under-

Returning US Vietnam Veteran, Hanoi

stand that Vietnamese who have had strong connections with Americans in the past might wish to hide that fact from representatives of the present government. In spite of a new Vietnamese glasnost, or openness, called *coi mo*, foreigners are still viewed with some suspicion by the Communist administration. A Vietnamese citizen might want to speak with a former American friend, but hesitate (concerned about being watched by local authorities) and perhaps even act as if the friendship had never existed. Listen carefully and observe body language; the intended meaning is often hidden between the lines.

PLANNING AHEAD

Planning ahead to arrange visits will accelerate the paperwork process. Visiting relatives and in-laws in Vietnam is possible. If an

THE RETURNING VIETNAM VETERAN

American husband or his Vietnamese-American wife, or both, would like to visit members of her family in Vietnam, the husband, wife, or both are permitted to make the arrangements. Americans may encounter some restrictions concerning movement within Vietnam, such as securing permission to cross district boundaries. Unauthorized visits to private homes are still not allowed.

Veterans considering a return trip to Vietnam will want to ensure an emotionally positive experience. Some veterans have experienced sadness and disappointment at what they saw and experienced on their return trip to Vietnam, and others have come home with a sense of relief that, although the country is poor and suffering from the effects of a long war, it is now at peace.

Tell-tale signs of emotional problems such as experiencing recurrent nightmares, "flashbacks," or unwanted thoughts related to veterans' wartime experiences, an acquired hatred for Vietnamese, sudden rages or guilt beyond what is considered reasonable should be addressed—it is advisable that veterans in this category discuss their plans with a Vet Center (now called Readjustment Center) counselor, or seek out a professional who is knowledgeable about such matters. There are over 350 local Vet Centers in the US. (The phone numbers of Vet Centers are listed in the phone book under "US GOV-Vet Center.") This type of preparatory dialogue might head off unreasonable expectations, pay off with an enriched travel adventure, and enhance the experience upon their return since they can sort out and share the emotional ramifications of their visit with a counselor who already knows them.

William Broyles, Jr.'s book about his return to Vietnam after many years, *Brothers in Arms, a Journey from War to Peace,* was called "healing of the highest order" by the *Chicago Sun Times.* Be advised that, although a return trip to Vietnam has the potential of being therapeutic as well as fun, it cannot substitute for competent therapy—if that is needed. Several groups are just now beginning to conduct research on the experiences of veterans returning to Vietnam.

WHAT TO EXPECT

Now that a return trip is possible, veterans wonder how they will be received by the citizens of a country that was once their enemy. Those who have gone back have had a warm reception. If there was any hostility expressed (and there are very few reports of this), it is probably related to residual anti-foreign feelings, and not related to the fact that the visitor is an American veteran.

Vietnamese guides, assigned to smooth the way for foreign visitors, vary in their willingness to discuss the war and to show visiting veterans places they wish to see. What the visitor sees often depends on the character and age of the individual guide. For example, in Hanoi, guides cannot understand why US veterans want to see the prison compound called the "Hanoi Hilton" where prisoners-of-war were held for many years under abominable circumstances. See section on Hanoi for more about the prison.

As a subject of media interest, the Vietnam war (the one involving the US) receives more coverage in the United States than in Vietnam. Since the US military left in 1975, Vietnam has been at war with its neighbor Cambodia and has had several military clashes with China. The Vietnamese are more intent on getting on with rebuilding their country than reminiscing about old wars. As an example, some guides would prefer to show tourists a tapestry cooperative rather than the underground tunnels at Cu Chi (an intricate network of hand-dug tunnels used by the revolutionaries to fight the French and, later, the US). The former American Embassy (its roof was the site of the last US helicopter's dramatic withdrawal from Saigon) is not indicated on maps sold to tourists. Western tourists are often diverted from the "War Crimes Museums," collections of US military implements of war, photographs of grisly torture and executions, and evidence of the disastrous effects of Agent Orange on women who had been exposed to the defoliate—deformed fetuses (many stillborn) staring out of glass jars. In Hanoi, there is a statue depicting an American pilot parachuting into a city lake after his plane was shot down by North Vietnamese anti-aircraft fire. Although the statue was built to honor the bravery of the North Vietnamese anti-aircraft crews, one tactful Vietnamese guide, eager not to offend American tourists, commented with a straight face that the statue is a "friendship monument."

A true "monument to friendship" was built by a group of Vietnam veterans in California who formed the Vietnam Veterans Restoration Project. These veterans donated their construction and labor skills to construct a 14-room hospital in Vungtau that was dedicated on April 1, 1989. The group is:

Vietnam Veterans Restoration Project
P.O. Box 69
Garberville, Ca 95440
tel. (707) 932-3357

Future projects will be tackled by subsequent teams of veterans.
A Canadian travel agency called "Good Morning Vietnam Tours" states that the main objective of their group is to assist Vietnam veterans who wish to return to Vietnam. The address is:

Good Morning Vietnam Tours
R.R.2
Brockville
Ontario, Canada K6V 5T2

A French travel agency has arranged tours for former French soldiers who served in the Indochina War and at this writing is putting together a tour specifically designed for American Vietnam Veterans and their families:

Logotour
"Le Jardin Tropical"
3 rue des Chenes Pourpres
95000 CERGY
France
tel. (1) 30.30.53.35

VIETNAMESE RETURNING FOR A VISIT

According to Vietnam's official tourism policy, Vietnamese who had left Vietnam are welcome to visit their mother country. This hospitality is extended to include the "boat people" and "walk people" who left Vietnam after 1975. For those Vietnamese who left Vietnam without going through regular legal exit visa channels and who are considering a return trip but fear punitive repercussions upon entering the country, reports by Vietnamese émigrés who have recently visited Vietnam have varied—some describe a warm and curious welcome while others experienced, at worst, bureaucratic aloofness.

OFFICIAL STATUSES

In addition to apprehension by many Vietnamese regarding a visit to Vietnam, inaccurate information has been circulating among Vietnamese communities concerning US immigration laws relating to return visits to Vietnam. Vietnamese legally living in the US have one of three official statuses: US citizenship, permanent resident (green card holders), or refugee. For Vietnamese who are US citizens or permanent residents, no matter whether their previous status was that of refugee, travel to Vietnam for tourism or a visit with relatives will not affect their legal status upon their return.

Vietnamese living in the US on a current refugee visa, however, cannot expect to visit Vietnam and maintain their refugee status upon return. The 1980 UN Protocol on Refugees defines a "refugee" (in part) as a person who has ". . . a well-founded fear of persecution . . ." if the individual were to return to the country from which he or she fled.

After living in the US for one year, persons on a refugee visa may apply for "green card" or permanent resident status. Once they receive a "green card" (permanent resident status), they are no longer considered legally a "refugee" and therefore may visit Vietnam without losing the "green card." Persons in doubt about making a trip should consult an immigration attorney for up-to-date information.

VIDEOS: GETTING A GLIMPSE
AHEAD OF TIME

There are several videos on the market that offer scenes of contemporary Vietnam which may be educational and enlightening when viewed prior to your trip.

"Vietnam Revisited: A Veteran Returns on Tour"
P.O. Box 888
Woodruff, WI 54568

Narrated in English.

"Vietnam: When Night Comes"

A 30-minute video of a two-week trip of former International Volunteer Service volunteers. The film won a bronze medal at the Houston International Film Festival in 1988.

Asia Resource Center
PO Box 15275
Washington, D.C. 20003
tel. (202) 547-1114

"VIETNAM: Through the Eyes of Nguyen Tua A"

There are three different videos available: Hanoi, Saigon, and one combined Dalat / Nhatrang. Random street scenes with natural background voices and sounds.

Viet Press
PO Box 2264
Westminster, CA 92683
tel. (714) 898-1018

"Vietnam—Tet 88"

Two-hour home-movie quality scenes of Tet celebrations in five cities. The photographer describes some of the action in Vietnamese.

Hang Ha
P.O Box 4584
Akron, OH 44310
tel. (216) 434-1774

"Indochina Revisited"

A moving, lyrical look at the countries of Vietnam, Cambodia and Laos in the late 1930s, as seen through the work of the French artist Jean Despujols. The film utilizes a variety of elements such as authentic dances by Royal Thai Dancer to recreate French Indochina as seen by Despujols. Also included in the film are excerpts from the artist's personal journals and an evocative music score that blends Despujols' original music compositions with those of others.

Meadows Museum of Art
Centenary College of Louisiana
2911 Centenary Blvd.
Shreveport, LA 71104-3335
tel. (318) 869-5169

Available for rent in 16mm film, 1/2″ VHS or 3/4″ video cassettes. Running time 28 minutes.

WHEN TO GO

I f you have the flexibility of choosing your travel dates, factors you may wish to consider are the weather, your plans upon your return, and the occurrence of Vietnamese holidays.

CLIMATE

Hanoi has a cold winter (no snow) and the temperature in June can reach 100° F (38° C). Ho Chi Minh City averages from 78° to 90° F (26°–32°C) year-round. As the rainy season starts in May and lasts until early December, the most favorable weather for a trip to Vietnam would be between the end of December and April. But by no means should you limit yourself by this suggestion. Since rain is an integral part of Vietnamese life, you may choose to experience how the people cope with the forces of nature. If you visit during the rainy season, it may help to recall the Vietnamese saying:

"Winds serve as brooms to clean the skies.
Rain is a silken curtain before heaven."

JETLAG

Since Vietnam is on the opposite side of the globe from the US, the effects of jet lag can be expected to be about as severe as possible. Traveling from east to west seems to result in less fatigue and time disorientation than traveling in the opposite direction. If your itinerary is from San Francisco to Bangkok, for example, you will experience waking earlier than usual with sleepiness in the late afternoon.

Before going into Vietnam, spending a few days in a city with a time zone similar to Vietnam's, such as Bangkok, Hong Kong, or Manila, will help your circadian rhythm (biological 24-hour time clock) to adapt. Even healthy young travelers returning from the Orient to the US require from seven to ten days to fully recover their time orientation. Given the wear of jet lag on the body, plan enough free time and schedule flexibility upon your return to readjust. Those who plan to return to work or school might plan to leave some time for afternoon naps. There are several books on the prevention of jet lag that the traveler can consult.

HOLIDAYS AND FESTIVALS

Holidays throughout much of Asia are based on the lunar calendar, which varies from the Western calendar. Celebration dates might fall on different days from year to year. In addition to national observances, there are many local rituals and festivals that pay homage to the tutelary spirits and the patron of the temple of a particular village.

Tet. The word is an abbreviation of Tet Nhat, meaning the first day of spring between the harvest and planting time. It occurs on the first new moon of the lunar calendar, falling between January 19 and February 20 of the Western calendar. New Year is officially a three-day holiday, but in practice the celebrations often last up to a week.

During the celebration of the Lunar New Year or Tet, visitors will find Vietnam in a festive holiday atmosphere, with dragon dances, fireworks, and flowers everywhere. Going at this time of year, however, also presents a few disadvantages. Many shops and museums are closed, not just for one day but in some cases for the whole week. Although Tet is the quintessential Vietnamese holiday, it is not representative of everyday life—children are out of school, people spend more lavishly, holiday clothing is worn, and special foods are prepared.

Tet is set aside as a time of rest. Offices, shops, and markets, as well as schools, are closed. Most of the population will be thinking of and actually celebrating the holiday with their families. Vietnamese people travel far to be with their families for at least the three most special days of Tet. Planes and buses are jammed. People are understandably sad if they are not able to get off from work. As a result, your guides and drivers might be preoccupied and therefore less enthusiastic to fulfill your special requests. This is not a criticism of the general helpfulness the guides provide, but a factor to consider when planning your trip.

In the south, the streets are filled with flowers, especially branches of the *mai* apricot—Tet apricot flowers are yellow in the south and rose-colored in the north. Miniature orange bushes are pruned so that they bear fruit just at Tet. Fireworks, although discouraged by the socialist government as a wasteful luxury, are heard for days.

On the night of the first new moon (considered the most important night), according to traditional beliefs, the household god

(called the hearth god or the stove god) returns to heaven to make his report on the household to the Jade Emperor. In preparation for this first night of celebration, everything is cleaned in advance, including the graves of ancestors—no cleaning is done during the holiday itself. The family altar receives special attention: incense, fruits, and flowers are offered to the spirits of dead relatives who are invited back into the family to enjoy a meal with the living.

In the north, a special square rice dish, called *banh chung,* is prepared with sticky rice. *Banh Tet,* a similar dish made in a round shape, is served in the south. These rice dishes are called rice cakes but are unlike "cakes" in the Western sense; they're made of meat and vegetables surrounded by a dense mixture of sticky rice and mung beans. These "cakes" are not sweet, either. For sweets, Vietnamese can choose from dried fruits such as winter melon, coconut shreds, and *mut hot sen* (sweetened lotus seeds).

The festive air permeates every available space. Hotels decorate lobby trees with lights and colorful papers, and the popular dragon dance often takes place in a town square (Lam Son Square in Ho Chi Minh City). When the dragon or unicorn dances in front of a shop or house, it is thought to bring prosperity.

Tet is everybody's birthday; on this day everyone becomes one year older. If a child is born one hour before the New Year, then one hour later the child is considered to be two years old. At Tet,

Public information posters: poster on left celebrates the 20th anniversary of the 1968 Tet Offensive; poster in middle states that citizens of Cu Chi oppose the making and drinking of moonshine booze; poster on right urges cooperation to increase production

children receive gifts or coins wrapped in red paper. Candies such as lotus seeds and sugared winter melons are popular. The first visitor of the New Year to enter the house brings with him good or bad luck. A common practice is to invite a respected person to visit at that time so that this turn of luck is not left to fate. Debts are also repaid at Tet.

Each year is "sponsored" sequentially by one of 12 animals of the zodiac: the rat, ox, tiger, cat, dragon, snake, horse, ram, monkey, cock, dog, and pig (e.g., the years 1964, 1976, 1988, and 2000 are dragon years).

Founding of the Communist Party of Vietnam. February 3.

Dong Ky Fireworks Festival. Fourth day, first lunar month. A competition of large firework creations is featured in Ha Bac and Ha Son Binh provinces.

Dong Da Day (fifth day, the first lunar month in the Oriental calendar, late January or early February in Western reckoning) is the celebration of the conquest of King Quang Trung over the Chinese in 1789.

Co Loa Festival, sixth day, first lunar month, commemorates King An Duong, the builder of the citadel, Co Loa, in 3rd century BC.

Lantern Festival on the first full moon (15th of the first lunar month) of the lunar year, in February.

Hoi Lim Festival or the alternating song contest, is held in Ha Bac Province on the 13th day of the first lunar month. Girls and boys carry on a courtship dialogue in song. The singers of one gender meet the singers of the opposite sex from another village to engage in a vocal contest which follows specific guidelines. For example, one melody can be used for only two verses of the song, encouraging extemporization. The songs incorporate daily events as they happen, and the singers practice during the year while they work at activities, such as weaving, fishing, or transplanting rice.

Trung Sisters Day (sixth day, second lunar month, usually late February or early March) celebrates the feats of the two sisters who fought the Chinese in AD 40.

Pagoda of the Perfumes Pilgrimage is celebrated on the full moon of the second lunar month in Ha Son Binh Province. Located 31 miles (50 km.) west of Hanoi, in a mountainous section, the pagoda complex contains streams, caves, and a forest-like apricot orchard. In the springtime, its sacred grottoes (especially the main one, Huong Tich) fill with visitors.

Buffalo Immolation Feast is a springtime ritual of the Tay Nguyen Highlands. A buffalo is killed and smoked over an open fire for a feast.

Thanh Minh Day (fifth day, third lunar month, April 5 to April 20) honors the dead. In China, this is the Ching Ming-pure-and-clear celebration. The link between death and life is a continuous interchange in traditional Vietnam, the dead relying on the living to provide them with the necessities of the afterlife, the living at the mercy of the dead who could return spiritually either to bring good advice and luck or to torment the living in the form of ghosts. On this day it is important to please one's ancestors. Graves are cleaned and whitewashed. If the fates have not been kind to the family, perhaps grandfather's grave is located in an unfavorable spot. To bring better times for the living, coffins of ancestors may be exhumed and moved to another, hopefully more auspicious, resting place.

Hung Vuong Kings Day, tenth day, third lunar month, around April 19, commemorates the historic founding of Vietnam by the Hung Vuong Kings. This celebration has a special significance in Vinh Phu Province where it is celebrated with water puppetry shows and wrestling matches.

The King Dinh Temple and Le King Temple festivals are held on the same day and take place in the same region of Ha Nam Ninh Province where the temples are located.

King Dinh Temple Festival 12th day, third lunar month, commemorates the unification of the country in the 10th century by King Dinh Tien Hoang (Dinh Bo Linh), who pacified and united competing warlords of 12 adjacent regions. The period of time before unification, when Vietnam was ruled by 12 separate states, is historically known as the Rule of the 12 Lords. As the founder of the short-lived Dinh dynasty, which ruled from 968–979, King Dinh Tien Hoang set up his capital at Hoa Lu in the province of Ninh Binh.

Le King Temple Festival commemorates King Le Dai Hanh, who defeated the Sung in AD 980 and founded the Early Le Dynasty (980–1005).

Re-enactment of a Legendary Marriage. Each spring the village of Trieu Phu hosts the yearly re-enactment of the legendary marriage of the daughter of the Hung Kings princess My Nuong Ngoc Hoa to the Spirit of the Mountain. On her way to her new home as the wife of the mountain king, the princess arrived at Trieu Phu village so homesick that she refused to continue. The villagers, seeing the plight of the princess, organized a party to help the bride overcome the blues. The festival, as enacted today, includes choosing a boy and a girl between 13 and 16 years old to represent the legendary couple, who are carried on palanquins through the town while singers, musicians, storytellers, and dancers entertain them.

Liberation Day, April 30, celebrates the anniversary of the liberation of Saigon from US control on April 30, 1975. Typically, there is a parade combining the military and school children (the nieces and nephews of "Uncle Ho"), with speeches by dignitaries. Government offices are closed.

May Day, May 1, Celebration of International Workers Day.

Defeat of the French at Dien Bien Phu celebrates the end of the first Indochina war, May 7, 1954.

Phat Dan Day (eighth day, fourth lunar month, usually early in May). Buddha's birthday, enlightenment, and death. This day of homage is not celebrated with as much formality as was once the case.

Phong Sinh, the festival of the doves' flight, occurs in early May. This ritual sets free captive fish and birds in honor of Buddha's birthday and is timed to coincide with the molting season of predator hawks. Since the birds of prey do not leave their nests, they pose no danger to the doves. The doves are organized in teams of ten and the teams are judged on their ability to stay together, to fly high, and to execute small, perfect circles in the sky.

Ho Chi Minh's Birthday, May 19, is one of the most important holidays of the Vietnamese year. Government buildings and schools are closed and ceremonies take place in remembrance of "Uncle Ho."

Tet Doan Ngo. Fifth day, fifth month, end of May or early June. This is the opening of the summer solstice, a time for harmonizing the complementary male and female principles of Nature, the *yin* and the *yang*. In Hanoi, one can see the morning sun cast the shadow of the Penbrush Tower (the male principle) onto the hollow in the stone of the Inkslab (the female principle) on the east side of the lake. There are various customs intended to assist nature in making a happy transition over this period and to protect man from the diseases common at this time of year. In China and elsewhere in East Asia, this is also the time of the dragon boat festivals.

War Invalids and Martyrs Day, July 28.

Weaver and the Shepherd Reunion, seventh day, seventh month (mid-August). Celebrates the start of the rainy season. The legend goes as follows:

A shepherd loved a pretty weaver girl. They enjoyed each other's company so much that they neglected their work. The Lord of Heaven separated them by placing them on opposite sides of the Milky Way galaxy. The Queen of Heaven had mercy on the lovesick couple and begged the King for a concession. Moved by his wife's pleas, the lord arranged that on one day of the year a flock of magpies would form a temporary bridge across the Milky Way upon which the couple could cross and meet. At their subsequent parting at the end of the day, showers of tears fall from heaven—the first autumn rains.

Independence or National Day, September 2, commemorates the founding of the Democratic Republic of Vietnam in 1945 on the day of the Japanese surrender aboard the USS Missouri.

Vu Lan Day (full moon or 15th day, seventh lunar month during August) is Wandering Souls or the Day of the Dead (*Co han*). Souls of the dead are remembered on this day by families visiting the graves of buried loved ones to perform the *Dan chay*, the incense and obligation offering to the souls of the departed. The ancestor's altar at home is also prepared. The altar has two levels: the higher is for Buddha, who receives offerings of incense, fruit, and rice; the lower portion of the altar is for departed relatives, who receive offerings of rice soup, fruit, and meat. It is best if the offerings include the *tan sinh*, the three living creatures, fish, meat, and shrimp, plus the *ngu qua*, the five kinds of fruit.

Con Son Temple Festival (tenth day, eighth lunar month). Held yearly in Hai Hung Province to commemorate the victory of

Le Loi and his advisor, Nguyen Trai, over China's Ming troops. Nguyen Trai wrote a famous Victory Proclamation, an early Declaration of Independence.

Children's or Harvest Festival or Tet Trung Thu (full moon / 15th day, eighth lunar month or the end of September, when the full moon on the horizon is at its largest of the year). Children parade happily in the street with candles, moon-shaped lanterns, and toys, while enjoying a special meat and egg "cake" called *banh trung thu*.

Tran Hung Dao Day (20th day, eighth lunar month). Anniversary of the victory of General Tran Hung Dao over the Mongols in 1284. It is celebrated with exceptional exuberance at the Kiep Bac memorial temple in Hai Hung province.

Le Loi Day (22nd day, eighth lunar month) celebrates the victory of Le Loi over the Chinese Ming invaders.

Double Nine (ninth day, ninth moon) marks the coming of winter frosts, the transition from fall into winter. Celebrated with kite-flying.

MAKING TRAVEL ARRANGEMENTS TO VIETNAM

The February 1988 Treasury Department ruling forbids US travel agencies from promoting or profiting from travel in Vietnam. Foreign travel agencies, however, do not have the same restrictions. US travel agencies may arrange, and collect a commission on, travel into and out of Vietnam using third-country carriers such as Air France, Philippine Airlines, or Thai Airways International, but not the Vietnamese national airlines, Hang Khong.

Some of the groups listed below arrange humanitarian trips, including medical personnel offering their services, groups bringing donations of medical supplies for hospitals, supplies for orphanages, and equipment for the handicapped. Others have academic leaders who lecture on historical sites; and one special interest group in particular studied Southeast Asian art while in Vietnam. It would be best to phone the American agencies listed below, since they are

MAKING TRAVEL ARRANGEMENTS

not permitted to send promotional information. Foreign agencies, however, will send informational brochures upon request.

Bookings in Vietnam will be made for you as part of a tour. Be sure you understand what your tour price includes. For example, does it include travel to Bangkok or Manila, the flight from these cities to Hanoi or Ho Chi Minh City, or in-country travel between cities?

AGENCIES TO CONTACT FOR TRAVEL INFORMATION

UNITED STATES

Asia Resource Center
P.O. Box 15275
Washington, D.C. 20003
tel. (202) 547-1114

Ben-Thanh Tours
210 Fifth Ave. Suite # 1120
New York, NY 10010
tel. (212) 633-8170

Bolsa Travelmart
9521 Bolsa Ave.
Westminster, CA 92683-
  5983
tel. (800) 333-6572
tel. (714) 531-3010

Florida Office of Indochina
  Communication Services
P.O. Box 3255
Homestead, FL 33034
tel. (305) 246-4898

Folkways Institute
14903 S.E. Linden Lane
Oak Grove, OR 97267
(503) 658-6600
tel. (800) 225-4666 in OR
Offers historian-led
educational and cultural
experience

Indochina Reconciliation
  Project
5850 Green Street
Philadelphia, PA 19144
tel. (215) 848-4200

Indochina Communications
  Services
631 Great Hill Road
Guilford, CT 06437
tel. (203) 457-0179

Travel Management
  International
18 Prescott Street Suite #4
Cambridge, MA 02138
tel. (617) 661-8187

continued

AUSTRALIA

Oribitours PTY. Ltd.
7th floor Dymocks Building
428 George Street
Sydney NSW 2000
GPO Box 3309
Sydney 2001 Australia
tel. (61-2) 221-7322
fax (61-2) 221-7425

CANADA

Good Morning Vietnam Tours
R.R.2 Brockville
Ontario, Canada K6V 5T2
tel. (613) 926-56126

Wings of the World Travel Inc.
653 Mount Pleasant Rd.
Toronto, Ontario M4S 2N2
tel. (416) 482-1223
(800) 268-8912

HONG KONG

Abercrombie & Kent
   International
Tai Sang Commercial
   Building, 27th floor
24-34 Hennessy Rd.
Wanchai Hong Kong
tel. 5-865-7818
telex 780-90 A Kent HX

THAILAND
(country code for Thailand
from the US is 662)

Air People Tours and
   Travel Co., Ltd.
Regent House Building, 2nd
   floor
183 Rajdamri Rd.
Bangkok 10500
Thailand
tel. 251-1534
telex 21132 GUE TH

Diethelm Travel
KianGwan Building II
140/1 Wireless Rd.
Bangkok 10500
Thailand
tel. 255-9150
telex 81183, 21763
   DIETRAN TH

Tri Tee Limited
TDI Building, 4th floor
42 Surawong Rd.
Bangkok 10500
Thailand
tel. 223-3604

FRANCE

HIT Voyages
21 rue des Bernardins
75005 Paris, France
tel. 43-54-17-17

Logotour
3 rue des Chenes Pourpres
95000 CERGY
France
tel. (1) 30-30-53-35

VISA FORMALITIES FOR VIETNAM TRAVEL

All foreigners visiting Vietnam must be in possession of a visa issued by the Vietnamese government. Visa applications must be completed in triplicate, with a 1-1/2 × 2-3/8 inch (4 × 6 cm.) photograph attached to each. One form is submitted to the local Vietnamese embassy or diplomatic representative nearest the visitor; the two remaining forms are retained for submission at Vietnam's embassy in the city of entry. At least 20 days prior to arrival in Vietnam, the local Socialist Republic of Vietnam Embassy must be supplied with a finalized name list for the entering group. Information to be supplied includes:

1. Name in full
2. Date and place of birth
3. Nationality
4. Passport number
5. Current occupation

Within 10 days of receiving the names, the local embassy will be advised by VietnamTourism-Hanoi if the entry permit has been approved.

If the visa has been approved, travelers must bring their passports and the two remaining visa forms to the Vietnamese Embassy in the city from which the tourist will fly into Vietnam (most commonly for Westerners, Bangkok, Manila, or Paris) where the visa is stamped onto the visitor's passport. Passengers leave their passports at the embassy in the morning (at which point flight departure information should be reconfirmed) and may pick them up with their approved visas the next morning; in some cases, visas may be approved on the same day. Travelers should note that this procedure requires them to arrive at Bangkok (or Manila) with at least one full business day available to complete the paperwork before flight departure for Vietnam.

Visa processing fees vary from country to country, but fall within the range of US$10–40 per applicant. In 1988, a visa-processing fee of 200 Thai baht was charged. Individuals or groups requesting special itineraries inside Vietnam are usually asked to provide additional information in a letter outlining the purpose of their trip and any special requests, including a short biography of each participant.

VIETNAMESE LIVING ABROAD

Vietnamese nationals residing overseas who wish to tour Vietnam as well as visit relatives (a minimum tour program is usually required prior to the visit with relatives) must submit their applications at least six weeks prior to arrival. Overseas Vietnamese must also supply the following additional information:

1. Date and number of exit permit (if acquired) or the date, purpose, and method of the original departure from Vietnam.
2. Name(s) in full, address(es), and occupation(s) of their relatives to be visited in Vietnam and their relationship to each.

PLANNING AN INDEPENDENT VIETNAM TRIP

Although most visitors go to Vietnam as part of a group tour, it is also possible to arrange your own travel.

Contact the Vietnamese Embassy in a country that maintains diplomatic relations with the Socialist Republic of Vietnam for information. Another option is to go directly to Bangkok or Manila and to make arrangements with either local travel agents or the Vietnamese Embassy there in person. In early 1989, visitors from the US traveled to Bangkok, went to the embassy of the Socialist Republic of Vietnam requesting a tourist visa and were referred to cooperative local tour agencies. The English-speaking tourists had to wait around Bangkok until a sufficient number of tourists had signed up before setting out. Even if your visa has been approved in advance, there is usually a wait of a few days before you can pick up the completed paperwork that is required before boarding the plane to Vietnam.

If you are in a country with access to a telex service to Hanoi, you might be able to get visa approval by sending a telex to 4269 tourism VT or 4552 tourism VT. In December 1988, the telex route did not work from the US or London: "No circuits to that country available." The cable address is VietnamTourism-Hanoi. In using the telex or cable method, be sure to include all the required visa information in your request.

DIRECTORY OF EMBASSIES OF THE SOCIALIST REPUBLIC OF VIETNAM ABROAD

Australia
6 Timbarrta Crescent, O'Mally
Australian Capital
   Territory 2606
tel. 866-059

Federal Republic of Germany
5300 Bonn 2
Konslantinstr. 37
tel. 357022
Vietnam Tourism maintains
an office in Bonn.

France
62 rue Boileau
75116 Paris
tel. (1-4) 524-50-63

Italy
Piazza Barbarini 12
00187 Rome
tel. 475-4098

Japan
50-11 Moto Yoyogi-Cho
Shibuya-ku
Tokyo 151
tel. 466-3311

Malaysia
4 Persiaran Stonor
Kuala Lumpur
tel. 248-4036

Mexico
Sierra Ventana 255
Col Lomas de Chapultepec
11000 Mexico, D.F.
tel. 540-1612

Philippines
554 Vito Cruz
Malate, Metro Manila
tel. 500364

Sweden
Orby-slattsvag 26
125 36 Alvsjo
tel. (8) 86-12-18

Thailand
83/1 Wireless Rd.
Bangkok 10500
tel. 251-7201

United Kingdom
12-14 Victoria Rd.
London, W8 5RD
tel. 937-1912

VIETNAM'S TRAVEL POLICY

Although the Vietnam General Commission of Tourism was established as early as 1979, it was not until the mid-1980s that Vietnam tourism policy made a perceptible shift toward the West, welcoming visits by Europeans and Americans through a general easing of restrictions on tourist travel.

By 1988, some 30 cities, towns, and districts had been opened to foreign tourism. Some travel by train is starting on the reconstructed rail system. "Opened" towns are set up with at least minimal lodging facilities and a government tourism office.

OPERATION OF TOURISM IN VIETNAM

The government body with direct authority over all policy-making tourism operations in Vietnam is the Vietnam General Commission of Tourism (more popularly known as VietnamTourism)—54 Nguyen Du Street, Hanoi; tel. 54574/52986/55963; telex: 4269/4552 TOURISM VT.

The head of VietnamTourism is Nguyen Quyen Chinh.

VietnamTourism (VT) sets up group and individual itineraries, sets fees, and is the official visa-issuing authority for foreign tourism. It maintains branches throughout the country (including representative offices in Hanoi and Ho Chi Minh City (Saigon). (See directory of individual cities for local branch addresses of VT.)

These branches, in turn, operate local itineraries (the branch in Ho Chi Minh City, still known as Saigontourism, conducts tours throughout southern Vietnam), function as intermediaries for hotel bookings, rent out staff-driven cars and buses and books for sightseeing, employ guides and interpreters, and provide most other major services required by tourists (including, in some cases, local distribution of soft drinks).

ITINERARIES

VT itineraries vary from seven to 21 days and invariably include international entry ports of Hanoi, Ho Chi Minh City, and/or the newly opened international terminal at Danang. Longer tours may include three- to four-day visits to Cambodia, with visits to Phnom Penh and the magnificent archaeologic site of Angkor, where the famous Angkor Wat temple is found. Side trips from Vietnam also include Laos, with stays in Vientiane and Luang Prabang. In 1988, VT was operating some 15 "set" itineraries (samples

VietnamTourism
(Du Lich)

VietnamTourism logo

---

below) for groups, with a multitude of variations if given ample notice. Among the favorite stops offered, apart from Hanoi and Ho Chi Minh City, were Danang, Hue, Halong Bay, Haiphong, Nhatrang, Dalat, Vungtau, and Cantho.

GUIDES AND INTERPRETERS

VT maintains a staff of national guides trained in nine languages: English, French, Russian, German, Polish, Japanese, Czech, Hungarian, and Bulgarian. Although ample numbers of local guides are employed at all major tourist towns and sites, few of these local guides speak but a smattering of foreign languages. The VT guide who accompanies the group throughout the country usually translates what the local guide has to say.

Personal guides are limited (VT employs only four German-speaking guides for the entire country). Consequently, Vietnamese teachers or other "amateur" interpreters may be drafted into service, or a guide speaking a similar or related language may be substituted as necessary. For long tours, securing an adequately trained interpreter becomes an all-important priority. Since the possibility exists that you may not be able to understand your guide fully, reading as much as possible about the place you plan to visit is strongly recommended.

DAILY SIGHTSEEING ITINERARIES

Although activities for a given day are usually set out in advance by the local VT office, requests for modifications are usually accepted cheerfully and genuine efforts are made to accommodate the special interests of teachers, medical personnel, art aficionados, and other professionals.

TOUR PACKAGES

Most private visitors to Vietnam (including tourist and business people—as opposed to guests of the government), whether traveling as individuals or as part of a group, are obliged to purchase a service package from VietnamTourism. A complete service package will include airport pick-ups and transfers, all domestic travel specified in the itinerary (including domestic airfare), guide/interpreter services, local transportation, cultural events, and luggage transport between airport and hotel. Since bellhops are still scarce, you may have to carry your luggage from the van to your hotel room. Although accommodations, meals, and cultural outings are determined by VT, Western tourists with hard currency (US dollars) generally receive the best services and facilities.

PAYMENT

Tourists traveling on their own (not part of a prepaid tour) will pay for accommodations, outings, drivers, and guides in US currency— payable upon arrival in Vietnam to VietnamTourism. While the preferred mode of payment is US dollars in cash, US-denominated traveler's checks may also be acceptable to VietnamTourism; expect a 2% bank fee service charge.

FLIGHTS INTO VIETNAM

In addition to securing your visa and arranging in-country tours, you or your travel agency will book flights into Vietnam. The following carriers fly to Vietnamese cities: Air France, Thai Airways International Ltd., Hang Khong Airlines (Vietnam Airlines), Philippine Airlines, Interflug (East German Airlines), Czechoslovak Airlines, and Aeroflot (Soviet Airlines). Garuda (Indonesia's airline) began weekly flights from Jakarta in June 1989. New flights and additional airlines are initiated each month.

Since May 1989, Vietnam Airlines, Thai Airways International, and Air France have been running three flights weekly on the Bangkok-Ho Chi Minh City and Bangkok-Hanoi routes. In addition, there is a weekly flight directly from Vancouver, Canada, to Ho Chi Minh City.

The following flights served Vietnam in the fall of 1988. These are used for references only. Check airlines for current information.

TO HO CHI MINH CITY

Air France flight #174: Mondays leaves Bangkok at 12:50 P.M.; arrives Ho Chi Minh City at 2:30 P.M. Thursdays leaves Bangkok at 11:15 A.M.; arrives Ho Chi Minh City at 12:55 P.M.

Aeroflot flight #569: Sundays leaves Moscow at 1:30 P.M.; arrives Ho Chi Minh City at 1:20 P.M. the next day. A flight every two weeks leaves Khabarovsk, Russia, at 11:40 P.M. and arrives 11:30 A.M. the next day.

Czechoslovak Airlines: special monthly flights from Prague.

Philippine Airlines flight #591: Tuesdays leaves Manila at 9:10 A.M.; arrives Ho Chi Minh City at 10:30 A.M.

Thai Airways International flight #200: Tuesdays and Fridays from Bangkok at 4:00 P.M.; arrives 5:35 P.M.

Hang Khong (Vietnam Airlines) flight #852: Tuesdays and Thursdays leaves Bangkok at 1:30 P.M.; arrives Ho Chi Minh City at 3:00 P.M. Flight #9034: every other Friday leaves Bangkok at 3:00 P.M.; arrives at 4:00 P.M.

INTO HANOI

Aeroflot flight #569: Sundays leaves Moscow at 1:30 P.M.; arrives Hanoi at 9:45 A.M. the next day. Flight #541: Mondays, Wednesdays, Thursdays and Fridays leaves Moscow at 6:00 P.M.; arrives Hanoi at 2:15 P.M. the next day.

Czechoslovak Airlines flight #516: Mondays, Wednesdays and Saturdays leaves Prague at 1:15 P.M.; arrives Hanoi at 10:30 A.M. the next day.

Interflug flight # 912: Every other Tuesday leaves Berlin at 9:00 P.M.; arrives Hanoi at 5:25 P.M. the following day.

Thai Airways International flight #682: Wednesdays and Saturday leaves Bangkok at 11:00 A.M.; arrives at 12:40 P.M.

Hang Khong flight #832: Fridays leaves Bangkok at 1:30 P.M.; arrives Hanoi at 3:10 P.M.

PREPARING TO VISIT VIETNAM

HEALTH PREPARATIONS

Consult your doctor or public health facility a few months before your trip for up-to-date information on precautions and immunizations. Although few immunizations are required legally to enter Asian countries, you should still be advised by a physician. Write to: U.S. Public Health Service, Center for Disease Control, Bureau of Epidemiology, Quarantine Division, Atlanta, GA 30333 for further information.

You probably will be advised to get immunized against tetanus, polio, typhoid, and yellow fever. A tuberculous skin test will be done as a baseline to establish whether or not you have been exposed to the disease. This may seem like a lot of shots and many doctor's appointments, but in many clinics these are routine and can be done quickly. Some immunizations, however, must be spaced over a period of time. For example, typhoid vaccine is given in two doses, at least four weeks apart, and is not given at the same time as the cholera, which also requires two doses from one to four weeks apart. Plan early so there will be enough time to complete your series of shots. Carry proof of immunizations (World Health Organization approved-yellow international certificate of vaccination) with you. Immigration officials in Bangkok or the US may ask for proof of vaccination when you return from a country where epidemics have occurred recently. If you arrive from an area infected with yellow fever or cholera, you may be required to show proof that you were vaccinated against these diseases.

A gamma-globulin shot is usually recommended to prevent contracting hepatitis. Discuss the pros and cons with your doctor of taking a broad-spectrum antibiotic while in Vietnam. Malaria, prevalent in Asia, is transmitted by the bite of a mosquito. Follow your doctor's recommendations. If malaria pills are suggested, you must start the course of prophylaxis *before* entering the malarial area and continue the medication for six weeks after leaving. Another medication, Fansidar, may be prescribed if signs of active malaria occur. Pregnant women should inform the doctor of their pregnancy prior to receiving any shots—some drugs are potentially harmful to the fetus.

WHAT TO TAKE ALONG

Packing for a trip to Asia requires a balance between bringing all you think you will need for your visit and packing as lightly as possible. You should be prepared to carry your own bags in Vietnam, so pack light and make each piece of clothing do double duty. For example, long-sleeved shirts can be used as underwear in the chilly north during winter. Hotel laundry service is quick and inexpensive, so you need take changes only for a few days at most. Appliances will have to be adapted for the electricity at 220 volts AC 50 cycles—the actual voltage usually varies at different times of day. Electric hair dryers and similar appliances should be left at home.

Make up a small medical kit consisting of aspirin, an antihistamine, anti-cough medication, band-aids, an antibiotic ointment for cuts and bug bites, an oral antibiotic to be taken as advised by your physician, and enough of any prescription medication you require. You will *not* be able to get a prescription refilled in Vietnam. For diarrhea, bring Lomotil and/or Pepto-Bismol. Women should anticipate their feminine hygiene needs and bring along their own supply—as a result of overseas travel, menstrual periods may start earlier than expected and may last longer than normal.

Travel packets of premoistened towelettes will come in handy; you will probably wish you had brought more. Carry an extra pair of eyeglasses and a copy of your lens prescription.

Carry an insect repellent (stick ones are convenient) and use the mosquito nets provided in most hotels. Insect repellent towelettes may be purchased in camping stores. One pats the towelette around areas exposed to flying insects. Some campers report that a skin moisturizer called Skin So Soft ™ from Avon Products acts as an effective insect repellent.

OTHER ITEMS TO TAKE

— Four extra passport photos in addition to the two needed to process your visa. You can get your photo taken in Vietnam if necessary, but it might require a valuable half day to accomplish the task.

— Sunscreen, soap, shampoo, tooth paste

— Small flashlight with extra batteries

— Extra batteries for cameras

— Notebook and several pens

— Travel sewing kit

— Large drain cover

— Toilet paper or tissue. The hotel rooms are supplied with toilet paper, but sometimes it is not available in toilets of restaurants and airports.

— A pack of peel and self-stick labels with your name and address imprinted on them. This will save you time when you want to give a new friend your address.

— For international news (in English rather than Russian or Vietnamese), bring a lightweight short-wave radio capable of receiving BBC international services.

— Several hundred clean and untorn US dollars in small ($5, $10, and $20) denominations. Some $100 traveler's checks may be useful to paying for large items. For example, if you rent a guide and a car for a week from VietnamTourism, they will accept travelers's checks at a good rate of exchange. Credit cards will be useless. Wearing a money belt is a good idea in any foreign country.

CLOTHING

You will be most comfortable in jeans or loose cotton slacks and your favorite comfortable soft shirts, even T-shirts are acceptable. It is advisable to bring a good pair of walking shoes. A hat with a brim is necessary protection from the intense sun in the south from December to May; from May to November, a lightweight rain poncho will keep you dry. Take along lightweight, long-sleeved shirts and at least one pair of socks for buggy evenings.

Bring jogging gear if you want to continue your morning runs and a swimsuit if you plan to be near a beach, e.g., Nhatrang, Vungtau, or Danang.

SAMPLE CUSTOMS DECLARATION FORM

GENERAL DEPARTMENT OF
   CUSTOMS

SOCIALIST REPUBLIC OF
   VIETNAM   HQ 60-87

Check Post: _____ Independence - Freedom - Happiness   19 × 27

CUSTOMS DECLARATION

No: _____

Date: _____

---

1 — Keep this declaration for presentation at the Customs upon re-exporting from or re-importing into Vietnam.

2 — Persons giving false declaration or having action of tricking will be dealt with according to Customs law of the Socialist Republic of Vietnam.

---

1 — Name in full _____ Sex _____ Nationality _____

2 — Passport number _____ Date of granting _____ / _____ / 198 _____
   Place of granting _____

3 — Place of departure _____ Place of destination _____

4 — Purpose of the journey (for mission, travel or private business) _____

5 — Accompanying family members under eighteen with their full names _____

---

6 — Luggage consisting of:

A) Disaccompanied luggage sent before import:

Consisting of _____ cases with Bill of Lading
   No.: _____

Consisting of _____ cases with Air way Bill
   No.: _____

B) Accompanied luggage:

Remarks of the checkpost Customs when consignee receives his goods:

1. Marine way:

2. Air way:

Consisting of _____ handpieces/cases _____ and _____ registered pieces/cases

DETAILS OF ACCOMPANIED LUGGAGE

I — Vietnam currency: Bills and securities in Vietnam currency

{ in cash: _____ dong
{ in bill: _____ dong

II — Foreign currency: consisting of all kinds of cash and cheque and securities in foreign currency:

Description of cash and cheque	Quantity		Control of the Customs	{Approval for the declaration or checking in detail
	In figures	In words		

III — Personal jewelry in precious metal (gold, silver, etc . . .) and precious stones

Description	Quantity	Weight	Control of the Customs	{Approval for the declaration or checking in detail

IV — Objects must be declared (give exact amount in figures and in words, if there isn't any, write clearly letter «No» following each name of the objects below):

Description (including mark)	Quantity	Control of the Customs	Description (including mark)	Quantity	Control of the Customs
1. Motorbike			16. Medicine		
2. Video cassette			17. Cigarette		
3. Video cassette tape			18. Wine/alcohol . . .		
4. Radio cassette			19. Sporting effects		
5. Radio cassette tape			20. Jeans (either shirts		
6. Shot (sporting) gun			or trousers)		
7. Airgun			21. T-shirt, pull		
8. Television			22. All kinds of cloth		
9. Radio-set			Super consumer goods		
10. Camera			not be shown above		
11. Film			1.		
12. Photo camera			2.		
13. Photo film			3.		
14. Photo paper			4.		
15. Watch/clock			5.		

PREPARING TO VISIT

V. Presents (gifts): Declare all of the presents.

- «Yes» (Declare detail in the index No «1» attached)
- «No» (If there isn't any, cross out letter «Yes» above)

VI Objects belonging to other person:

- «Yes» (Declare detail in the index No «2» attached)
- «No» (If there isn't any, cross out letter «Yes» above)

VII. I guarantee there is no accompanied effects belonging to effects (commodities) prohibited by the Vietnam government.

Remarks of the Customs: *The Declarant:*

— Hand luggage and registered luggage . . . . cases.   (Give full name and signature)

— Quantity of cases being checked already . . . . cases.

— Result _____

_____

_____

Customs Officer: *Decision of the Customs Director of the Checkpost*

(Give full name and signature)   (Give full name and signature)

Foreign money spent during your stay in Vietnam			
Kind of money	Quantity	Document No	Control of the Customs

III

TRAVELING IN
VIETNAM

CUSTOMS

Arriving travelers will pass through Vietnamese customs and immigration procedures where they will be asked to declare US dollars, plus such items as cameras, tape recorders, and jewelry. Luggage of foreign tourists generally is not searched. On the other hand, luggage and handbags of Vietnamese returning for family visits are carefully inspected for undeclared or illegal items. Customs inspectors examine film containers, unwrap chewing gum packages, and open sealed soap wrappers. They are looking for hidden gold and undeclared large denomination US currency. It is illegal to bring in drugs or weapons.

A 1988 regulation empowered the Vietnamese COSEVINA Corporation to collect taxes at Tan Son Nhut airport on gold that is brought in for families and friends. The taxes, called contributions to the public welfare, are collected in foreign currency at the rate of 1.6 US dollars, 10.6 French francs, or one British pound for each gram of gold regardless of its purity.

You will be asked to declare and itemize articles designated as gifts. You, or the person receiving the gift, may have to pay an import duty on the item. In January 1989, an import duty of $200 was levied on a VCR declared as a gift. It seems that there is no posted fee schedule and the amount to be paid depends upon the discretion of the customs officer. Medical equipment, textbooks, and medicines brought into Vietnam as gifts for one of their hospitals may also be taxed by the customs authorities.

After customs, travelers will be taken care of by sponsors or VietnamTourism.

SAMPLE ITINERARIES

Program #1.   20 nights/21 days   Cities visited: Hanoi/ Hasonbinh/Halong/Danang/Hue/Quinhon/Dalat/Vungtau Mytho/ Ho Chi Minh City

Day 1   Arrive Hanoi
          Hotel check-in
          Free time

Day 2   Ho Chi Minh Mausoleum
          One Pillar Pagoda
          Van Mieu (Temple of Literature)

SAMPLE ITINERARIES

Day 2   Army Museum
(cont.) Lake of the Restored Sword
         Variety show

Day 3   Hanoi-Mai Chau
         Visit to a Thai minority village

Day 4   Muong village
         Tram Gian Pagoda
         Return Hanoi

Day 5   Hanoi-Haiphong
         City tour—Haiphong
         Haiphong-Halong Bay

Day 6   Cruise—Halong Bay
         Return Hanoi

Day 7   Co Loa archaeologic site

Day 8   Flight to Danang
         Cham Museum
         Marble Mountain
         Beach

Day 9   From Danang to Hue by bus or van via Hai Van pass
         Citadel and Imperial City
         Tu Duc Mausoleum
         Khai Dinh Mausoleum

Day 10   Boat ride on the Perfume River to the Linh Mu Pa-
            goda
         Minh Manh Mausoleum
         Return to Danang

Day 11   Danang to Quinhon
         City tour of Quinhon

Day 12   Quinhon to Nhatrang
         City tour of Nhatrang
         Beach

Day 13   Po-Nagar Tower
         Hon Chong Rocks
         Tri Nguyen Aquarium

Day 14   Nhatrang to Dalat
         City tour Dalat

Day 15   Lover's lane
Xuan Huong Lake
Shopping at Market

Day 16   Dalat to Vungtau
Penn Falls

Day 17   Buddhist shrines
Beach

Day 18   Vungtau to Ho Chi Minh City
Variety show

Day 19   City tour Ho Chi Minh City
Thong Nhat conference Hall
Zoo and Botanical Gardens
Cu Chi tunnels

Day 20   Ho Chi Minh City to Mytho
Boat trip on the Delta to plantation

Day 21   Free time in Ho Chi Minh City
Departure

Program #2.   8 nights/9 days   Cities visited: Hanoi/Halong/
Danang/Hue/Ho Chi Minh City

Day 1   Arrive Hanoi
Hotel check-in
City tour

Day 2   Ho Chi Minh Mausoleum
One Pillar Pagoda
Van Mieu (Temple of Literature)
Trip to Halong Bay

Day 3   Cruise—Halong Bay
Return Hanoi

Day 4   Tay Phuong Pagoda
Thay Pagoda
Variety Show

Day 5   Flight from Hanoi to Danang
Cham Museum
Bus from Danang to Hue

Day 6   Citadel and Royal Palace
Boat ride on the Perfume River to the Linh Mu Pagoda

Day 6   Tu Duc Mausoleum
(cont.)   Return to Danang
             Marble Mountain
             Beach

Day 7   Flight from Danang to Ho Chi Minh City
             City tour

Day 8   Thong Nhat Conference Hall
             Zoo and Botanical Gardens
             Cu Chi tunnels
             Variety Show

Day 9   Free time in Saigon
             Departure

Program #3.   Historic North: 7 nights/8 days   Cities visited:
Hanoi/Hasonbinh/Ha Nam Ninh

Day 1   Arrival and hotel check-in

Day 2   Ho Chi Minh Mausoleum
             One Pillar Pagoda
             Van Mieu (Temple of Literature)
             Fine Arts Museum
             Quan Thanh Pagoda
             Lake of the Restored Sword
             Variety show

Day 3   Hanoi to Hoa Binh
             Muong village

Day 4   Hoa Binh to Mai Chau
             Thai village
             Return to Hanoi

Day 5   Hanoi to Nandinh (Ha Nam Ninh Province)
             Tran Dynasty Temple
             Tower Pagoda (Pho Minh)
             Co Le Pagoda

Day 6   Tam Coc Cave
             Bich Dong Pagoda
             Dinh and Le Dynasty Temple
             Return to Hanoi

Day 7   Tay Phuong Pagoda
Thay Pagoda
Free time in Hanoi

Day 8   Departure

Program #4.   The South: 7 nights/8 days   Cities visited:
Ho Chi Minh City/Binh Long/Cantho/Vungtau

Day 1   Arrival and hotel check-in
City tour

Day 2   Thong Nhat Conference Hall
Thien Hau Temple
Cu Chi tunnels
Variety show

Day 3   Ho Chi Minh City to Vinh Long
Boat trip to plantation and orchards

Day 4   Vinh Long to Cantho
Agriculture projects

Day 5   Military Museum or Cantho University

Day 6   Ho Chi Minh City to Vung Tau
Orphanage
Buddhist shrines
Beach

Day 7   Return to Ho Chi Minh City
Lacquer workshop

Day 8   Free time in Ho Chi Minh City
Departure

Program #5.   Side trip to Cambodia: 7 nights/8 days Cities
visited: Ho Chi Minh City/Mytho/Cu Chi/Angkor/Phnom Penh/Ho
Chi Minh City

Day 1   Ho Chi Minh City to
and 2   Siem Reap, Cambodia, by air

Day 3   Visit Angkor
Angkor to Phnom Penh

Day 4   Sightseeing in Phnom Penh
Toul Tum Pouing Market
National Museum
Royal Palace
Silver Pagoda

Day 5   Hoa Hong Kindergarten
          Tuol Sleng Museum
          Return to Ho Chi Minh City by air

Day 6   Ho Chi Minh City to Mytho
          Boat trip on the Tieng River
          Local plantations and orchards

Day 7   Cu Chi tunnels
          Free time in Ho Chi Minh City

Day 8   Free time
          Lunch
          Depart Ho Chi Minh City

DOMESTIC TRANSPORTATION

Transportation will be provided by VietnamTourism between the airport and hotels and to and from tour sites. If you are a guest of a government ministry, such as the Women's Association or the Ministry of Health, you can expect a representative of that group to meet you with transportation at the airport and escort you to your temporary residence. Once in Vietnam, you will be assigned a bilingual guide from VietnamTourism. They are friendly, creative, eager to please, and unabashedly curious about you.

If you are traveling on your own, be sure to discuss your plans at the tourism office to make arrangements for a guide and car. If you would rather drive than fly between cities, the tourist office can also accommodate your wishes. Saigon taxi service was initiated in July 1989. It is the first taxi service since 1975 using Nissan and Eastern Bloc vehicles. City visitors can also travel by human-powered pedicabs—tricycles which push a double seat perched in front of the handlebars. The seat is ample enough for one Western man, but an amazing number of Vietnamese can manage to pile into one seat, as many as eight children in one pedicab.

Car rental agencies and bicycle rentals are not yet fully operational in all cities. A traveler willing to make a few inquiries can make private arrangements for the use of a bike within the city. Unescorted visitors are not permitted on the railroads that run along the coast; plans were on track in 1989 to accommodate tourists by providing them with special tourist coaches on the rail system. Hospitality is not always consistent: in Hanoi, some Western visitors were welcomed to ride the electric tram car free of charge. Another

DISTANCES IN MILES & KILOMETERS BETWEEN CITIES

	Ho Chi Minh City	Haiphong	Danang	Nhatrang	Vientiane	Phnom Penh
Hanoi (mi.)	1,094	64	487	814	601	1,242
Hanoi (km.)	1,764	103	786	1,313	970	2,004
HCM City (mi.)		1,092	606	280	839	149
HCM City (km.)		1,761	978	451	1,354	240

time, a foreign visitor attempting to board a tram was waved away. There are public buses running between some cities, and one adventuresome Western traveler recently piled in with the chickens and the vegetables to survive a bus trip from Ho Chi Minh City to Mytho. Bus schedules are not published in English and there are restrictions on out-of-city travel, even for the Vietnamese.

Hang Khong Vietnam, Vietnam's airline, flies between Ho Chi Minh City/Danang/Hanoi/Dalat. No two cities in Vietnam are further apart than about two hours by air. You need not worry ahead of time about booking in-country flights between cities because your tourism guides will help you make your air connections.

Take along something to eat and drink on your plane trips between cities and on lengthy bus excursions. It is convenient to carry a safe water supply in a plastic bicycle bottle (the type with the nipple-shaped spout that locks to resists leaks). A welcome snack on day trips are oranges; their sweet juiciness will hit the spot at those inevitable junctures when your van is being repaired or when the paperwork of Vietnam's travel bureaucracy seems to take forever. At certain times of year, watermelons, coconuts, pineapples, and other fruits are sold on the roadside. You may request the tour van to stop to purchase these refreshments.

TIME

The time in Vietnam year round is Mean Greenwich time plus 8 hours. In summer when US clocks advance one hour for daylight savings, Vietnam time remains the same.

London: 5 A.M. Monday
New York: Midnight Monday
San Francisco: 9 P.M. Monday
Hanoi: Noon Tuesday

HOTEL FACILITIES

At present, hotels are preassigned. The Vietnamese seem to have set aside some hotels for Westerners and others for East bloc visitors, but this is not a hard and fast rule, and Soviets and Cubans can be seen in any hotel. Most hotels in Vietnam are renovated older hotels dating from the French or American era. Two hotels in Hanoi have been built since 1984: the Thang Loi (Victory) and the twelve-story Thang Long.

Your hotel will provide meals (see "Dining in Vietnam," below). Most have a souvenir shop. The rooms vary in size from large suites in the colonial style at the Metropole in Hanoi and the Cuu Long in Ho Chi Minh City, to smaller single rooms. While many rooms are equipped with air-conditioning, most lodgings will not have a TV or phone. Some rooms have tubs, others have showers. The most comfortable hotel in the capital city is the Thang Loi Hotel in Hanoi, which features rooms with television sets, heat and air-conditioning, phones that work, and Western-style showers. In the Orient, one frequently sees a shower arrangement in which there is not a separate shower stall but in which the water flows from a flexible faucet attached to the wall set adjacent to the sink or toilet, without a curtain or divider. A drain in the floor catches the water. In some hotels, the hot water must be turned on by the guest from inside the bedroom. It is a little tricky in some cases and you might want to ask at the reception desk for a demonstration in advance if the control system is unclear.

Small lizards called geckos commonly traverse the walls of homes and hotels. These harmless creatures are part of a tropical ambiance, and the frequent Asian traveler learns to enjoy their soft clicking sound because their diet is made up exclusively of mosquitoes and other tiny pests. Vietnamese believe that their presence prevents asthma attacks.

TRAVEL DECORUM

If you are with a tour group, outings to historical and cultural sites will be part of your pre-planned program, but there are free days or half days during which time you can explore on your own. Even if you are part of a tour group with a planned schedule, you may be able to visit a site not originally on the tour if you inform your tourism representative early in the trip. Limitation on travel does exist, partly for the safety of the visitor, and partly for government security reasons. It is wise to recall and take the lead from the Vietnamese proverb: "The emperor's rule stops at the village gate." In modern terms, one could say suspicion and hostility toward government agents and foreigners (no matter how friendly) still exist in rural areas of Vietnam. The foreign traveler will not be allowed to venture unescorted beyond urban limits and is forbidden to enter private homes. Vietnamese guests are not allowed in hotel rooms. If you wish to look up an old friend, a bit of intrigue enters the experience when you send a note by pedicab driver (private phones are few) to arrange a meeting in a hotel lobby or in a public restaurant.

PHOTOGRAPHY

You will have many opportunities to take stunning and unique photographs. Most citizens of Vietnam love to be photographed, including monks, nursing mothers, and police. No cameras or large bags are allowed in Ho Chi Minh's Mausoleum. You should be aware that areas considered of military importance, military installations, bridges, police stations, and prisons are off-limits to photographers. When you are photographing an attractive French-style building on a quiet residential street, a guard may appear suddenly and ask that you put away your camera. The government has recently lifted the requirement that all exposed film be processed before leaving the country. One deviant photographer in a group, however, might cause the film of the entire group to be impounded. Most experienced travelers are aware that X-ray security machines will white out (make useless) both fresh and exposed film. To avoid damage, use a lead-lined bag or better yet, request that the inspector hand-examine your film.

Although film can be purchased in Vietnam, it is expensive and probably outdated. Your best bet is to bring enough film with you. A Polaroid camera, although adding to your baggage weight, will make you popular and will help to relax your subjects who may then be more agreeable to pose for your 35-mm camera. If you give one child an instant Polaroid shot, many more eager open palms will beg you for a photo from the magic camera. Your film can be developed during your stay in Ho Chi Minh City by the camera shop on Dong Khoi Street next to the Air France offices. Tell the camera shop your time schedule to be sure your film is processed before you

Amerasian Young Pioneers, Dong Khai Street, Ho Chi Minh City

have to leave. Videocameras are allowed but also are weighty and bulky (new camcorder-type videocameras are much lighter).

Visitors from the Soviet East bloc countries are common in Vietnam. Russian and Soviet bloc advisors and vacationers will be seen at hotels and around town. Most of the Soviets keep to their own groups, shy away from interacting with tourists of other nationalities, and seem to prefer their own highly scheduled and regulated travel programs. Perhaps this attitude will change with the much touted nascent "glastnost" policy now favored by Moscow. In putting aside generalities, some East bloc advisors are quite lonely and welcome a smile and any attempt (even simple sign language) at starting a conversation.

Most pre-adolescent children in Vietnam have never seen Americans and they have not yet learned to distinguish between

Soviets and other non-Asian nationalities. They will call all Caucasians *"Lien Xo "* —Russian. If you wish to correct this impression, you might say, "No, I am an American.": *"Khong phai Lien Xo, Toi la nguoi My."* Conversely, if you do not want to be followed by begging children, say, "Yes, I am Russian": *"Da phai, toi lien Xo."* Russians are considered to be "Americans without dollars."

CURRENCY

The Vietnamese monetary unit is the *dong*; as the *dong* does not float on the world market, it is difficult to know just what a US dollar is worth in *dong* before you go. During 1988, visitors recieved exchange rates varying from 80 to 5000 *dong* to the dollar—an enormous gap due the *dong* being devalued in November 1988 to bring it in line with the black market rate.

A 5,000 *dong* bill has been introduced; the smallest bill is a 50 *dong* bill. The exchange rate varies from city to city and from hotel to hotel within the same city. Ho Chi Minh City gives the best rates and Hanoi gives the lowest rates of exchange. At one time, visitors were advised not to change dollars for *dong* illegally. More recently, however, some guides have been turning their heads at illegal black-market money changing by foreign visitors. When departing Vietnam, you will be asked to account for all foreign currency brought into the country, so keep the receipts given when you convert your money into *dong*.

SHOPPING

Vietnam is not thought of generally as a shopper's paradise. While you will not find the abundance and quality of merchandise encountered in Bangkok or Hong Kong, there are treasures to be found if you are willing to search carefully. Prices are astonishingly low and most market or street-stall items are handmade and unique. It is difficult at this stage of Vietnam's developing economy to give general advice; when it comes to shopping, it is safe to say that if you like it and can both afford and carry it, snap it up. You may not see a similar item, particularly a craft item, again.

There are more goods to choose from in the south, with the scope of merchandise generally decreasing as one moves north. Hanoi is an exception; many items are produced specifically for local market-areas that constitute the overall urban market—few products leave the district in which they are produced. Although prices may be higher in the south, the cost factor of merchandise is somewhat offset because the exchange rate is better—in other words, if you are allowed to pay in local currency, do so. If you enter Vietnam through Ho Chi Minh City, as has been the precedent in recent years, the exchange rate will be the best you will see for the rest of the trip.

ANTIQUES

Sales of antiques are restricted; they must also be bought in government shops. An official receipt is required for customs when you leave the country. The Perfume Hotel in Hue has lovely antiques, but these vintage objects are selling fast at prices that seem to rise with each tour group.

BOOKS

English language books are in high demand and sell out quickly. Although there are few souvenir books of good quality, the traveler might enjoy a handsome, well-done photobook of Vietnamese scenes with a text in Vietnamese, called *Vietnam* and published by Nha Xuat Ban Hoa Book Company in Hanoi. The photos were taken by Russian photographer Yevgeny Glazunov.

CERAMICS

Bright colors and bold designs are typical of contemporary Vietnamese ceramics. Large ceramic elephants may still be familiar to US military personnel who once bought them as ornaments for their patios or to use as end tables in their homes in the States. High quality ceramics are kiln fired at Bat Trang, Tho Ha, Quang Ninh, Song Be, Dong Nai, and in Ho Chi Minh City.

CONICAL HATS

The typical Vietnamese conical hat called *non la*, is made throughout the country. They make bulky but certainly representative souvenirs. Chuong village in the north and Hue in central Vietnam are known to make the most aesthetic hats. A Hue hat may contain any number of traditional designs such as paper cutouts of poetry, pagodas, birds, or flowers carefully inserted between the layers.

SHOPPING

When the hat is held up to the light, these motifs appear inspired subliminally. Some hats are signed by the artist. Ribbons to be attached to the hats are chosen separately, giving a buyer the option of choosing the color of ribbon. Some military buffs may wish to purchase inexpensive pith helmets which were worn by the North Vietnamese military.

EMBROIDERY

Blouses and women's lounging suits with hand-embroidered designs make attractive gifts. The costly, gorgeous, intricate embroidery of dragons and phoenixes on the traditional *ao dai* (pronounced ow zai) has been toned down in the last ten years. Few Vietnamese women can afford them and displays of luxury in public are discouraged amidst poverty and government policies toward moderation. Nevertheless, a selection of hand-embroidered fabric lengths for making the traditional *ao dai* are still available on Dong Khoi Street and in the large Cho Ben Thanh market in Ho Chi Minh City. Generally speaking, Vietnamese women do not purchase ready-to-wear dresses off the rack. Instead, they purchase a piece of *ao dai* fabric about two-and-a-half yards (60 cm.) long from which a dress is hand-tailored to fit.

JEWELRY

Hand-tooled silver bracelets, rings, and earrings are exotic, even if the designs are somewhat crude. The thin layer of silver may eventually rub off to expose the brass beneath. Bead necklaces of bone (not ivory) are fun to bargain for in the street markets. Ivory is also sold inexpensively, although the importation of elephant ivory is illegal in many countries. Hotel shops charge more than double the street price for jewelry—but even at that rate, such objects remain a bargain.

LACQUERWARE

Oriental lacquerware is usually associated with decorated practical objects such as boxes, trays, and screens. In Vietnam, lacquerware is considered an art form in itself. Although lacquerware sometimes cracks when introduced to a climate with a different humidity, the staff at the state-run lacquer factory in Ho Chi Minh City maintain that their pieces, some of which are immensely large and intricately beautiful, are kiln-dried and carefully prepared so as not to warp or flake regardless of the moisture content of the air. Vietnamese lacquerwork often features goldfish that appear to swim just below the black surface and are so subtle and striking that it will be difficult to resist purchasing a few small boxes or vases.

PAINTING AND OTHER ART WORK

Paintings on silk, block prints, simple ink drawings, and water colors are traditional artworks readily available for purchase. Hand-painted silk note cards are elegant and a recommended buy. The Thang Loi Hotel in Hanoi features works of a variety of artists worth investigating. The mattings might become a bit wrinkled during the trip home, but you will probably want to remat them to suit your taste anyway. The Tan Son Nhut airport shop in Ho Chi Minh City shows some large modern paintings that might enhance an eclectic decor. There are many art galleries to explore up and down the streets near the Cuu Long Hotel on the waterfront in Ho Chi Minh City and around the old French Opera House in Hanoi.

TAPESTRIES

Tapestry weaving made its appearance in Vietnam in the 1930s. The Dong Da factory in Hanoi, established in 1961, weaves woolen carpets and wall hangings for export and sale in government shops under the trade name Tada.

Note: The US Treasury will allow US citizens to bring back only $100 worth of goods from Cambodia and Vietnam. Keep your receipts.

TELECOMMUNICATIONS AND POSTAL SERVICE

TELEPHONE

International phone calls can be made from some hotels and specially designated public buildings in Hanoi and Ho Chi Minh City. (Some hotels as well as the main post office in Ho Chi Minh City have conveniently located long-distance phones plus *fax* and telex capabilities.) To avoid frustration, however, it might be best not to promise to call home while in Vietnam. If the phones are working, your family or friends will have a surprise. Phone calls from the US to Vietnam are possible, but difficult.

MAIL

The selection of attractive postcards from Vietnam is limited, but if you wish to send cards or letters home, do so early in your trip. As a metered stamp from the post office is necessary, I suggest queuing up with everyone else while maintaining an easy attitude—the horrendous wait during certain times at the post offices may try the patience of Buddha himself. Stamp collectors can bypass waiting lines to purchase colorful Vietnamese stamps in shops and street stalls outside the post office building. Vietnamese stamps cannot be bought in stamp shops in the US and make a welcome gift for a collector.

Vietnamese stamps do not have glue on the back; glue has to be applied and the letter taken to the post office where, if the postage is deemed insufficient, another receipt may be applied in addition to your stamp. Mail should arrive in the US in less than three weeks; packages can take up to six weeks. Money orders can be sent to another district by special arrangement. If, for example, you have a friend in the delta and your tour is not going there, you may wish to send your friend cash via a money order.

DINING IN VIETNAM

Your tour package rate includes fixed menu meals; you will not leave the table hungry. While hotels offer the option of Western or Vietnamese style dishes, Vietnamese cuisine is prepared best. Vietnamese food contains little fat, even when a particular food is fried. Southern Vietnamese cooking, influenced by the culinary arts of India, China, and France, can be quite spicy.

TYPICAL FARE

Perhaps the best-known Vietnamese seasoning agent is a fish sauce called *nuoc mam* (pronounced nook mom). The concentrated form of this sauce (it needs to be diluted and spiced up before it is served) provides a base for *nuoc cham*, which is what finally appears in a small dish on your table. *Nuoc cham* sauce is prepared from the *nuoc mam* by adding sugar, lime juice, vinegar, chopped shallots, garlic, and carrots. (See section on Nhatrang for how the fish sauce is made.)

Sliced peppers are a staple condiment at most meals. Spices such as coriander, lemon grass, mint, black pepper, and a local, basil-like herb call *rau ram* add a light and subtle flavor. Fresh vegetables and fruits are characteristic of southern Vietnamese cooking, which differs from Chinese cooking in that soy sauce is rarely used. The cuisine of the North relies more on thickening agents with less emphasis on fresh ingredients and spices.

French bread is excellent and delicious with jam (ask for comfiture) in Ho Chi Minh City and a rare treat in Hanoi. Baked goods (other than French bread) are rare because cooking, as elsewhere in East Asia, is not done in ovens but over a flame. On occasion, a loaf of bread may harbor a tiny weevil—they are harmless (and possibly even nutritious) if eaten, but the more finicky patron may wish to pick them out before the bread is eaten.

The Vietnamese use chopsticks as utensils. Meals often consist of many dishes: soup, fish, fowl, and perhaps a beef dish. A small dish or shaker of white crystal on the table is more likely to be monosodium glutamate (MSG) than sugar or salt. After the meal, your Vietnamese friends will select a toothpick from the container provided at the table, discretely cup the mouth to hide the process, and proceed to clean their teeth.

DRINKS

You will not find fresh milk or any dairy products in Vietnam. Coffee is served with sweetened condensed milk if ordered *sua* (with milk). At receptions and meetings, strong tea in tiny cups is ritually served as a form of hospitality. The visitor is advised to drink the

Sugar cane juice vendor, Cholon

tea offered out of deference to the host and because it is a safe opportunity to take in liquids (the boiling presumably kills any bacteria).
Tea is sometimes mixed with dried flowers, such as jasmine or chrysanthemum.

The Vietnamese beer label called "33" or Ba Muoi Ba is disappearing and is being replaced with "Hanoi" and "Saigon" brands—
essentially the same brew—it's light and an ideal hot-weather fluid.
"Gas beer" is a draft beer purchased by the pitcher in bars frequented
by Eastern Europeans. Vietnam also has strong rice liquors called Ba
Xi De (or Ruou De or Ruou Nep), sold in outdoor cafés. A refreshing and safe (for tourists) fluid is the local natural mineral water
that is carbonated and contains minerals to replace what you may
have lost due to perspiration. Nuoc Khoang is a popular brand of
mineral water served in hotels.

SOUPS

Soups are a fast snack and can be paradoxically refreshing on either
a hot or a cold day. Since soups have been boiled, they are safe to
eat (but you might pass up the garnish of fresh greens, which have
not been sterilized). Edward Landsdale, Chief of US Psychological
Operations in Vietnam in the 1950s, had this to say about the soups
of Vietnam:

> Anyone who wants to see the Vietnamese at their gregarious best
> and to find out what the public is saying about current events
> needs only to go on a gastronomical excursion among the soup
> stands. It's a delicious way to take a political survey.

Pho is a hearty noodle soup, a meal in itself, eaten by the
Vietnamese for breakfast.

Bun Bo Hue is a peppery beef soup with noodles. Tears in the
eyes indicate that it is being enjoyed properly.

Bun Reu is a noodle soup with shrimp and vegetables, less
spicy than *Bun Bo Hue*. Sometimes called Soupe Chinoise, it is
a delicious quick snack sold in street stalls.

Canh Chua Dau Ca is a sour fish soup made from fish pieces.

Asparagus soup with crab is a wonderful remnant of French
cuisine.

SNACKS

The south has a selection of delightful fruits: watermelons, pineapples, and small, wrinkled but suprisingly sweet oranges. Pomeloes
are large, green grapefruits with a thick skin. Jackfruit, carambola,

durian, papaya, *chom chom,* and *long nhan* are tropical fruits found in the markets and on roadside stands in the south. Apples and grapes are rare. While oranges and bananas are served in the north, other fruits are not available. Snacks include peanuts and watermelon seeds, dried and often dyed red.

A fast food sold from pushcarts is *Com Tay Cam,* a sandwich of French bread with slices of chicken, pâté, fish or pork, onions, and vegetables, spiced with ginger or hot pepper.

TRADITIONAL VIETNAMESE DISHES

Cha Gio (spring rolls) are lightly fried rice-paper rolls, smaller and crispier than Chinese egg rolls but more flavorful. *Cha Gio* are filled with highly seasoned morsels of crab, shrimp, chopped vegetables, sprouts, and transparant cellophane noodles (also called mung bean threads). On the ritual of eating *Cha Gio* as finger food wrapped with fresh greens and dipped in *nuoc cham,* Norman Lewis, a Western journalist traveling in Asia, had this to say:

> *Cha Gio* consists fundamentally of very small, highly spiced meat rolls, which are transferred easily enough with chopsticks from the dish to one's plate. But this is nothing more than a preliminary operation, and many dexterous manipulations follow. Two or three kinds of vegetable leaves are provided as salad, plus minute spring-onions. A leaf of each kind is picked up, and this is not so easy, placed in superimposition on one's plate and garnished with an onion, ready to receive the meat-roll in the middle. And now comes the operation calling for natural skill or years of practice, since the leaves must be wrapped neatly round the narrow cylinder of mincemeat. The *Cha Gio,* now fully prepared, is lifted with the chopsticks and doused in the saucer of *nuoc mam.* On this occasion, the Europeans soon gave up the struggle, throwing dignity to the winds, and dabbled happily with their fingers. A spirit of comradeship was noticeable, a democratic kinship born in an atmosphere of common endeavor, frustration, and ridicule.

Cha Tom is ground seasoned shrimp grilled on thin sugarcane skewers that add a sweetness to the shrimp as it is cooked to perfection.

Bo Bay Mon is "'beef seven ways." There are restaurants in Saigon specializing in these beef dishes that begin with beef fondu marinated in vinegar; the last course is usually beef rice soup.

Banh Hoi is a tiny noodle eaten with *nem muong* (barbecued pork balls) served with *nuoc mam* and fresh vegetables.

Banh Chung or New Year's rice cakes, a specialty for Tet, are moist rice squares wrapped in banana leaves, which give a desired light green color to the rice. In the south, the cakes are called *Banh Tet* and are round (see section on Tet celebration). Many Vietnamese attribute their victories in historic battles to the *Banh Chung*, the present-day equivalant of C-rations. For days, in either hot or cold weather, the rice packet remains unspoiled. Eaten with some locally picked mint leaves or greens, the rice concoction provides a balanced diet. In the battle of Dong Da, for example, individual portions of *Banh Chung* tied around the soldiers' waists allowed Emperor Quang Trung (Nguyen Hue) to travel quickly, and thus surprise the Chinese—lending further credibility to the adage that an army does, indeed, travel on its stomach.

Xeo means "singing" and is the word used to describe foods which sizzle during their preparation, such as *Banh Xeo*—a sizzling pancake.

Inquisitive diners may wish to try pig fallopian tubes, served chopped up with chillies and other spices. Other exotic selections include cartilage of pig's ear served spicy and cold, duck's-blood custard, or sea swallow-nest soup.

DE GUSTIBUS

IN HANOI

Fredric M. Kaplan

"Have you tried the veal?" Mrs. Heathcote asked brightly as I sat next to her for dinner at Hanoi's Thang Loi Hotel, which is built on a lake. Mr. and Mrs. Heathcote, exuberant tourists from London, had arrived a few days earlier and were the only other English speakers in the Thang Loi, which was otherwise packed with animated Cubans, dour Soviets, and some 200 thumping Bulgarians.

"Veal?" I was mildly surprised that Vietnam, with its so evident food problems, could manage to raise small calves to feed tourists.

"Very nice," Mrs. H. encouraged. "Had it every night here."

Lightly sautéed to the requisite golden beige, the small morsels were indeed tasty and tender, done in an aura of garlic. At the following night's dinner, the veal bits returned, this time prepared with slivers of ginger. I was not unpleased, but was frankly looking forward to more variety in the cuisine.

On the third night another veal creation was placed before me.

The dish was prepared in a bean sauce with onions. I spoke to the maitre d' through my guide and suggested that I would enjoy some fresh fish which is so good in Vietnam. He told me that the meal before me had been caught from the lake one hour ago. Very fresh!

My senses were now on alert as I returned to the pleasant-tasting bits. Not fish: wrong taste, no fish texture, no fish smell whatsoever. And then the bones. Not at all like fish bones. White, delicate, brittle and tubular. Hmmmmm.

After dinner, I lingered on the walkway along the edge of West Lake. The stillness of the serene and humid night was broken only by the rattling of a motorbike, and the croaking of . . . BULL-FROGS!

STAYING HEALTHY WHILE IN VIETNAM

If you have informed yourself on health preparations and follow proper precautions, chances are you will experience no, or at most mild, health problems. The most common travel-related health problem is diarrhea.

DIARRHEA

This ailment is debilitating and especially annoying on a trip when your ability to move about freely is part of the adventure. It is amazing to see even experienced travelers disregard the well-known warning: DO NOT DRINK THE WATER. DO NOT USE ICE IN YOUR DRINKS. Drink only bottled water, canned sodas, beers, and boiled tea. If you pass through Bangkok, you will want to start water precautions in that city. Although bringing along your own water-purifying chemicals is a healthy concept, once you are in the country and traveling from hotel to hotel, the practicalities involved get rather bothersome.

Tea made from boiled water is safe. Bottled carbonated mineral water in Vietnam is readily available and served with meals (Nuoc Khoang is a popular brand). Usually the water in the thermos provided in your hotel room will still be hot from boiling. If, however, you have any doubts about the room water provided and you have not brought a supply of purified water from Bangkok, use the local bottled mineral water to brush your teeth with.

Night soil (human excrement potentially containing disease-causing bacteria and the hepatitus virus) is still used as fertilizer on crops in some places, so be careful about consuming fresh vegetables such as tomatoes and lettuce—which is especially tempting since the delicious little rolls called *Gia Cho* are served with lettuce and fresh greens in which to wrap them. Eating clams or oysters in Vietnam is asking for hepatitis.

Keep your hands clean and wash with soap frequently, especially before eating. Packets of antiseptic wipes are handy for times when you are on the road or the water in your room is temporarily turned off.

If you come down with diarrhea, treat it seriously. Drink plenty of safe water to prevent dehydration. Some victims swear by drinking warm Coke that has gone flat. The Chinese and the Vietnamese people stop drinking tea when stomach problems occur and eat only rice congée—the creamy white broth that results after rice has been boiled a long time. In most cases, a day or two of this diet will cure the problem. As it takes time for the kitchen to prepare the congée, guides must be reminded that you require the congée at each meal. Some experienced travelers take a teaspoon of Pepto-Bismol each day and believe that it "coats the stomach"—in all probability, however, this medication causes constipation that counteracts a mild diarrhea.

You will notice during your travels that the Vietnamese frequently offer moistened hot or cold cloths as a way of refreshing yourself after returning to your hotel, or before meals. Be careful not to rub the damp cloths around your eyes or on your lips. Some organisms that are harmless on the skin may penetrate mucous membranes.

MOSQUITOES

Malaria is prevalent in Asia. Even though you may be taking malaria prophylaxis at your doctor's suggestion, you will want to avoid mosquito bites. Use insect repellent in the evening, and be sure to wear socks and long sleeves as well. Sweet-smelling colognes and shaving creams may actually attract insects. Hotels not equipped with air-conditioning will supply a mosquito net over the head of the bed. The netting spreads out over the bed and tucks in under the mattress. Use it.

Lighting a few sticks of incense near your bed may also keep mosquitoes away during the night. While mosquito coils are readily available and frequently used by the Vietnamese, some of these coils contain poisons which adversely affect humans—the smoke is not good for one's lungs, either. You can fumigate your room and avoid the toxins by burning the coil while you are out, with the windows and doors closed. Upon returning, air the room out a bit and place the stick or coil under your bed—mosquitoes like to congregate in dark and damp areas. Citronella oil-based candles also have a reputation as an effective insect repellent.

For those Westerners who are extremely sensitive to the bites of Asian insects, a local ointment will be a great help in soothing the swelling and itching. The Vietnamese salve—Golden Water is one brand—smells like Vicks rub and is sold in a small red tin (like the Chinese product "Tiger Balm"). If you think the bite has gotten infected from scratching, use an antibiotic ointment at once—it is important to attend to even the slightest wound in the tropics to prevent infection or to keep an infection from getting serious.

The medical system in Vietnam is still recovering from wartime shortages. If you are not seriously ill you may wish to experiment with the herbal and traditional medicine methods practiced in Vietnam. If, however, any of the following symptoms occur, consider arranging emergency transportation to a nearby country (such as Bangkok, Thailand) with more modern facilities. The symptoms listed below are medical emergencies requiring immediate action:

- persistent abdominal pain
- swollen abdomen
- shaking chills and fever
- fever over 104° F
- blood in stool or vomit
- coughing blood
- fainting
- severe weakness
- persistent headache and stiff neck
- chest pain

If you develop a fever, have persistent stomach problems, or develop other symptoms after you return from your trip, be sure to tell your doctor in which countries you have traveled. Symptoms of some disorders do not show up until months, or even years, after exposure.

IV

THE VIETNAM

TOUR:

CITIES AND

SITES

Hanoi

NORTHERN REGION

H anoi, the capital of Vietnam, is a quietly busy, crowded city of three million. Its average density of 3,570 persons per square mile (1,373 persons per sq. km.) makes it the country's second largest urban center, after Ho Chi Minh City. Hanoi Municipality, Ho Chi Minh City, and Haiphong are Vietnam's three self-administrating cities.

A legacy of foreign occupation still pervades Hanoi in the inescapable, anachronistically charming form of French-colonial architecture that dominates the capital's narrow, tree-shaded streets. The absence of modern buildings and the predominance of bicycle traffic also evoke an old-world ambience and tranquillity.

ARRIVAL

Noi Bia Airport is 40 miles (65 km.) to the north of Hanoi. Along the landing approach, airline passengers can peer out the window to catch a glimpse of dozens of round, water-filled bomb craters dotting the surrounding fields below, the pockmarked earth being a reminder of less peaceful times. Interestingly enough, some of these craters have been put to use as fish breeding ponds.

Because the public toilets in Hanoi, including airport facilities, are primitive (many appear to be closed permanently), it's best to try to plan ahead and use the lavatory on the plane. The drive into town takes well over an hour.

The small airport souvenir shop gladly accepts US dollars as does most of Vietnam. A good collectable worth buying here (it is seldom found in the city) is a ceramic vodka bottle imprinted with the "Air Vietnam" label that features a chubby Buddha. Vietnam began producing inexpensive vodka in the late 1970s to supply the large contingent of Soviet personnel in the country. The degree of Soviet influence can be gauged by signs at airports and hotels which are written in Vietnamese, Russian, English, and French—in that order.

Immigration and customs procedures are surprisingly swift and perfunctory.

The trip from the airport to the city crosses the flood plain of the Red River. Except for an occasional tree, a rock outcropping,

Red River flood plain, outside Hanoi

or small village, flat unrelieved plains of rice paddies stretch out to the horizon. Each year during the wet season (mid-May to mid-September), both Haiphong and Hanoi are routinely inundated by the floodwater of this river. West of the river at the Chinese border stands the highest mountain in the country, Phan Si Pan (elevation: 10,300 feet (3,000 m.)).

HANOI'S HISTORY

In 1010, Ly Thai To, founder of the Ly Dynasty, moved his capital to the confluence of the Red River and the To Lich River, the site of present-day Hanoi. Known as Thang Long until the 19th century, Hanoi was also called Dong Kinh, which the French corrupted to Tong Kinh or Tonkin.

Architectural Features. Thang Long was a swampy area of interconnecting lakes and ponds inhabited by large turtles—creatures that also have crept ubiquitously into the culture's folklore and legends. An elaborate dike system not only protected the city from foreign attack and flooding, it also demarcated Hanoi's urban boundary. Dike maintenance was the responsibility of all citizens, an obligation that included the toil of scholars at the Quoc Hoc School who were exempt from all other forms of labor. With time and population growth, Thang Long's city limits eventually expanded beyond the dike network. Vestiges of these dikes can be seen along the Red River near the Long Bien Bridge.

The active port of Dong Bo Dau on the Red River, east of the citadel fortification at Thang Long, must have seemed much like the maritime state of Venice. Merchants and buyers crowded into thriving markets, while ships from lands as far off as Java and Japan moored at the wharves, and perhaps a nobleman from a remote province could be seen here traveling to court with his royal entourage. In 1680, an Italian visitor to the Imperial Palace of Thang Long wrote: "The palace alone occupied an area with a perimeter of six or seven miles. The marble paved yards, the doors and the ruins of the apartments testified to its former magnificence and caused people to regret the destruction of one of the most beautiful buildings in Asia."

Bridges of Hanoi. The Thang Long Bridge crosses the Red River northwest of metropolitan Hanoi. This two-deck bridge, the most modern in Vietnam, was inaugurated on Ho Chi Minh's birthday, May 19, 1985. The lower deck carries rail tracks and a lane for motorscooters and bicycles.

The older bridge crossing the Red River is the Long Bien, formerly called the Paul Doumer Rail and Highway Bridge. Built between 1896 and 1902, the bridge was named for the Governor-General of French Indochina who conceived the 1,300-mile (2,093-km.) narrow gauge rail system—the Trans-Indochinese railroad—connecting Saigon and Hanoi. (Doumer was later elected president of France and assassinated while still in office.) In the 1960s all supplies coming into Hanoi by rail passed over this mile-long steel bridge that carried the crucial rail line running to the steel foundry in Thai Nguyen, 60 miles (96 km.) to the north. A rail line running northwest to Kunming, China, and another northeast to Beijing came together just north of Hanoi and entered the city by this bridge.

"They got a little place just south of the Ridge
Name of the place is the Doumer Bridge . . ."

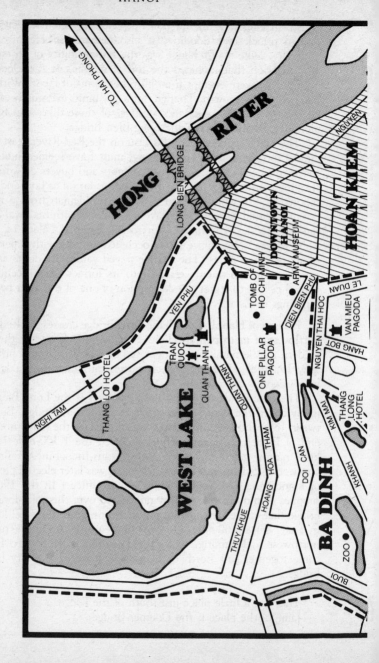

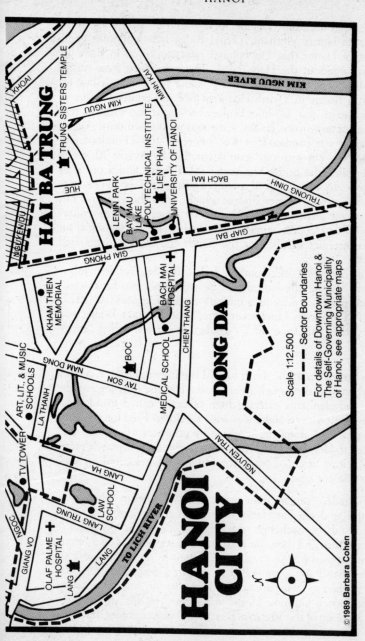

HANOI CITY

HAI BA TRUNG

DONG DA

KHOAI
TRUNG SISTERS TEMPLE
NGUYEN DU
HUE
KIM NGUU
MINH KAI
KIM NGUU RIVER
LENIN PARK
BAY MAU LAKE
POLYTECHNICAL INSTITUTE
LIEN PHAI
UNIVERSITY OF HANOI
BACH MAI
TRUONG DINH
GIAP BAI
GIAI PHONG
KHAM THIEN MEMORIAL
BACH MAI HOSPITAL
CHIEN THANG
BOC
MEDICAL SCHOOL
NAM DONG
TAY SON
ART, LIT., & MUSIC SCHOOLS
LA THANH
TV TOWER
NGOC
LANG HA
LANG TRUNG
LAW SCHOOL
GIANG VO
OLAF PALME HOSPITAL
LANG
TO LICH RIVER
NGUYEN TRAI

Scale 1:12,500

- - - Sector Boundaries

For details of Downtown Hanoi & The Self-Governing Municipality of Hanoi, see appropriate maps

© 1989 Barbara Cohen

These lines are from "Doumer Bridge Blues," a song about the air war over North Vietnam. (Thud Ridge is a mountain chain northwest of Hanoi that US bomber pilots followed in their approach to targets in the Hanoi area. The mountains were rugged and usually free of anti-aircraft fire.) While the Dragon's Jaw (or Ham Rong) Bridge in Thanh Hoa Province was bombed earlier in the American air war, Doumer Bridge, because it was within a ten-mile radius of downtown Hanoi, remained untouched until August 1967 when it was bombed by US Air Force F-105 Thunderchiefs. The Bridge was cut with one span down. But by August 30, recon photos revealed the bridge was under rapid repair and a rail ferry three mile south was already in service. During 1967–68, 177 sorties were flown against Doumer Bridge, which, with the Dragon's Jaw Bridge, became a symbol of the North Vietnamese peasants' endurance as well as US determination, backed by highly technical air power, to interdict supplies for the South and force a negotiated settlement.

In March of 1968, the bombing halt called by President Johnson, on the day he announced that he would not run for re-election, protected the bridge as a military target. On May 10, 1972, as part of "Operation Linebacker One," the Doumer Bridge was again attacked, this time by TV-guided munitions called "smart bombs."

Grass Street. From the south toward the Imperial Palace, a road was constructed wide enough to accommodate the ongoing parade of horses and elephants carrying high officials, called mandarins, and other dignitaries to audiences with the king. Feed for the animals was provided along the roadside by prisoners who busily cut and stacked fodder, providing the origin of the thoroughfare's present name, Grass Street. Today, the rail station is located on this well-worn ancient lane.

Early Trade. Foreign trade with the West began when the Dutch ship Ryp docked at Hanoi in 1626. A trading post was soon established and the exchange of goods and ideas officially began. Later, in the 16th and then the 17th century, restrictions on foreign trade were imposed by the royal court. Then, in the 18th century, foreign merchants were compelled to live in a designated zone to the south of the city's lake area called Pho Hien or "foreign concession." The French Customs House was located in this area at one time; the Museum of the Vietnam Revolution now occupies the site.

Rapid Expansion. The city expanded rapidly under the Le-Trinh period of rule (17th-18th centuries) and the lake area became the hub of the capital. The Trinh lords reviewed their navy on the lake, known at the time as Ho Thuy Quan, or Lake of the Navy. The lake was much larger then and was connected to the Red River and numerous small lakes through canals that were spanned by bridges. Later, the lake was renamed Hoan Kiem, or Restored Sword Lake, in honor of Vietnamese hero Le Loi's victory over the Chinese in the 15th century.

When Gia Long, the first Nguyen Emperor, came to power at the turn of the 19th century, he established his capital in Hue to the south; the power of Thang Long was reduced to that of a chief city of the northern province. In 1805, Gia Long ordered the ancient citadel of Thang Long to be torn down and replaced by a smaller fortification constructed in the Western style of the French military architect, Sebastien Le Prestre Vauban (1633-1707). A single watchtower is all that survives of Gia Long's citadel complex at Thang Long.

In 1902, when the various French protectorates and colonies of Southeast Asia merged, Hanoi (Thang Long) was chosen as the capital of the French Indochinese Union. Several factors made Hanoi a logical choice. The Red River region had the greatest population and Hanoi had been the base for the exploration of an overland and water route to China. Climate was another consideration. With warm summers and cool winters, Hanoi was more like Paris. Saigon, on the other hand, was typically hot and humid year-round.

HIGHLIGHTS
FOR TRAVELERS

THE FOUR SECTORS OF HANOI

The Municipality of Hanoi, a metropolitan area, includes various former provinces containing several fairly large towns. Commonly and traditionally thought of as "Hanoi," Hanoi City is today divided administratively into four sectors: Hoan Kiem, Ba Dinh, Hai Ba Trung, and Dong Da.

1. Hoan Kiem—The Restored Sword
2. Ba Dinh—The fortification which held out against the French in 1886-1887
3. Hai Ba Trung—The Two Ladies (the Trung Sisters)
4. Dong Da—Dong Da Hillock—place where King Quang Trung defeated the Chinese Manchu invaders in 1789

Hanoi municipality includes 11 outlying suburban districts: Thanh Tri, Tu Liem, Dong Anh, Gia Lam (where the Gia Lam Airport is situated), Ba Vi, Thach That, Phuc Tho, Hoai Duc, Dan Phuong, Me Linh, and Soc Son (where the Noi Bai International Airport is located).

HOAN KIEM SECTOR

This is the oldest and most densely populated of the four sectors of Hanoi City. Beneath war-weary and fading exteriors, the inherently beautiful French colonial buildings of Hoan Kiem stand proud and intact. Architecturally elegant, these gracious-looking structures appear as if they had been transplanted from an old Parisian neighborhood, which is not surprising, as entire blocks were built by French building contractors. Window shutters, traditionally painted green, complement cream-colored stucco facades streaked from nature's palette with tears of moss and rust. The romance of Hoan Kiem is further enhanced by wide, quiet thoroughfares that flow gracefully beneath tall tamarind trees. The streets are alive with streetside entrepreneurs. Barbers routinely set up their mirrors and seats against a convenient wall, while bicycle mechanics ply their trade on the sidewalks.

Many bicycles and few motor vehicles make for surprisingly quiet streets and few traffic signals; those lights that do operate are permanently set on either red or amber and are systematically ignored. The French-built electric tram system still weaves through this sector. Although superficially battered, the tram cars continue to provide essential daily transportation within the city for thousands of commuters.

Restored Sword Lake. The center of this section and the site from which it takes its name is the Restored Sword Lake (also known as Hoan Kiem Lake or Petite Lake). The lake area has long provided the crowded population with a quiet and peaceful spot, like Central Park in New York City, in the busiest part of town. Its waters reflect lovely willows and brilliant flame trees. At one time, at the edge of the lake, there was a "street of flowers" (now located

Restored Sword Lake with Turtle Pagoda in the center of the photograph

on Comb Street near the crowded Dong Xuan market) where women in flat, wide-brimmed hats sold flowers to French passers-by for a few coins—a scene the French impressionist, Claude Monét, might have painted. In contrast, the area is now inhabited by youths in jeans, T-shirts, and long hair standing around the lakeside cafes listening to raucous taped rock music.

Individual bomb shelters that had been built beneath the sidewalks during the 1960s are now gone. The lake continues to play its role as an integral part of the community by hosting events such as bike races, dove competitions (teams of trained doves performing inflight maneuvers), and festivals throughout the year.

Every Vietnamese child knows the legend of Le Loi, the hero who asked the heavens for help in resisting the advances of the Chinese in AD 1418. The tortoise of Hoan Kiem Lake responded to his pleas with a magic sword that flashed lightning from its blade. Sword in hand, Le Loi drove off the invaders. With the Chinese vanquished, the tortoise rose again from the lake; the sword leapt from Le Loi's scabbard and flew back into the watery depths. There is a striking similarity in themes between Le Loi's exploits and medieval British lore concerning King Arthur, the national hero of his time, who defeated his enemies by possessing the magical sword, Excalibur, given to him by the mysterious Lady of the Lake.

The lake's temple-shrine, now open to the public, is located on the northern shore. These words are chiseled on the shrine: "If you want to serve your country, take care of the common people."

Also found on the historic grounds is Huc Bridge, a curved wooden bridge built in 1855. Huc has been variously translated as "To Keep the Morning Bright," "Perch of the Morning Sun," "Rainbow," or "Sunshine." The entrance to the bridge is highlighted by two imposing structures called the Penbrush and Inkslab towers. These monuments were erected in 1864 on a knoll on the east side of the lake to honor the scholar Nguyen Van Sieu. A tower 30 feet (9 m.) high with a pointed peak represents the brush. Nearby, a hollowed rock in the shape of a peach is held aloft by three frogs, forming the formidable inkslab. Each year, in the early summer on the fifth day of the fifth month (the Tet Doan Ngo), the morning sun is in such a position that the shadow of the "brush" points deep into the center of the hollow of the inkslab.

The lake itself provides a liquid landscape for yet another shrine. Dedicated to education and scholars, a graceful three-story temple pagoda rises from the mists in the middle of the lake. From the pagoda landmark, one can set out to explore the ancient commercial section of Hoan Kiem to the north and the former French section to the south.

Commercial Section of Hoan Kiem. Hanoi's most ancient and wealthiest quarter is located between the lake, which forms its southern boundary, and the Long Bien Bridge to the north. The commercial section of Hoan Kiem extends westward to the old citadel wall marked by Ly Nam De Street. On the east it extends to the Red River.

Hanoi (called Thang Long in ancient days) was originally a collection of villages clustered around the walled palace that served as workshops for the royal court. At one time, there were 36 "quarters" or handicraft centers located in the town's outlying areas where the artisan guilds (Phuong) worked and resided in groups according to their crafts. For example, copper founders worked in Ha Bac village on the bank of the west gate, embroidery was done in Quat Dong village, and lacquerwork took place in Ha Vi village. Guilds arranged for the transportation and sale of their products on a designated street (e.g., Silk Street, Cotton Street, Paper Street, and so on) of the business section in town.

Guild Temples. Temples dedicated to the patron saint of a given craft are still active—Hang Bong Street has five such temples and pagodas. The Phuc Hau Temple at 2 Hang Bong Street was dedicated to the founder of the mirror-making craft; the Luong Ngoc temple at 68 Hang Bong honors a tutelary village spirit; the Kim Hoi at 95 is dedicated to Tran Hung Dao, a Vietnamese hero who routed the Chinese in the years 1285-1288; the Vong Tien at 120B commemorates the spot where in legend King Le Thanh Tong met a beautiful spirit woman; and the Thien Tien Pagoda at 120 Hang Bong was dedicated to Ly Thuong Kiet, the hero who defeated the Chinese Sung invaders in the 11th century.

There are two ancient pagodas on Hang Can Street; Hang Dao Street has five pagodas and small temples; and there are two temples with the Dong Mon Pagoda at 38B Hang Duong. The White Horse Pagoda is on Hang Buom.

Noteworthy Streets. Starting at the northern tip of the lake and walking north will lead you to Hang Gai, the street coming in from the left, once the area of canvas makers. The large street leading directly north from the lake is Hang Dao. Hang Ngang and Hang Dao streets link the lake to the Dong Xuan Market.

At the turn of the 20th century, 10 Hang Dao headquartered a movement called Dong Kinh Nghia Thuc—its membership of patriotic scholars attempted to reform the French colonial regime and modernize the thinking of Vietnamese mandarins who lingered on at the court of Hue. The Dong Kinh Nghia Thuc founded an educational institution in 1907 called the Free School of Tong Kinh. Scientific knowledge, especially chemistry and engineering, was extolled as a key to national independence. In addition to studying the sciences, students were encouraged to read French political writers such as Montesquieu and Rousseau. In a demonstration of asserting their independence, leaders of the Free School cut off their traditionally long hair worn in buns; women were also welcomed into their enlightened school.

The French considered the development of a progressive, self-directed, educated Vietnamese elite as dangerously subversive to colonial rule. If the "natives" looked upon education as a means to liberation, then there would be no education at all. The French closed the school and arrested its teachers.

At the start of the war against the French, the streets in this section were barricaded with sandbags, overturned cars, and furniture. The walls of Vietnamese homes facing the street were broken through and interconnected to provide easy access for the rebels from one building to another in order to escape the French. At 48 Hang Ngang Street, President Ho Chi Minh wrote the Vietnamese Declaration of Independence. He publicly read the document on September 2, 1946 (Vietnam's National Day), when he declared Vietnam's independence from France.

Architecture. Most private homes in the Hoan Kiem section date from the 19th century. While houses in the countryside had the available space to spread out laterally, congested city homes were long and narrow. The art of *bonsai* was prevalent in old Hanoi so that small inner courtyards could contain miniature mountains landscaped with tiny trees. Traditional construction practice dictated that attic storerooms must not look out onto the street and, out of respect, must not be higher than a passing mandarin's palanquin.

Ramparts or strong walls surrounded the city to hold back the river at flood time. Wooden gates (*Cua O*) that surmounted the ancient dikes were placed at intervals along the city walls. In the 16th century, 16 huge wooden gates led into Hanoi. The Dong Ho gate, popularly known as the Quan Chuong gate, can still be seen at the river end of Hang Chieu Street.

The Covered Market. Built by the French, the Cho Dong Xuan market is an adventure for the wanderer who stops to examine the wide array of food and goods for sale. Note the women carrying goods in baskets hanging from poles balanced on their shoulders—the carrying pole requires a stately and graceful posture to maintain its equilibrium.

Old French Section of Hoan Kiem. The following is a suggested walking tour of the old French Section. Numbers in parentheses refer to the location of a building on the detailed downtown Hanoi map. Note: the French administrative buildings were once located south of the lake.

A few steps south of the Pagoda of the Restored Sword you will find the former French mayor's residence and town hall, which is now Party headquarters on the corner of Le Lai (1). The French-style building adjacent to the town hall is now called Uncle Ho's House (2). It was here, on March 6, 1945, that Ho Chi Minh signed an agreement with the French representative, Jean Sainteny, recognizing the Democratic Republic of Vietnam as "a free state in the Indochinese Federation and the French Union." Later a report came to light from the French High Commissioner in Hanoi to the French Prime Minister which said: "It is my impression that we must make a concession to Vietnam of the term Independence; but I am convinced that this word need never be interpreted in any light other than as a religious verbalism." Uncle Ho's House, once the French Treasurer General's villa, contains displays depicting the life of Ho Chi Minh. Plays and dances are staged in front of this building during holidays.

One block east on Ly Thai To you will find the six-story Children's Palace or Young Pioneers' Cultural House, which was established in this building in 1957 (3). (Such cultural houses throughout the country provide after-school enrichment programs for the children of workers and government officials. Programs foster art, music, dance, sports, and various hobbies. There are over 60 Children's Palaces in the country.)

The former Bank of Indochina was once located at 7 Le Lai Street, now home to the Savings Fund for Socialism (5). The State Bank (Vietbank) has a foreign-exchange department and is located at 49 Ly Thai To. This address also houses the Vietcombank, the official bank for foreign trade.

Across nearby Le Lai Street is the recently renamed Indira Gandhi Park (4). The main post office is located south of the park and the government guest house is located at 2 Le Thach. One block

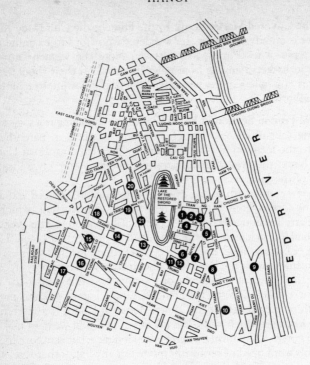

Note: Information in parentheses refers to former name.

1. Hanoi City Party Hdqtrs (Town Hall)
2. Uncle Ho's House Museum (Treasury)
3. Children's Palace
4. Indira Gandhi Park
5. Savings Fund for Socialism (Bank of Indochina)
6. Museum
7. Thong Nhat Hotel (Metropole Hotel)
8. Theatre (Opera House)
9. Historical and Archaeologic Museum
10. College of Pharmacy
11. Department Store
12. Club (Paix Club)
13. Vietnam Airways Office (Int'l Bookings)
14. Central Library and Archives
15. Prison ("Hanoi Hilton")
16. Quan Su Pagoda
17. Fine Arts School
18. VN-German Hospital (Yersin Native Hosp.)
19. Cathedral
20. Wood-block artists' studios and shops
21. Duc San restaurant

further south, at 15 Ngo Quyen Street (7), is the Thong Nhat Hotel (the former Metropole).

Between the lake and the Thong Nhat Hotel is the Bac Bo Palace, a huge building that once housed the offices of the French Governor-Resident of Tonkin. During World War II, the palace was the headquarters of the puppet government set up by the Japanese. The former palace now contains government offices. A museum and theatre (6) are located one block southwest on Trang Thi.

At 19 Hai Ba Trung Street is a large, light-green villa that once housed the US Consulate during the French-colonial period. During the Vietnam War, the villa was used by the National Liberation Front delegation (the "Viet Cong"). Robert Shaplen (1917–1988), the prominent US journalist who wrote extensively about Indochina, was informed by Vietnamese government officials in 1988 that the villa is ready for reoccupancy by US diplomats as soon as the US and the Socialist Republic of Vietnam establish official relations.

At the southern tip of the lake, one comes to a once-elegant street that was called Rue Paul Bert, named after a Governor-Resident of Annam and Tonkin. It is now three streets: Trang Thi, Trang Tien, and Hang Khay. At the intersection of Ngo Quyen and Trang Tien was the Paix Café (12), popular with the French for playing the card game, *"quatre vingt et un."* Another club now occupies the location. The department store at Trang Tien and Hang Bai Dinh (11) has few items that would appeal to foreigners, but a brief inspection will provide an indicator of the city's current economic situation. Hanoi's main bookstore is next door at 32 Hai Ba Trung. Occasionally, one may find books in English that appeal mainly to readers with a special interest in contemporary Vietnamese policies.

Opera House. One block east on Trang Tien is the Opera House, built in 1911 as a replica of the splendid Paris Opera (8). In 1945, at the close of World War II, a committee of Viet Minh commandeered public buildings, including the Opera House. From the balcony of this ornate building, the Viet Minh announced the success of their "August Revolution" in seizing power from the French and Japanese. Antique stores and art galleries surround the theater. Art galleries display traditional paintings on silk and contemporary oil paintings. Although one can browse here for antiques to get a general idea of what is available and at what cost, tourists should buy antiques only from approved government shops that issue official customs receipts.

Museums. The Historical and Archaeological Museum, formerly the Musée Louis Pinot, is one block east of the Opera House (9).
The focus here is the collection of ancient bronze objects. Of specific interest are large bronze drums that are vestiges of Vietnam's
Bronze Age, which flourished in the area around 3,000 BC. The
Vietnamese stress that their early Bronze Age culture preserved its
originality throughout the Chinese occupation. Ceramics displayed
in the museum from the Ly and Tran Dynasties reflect a distinctive
cultural identity. Early Ly wares were characterized by incised and
painted decorations with a brown design on a white body.

In addition to bronzes and ceramics, the museum has some rare
thousand-year-old Cham gold ornaments from the My Son site of
the Cham capital near Danang.

The Museum of the Revolution, across from the Museum of History and Archaeology, occupies the old French Customs House. The
museum was founded in 1959 and portrays Vietnamese struggles
against the French, Japan, and the US, as well as Vietnam's age-
old continuing struggles with China. The historical treasury contains relics of earlier guerrilla wars, including huge sharpened spikes
implanted in the riverbed to impede the invasion of Chinese war
junks. Hanging above one of the displays is a poem attributed to
General Ly Thuong Kiet, ca.1077. Le Duc Tho, the North Vietnamese negotiator at the Paris Peace Talks, quoted this poem to
Henry Kissinger, who represented the US:

Over the mountains and rivers reigns the Emperor of Vietnam,
As it is written in the Book of Heaven.
How is it that you barbarians dare invade our land?
Your armies, without pity, will be annihilated.

Also on display in bronze are the opening words of Ho Chi Minh's
Independence Day speech, given on September 2, 1945: "All men
are created equal. They are endowed by their Creator with certain
unalienable Rights, and among these are Life, Liberty and the Pur-
suit of Happiness."

South of the History Museum, at 33 Pham Ngu Lao Street, is
an old French villa where in March 1974 Hanoi's military leaders
reached the decision to make an all-out military effort in the South.
The subsequent effort culminated in the fall of Saigon in April
1975.

Other Sites of Interest. At 13 Le Thanh Ton Street is the Hanoi College of Pharmacy (10). Once the site of the Hanoi College

of Medicine and Pharmacy, the Medicine branch moved to larger quarters in the Dong Da section. Alexandre Yersin was instrumental in founding this college in 1902 (for more about Yersin see the section on Dalat).

Returning toward the lake via Ly Thuong Kiet Street, you will pass the Australian Embassy at 66 and the British Embassy at 16. A lycée for young girls once stood at the intersection of Ly Thuong Kiet and Hang Bai streets. Turn north on Ba Trieu Street to reach the lake. Walk west past the Vietnam Airways Office on Hang Khay (13) until the street becomes Trang Thi, where you will find the Central Library and Archives (14).

"Hanoi Hilton." One block south and two blocks west is the infamous "Hanoi Hilton" (15). Located on Hoa Lo Street (the Vietnamese name is Hoa Lo Prison), off Hai Ba Trung Street, this grim, high-walled structure is where US prisoners of war were incarcerated during the war. The prison's central location in Hanoi, in an otherwise pleasant-looking commercial district, comes as something of a shock. Built by the French in the early 20th century, the structure

Hoa Lo Prison, "Hanoi Hilton"

is a triangular complex with barred windows and barbed wire atop
15- to 20-foot (4.5- to 6-m.) walls. Glass shards are cemented into
the walls with electric wires running along the length of the fortification's perimeter.

Hoa Lo still functions as an active prison today and inmates
dressed in dark blue prison garb can be seen peering out of the barred
windows. Taking photographs of this building is not allowed.

American prisoners gave the configurations inside the prison
compound names such as "Heartbreak Hotel" for the 35-foot-long
building containing eight individual cells, each 6 × 6 feet (under
2 × 2 m). Other areas were descriptively labeled the "New Guy
Village," the "Knobby Room," and "Little Vegas." North Vietnam
contended that Americans detained there were not protected by the
Geneva International Convention on Treatment of Prisoners of
War because the US had not made an official declaration of war.
High-ranking or highly "resistant" prisoners were taken from Hoa
Lo prison to a tight security zone to the northeast (behind the Min-
istry of Defense) known as "Alcatraz"—across the street was the
"Plantation" or "Citadel." Another prison (the building had once
been a movie studio) in the Tu Liem outskirts of Hanoi was nick-
named the "Zoo" or "Zoo Annex" by American captives held there.

Quan Su Pagoda. Located a block south of the prison at 73
Quan Su Street, the Quan Su Pagoda was built originally as a guest
house for ambassadors to the court of the Le kings (16). The pagoda
has two sections: the forecourt serves as a Buddhist place of worship;
the rear section is devoted to a monk who was awarded the title of
Quoc Su because he had cured King Ly Than Tong of a serious illness. In the final days of the Le Dynasty, all major pagodas of Thang
Long, with the exception of Quan Su, were destroyed during the
conflict for power. In 1934, the Northern Vietnam Buddhist Association was headquartered in the Quan Su Pagoda. Work to build an
entirely new pagoda was completed in 1942. The wall of the right
corridor features a depiction of the enlightenment of Sakyamuni,
one of the incarnations of Buddha.

Workers' Cultural Palace. Continuing on Tran Hung Dao (formerly Rue Gambetta), the modern four-story (120-room) Workers'
Cultural Palace comes into view. Constructed with Soviet aid, it
stretches from Yet Kieu Street to Tran Binh Trong Road. The white
stone columns lend the massive building an open, airy look; the
imposing structure is surrounded by trees and benches, ornamental
plants, and grassy areas. The building contains clubs where after-

work leisure activities take place, classrooms, and libraries, as well as a 1,200-seat movie theater. Since it is also the highest building in Hanoi, the view from the roof is panoramic. The Maurice Long Museum formerly occupied the site.

The French Embassy is at 57 Tran Hang Dao Street. During the French era, the busy Hotel Terminus et de la Gare stood next to the railroad station on Tran Hung Dao Street. The Fine Arts School is also near the rail station on the south end of Yet Kieu Street (17).

Returning to the west side of the lake, there's the tree-lined Trang Thi street. At 40 Trang Thi there are the pale yellow pavilions of the Viet-Duc (Vietnamese-East German) Surgical Hospital (18)—formerly called the Native or Yersen Hospital—built and equipped by the East German government. Across Trang Thi Street is the Maternity (Mother and Infant) Hospital, formerly the Radium Hospital.

The Catholic cathedral is one block west on Nha Tho and Nha Chung streets (19). The Duc San Restaurant is across the street from the Cathedral (21). Walking north from the cathedral leads to Hang Trong Street (Drum Street), where wood-block artists have come to sell their works (20). In Dong Ho, the town in central Vietnam noted for woodblocks, artisans chisel patterns on wooden plates. The designs are then printed on a white-alloy coated paper that is finally colored with dark green or yellow. The craftspeople on Hang Trong Street paint or print their pictures in black and then apply the colors.

The editorial offices of the Nhan Dan party newspaper are at 71 Hang Trong, formerly the residence of a French commandant.

Street Names. Some of the old commercial streets of Hoan Kiem retain their former names, still selling the product that describe the avenue.

STREET LOCATION	GUILD PRODUCT
Hang Bac	silver
Hang Be	rafts
Hang Bo	baskets
Hang Bong	flower or cotton
Hang Buom	sails
Hang Ca	fish
Hang Can	scales
Hang Chieu	mats
Hang Cot	mats
Hang Da	leather

Hang Dau	oil
Hang Dao	dyer's special red dye peach
Hang Dau	beans
Hang Dieu	pipes and smoking paraphernalia
Hang Dong	brass
Hang Duong	sugar
Hang Ga	chicken
Hang Gai	hemp (canvas)
Hang Giay	paper
Hang Hom	coffins
Hang Khoai	sweet potatoes
Hang Luoc	combs
Hang Ma	paper items to burn for the dead (this street now sells all types of paper products: paper lanterns, flowers, and papier mâché puppets)
Hang Mam	fermented fish
Hang Manh	bamboo shades and blinds
Hang Muoi	salt
Hang Ngang	cross street
Hang Non	hats
Hang Phen	alum, used medicinally and as a purifier for water
Hang Quat	fans
Hang Ruoi	worms
Hang Than	charcoal (now noted for banh com, a dense sticky rice patty filled with green beans, lotus seeds, and coconut strips)
Hang Thiec	tin products
Hang Thung	casks or barrels
Hang Tre	bamboo
Hang Trong	drums
Hang Vai	fabric
Hang Voi	lime calcium oxide used in the betel-chewing process, not the citrus

BA DINH SECTOR

The Ba Dinh sector embraces the large West Lake or Ho Tay, as well as the citadel that once enclosed the Imperial Palace. As a form of relief from the hot, humid weather, a favorite pastime among Europeans was the 15-mile drive around the lake's perimeter, called the *promenade circulaire*. The drive, especially popular at sunset, took in the colorful and fragrant villages of flower growers: Huu Tiep, Yen Phu, Quang Ba, and Thuy Khue. *Nhat Tan* village is noted for its peach trees; its flowers are used to adorn almost every house during the holidays.

Pagodas. Tran Quoc, the oldest pagoda in Hanoi, is within walking distance of the Thang Loi Hotel. Turn right on the street in front of the hotel, which happens to run on one of the old city dikes. Making another right turn by the bus depot puts you on the causeway crossing West Lake toward the focus of Ba Dinh sector: the Ho Chi Minh mausoleum. If you continue on past the bus depot instead of turning right, you will eventually arrive at the Restored Sword Lake in the Hoan Kiem section of Hanoi.

The lotus plant is especially thick around Ca Vang (goldfish) Islet that supports the Tran Quoc, a 1,400-year-old pagoda, the oldest still standing in Hanoi. Originally built on the banks of the Red River in the time of King Ly Nam De in the 6th century, Tran Quoc was a monastery for high-ranking monks of the courts. When the bank of the river eroded in the 17th century, the pagoda was moved to the islet. In the summer, lotus flowers on the lake blossom in a great mass of color that appears to lift the pagoda into the air.

Continue south past the pagoda to a stone monument depicting a plane's torn-off wing and a parachuting pilot. The memorial honors the North Vietnamese anti-aircraft units stationed around West Lake. (Some guns can still be seen on the banks.) On October 26, 1967, Navy Lt. Commander John Sidney McCain III parachuted from his incapacitated A-4 Skyhawk into West Lake. He survived serious injuries and five-and-a-half years of torturous prison life. In 1982, he was elected to congress from Arizona and has since returned to Hanoi on missions concerning MIAs and POWs. (See description of "Hanoi Hilton" in Hoan Kiem sector.) As a senator, McCain has continued to work toward establishing a "US interest section," an in-country office in Hanoi staffed by US officials who would facilitate communication and cooperation on issues of mutual concern.

The Pagoda of the Grand Buddha (Chan Vu) at the intersection of Thanh Nien and Quan Thanh (once called Avenue of the Grand Buddha) is situated on the south end of West Lake at the location of one of the old city gates called the Youth Promenade. The remnants of the gate are covered with light purple blooms in late spring. Thanh Nien becomes Hung Vuong Street and will take you to Ba Dinh Square.

Ho Chi Minh's Mausoleum. The dark-gray marble building housing the embalmed body of Ho Chi Minh stands out starkly in the spacious square. The tomb is built with marble from Marble Mountain near Danang and stone from other provinces.

As you face the entrance to the mausoleum, the National Assembly and Party Headquarters buildings will be at your back. Foreign visitors are given priority and are escorted into the imposing building by stiffly formal uniformed guards. Over the entrance is Ho's famous and moving quotation, "Nothing is more precious than independence and freedom." Cameras or large bags are not allowed in the mausoleum. Visitors are asked to remain silent and keep their hands loosely at their sides while viewing the body. Inside the air-controlled tomb, attended constantly by four guards, is Ho's frail body on a glass-enclosed platform lit by a pink light—giving his face a peaceful, quiet glow. Ho's attire consists of a coarse gray shirt, and his hands are folded over his chest. Tears stream from the eyes of

Ho Chi Minh's mausoleum

many of the 15,000 school children and workers from other provinces who pass through each week.

Ho Chi Minh, the patriot, elicited strong feelings in the people of the North. Whether his actions were planned as brilliant public relations maneuvers or motivated by sincere empathy for the plight of his suffering countrymen, Ho Chi Minh was more than a leader; he was loved as a favorite and respected "Uncle Ho."

Governor General's Residence. This mansion once housed the French administrators of Tonkin. The gardens surrounding the mansion contain botanical specimens from all over the world. The building is still used for formal receptions and other government affairs. Ho refused to live in this building when he came to power in Hanoi but chose instead to live on the site of the gardeners' and servants' quarters.

Ho Chi Minh's House. A terrace of steps on the grounds behind the former governor general's residence leads to a small pond stocked with koi carp. Ho would clap his hands and the fish would come to him. The simple two-story wooden house in which Ho Chi Minh lived during the war is situated among banyan, frangipani, poinciana, and milkweed trees. The lower level of the house served

Ho Chi Minh's house

as a conference room; on the wooden conference table are books written by Woodrow Wilson, the *One World* of Wendell Willkie, and a book by the American anti-war activist and pediatrician Dr. Benjamin Spock. There are two simple rooms upstairs: a bedroom and a study area. Note the bomb shelter on your right as you leave the house.

One Pillar Pagoda. The Chua Mot Cot, a miniature pagoda once called the Temple of Love, was built in 1040 on a pillar constructed of a single large tree trunk. Today, the pillar has been re-

One Pillar Pagoda

constructed in more durable cement. The temple was built to honor Buddhist advisors who had been loyal to King Ly Thai To and had travelled with the monarch to the new capital from Hoa Lu. On the first and the fifteenth of the lunar month, the Ly kings went to honor Buddha at the pagoda, which some say resembles Buddha sitting on a lotus blossom growing out of the mud. A glass disk held between two dragons rests at the top of the pagoda's peaked roof; the disk is a symbol of the Emperor as the sun shining brightest at high noon.

In 1954, as the victorious Viet Minh entered Hanoi, the retreating French burned the temple. By April 1955, the One Pillar Pagoda had been restored, and a Bo tree was planted nearby in 1958 as a gift from India. As the ancient story goes, it was under a Bo or Bodhi tree that Buddha gained enlightenment—he sat and watched the current of life pass before him: birth and death, grief and joy, pain and tranquility.

National Assembly. Opposite the square from the mausoleum entrance is the four-story National Assembly Hall and Party Headquarters where government congresses meet. A legend over the entrance announces: Peace, Independence and Freedom of the country.

The Foreign Ministry is one of the most graceful old colonial buildings on Ba Dinh Square.

Taking Dien Bien Phu Street toward the old tower leads to the Army (War) Museum. Foreign embassies are located south of the mausoleum on the short street intersecting Khuc Hoa Street. The Soviet Embassy is the large walled compound, one block south at 58 Tran Phu Street.

Army (WAR) Museum. Defense is a major theme in Vietnamese history; today, Vietnam maintains the world's fourth-largest army. Military service is compulsory and a typical tour of duty lasts three years. In 1985, there were over one million soldiers in the Armed Forces. Another three million people are in paramilitary units such as border defense, regional forces, and Armed Assault Forces.

The displays begin with depictions of ancient wars with China and the Trung Sisters' rebellion in the first century. Next, the French colonizers and the battles that defeated them in 1954 are described (one depiction puts on a light display illustrating the tactics of the battles of Dien Bien Phu) as are the struggles with South Vietnamese president Diem and his American supporters.

Watchtower of Old Citadel on grounds of Army Museum

That is not the end of Vietnam's war experiences. The history of enemy attacks and the means the Vietnamese took to repel them goes on to include the Pol Pot border incursions and the 1979 invasion of the Northern border by China to "teach the Vietnamese a lesson" for its military actions in Cambodia against China's ally, Pol Pot.

The museum's historical perspective presents Vietnam's combat with the Americans as an interlude, a mere dot on the time chart of their history of war. Among the displays is a model of the modified bicycles called "steel horses," used on the Ho Chi Minh trail to transport tons of war supplies into the south.

Outside, in the courtyard, across from the huge pile of metallic debris that was once an American B-52, are the remains of the Nguyen Dynasty Citadel. The watch tower, a 65-yard-high (60-m.), narrow hexagon, tapers as it rises. When it was functional, each story of the Citadel had apertures for light and ventilation with guard posts at the gates in outlying areas to protect the structure. The roof was used as a platform from which soldiers, using lights, signaled distant receiving stations.

In a building outside, next to the museum entrance, eight- to ten-inch chunks of twisted metal from downed American planes are for sale as souvenirs. Debris from US planes is not as popular with American visitors as are the inexpensive, colorful enameled campaign medals—one from Dien Bien Phu and another from the border battles with the Chinese.

Opposite the Army Museum, across Dien Bien Phu Street, stands a statue of Lenin in Chi Long Park.

The Fine Arts Museum. Located at 38 Cao Ba Quat, the Fine Arts Museum is housed in a huge French-style building and contains artifacts from the cultural history of the country. The top-floor exhibition features classic works of art. Also on display are the tools and costumes of more than 60 ethnic minority groups in Vietnam. Periodic special displays, such as musical instruments or ethnic costumes, are shown for limited engagements.

The lower floor exhibits more recent works of socialist realism, "combat art" and modern sculpture. The wooden statues of *arhats* (lifelike statues of enlightened monks made of lacquered wood) from the Tay Phuong Pagoda are worth the trip to the museum. These figures often portray poignant scenes depicting life's suffering.

The Thu Le Park in the western section of Ba Dinh contains a small zoo.

HAI BA TRUNG SECTOR

The foreign concession in this sector by the river was once an enclosed area to which foreigners were restricted during the 17th century (the emperors were suspicious of foreign religions and influences on the people).

Workers Palace. The huge Workers Palace faces Lenin Park, where the state circus sometimes performs. Each morning, between

5 and 6 A.M., senior citizens gather in Lenin Park to do graceful Tai Chi-like exercises. The Pasteur Institute was in this section at one time, bounded by the street still named Yer Xanh after Dr. Yersin, founder of the institute. Yer Xanh remains one of the few French-named streets unchanged by the government. The new Viet-Soviet Hospital is just to the north.

Hanoi Polytechnic Institute. The school is located on the southern tip of Seven Mau Lake (one mau = 3,600 square meters or nine-tenths of an acre; seven mau is not the true size of the present lake). Situated along four blocks of buildings that once accommodated the former Indochinese University campus, the institute was used by the French as a barracks during the Indochina War. The school had barely completed Soviet-aided reconversion to an educational institution in 1965 when US bombing started; classes and laboratories were evacuated to safer quarters in the countryside. The school now has five departments: engineering, electricity, radio, chemistry, and metallurgy.

Trung Sisters Pagoda. The first Vietnamese state was subjected to Chinese feudal domination for a thousand years (111 BC–939 AD). The first of the many uprisings of the people was led by the Trung Sisters (first century), who succeeded in "taking 65 citadels" but were defeated in the end. Grateful posterity erected a temple south of Hanoi in 1142 to honor the national heroines. It is located on 337 Street.

DONG DA SECTOR

Dong Da, the largest sector in Hanoi, is known primarily for its schools and hospitals.

Van Mieu. The most important historic site in the Dong Da section is the Van Mieu or Temple of Literature, the oldest school in the country. The term Van Mieu, translated perhaps more correctly as Temple of Civility, is applied to temples in each province that were dedicated to teaching the proper Confucian ways of thinking and behaving. The Vietnamese tradition of respect for learning is concretely represented in the Van Mieu complex of buildings erected at the southern gate of the old city of Thang Long—now located between Hang Bot and Nguyen Thai Hoc Streets. The temple was established in 1072 on this site to honor Confucius and 72 wise men who served as exemplary models in correct thinking. Scholarly Chinese texts were also studied in the temple.

In 1076, Vietnam's first university, Quoc Tu Giam, was founded

Temple of Literature, Van Mieu

and located in the Van Mieu complex of buildings. The sons and daughters of the emperor and of high-ranking officials attended the school. In pre-Confucian times, private tutoring was customary and Buddhist clergy were responsible for the education of youth. By the 11th century, Confucianism successfully competed with Buddhism. The university broke the Buddhists' monopoly on education, allowing Confucianism to expand and reinstate the "eight-legged" examination system from an earlier time.

A new type of examination was held in the 1230s under the Tran Reign, and in 1253 the school was enlarged and renamed Quoc Hoc Vien, or National Institute. The school became accessible (in theory) to children of commoners who had achieved high scores on regional examinations. Once underprivileged, these graduates of the common people began to hold public offices. From its inception, Confucian scholarship was intertwined with professional rank. Consequently, the Van Mieu is a place both of worship and of training for state office.

Under Le Loi, the university expanded to include a new library and lecture halls. Examinations were refined to include poetry competitions. Le Loi is also noted for a comprehensive legal code aimed at bringing some structure to the chaos in Vietnam after the Chinese were finally routed. Efforts were made to restore written works of history and literature destroyed or stolen in the war against the Mings.

Successful candidates in the triennial examinations were recognized by having their names, places of birth, and achievements recorded permanently on stone slabs, called steles. This practice continued until 1778 and, during that time, 116 examinations were held. Eighty-two steles remain, each carrying 20 names of outstanding laureates. The oldest of these slab dates from 1443.

Students at the Van Mieu used an ideographic writing called *Chu Nho* or scholar's language. Long after the Chinese were driven from the country, Chinese characters were employed exclusively for governmental and educational purposes. For less formal writing, the Vietnamese used an ideographic writing system based on Chinese characters called *Chu Nom*.

Emperor Gia Long re-established the school in his new capital at Hue, but this system of recruiting civil servants finally ended in 1915 in the North, and in 1919 in central Vietnam. The French encouraged the simpler *quoc ngu* form of writing, which was more suited to Western printing capacities.

Because the Van Mieu was set in a grove of old mango trees which sheltered flocks of crows, the French later called it *Pagoda des Corbeau*, or the Pagoda of Crows.

The main building of the Van Mieu and its ancillary buildings cover an area 380 yards (350 m.) long and 76 yards (70 m.) wide that is surrounded by a brick wall a quarter of a mile long. The entrance gateway has a second story called the Poet's Balcony where poetry recitals are still held on special occasions. Beyond the entrance in the first and second courtyards, now bare of buildings, stood wooden hostels for students and teachers. The third section contains the steles around a pond. The fourth area is the temple dedicated to the memory of Confucius and his learned disciples. This section has dragons on pedestals and bonsai plants in colorful pots. A fifth section, a library, beyond the temple, was destroyed by bombs in 1954.

Next to the Van Mieu is an amusement park where families enjoy the rides on weekends and holidays.

Other Sites of Interest. The Huy Van Pagoda, dating from the 15th century, is located in the section of town known as Van Chuong village. The pagoda is on Huy Van, a small street off Hang Bot Street, and is associated with the tribulations of the royal concubine Ngo Thi Ngoc Dao and her son, King Le Thanh Tong.

Further south on Hang Bot Street is Kham Thien—an area heavily damaged by US Air Force B-52s aiming for the railway station during December 1972. Called Nixon's "Christmas bombing" or Linebacker Two, this was the first and only B-52 bombing over Hanoi. One month later, the final settlement of the Vietnam War was reached in Paris between Henry Kissenger, representing the US, and Le Duc Tho, representing the North Vietnamese.

There is a monument on Kham Thien Street commemorating the civilians who were killed by the bombs. The homes in the area have since been rebuilt and no evidence of the bombing can be seen today.

HOTEL
ACCOMMODATIONS

HOAN KIEM SECTOR

The **Thong Nhat** (Metropole) is located at 15 Ngo Quyen, tel. 52785-52767. Its high ceilings and wide windows that look out on balconies give it a truly colonial appearance. Plumbing fixtures from the 1920s still bear the emblem of the French manufacturing company: Jacob Delafon. Its high bar lined with sheets of shiny zinc was frequented by senior French officers, their wives, and their girlfriends. A recent visitor described the hotel as "an evocative dump." Since that visitor's stay, France's Pullman International Hotels has taken on the task of renovating the 110-room hotel. The writer Somerset Maugham stayed at the Metropole on his visit to Indochina in 1922-23. Maugham's trip resulted in his book "The Gentleman in the Parlour."

BA DINH SECTOR

The 12-story **Thang Long** Hotel has little to offer other than a conference room that accommodates large meetings and has facilities for simultaneous (language) translations. There is a bar, restaurant, and gift shop in the hotel, and a state-run intershop a block away. Catering exclusively to Westerners, intershops, sometimes called Dollar Shops because they accept only $US dollars, sell such items as toiletries, liquors, foreign-brand cigarettes, and other products not readily available to Vietnamese citizens. Several blocks to the south is an exhibition hall where products of all the provinces of Vietnam are on display. The Swedish Embassy compound is within walking distance across Giang Vo Street.

The **Thang Loi** or Victory Hotel (tel. 58211) is on West Lake. Built by Cuban contractors, it is the most modern hotel in town, with conveniences such as heaters, refrigerators, and television sets that receive two channels of programming—news, classical works, and special features—one in the Russian language, the other in Vietnamese. There is dancing in the International Bar twice a month. In the bar across from the restaurant, guests can strike up conversations with visitors from socialist countries as well as travelers from Western Europe. While in the bar, try a Saigon (yes, Saigon) cocktail made with egg, Kahlua, condensed milk, orange liquor, vodka, and cognac.

FRENCH-STYLE VILLAS

The following are small hotels in French-style villas:

Hoan Kiem
25 Tran Hung Dao
tel. 54204
Eight rooms in the center of town.

Hoa Binh
27 Ly Thuong Kiet
tel. 53315

Dan Chu
29 Trang Tien
tel. 53323
Located opposite the Opera House, the Dan Chu Hotel was formerly the French Paix Hotel.

RESTAURANTS

Although many private restaurants catering to Western tastes have closed, others have opened. Ask your guide or hotel clerk for the latest information. The **Quan An Duc San** restaurant on Nha Chung Street, near the old cathedral, is a privately run restaurant popular with Westerners which has recently reopened. There are perhaps three or four tables and the Crab Farsi is delicious.

Two restaurants located very close to each other in the area of the Dong Xuan Market are the **Cha Ca Restaurant** and **Hang Can**

Restaurant. There are no signs outside either of these, and they can be easily missed. The Cha Ca Restaurant is located on 14 Cha Ca Street. Cha Ca means fried fish, and it is the speciality of the house. The Hang Can on the second floor of 22 Hang Can Street has re-opened and is known for its crispy fried fish. You will pass the kitchen on your way up the stairs to the small dining room and intimate terrace.

Two other restaurants are the **Rail Station Restaurant** and **Restaurant 202.** The Rail Station Restaurant is opposite the rail station on Tran Hung Dao Street, on the site of the former French Hotel Terminus et de la Gare. Restaurant 202, located at 202 Hue Avenue in the Hai Ba Trung Sector, has Vietnamese specialities as well as French-style dishes.

NIGHTLIFE AND ENTERTAINMENT

If you would like to meet Westerners living in Hanoi, visit the bar at the Australian Embassy, where you might hear the latest gossip about the international scene. Although a small membership fee is required, it may be worth joining if you are staying more than a few days.

The Swedish Embassy compound has disco dancing on some evenings. The entire compound, including the disco, apartments, swimming pool, and tennis courts, was shipped prefabricated from Sweden.

HANOI DIRECTORY

FOREIGN EMBASSIES	Telephone
Australia, 66 Ly Thuong Kiet, Hoan Kiem Sector	52763
Belgium, 51 Nguyen Du, Hoan Kiem Sector	52176
Federal Republic of Germany (West Germany), 25 Phan Boi Chau BP 39, Hoan Kiem Sector	53663/55402
France, 57 Tran Hung Dao, Hoan Kiem Sector	54368/52719/54367
Holland, 181 Ba Trieu, Hoan Kiem Sector	
Italy, 9 Le Phung Hieu, Hoan Kiem Sector	56246/56256
Philippines, 4 Ho Xuan Huong, Hai Ba Trung Sector	
Soviet Union, 58 Tran Phu, Ba Dinh Sector	
Sweden, #2 358 Street, Ba Dinh Sector	
United Kingdom, 16 Ly Thuong Kiet, Hoan Kiem Sector	52349

GOVERNMENT OFFICES	Telephone
The Department of Foreign Nationals, Dien Bien Phu	58131
The Department of Propoganda and Education of the Communist Party of Vietnam	58261
The Foreign Relations Commission of the Party Central Committee	53764
The Office of the Party Central Committee, Hoang Van Thu	58261

AIRLINE BOOKINGS	Telephone
The Domestic Airline Booking Office, 16 Le Thai To	55283
The International Airline Booking Office, 25 Trang Thi	53842

POST OFFICES	Telephone
The Central Post Office, 75 Dinh Tien Hoang	57036
The International Post Office, 75 Dinh Tien Hoang	54413

SHOPS	Telephone
The Department Store, 5 Nam Bo	55814
The General Department Store, Trang Tien	53042
The Fine Arts Shop, 25 Hang Khay	55845
The Giang Vo Intershop (US dollars only), Giang Vo	56644
The Souvenir Shop, 30a Ly Thuong Kiet	55516
The Souvenir Shop, Ngo Quyen	52785
Xunhasaba (subscriptions to English language periodicals published in Vietnam, plus stamps and paintings), 32 Hai Ba Trung	54067

BOOKSHOPS	Telephone
The Foreign Languages Bookshop (English, Russian, French and Spanish language books), 61 Trang Tien	57043
The State Bookshop, 40 Trang Tien	54282
The Thong Nhat Bookshop, 17 Ngo Quyen	57351

LIBRARIES	Telephone
The Army Library, Ly Nam De	58101
The National Library, 31 Trang Thi	52643
The Technical and Social Sciences Library, 26 Ly Thuong Kiet	52345

MUSEUMS	Telephone
The Army Museum, Dien Bien Phu	58101
The Fine Arts Museum, 66 Nguyen Thai Hoc	52830
The Ho Chi Minh Museum	58241
The Memorial House of President Ho Chi Minh, 48 Hang Ngang	52622
The Museum of History, 1 Pham Ngu Lao	53518
The Museum of the Vietnamese Revolution, 25 Tong Dan	54323

EXHIBITIONS	Telephone
The Giang Vo Exhibition Center, Giang Vo	55920
The Van Ho Exhibition, Van Ho	54809

THEATRES	Telephone
The Central Theatre, Trang Tien	54312
The Dai Nam Theatre, 89 Hue	57218
The Hong Ha Theatre, 51 Duong Thanh	52803

CLUBS	**Telephone**
The Ba Dinh Club, Hoang Van Thu	53024
The Children's Cultural House, Ly Thai To	55833
The Labor Club, Tang Bat Ho	54223
The International Club, 35 Hung Vuong	52820
The Vietnam Committee for Solidarity and Friendship with the People of All Countries, 105a Quan Thanh	

COMMERCIAL ENTERPRISES	**Telephone**
Artexport (Handicrafts and art objects), 33 Ngo Quyen	
Barotex (Bamboo and rattan), 37 Ly Thuong Kiet	
Hanoi Export and Import Corporation, 41 Ngo Quyen	54506
Machinoimport (Imports tools and laboratory equipment and exports rubber goods and hand tools), 8 Trang Thi	
Mecanimex (Mechanical products), 36 Ba Trieu	
Naforimex (Forest and native produce), 19 Ba Trieu	
Petrovietnam (Oil and Gas), 80 Nguyen Du	
Technoimport (Large equipment), 16–18 Trang Tri	
Tocontap (Sundries), 36 Ba Trieu	
Vegetexco (Vegetables and fruit), 46 Ngo Quyen	
Vietcochamber (Chamber of Commerce), 33 Ba Trieu	
Vietnam National Bank, 47 Ly Thai To	52831

TOURISM	**Telephone**
The Hanoi Tourist Company (Local City), 32 Ba Trieu	52986
VietnamTourism (National), 54 Nguyen Du	54674
The West Lake Boat House, 30 Thanh Nien	57105

UNIONS	**Telephone**
The Vietnam Federation of Trade-Unions, 82 Tran Hung Dao	58181
The Vietnam Women's Union, 39 Hang Chuoi	53436

COMMUNICATIONS	**Telephone**
Foreign Press Center, 10 Le Phung Hieu	51697
Ministry of Culture, The Foreign Languages Publishing House (publishing company), 46 Trang Hung Dao	53841
The Central Film Production, 67 Tran Hung Dao	52340
The Central Information House, 93 Dinh Tien Hoang	53072
The Hanoi Cinema State Company, 45 Hang Bai	54483
The Literature and Arts Association, 51 Trang Hung Dao	52140
The Nhan Dan Daily Printing House, 24 Trang Thi	52667
The State Company of Distribution of Foreign Language Books (Import/export/marketing foreign language books), 66 Trang Tien	57376
The Vietnam Broadcasting and Television Commission, 58 Quan Su	54134
Radio Vietnam (The Voice of Vietnam), 58 Quan Su	54134
The Central Television Studio, Giang Vo Sector	55931/55933
The Vietnam Journalists' Association, 59 Ly Thai To	53608
The Vietnam Writers' Association, 65 Nguyen Du	53985
Vietnam News Agency (VNA), Ly Thuong Kiet	52931

SCHOOLS/EDUCATIONAL INSTITUTIONS	**Telephone**
Hanoi University, Thuong Dinh, Dong Dinh Sector	
The Banking College, Chua Boc, Dong Da Sector	

The International Relations and Law School, Lang Trung, Lang
   Trung Sector
The Institute of Archaeology, 61 Phan Chu Trinh	53203
The Institute of Cybernetics, Nghia Do	53126
The Institute of Earth Sciences, Nghia Do	58333
The Institute of Educational Science, 101 Trang Hung Dao	52108
The Institute of Ethnology, Tran Xuan Soan	55380
The Institute of History, 38 Hang Chuoi	53200
The Institute of Linguistics, 20 Ly Thai To	57406
The Institute of Literature, 20 Ly Thai To	52895
The Institute of Mathematics, Nghia Do	56254
The Institute of Philosophy, Tran Xuan Soan	57241
The Institute of Physics, Nghia Do	52129
The Institute of Social Sciences Information, 38 Hang Chuoi	52345
The State Committee of Social Sciences, 27 Tran Xuan Soan	54773

The State Committee for the Protection of the Mother and Infant
   59 Ly Thai To   53609
The State Committee of Sciences and Technology, 39 Trang
   Hung Dao   52731

HOSPITALS	Telephone
Hospital for Mothers and Newborns, Trang Thi	56321
St. Paul's Pediatric Hospital, Chu Van An	52691
The Bach Mai Hospital, Nam Bo	53731
The E Hospital, Co Nhue	53561
The K Hospital (cancer), 43 Quan Su	52143
The International Hospital	54373
The Institute of Ophthalmology, 38 Tran Nhan Tong	53967
The Traditional Medicine Hospital, 29 Nguyen Binh Khiem.	52850

The Vietnam-Cuba Friendship Hospitals, 92 Tran Hung Dao
   and 37 Hai Ba Trung   57374 and 52243
The Vietnam-Germany Friendship Hospital (Viet-Duc), 47
   Trang Thi   53531
The Vietnam-Soviet Union Friendship Hospital (near the former
   Yersin Institute), Tran Khanh Du   52231
The Vietnam-Swedish International Children's Hospital (formerly
   the Olaf Palme Children's Hospital), Lang Thuong Sector,
   Dong Da District   54373

INTERNATIONAL ORGANIZATIONS

United Nations Development Program 27–29 Phan Boi Chau

HANOI REGION:
ANCIENT CAPITALS OF VIETNAM AND OTHER SITES OF INTEREST

The region surrounding Hanoi is the cradle of the Vietnamese civilization. A flourishing Bronze-Age society developed around 3,000 BC on the Ma River, a Red River tributary. Since that ancient society was near the town of Dong Son, it was called the Dong Son culture. Dong Son was the center of a rich and complex civilization built by the Lac Viet people whom the Vietnamese acknowledge as their direct ancestors. The casting of a single drum of the Dong Son type required smelting more than seven tons of copper ore. The Lac Viet practiced a sophisticated bronze and iron craft long before they were incorporated into the Chinese empire, and thus developed this technology independently of Chinese influence.

As the Red River area could be reached easily from China by sea and along natural land routes, migrants from southern China, in search of fertile land, settled the Red River area. Later, Chinese military expeditions usurped the region from the indigenous Lac Viets and established fortified administrative centers.

Toward the end of the Bronze Age, 257–179 BC, the Lac Viets, ruled by King An Duong, moved 9.5 miles (15 km.) north of present-day Hanoi and built his capital at Co Loa.

CO LOA

Of the nine original earthen ramparts that once protected this ancient capital, only three remain—some as tall as six yards (5.5 m.) high and surrounded by moats filled by a tributary of the Red River. The first line of defense was an enclosure covering an area of four square miles (10.4 sq. km.). The walls of the second enclosure were taller than those of the first. In the center of this defense system was the citadel, called **Co Loa** or "snail," because the protective ramparts and moats were constructed in a labyrinthine fashion that resembled the spiral core of a chambered nautilus. Surrounded by guards' quarters, the citadel includes a parade ground and the Imperial Palace.

A popular legend tells of a royal drama that included King An Duong of Co Loa and his daughter, Mi Chau, who committed the first recorded betrayal in Vietnamese history. While her father did

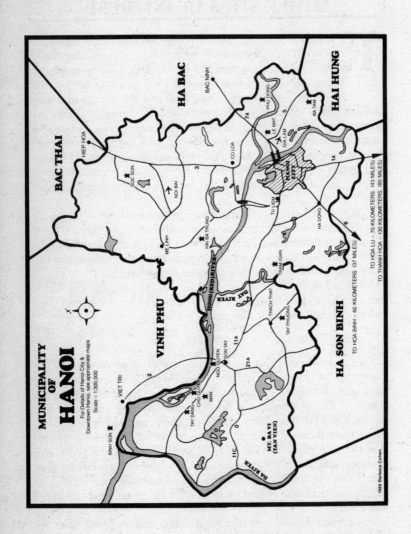

MUNICIPALITY
OF
HANOI

For Details of Hanoi City &
Downtown Hanoi, see appropriate maps

Scale = 1:300,000

BAC THAI

HA BAC

HAI HUNG

VINH PHU

HA SON BINH

BINH SON

VIET TRI

SOC SON

NOI BAI

HIEP HOA

BAC NINH

PHU DONG

LE MAT

GIA LAM

BA TAM

CO LOA

HANOI
CITY

ME LINH

HAI BA TRUNG

TU LIEM

HA DONG

TRAN GIAN

TRACH THAT

TAY PHUONG

HONG (RED) RIVER

DAY RIVER

TAY DANG

CHU QUYEN

MAN

NGO QUYEN

SON TAY

11A

21A

11C

DA RIVER

MT. BA VI
(TAN VIEN)

1A

7A

3

5

6

2

0

TO HOA LU – 70 KILOMETERS (43 MILES)
TO THANH HOA – 130 KILOMETERS (80 MILES)

TO HOA BINH – 60 KILOMETERS (37 MILES)

N

1989 Barbara Cohen

Karst land formation, southwest of Hanoi

battle with the Chinese General Chao T'o, Mi Chau fell in love
with her enemy's son and revealed defense secrets to her lover. The
fortress soon fell to the enemy as a result of her betrayal. (See Appendix for full story of Mi Chau.)

The entrance to the Co Loa citadel has statues of King An Duong and Mi Chau. More than a thousand years after their deaths,
local residents still honor the memory of the ancient king and his
treacherous daughter. After the military occupation of the Lac Viet
territory by the Chinese, a Chinese province of **Giao-Chi (Chiao
Chih)** with its capital at Luy Lau was established. Luy Lau is on a
plain south of the hill of Long Bien east of present-day Hanoi.

ME LINH

Early in the first century, the brutal treatment of the Lac Viets at
the hands of the Chinese imperialists incited the native people to
rebellion. Trung Trac and Trung Nhi, popularly known as the
Trung Sisters, led one such uprising in AD 40. The sisters lived at
Me Linh, 40 miles (64 km.) northwest of Hanoi city. Vestiges of
citadels built by the Trung sisters still remain at Me Linh. The Den
Citadel or "The Citadel with Three Ponds" is believed to have been
the headquarters of Trung Nhi. The remnants of the walls of this
fortress, built on a hill overlooking a plain, are 11 yards (10 m.)
thick. The swamp to the west connects with the Nguyet Duc and
Red rivers, a route of communication for the citadel's inhabitants.
A pagoda honoring the heroic sisters, the Pagoda of Hai Ba Trung,

is located on Route 2 between the Thang Long bridge and the town of Me Linh.

While they ruled, the sisters initiated reforms and reduced the oppressive taxes levied by the Han Dynasty Chinese administrators. A few years later, the Chinese returned with reinforced troops and defeated the sisters, who committed suicide by drowning in the Day River. After the Trung Sisters' insurrection, the Lac Viet lords lost power and the Chinese dominated the area.

A woman taking up arms for her country after the battlefield death of her husband is a popular theme in Vietnamese literature. There is, however, no historic documentation that Trung Trac's husband had been killed or even that she had been married.

HOA LU (ALSO WRITTEN HOA LOA)

The Chinese controlled the Hanoi area until the tenth century. Hoa Lu (Ninh Binh in present-day Ha Nam Ninh Province) was the first Vietnamese capital free of Chinese domination. King Dinh Tien Hoang (968–979), founder of the Dinh dynasty, moved his capital to Hoa Lu from Co Loa. At that time the country was called Dai Co Viet. To avert another Chinese invasion, massive fortifications were built and the king constructed a splendid palace decorated with gold and silver. After 1010, the capital of Vietnam was at the site of present-day Hanoi.

PAGODAS IN HANOI REGION*

But Thap Pagoda. Constructed in 1648 under the Le dynasty, the But Thap Pagoda is 12 miles (20 km.) from Hanoi and surrounded by countryside typical of the Red River delta. The pagoda features a one-span bridge, a five-story tower, a statue of the thousand-arm and thousand-eyed Buddha, and an elaborate altar piece with wooden statues of Buddhist holy men.

Dong Co (Bronze Drum) Temple. Built in 1028, Dong Co Temple is one of the most famous temples of the country. Every year, a major festival occurs here on the fourth day of the fourth month—the time of year when the king and his mandarins arrived to renew their oaths of loyalty.

Phu Dong Temple. Phu Dong Temple is located on the Duong River, east of Hanoi. It commemorates the deeds of the legendary hero, Giong, who miraculously grew from a speechless child into a

---

*Pagodas that can be visited in downtown Hanoi are discussed earlier in the book.

powerful giant and saved his country by routing invaders from the north.

Phung Hung Temple. Phung Hung seized the capital from the Chinese in 791 and managed to control it for a few months. After his death, these words were written on his temple: "Great king, father and mother of the people." This temple is located in Trieu Kheu village in Thanh Tri district, south of Hanoi.

Tay Dang Communal House. Built at the end of the 15th century, this house is one of the oldest remaining communal houses in the country. It is noted for numerous wood carvings, especially that of the jumping elephant.

Tay Phuong Pagoda. The Tay Phuong Pagoda is located west of Hanoi, near Thach That. It was started in the third century, rebuilt in the ninth and enlarged over time to its present size. The layout

of the complex is as follows: a square enclosure encompasses three ancient wooden two-story houses with basins of water between them. The water reflects sunlight into the pagoda, illuminating the inside with an almost supernatural air of sparkling light. The curved roofs are covered with thick, leaf-shaped tiles. There are ceramic statues of the four sacred animals on the roof tops. Rafters are covered with bas reliefs of dragons, phoenixes, lotuses, sun rays, and moon beams. The stone pillar supports are decorated with carved lotus petals. Among other treasures, the pagoda retains masterpieces of wood sculpting. The originals of the most unusual ones are 16 life-like statues of *arhats*—Buddhist holy men who have obtained enlightenment—and are now displayed in the Hanoi Fine Arts Museum.

Thien Phuc Pagoda. This pagoda contains many lacquered statues of monks.

Thuong Temple. Located 12 miles (19 km.) from Hanoi, Thuong Temple is dedicated to General Dao Truc, who fought the Sung Dynasty troops in 981.

Tram Gian Pagoda. Tram Gian Pagoda is near Hoai Duc, west of Hanoi city. Bricks are decorated with real and mythical animal figures: dragons, horses, elephants, and birds. A winged horse figure, dating from the 17th century, is carved on the brick side wall.

HA DONG

Ha Dong City, in the south of Hanoi municipality, is known for its Van Phuc silks and exquisite brocades. The memory of the patron saint of weavers, Le Thi Nga, has been venerated in this city since the 11th century. The area also produces rattan and bamboo articles, Chuong conical hats, Vac fans, and wood products from the workshops of the Nhi Khue wood turners. Chuyen My commune, in the Phu Xuyen district on the bank of the Nhue River, carries on the centuries-old tradition of mother-of-pearl inlay.

The process of inlay involves the following basics: shells are broken and ground until they are quite thin. Pieces are then selected on the basis of color, luminescence, and size, prior to being cut and ground again. The refined fragments are assembled into a picture engraved on a wood panel. Finally, the shell pieces are fixed with lacquer and polished to a high gloss. The shells from Nam Dinh produce the best pinks, while those from Bac Giang produce the deepest violets.

HA BAC PROVINCE

As this region contains 22 major historic sites, it is appropriate that Ha Bac was the first province to implement the 1986 state ruling for restoring and preserving the country's historical and cultural remains.

This area is also noted for the **Tho Ha comunal house** and the

Phi Tuong Pagoda. The communal house of Tho Ha, the country's largest surviving *dinh,* located on the northern bank of the Cau River, is typical of 18th-century Vietnamese buildings. Because of its location on the riverbank, however, it is frequently (partially) submerged during the annual flood season. A stone stele engraved with a Buddha, dating from 1697, can be seen at the Phi Tuong Pagoda. The inscription on the stele indicates that the female Buddha is accompanied by the four symbols of her power: thunder, clouds, rain, and lightning.

Dong Ho, 25 miles (40 km.) northeast of Hanoi, is famous for its folk wood-block prints. The region is also noted for its lacquerware, Tho Ha pottery, and Dai Bai bronze.

The **Thuan Thanh** district of Ha Bac has a commune for the disabled. One hundred seventy disabled persons live there: some were wounded in the war, others were handicapped due to accidents, polio, cerebral palsy, or other illnesses. Humanitarian aid from friendship groups abroad helps them overcome their physical limitations.

Mai Dong has a wrestling and martial arts school founded by Tam Chinh, the patron saint of the wrestling school. He commanded the assault on Luy Lau citadel and defeated the Chinese. The "old ring" at the school is several hundred years old.

The **Yen The** district of Ha Bac is associated with the national hero De Tham (Hoang Hoa Tham), who led a peasant's uprising from 1893 to 1913. In Yen The, one can see De Tham's main stronghold, the Phon Xuong fort. The nearby communal house, once a meeting place of insurgents, is now a museum. Phan Boi Chau, the revolutionary kept under house arrest in Hue by the French, said of Phon Xuong: "For the victims of harsh treatment by the French this locality was an oasis of Freedom."

HAI HUNG PROVINCE

The **Giam Pagoda** was built during the Tran dynasty (1225-1400). Once the monastery of the traditional medicine practitioner, Tue Tinh, the pagoda features an unusual hexagonal wooden box with a nine-petal lotus motif. A yearly festival celebrating the accomplishments of Tue Tinh occurs there on the 15th day of the second lunar month.

The **Xu Dong** area of Hai Hung Province is noted for its active intellectual life. During the Ly, Tran, and Le Dynasties, this region produced many scholarly mandarins whose names were engraved on the stone steles at the Van Mieu. One small village, Mo Trach, called Doctors' or Scholars' cradle, had so many successful candidates in the civil service competitions that the examining officials suspected a hoax. The traditional village communal house, or *dinh*, of Mo Trach still stands.

HA NAM NINH PROVINCE

The capital of this province, **Nam Dinh City,** is an industrial center lying 20 miles (32 km.) inland from the coast and is the third largest city of the north after Haiphong and Hanoi.

Ha Nam Ninh Province contains many archaeological points of interest. The excavation site of **Phu Luong,** for example, is rich in vestiges of the Bronze age state called Van Lang, which thrived under the Hung kings over 3,000 years ago. Also situated in this province is **Hoa Lu,** the ancient capital (after Co Loa) of the Dai Co Viet nation from AD 968–980.

The area was also the Tran dynasty capital during the 11th to 13th centuries and a temple from this period remains. **Phat Diem**

Stone steles engraved with scholars' names, Van Mieu

Street market scene

market displays locally made items, especially piles of woven rush. Other places of interest in this historical area around Hanoi include **Pho Minh Tower Pagoda, Co Le Pagoda, Bich Dong Pagoda,** and **Doi Pagoda.**

HA SON BINH PROVINCE

The center of the ancient Hoa Binh culture was about 40 miles (60 km.) southwest of Hanoi. Hoa Binh was a bronze-working society that developed 6,000 years ago. Especially striking were the uniquely shaped and decorated bronze drums of which the Ngoc Lu drum, in the Hanoi History Museum, is an excellent example.

The **Thay Pagoda** (Master's Pagoda), 22 miles (35 km.) from Hanoi, was built during the reign of Ly Nhan Ton (1072–1128). The pagoda is dedicated to three cults. From the top of the Sai Son Hill, one can enjoy a beautiful view of the surrounding area, including a small stage, built on stilts in the middle of a pond, which was used for water-puppet shows on festive occasions.

Huong Pagoda (Perfume Pagoda), located 37 miles (60 km.) from Hanoi, is the site of a popular spring pilgrimage. The area is reached by a sampan ride on the Yen River. On the sides of the stream are caves, grottoes, and strangely shaped hills with names such as "Haystack" and "Kneeling Elephant". The trail from the landing stage to the main pagoda rises and descends past small temples, such as "Heavenly Kitchen" and "Justice Repaired," and finally reaches the Huong Pagoda, where offerings are made in honor of Buddha.

Cuc Phong National Park is a wildlife preserve 120 miles (193 km.) southwest of Hanoi. Narrow canyons within the park prevented the hill people from practicing their destructive slash-and-burn agricultural methods. The park is also a temporary haven for large and colorful butterflies that swarm into the area during April and May.

The slopes of the canyon are composed of a type of limestone (really dolomite) of the Triassic period. Over the centuries rain has dissolved the calcium carbonate from the dolomite to form caves. Five miles (3 km.) downriver from the dam is a large cave (covering 1200 square yards (1008 sq. m.)) containing strangely shaped stalactites. Another cave located in the park was found to contain Neolithic tools, ancient art work etched on the walls, and skeletons thousands of years old.

Vietnamese officials delight in showing tourists the massive hydro-electric complex on the Da River at Hoa Binh. The project, under construction with Soviet aid, is scheduled for completion in the mid-1990s.

Tam Coc (Three Caves) is 75 miles (120 km.) south of Hanoi. A scenic two-hour journey by boat will take you first to the Thai Vi Temple where King Tran Nhan Tong (1279–1293) spent the end of his life as a monk. The boat passes Tuan Cao, the harbor for imperial ships. Before long, mountains of unusual shapes loom overhead: Mount Quan Van (the scholar), Mount Quan Vo (the General), Go Mung, and Nen Gio. Finally, the trip downriver passes three caves: Hang Ca, Hang Hai, and Hang Ba.

While in Ha Son Binh, many tourists, interested in the daily life of various ethnic minorities, visit the Muong village with its authentic stilt houses.

The **Dai Phung** communal house features rare 17th-century wooden statues of which the elephant is a witty example.

THANH HOA PROVINCE

Thanh Hoa province has many archaeologic sites of the Bronze Age Dong Son culture; the province is also the birthplace of legendary Vietnamese hero Le Loi (born 1385 in Lam Son). With the help of his scholarly advisor Nguyen Trai, Le Loi launched a successful guerrilla movement against the Chinese Ming invaders. Ruins of Le Loi's capital at Lam Kinh still remain.

Another historic site in this province is the Ly Cung palace. Built during the Tran Dynasty of the 14th century, the palace (located in the area of Thanh Hoa city) is currently being excavated.

Thanh Hoa became known to Westerners during the American air war against the North. The Thanh Hoa Rail and Highway bridge was also known as Ham Rong or Dragon's Jaw bridge. Located just north of Thanh Hoa city, the bridge was a strategic target (a "choke point" in military slang) of US bombing that attempted to cut off the flow of supplies from the north to the guerrillas fighting in the south. Although the bridge was destroyed by intense bombing by US aircraft during the war, it was subsequently and quickly rebuilt several times by teenage volunteers called Youth Brigade Teams.

Thanh Hoa province is noted for Nga Son rush mats, Quang Xuong rattan, and bamboo basketry; the Mount Nuong region fabricates iron tools.

NGHE TINH PROVINCE

Nghe Tinh province, located in the narrow "panhandle" region of the North, is one of the poorest regions in Vietnam. The capital of this historically important province is Vinh.

Nghe Tinh province was favorable to the breeding of scholars and revolutionaries. From the Ru Thanh, a hill overlooking the plain, there remains traces of a Chinese citadel erected during the time of the Chinese occupation. Le Loi and his troops operated in this region. A temple is dedicated to him nearby. Nguyen Du, the author of the great Vietnamese masterpiece, the *Kim Van Kieu*, was born in this province as well as revolutionaries Ho Chi Minh and Phan Boi Chau.

Nghe Tinh province is where the first worker–peasant self-defense units of Vietnam rallied when the Indochinese Communist Party was formally established (February 3, 1930) and called for armed struggle against Imperialist domination. In 1930 the economic conditions were at a low point. The new Communist Party organization pressed for a campaign of direct action and bred revolts among the peasants of Nghe Tinh against the French and large landholders. The revolts resulted in the brief overthrow of the French colonial administration. Large estates of Nghe Tinh Province were divided into communally worked farms called "soviets." Debts were voided, the colonial tax system was abolished, and a literacy cam-

Farmers returning from work

---

paign was set into motion. Within the year, the French reacted brutally by imprisoning or executing rebel leaders. Vinh was also the site of heavy French artillery bombardment between 1947 and 1954.

The area of Vinh was one of the targets attacked by US air raids after the Tonkin Gulf Decision in August 1964. The Tonkin Gulf Decision authorized US President Johnson to bomb selected targets in North Vietnam in response to a North Vietnamese torpedo boat attack on a US ship sailing in the Tonkin Gulf. Vinh, situated right on the north–south rail line, had been a supply center for North Vietnamese troops heading south to aid southern guerillas. Supplies were trucked, pushed along by modified bicycles, and carried in backpacks upstream along the Lam River and through the (Na Pe) Keo Nua pass into Laos. From there the supply caravans rode on many small trails (called collectively the Ho Chi Minh Trail) into South Vietnam. Vinh's civilian population was dispersed to countryside villages and most of the work of war supply was carried on at night to avoid detection in the air by US reconnaissance planes.

In 1972 the port surrounding Vinh was mined as part of the US Air Force Linebacker II offensive. After the war, the citizens returned to rebuild their homes.

Five miles (8 km.) to the northwest of Vinh at Kim Lien is Ho Chi Minh's hometown. The houses in the area, similar to the one in which Ho was born, have a rectangular shape, are of wooden construction, and have simple thatched roofs. Ho Chi Minh was born Nguyen Sinh Cung in 1890 and later, as is the Asian custom, took different names to reflect different life stages.

Tea is grown in this area; "April 20" is one of the State Tea plantations. The Kh'mu ethnic minority group, whose ancestors are from upper Laos, live in the province's western hilly regions. The Kh'mu play the Hun May, a bamboo musical instrument that sounds like a cicada.

THAI BINH PROVINCE

Thai Binh Province has a temple dedicated to a woman warrior—Lu Phuong Dzung who fought in the army of the Trung Sisters' during their revolt against the Chinese. This region is known for mulberry trees and silkworm raising. The Red River floods this province from June to October.

Khuoc village of this district supports a "Cheo theater" troupe which propagates classic Vietnamese theater. Everyone in the village participates in these theatrical productions.

The coastal village of Dong Sam is noted for its tin, bronze, silver, and goldsmiths. These craftsmen (only male family members are taught these skills) now export their handiworks abroad.

VINH PHU PROVINCE

At the end of 1952, the capital of Vinh Phu, Viet Tri, was the location of the French military operation called "Lorraine." The French forces had thrust deep into the Viet Minh communication system along the Red River, assuming (wrongly) that the Viet Minh's response would be to withdraw their main assault division to defend their rear. The French were attempting to maneuver Vietnamese Commander Giap's hard-core regular division into a decisive battle in which superior French fire power and air capability could be used to engage and route the Viet Minh forces.

Operation Lorraine was outfitted with the largest number of forces allotted by the French command for a single operation. With the aid of Soviet-built Molotov tanks, the Viet Minh fought hard to stop the French offensive before it reached their supply centers at Yen Bay and Thai Nguyen. As the French withdrew and entered Chan-Muong gorge on route #2, they were ambushed by the Viet Minh from the nearby cliffs. The French reorganized in the relative safety of the De Lattre line near Viet Tri and waited another year to try again—at Dien Bien Phu.

The Vinh Phu Pulp and Paper Mill built with Swedish assistance is located in this province. Vinh Phu province was one of the first to experiment with the government's 1986 production contract system aimed at reaching increased national agricultural and industrial goals. Under this system, contracts with farm cooperatives are made by province authorities. Local planning and removal of some restrictions on the free market offers workers incentives to higher production. Despite some positive results, this system has not yet solved the problem of farmers leaving their land to find work in Hanoi.

Each spring the provincial village of Trieu Phu re-enacts the legend of the marriage of the sea god and the mountain spirit, Princess My Nuong Ngoc Hoa. A festive procession honors a teenage boy and girl chosen to represent the legendary couple.

HOTEL
ACCOMMODATIONS

HA NAM NINH PROVINCE

Hotel Vi Hoang
115 Nguyen Du
tel. 439-362
Nam Dinh

HA SON BINH PROVINCE

Hotel Hoa Binh
tel. 01 HOA BINH
Located near the reconstructed Muong minority village.

Hotel Huong Son. Located near the Perfume Pagoda, this is a small, five-room hotel for foreign visitors in My Duc.

Hotel Song Nhue Hadong
tel. 340 HA DONG
New, but not for Western tourists.

THANH HOA PROVINCE

A tourist hotel occupies the same address as the Tourism Office. The **Sam Son Beach Hotel** (tel. 298) is located at Sam Son Beach.

NGHE TINH PROVINCE

Cua Lo Hotel
13 Cua Lo
Nghe Tinh
A small beach hotel with eight rooms.

THAI BINH PROVINCE

Dong Chau Hotel
Dong Minh Beach
Tien Hai

Huu Nghi Hotel
Ly Bon
Thai Binh
tel. 270

VINH PHU PROVINCE

Tam Dao Resort. This complex is located at an elevation of 3,300 feet (1,000 m.) above sea level and 50 miles (80 km.) from Hanoi. The beautiful Thac Bac (Silver) falls is a distinctive feature of the resort's landscape.

Cha Pa. Cha Pa is another lovely hilltop resort at an elevation of 4,500 feet (1,365 m.).

Hotel Vinh Yen
Ngo Quyen Square
Vinh Yen

Hotel Lam Thao
Cao Mai, Phong Chau
Vinh Phu

Song Lo
Tan Dan Square
Viet Tri
tel. 318 VIETTRI

HANOI REGION DIRECTORY

	Telephone
HA BAC PROVINCE	
Ha Bac Tourist Office	209-9913
HA NAM NINH PROVINCE	
Ha Nam Ninh Tourist Office, 115 Nguyen Du, Nam Dinh	439-362
HA SON BINH PROVINCE	
Ha Son Binh Tourist Office, 24 Tran Hung Dao, Ha Dong	37
THANH HOA PROVINCE	
Thanh Hoa Tourist Office, 21A Quang Trung	298
NGHE TINH PROVINCE	
Nghe Tinh Tourist Office, Truong Tri Square, Vinh	692 Vinh
THAI BINH PROVINCE	
Tourist Office, Ly Bon, Thai Binh	270
VINH PHU PROVINCE	
Vinh Phu Tourist Office, Viet Tri, Vinh Phu	245

Haiphong:
Hai Duong Province

WITH a population of 1.5 million, Haiphong is the capital of Hai Duong province and the third largest city (64 miles (102 km.) east of Hanoi) in the country, as well as the north's most important seaport. The central area of the municipality is made up of the three districts of Hong Bang, Ngo Quyen, and Le Chan, with 33 city wards. The suburban area comprises seven districts: Thuy Nguyen, Vinh Bao, An Hai, Do Son, Kien An, Tien Lang, and Cat Hai, with 161 villages and four towns: Quan Toan (An Hai district), Do Son (Do Son district), Kien An (Kien An district), and Cat Ba (Cat Hai district).

The suburban area also includes a number of islands such as Long Chau, Bach Long Vi, Cat Ba, and Dinh Vu. Cat Ba is the largest island and is known for its beautiful landscape and natural waterways. Dinh Vu island, which is linked to the city by a dam on the Cam river, will soon include a trade center and summer resort.

The five-hour ride from Hanoi to Haiphong, on Route 5, offers the visitor a chance to observe stages of rice cultivation on the flat and treeless Red River delta. The fertile area around Hanoi produces two rice crops a year, so the transplanting process can be seen in late January/February and in July/August. (See rice cultivation section in Vietnam Economy.)

Hai Duong province also grows red litchis and is noted for the production of mother-of-pearl used for inlay-work and for crafting fine china. In the spring, flamboyant trees flash a bit of color along the city streets.

HISTORY

Haiphong has witnessed the coming and going of many conquerors. The port of Van Don near Haiphong was the first commercial seaport of Vietnam that prospered under the Tran Dynasty.

Jules Ferry, the premier of France in 1883–85, was France's empire builder. Ferry's foreign policy was dominated by his concern for colonial expansion, favoring industrialization at home and opening up markets abroad. During the French colonial war against the Vietnamese, a defeat for the French troops at Lang Son meant political doom for Ferry, who was later assassinated. The street leading from the public works buildings' wharf to the Bank of Indochina was once aptly called rue Jules Ferry, but has since been renamed Cu Chinh Lan.

In June 1940, the Japanese gave an ultimatum to Georges Catroux, the French governor-general of Indochina. They demanded that he stop the flow of fuel and war materials from Tonkin to China and that he admit a Japanese military mission to supervise the closing of the supply channel. General Catroux had neither the troops nor the equipment to resist the Japanese, who landed at Haiphong in October 1940 and, throughout the rest of World War II, used the French-built transportation channels to export rice, coal, rubber, and mineral resources to Japan.

In November 1946, after Ho Chi Minh's government was granted "independence within the French Union," an incident occurred in Haiphong that started the eight-year war between the Viet Minh and the French. Between 500 and 1,000 Vietnamese were killed by French air and artillery bombardment of the port in a clash over who had the right to enforce customs regulations, the French or Ho Chi Minh's government.

After the French defeat at Dien Bien Phu and the Geneva accords, nearly one million North Vietnamese accepted the opportunity permitted by the accords to leave for the south. Many received transport on US Navy ships docked at Haiphong harbor. A US Navy physician, Thomas Dooley, was aboard the USS Montague, the first American ship to arrive in July 1954. In his book *Deliver Us From Evil*, Dr. Dooley publicized the flight of the refugees, most of them Catholic.

Virtually the only seaport in North Vietnam capable of receiving foreign aid, Haiphong was a major target of the US Air Force and Navy. In May 1972, Haiphong harbor was mined. On December 1972, President Nixon, in an effort to coerce North Vietnam to return to the negotiating table, ordered "Operation Linebacker Two," commonly referred to as the Christmas Bombing. US B-52s and other aircraft were deployed to bombard the area between Haiphong and Hanoi, causing many civilian deaths.

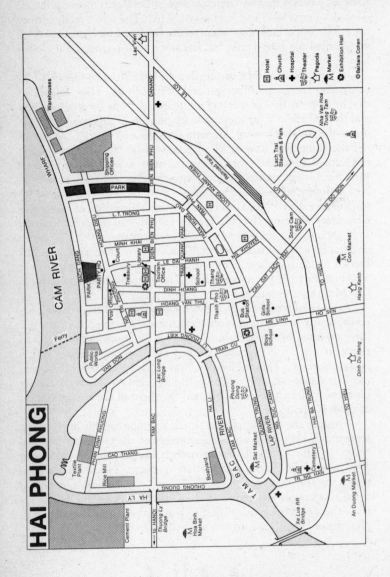

HIGHLIGHTS FOR
TRAVELERS

MOUNT ELEPHANT

Legend tells of deities playing chess atop Mount Elephant, a rocky hill on the outskirts of Haiphong. Halfway to the top is the communal house of Chi Lai, now a museum that displays Neolithic and bronze artifacts from the primitive societies that once thrived in the area. The caves in the dolomite-karst rock of Mount Elephant were used as guerrilla base camps during the war of resistance against the French. In 1967, an American jet fighter was downed by women gunners stationed on Mount Elephant.

DOWNTOWN HAIPHONG

Sites to visit in Haiphong include the museum, the Hang Kenh communal house, the Cho Sat market, Ben Binh harbor, and the large cement works established by the French. There are also functioning pagodas and Catholic churches.

The **Thien Phuc** pagoda has a large stone statue of Queen Mother Tra Huong which dates from 1551. The **Linh Quang** pagoda, built in 1709, exhibits wood carvings, including one representing a long-tailed cat poised to leap on a large carp. The **Le Chan** temple is dedicated to Le Chan, the first-century female military commander. **Du Hang** pagoda is a 300-year-old pagoda constructed of traditional Vietnamese architecture and sculpting.

Haiphong is also an industrial city with a woolen mill that manufactures carpets for export, glass-works, shipyards, and fish-canning factories. The town has two naval schools: Maritime Navigation College and River Transport College. There is also a French opera house facing a large square. In 1927, Helen Churchill Candee, an American writer, said of the opera house: "Haiphong has a fine theater in which bewildered companies try to feel the thrill of art in a climate like a sponge dipped in hot water."

Among the many bridges in Haiphong, the Thuong Ly bridge is the main bridge spanning the Tam Bac River. A busy railroad surrounds the downtown area.

Local seafood dishes are delightful, especially the crab soup.

HOTEL
ACCOMMODATIONS

Huu Nghi Hotel
62 Dien Bien Phu
tel. 47206
This hotel, built by the French, is old and not recommended for Westerners.

Duyen Hai Hotel
5 Nguyen Tri Phuong
tel. 47657
The Duyen Hai Hotel, which recently rebuilt 20 of its rooms, is considered to be the best lodging in town.

Bach Dang Hotel
42 Dien Bien Phu
tel. 47244
A hotel for domestic (locals only) use.

Do Son Resort
Do Son Beach
tel. 10
Formerly the Union Hotel, this resort is located on a point of land about 13 miles (20 km.) southeast of Haiphong on the Gulf of Tonkin.

HAIPHONG DIRECTORY

Central Post Office, Nguyen Tri Phuong and Hoang Van Thu (crossroads)
Exhibition, Nguyen Duc Canh
General Department Store, Dien Bien Phu and Minh Khai (crossroads)
Library, Dien Bien Phu and Minh Khai (crossroads)
Museum, Dien Bien Phu
Theatre, Tran Hung Dao
The Hospital for Gynecology and Obstetrics, Tran Quang Khai
The Traditional Medicine Hospital, Nguyen Duc Canh
Stadium, Lach Tray

COMMERCE AND TOURISM

Haiphong Tourism, 15 Le Dai Hanh
Haiphong Branch Office of the Vietnam Foreign Trade
  Transportation Corporation, 6 Tran Phu
Haiphong Foreign Trade Forwarding and Warehousing
  Corporation, 5 Hoang Van Thu
Haiphong Branch Office of the Vietnam Superintendence and
  Inspection Company, 36 Pham Minh Duc
Haiphong Branch Office of Vietnam National Agricultural
  Produce and Foodstuffs Export/Import Corporation, 20 Luong
  Van Can
Haiphong Representative Office of the Vietnam National Forest
  and Native Produce Import/Export Corporation, 11 Hoang Dieu
Haiphong Branch Office of the Handicraft and Art Articles for
  Export/Import National Corporation, 23 Danang
Haiphong Export/Import Corporation, 18 Cu Chinh Lan
Haiphong Union of Tourism Companies, Tran Quang Khai
Shipping General Department, 11 Vo Thi Sau
Units under the Shipping General Department:
  Haiphong Port, 13 Hoang Dieu
  Vietnam Ocean Shipping Company (VOSCO), 15 Cu Chinh
    Lan
  Vietnam Coastal Shipping Company (VIET-COSHIP), 1
    Hoang Van Thu
  Maritime Insurance Service, 31 Danang
  Transmission Station and Maritime Communication Group, 2
    Nguyen Thuong Hien
  Haiphong Insurance Branch Office, 24 Dien Bien Phu
  Vietnam Container Transport Corporation, 5 Vo Thi Sau
  Vietnam Ocean Shipping Agency, 11 Tran Phu
  Vietnam Ship-chandler Company, Tran Quang Khai

GOVERNMENT OFFICES

Headquarters of the Haiphong Party Committee of the Communist
  Party of Vietnam, Dinh Tien Hoang Street
Haiphong People's Committee, Hoang Dieu Street

Ha Long:
Quang Ninh Province

Quang Ninh Province is known mainly for the spectacular beauty of Ha Long Bay, but this province is also the source of yellow anise used as a flavoring in foods, beverages, and toothpaste. Aniseed is used in making herbal medicines, treating digestive disorders, and allaying arthritis pain.

Cao Ba Lanh is a mountainous region in northern Quang Ninh Province where minority groups such as the Tay, the San Chi, and the Zao make their homes.

The Hon Gai anthracite mine is located in this province.

HA LONG BAY

A ferry travels 12 miles (23 km.) from Haiphong to Cat Ba Island, where one boards another vessel for a tour of the stunningly beautiful Ha Long Bay.

HISTORY OF HA LONG

Ha Long Bay is called Bay of the Descending Dragon because fishermen in ancient times reported sighting dragons in these waters. (In contrast, Thang Long, the former name of Hanoi, means Ascending Dragon.) Six hundred years ago, Vietnamese naval ships took advantage of the large caves as natural hiding places to lie in ambush for Chinese warships.

In 1948, after the Viet Minh war with the French, former emperor Bao Dai tried to come to some agreement with the French. He signed what is called the Accord of Ha Long (June 5, 1948), in which the French agreed to recognize the "independence of Vietnam." The previous agreement signed between the French and Ho Chi Minh had characterized Vietnam as a "free state . . . belonging to the French Indochinese Federation and the French Union." But, by the provisions of the Ha Long accord, the southern part of Vietnam, Cochinchina, would remain a French colony unless the territorial assembly (made up mostly of French settlers) voted to return to Vietnam. Bao Dai refused to re-establish residence in Vietnam until Cochinchina was integrated with the rest of the country.

A cemetery for Vietnamese soldiers who fought with the French against the Viet Minh is located on one of the islands in Ha Long Bay.

Cat Ba and the surrounding islands were settled by Chinese merchants and fishermen. After Vietnam's break with China in 1979, 10,000 Chinese who had lived on Cat Ba departed for China.

HIGHLIGHTS FOR

TRAVELERS

GEOLOGY OF HA LONG

The aquatic terrain here is unique in the world. According to the legends, a great dragon plunged into the sea from his home in the mountains, twisting and turning along the way. His flailing tail gouged out huge crevices as he thrashed about, and when he finally reached the sea, the water he had displaced rushed into valleys, filling them up and leaving only the peaks which emerge from the surface to form over 3,000 "karst" islets covering an area of around 577 square miles (1,500 sq. km.). Note: Dragons in Vietnam and many other Asian countries are generally considered sacred and symbols of royalty.

Forty percent of the world's petroleum reserves are in limestone and dolomite deposits (the other 60% are in sandstone). "Karst topography" describes the bay, which is a remnant of an ancient limestone and dolomite sea bed that has eroded to the point of exposing these remaining peaks. The rocks consist mainly of dolomite—the sedimentary rock is composed of organic matter from plants and sea animals compressed by the pressure of the water over thousands of years. When calcium and magnesium carbonate in the rocks dissolve from rain and underground streams, the process forms caverns and bizarrely sculpted shapes. This type of topography runs into south China and is at its most spectacular around Guilin. Erosion of the rocks of Ha Long Bay is also due to the persistent pounding of the waves as well as the constant rasping of tiny mollusks living at tide level.

The scene in Ha Long resembles a Chinese ink painting: an ever-changing fantasy of one wonder after another. Vegetation is sparse, and what manages to grow on the islands is stunted and twisted into odd shapes. Many of the islets have been given individ-

Harvesting sea swallows nests in caves

ual names, such as Father and Son Rock, the Unicorn, and Fighting Cocks. One tunnel, called Hang Hanh, winds for nearly two miles before opening onto the sea. Some of the larger islets have marvelous little beaches and grottoes with names like Surprise Grotto and Customs House Cave. One island is inhabited by yellow-haired macaque monkeys from which a vaccine is prepared for export. Pelicans and sea swallows nest on the ledges and in the caves of these islands.

Earlier this century, one visitor (Crosbie Garstin) to the area wrote: "A fence of mighty stone pillars, each one separate, starting sheer up out of the sea to a height of cathedral towers, the chain enclosing an area of nearly 100 square miles (160 km.). Islands that took on human profiles, others that looked like crouching frogs, sugar loaves, and ships under sail. There were prehistoric monoliths, church spires. It was as though the architectural giants of the world grown senile, eaten with age and weather, had been dumped down here to crumble quietly away."

Garstin also visited the Cavern of the Marvels inside one of these small islands and wrote that it was capable of holding two or three thousand people: "Stalactites hung from the ceiling to the floor, strings of them, glistening white, a yawning mouth with strings of nougat."

MAIDEN GROTTO

A grotto, called the Maiden Grotto, owes its name to the following folk story: A fisherman and his wife, too poor to own a boat, rented one from a rich old man. The couple had a very beautiful daughter named Nang He. When her parents could not pay their debt, the wealthy boat owner forced Nang He to marry him. When she refused to share his bed, the old man had her beaten by servants. Then, when she still refused his attentions, he ordered her taken offshore to a grotto to starve. Fishermen found her body and buried her. At her burial site, a rock miraculously emerged resembling the lovely shape of Hang He.

HON GAI MINE

The country's largest anthracite mine at Hon Gai is on the north side of Ha Long Bay. Under French supervision, tens of thousands of laborers were recruited from the countryside to operate the mine. Intolerable working conditions sparked protests and rebellions against the French managers.

A temple dedicated to Tran Quoc Tang at the coal-loading port of Cua Ong overlooks the bay of Bai Tu Long. It was on this strategic point that the prince's father, a Tran emperor, defeated three Yuan (Chinese) invasions in the 13th century. The temple was built in the time of the Le Dynasty, but was later renovated in Nguyen style. A festival in Tran Quoc Tang's honor is celebrated on the first to the tenth day of the second moon.

HOTEL
ACCOMMODATIONS

All accommodations are on the beach. Hotels other than those listed here are for government use only.

Villa Hotel
Bai Chay Road
Ha Long
tel. 235

Ha Long Hotel
Bai Chay Road
Ha Long
tel. 238
A good old French hotel.

Bach Long Hotel
Bai Chay Road
Ha Long
tel. 281

Hoang Long Hotel
Bai Chay Road
Ha Long
tel. 264

Son Long Hotel
Bai Chay Road
Ha Long
tel. 254

QUANG NINH DIRECTORY

	Telephone
Quang Ninh Tourism, Bai Chay, Ha Long	08

Hue: Binh Tri Thien Province

H ue, the capital of Binh Tri Thien Province, is located in the geographic center of Vietnam. Because the mountains are dramatically close to the sea near Hue, the area has the highest rainfall of all the cities in Vietnam: 109 inches (277 cm.) a year. The climate is cool and foggy, similar to that of San Francisco. Moisture damage is evident on the old French and ancient imperial buildings. Erosion, moss stains, and rust give the historic Citadel and the Imperial Palace an otherworldly, timeless appearance.

With 12 schools of higher learning, Hue is the country's intellectual center. Citizens from other parts of the country sometimes think of people from Hue as intellectually aloof. Hue maintained its cultural identity while other cities were accommodating foreign influences. The essence of Hue's pure aloofness is summarized in the well-known poem:

Near the mud, the beautiful lotus
Green leaves, white petals, golden center:
Golden, white and green.
Close to the mud but not stinking of the filth.

HISTORY

Once an outpost of the Kingdom of Champa, the area around Hue was later conquered by the Viets from the north in the fourteenth century. In time, a Vietnamese princess married a Cham king and Hue was ceded to the Vietnamese. By 1687 the Vietnamese had moved their capital to Hue and from there continued their unrelenting southern expansion into Cham territory. Under the last (Nguyen) dynasty, Hue was the capital of Vietnam until 1945 (see chart of Nguyen Kings).

Hue is one of Vietnam's chief tourist centers. This small, quiet city is widely known for its magnificent architecture of citadels, palaces, royal tombs, pagodas, and temples erected under the Nguyen dynasties—all against a poetic background of greenery that carpets the banks of the Perfume River.

HIGHLIGHTS FOR
TRAVELERS

PERFUME RIVER EXCURSIONS

Hue's central location on the Perfume (Huong) River offers sightseeing excursions to either the north or south bank. The Citadel and the Linh Mu pagoda are on the north side of the Perfume River. The south side contains the foreign quarters (during the French colonial occupation) and the Imperial Tombs. The trip along the Perfume River itself is delightful. You will enjoy watching the graceful motions of the oar person propelling a forty- or fifty-foot-long sampan with a rounded roof of woven palm or bamboo. On warm nights, boatwomen sing songs of old heroes who resisted the French or of patriots who fought the Chinese.

THE NORTH BANK OF THE PERFUME RIVER

The Citadel. This side of the Huong river is taken up by the Nguyen Dynasty Citadel. The citadel is a small city of more than two square miles (5.2 sq. km.) covering 1,300 acres (525 hectares) that are enclosed by huge stone walls. Within these outer walls is a moated and walled enclosure, 700 yards on each side, called the

Barge on Perfume River

Imperial City, another small city in itself—and again, within that fortification is the Forbidden City or the Great Within, the living quarters of the emperor's family.

The Citadel is not "ancient," despite that word creeping into some descriptions. The misunderstanding is probably due to a mix-up in translating the French word *ancien*, meaning "former," not "ancient." Construction on the citadel was started in 1804 by Emperor Nguyen Anh (who took the name Gia Long), the first of the Nguyen emperors. The emperor's major achievement was consolidating the country after two centuries of civil war. Gia Long had many French advisors, including the Bishop of Adran, who assisted in building a strong navy and walled fortress-cities that incorporated many French fortification techniques. Gia Long also began work on a new citadel in Hanoi on the site of an ancient stronghold. Employing thousands of conscripts over the years, construction of the building compound was continued for decades by his descendants. The Hanoi citadel has now almost completely disappeared.

Stationed in front of the Citadel's main gate is a flagpole, once called the King's Knight, which became famous to TV viewers in the US and all over the world when the "Viet Cong" raised their flag (gold star on a red and blue background) during the 1968 Tet offensive.

The emperor entered the citadel by the King's Road through the main gate, the Ngo Mon or the Noon gate, on the southeast wall. It is named "Noon" because the emperor is symbolized by the sun which is at its brightest at high noon. The main gate structure contains three openings with the central door reserved exclusively for the emperor. Today, ordinary citizens may pass through the gates and stand amazed at the thickness of the stone walls.

On top of the Noon gate is the five-phoenix building. The emperor appeared in this building on national holidays, such as The Sowing of the First Seeds, and the Promulgation of the Calendar. It was in this building in 1945 that Emperor Bao Dai gave up the golden seal of the empire to a representative of Ho Chi Minh. The golden seal weighed 22 pounds (10 kg.); The whereabouts of this treasure is currently unknown. The east wing of this building was heavily damaged during the battle of Hue in 1968, but has since been repaired (see Tet offensive below). In addition to man-made disasters, nature has also been cruel to these buildings. The rains have induced rot, vegetation sprouting between the mortars is cracking the structure itself, and termites are destroying what the Tet battles had not. Restoration is proceeding with the aid of UNESCO and Hue's Preservation Service.

From the Noon gate we cross the bridge of Golden Waters over a lotus-filled moat leading to the gold-roofed Throne Room, or Palace of Supreme Harmony. The other buildings around the courtyard are roofed in green tiles. On the stone tiles of the two-level courtyard in front of the throne room, mandarins from all provinces genuflected to the emperor. The upper esplanade was used by the highest ranking mandarins and the lower by those of lesser rank. The civil mandarins stood on the left and the military on the right.

Imagine the courtyard filled with the spectacle of scholars dressed in colorful *ao dai* dress. This traditional costume is worn more by women now, but in the countryside older men might still be seen wearing one on a special occasion. The tile floor inside the Throne Room reflected a forest of dark red lacquer columns entwined with brilliant golden dragons. (Today, the room is a bit faded and one column has a splintered wound from rifle fire on it.) The once brilliant red and gold throne, inlaid with mirrors to ward off evil spirits, dazzled the mandarins who traveled here yearly from all over the kingdom. This is how Garstin saw the scene in the audience hall of former times: "The sword bearers in flowered purple, perfume-bearers in royal blue, fan-bearers in sky blue, waving enormous yellow feather fans, musicians and guardsmen, and the ranks

South gate to Imperial City

of mandarins, in their curious hats and gorgeous dragons-embroidered purple down on their noses kowtowing amid clouds of incense—and all that in a setting of blood-red lacquer scrawled with gold."

Physical Layout. Before going on, let us orient ourselves to some of the other buildings in the compound. Down a walled road behind and to the east (your right), as you face the Throne Room, is the former Royal Treasury building, now the Hue College of Fine Arts. Immediately behind the Throne Room, on the left and right sides of it, are royal offices where the administrative work of the empire was once done. In the building to the left behind the Throne Room, there is evidence of artillery shelling on the walls and on the blue tile floors. Twelve pillars hold up the roof and a large French-style mirror still hangs on the wall. Tall wooden French doors suggest the former glory of the building.

To the left of the patio of this "office" is a grassy area that was once the private living quarters of the emperor's family, his eunuchs, and his lovely concubines. The royal house had many names: the Great Within, *Dien Tho*, Everlasting Longevity Palace, the royal residence, the Forbidden Purple City. But by any name, it no longer exists. The site is now an overgrown meadow where cows sometimes graze.

Five hundred and fifty yards (500 m.) north of the Great Within, through that overgrown field, is the Serenity of Heart Lake and

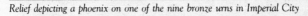

Relief depicting a phoenix on one of the nine bronze urns in Imperial City

a small airstrip, built by the French and later used by the US military. Much of the land around these buildings has been turned into vegetable or flower gardens. The mother of Bao Dai, the last Emperor of Vietnam, lived in Hue (although outside the palace grounds) until her death in 1980 at the age of 91. Before she died she contemplated the condition of the Imperial Palace: "I am sad, exceedingly sad. When I was young, Hue was beautiful. Then it was ruined."

Phung Tien Palace. A quiet path to the west (left when facing the throne) of the throne area, along a crumbling brick wall, leads to an enclosure called the Phung Tien Palace. This complex contains the The Mieu and the Hung Mieu, two ceremonial buildings. Just as you enter the courtyard between these two buildings, an ancient pine tree looms overhead. Frangipani and rich pink cassia trees also overhang the paths and are abloom in the spring.

Nine huge bronze dynastic urns, which were cast between 1835 and 1837, are the main feature of this compound. Placed in front of the Mieu, each urn (about nine feet/three m. tall) represents the exploits and achievements of the Nguyen Dynasty. The middle one

Dynastic urns

is on longer legs and set apart from the others. Each urn has a name and is unique in the 17 relief etchings on its bulbous belly. Note, for example, the details of the second urn in from the west, called Thuan. It depicts sabers, a waterfall, a pirogue (canoe) with nine pairs of rowers, trees, a water buffalo, and fish. Damage from rifle fire is visible on several of the urns. Legend has it that these urns were huge pots used to boil the emperor's enemies in oil.

Dinh Bo Linh (923-979) displayed in the courtyard of his palace at Hoa Lu a huge kettle and a caged tiger. He decreed that "Those who violate the laws will be boiled and gnawed." As a result of Dinh Bo Linh's decree, the large urns became symbolic of the emperor's power—these urns, however, show no evidence that they were ever used for this purpose.

The Phung Tien palace buildings built as a chapel to honor Gia Long, the founder of the dynasty, are now a museum displaying royal paraphernalia such as ten royal umbrellas plus altars of red and gold to honor the spirit of each Nguyen ancestor.

Tet Offensive. Remaining pretty much isolated during the wars with both the French and Americans, Hue, in 1968, was the site of fierce and prolonged fighting during a countrywide offensive by the People's Liberation Army and the North Vietnamese Army (NVA). On the night of January 31, the start of the Lunar New Year (Tet) celebration, fireworks not only ushered in the New Year of the Monkey, but drowned out the sound of gunfire. Soldiers of the 6th regiment of the NVA had attacked and occupied the eastern sectors of the citadel. The American MACV (Military Assistance Command-Vietnam) headquarters in the southern sector was also attacked. Assaults were simultaneously aimed at police headquarters, radio stations, homes of Americans, and those considered collaborators. On February 1, the Viet Cong flag flew from the tall and impressive flagpole on the southeast wall of the citadel and remained aloft for 24 days.

In the meantime, the hospital on the south bank of the river became a Communist command post; the Quoc Hoc school was commandeered and 2,000 prisoners were freed from the prison on the next block and given weapons to fight the Saigon troops. The Throne Room was taken over as a base of operations for a commando unit.

Company A of the First Battalion, First Marine Division, (Alpha 1/1) was sent from Phu Bai to retake the city. The marines quickly found themselves pinned down by enemy fire. Golf Company 2/5 arrived to help with longer-range weapons and found the thick stone walls of the citadel protected the enemy positions inside. The fighting was difficult and the advantage went to the revolution-aries because the marines, experienced in jungle warfare, were inexperienced in street fighting. To make matters worse for the Americans, the terrain was unfamiliar since no US units had ever been stationed inside the citadel. American and South Vietnamese commanders held back the heavy artillery to avoid destroying historic buildings, hoping the enemy would be quickly routed. The battle became a house-to-house fight. Units of the First Air Cavalry and the 101st Airborne Division were mobilized. Casualties on both sides were high, and thousands of civilians fled the fighting, quickly overtaxing makeshift relief facilities on the south bank.

After ten days of warfare, 60% of the citadel still remained in NVA/VC control and restrictions against bombing the historic citadel were lifted. In the days that followed, the citdadel was bombarded by US ships in the South China Sea and by 500-pound bombs dropped by Air Force F-4 Phantoms backed up by South Vietnamese A-1 Skyraiders. The fighting was followed daily by the American public in the press and on TV. After the citadel was retaken, American public opinion and President Johnson's own advisors put pressure on him to make stronger efforts to end the war. In March, Johnson announced he would not run for a second term as president.

The 1968 offensive recalls an earlier "surprise" Tet offensive in 1789. In Hanoi, King Le had asked the Chinese for military aid to help quell local rebellions led by Nguyen Hue. News of reinforcements by Chinese forces reached Nguyen Hue (later he became Emperor Quang Trung) in his capital at Hue. After rapidly recruiting an army of 100,000 men and 80 elephants, Nguyen Hue raced north at a remarkable speed. His men did not stop to eat but carried along *Banh Chung,* nutritious rice and meat cakes which resisted spoiling. Nguyen Hue's troops attacked the unprepared Chinese army while they were merrily celebrating the Lunar New Year.

Linh Mu Pagoda. Three miles west of the citadel on the same bank of the river is the stately seven-story Phuoc Duyen Tower or the Pagoda of the Heavenly Lady (sometimes called the Elderly Goddess). This pagoda, which has become symbolic of Hue's peaceful beauty, was built in 1844 on the site of an older 17th century pagoda, the Linh Mu. Each level is proportionately smaller than the one below it, giving the building a graceful, uplifting feeling. Each story has eight sides and a balcony around each level. Although the original pagoda building is gone, a stone stele from the Temple of Letters (which was once nearby) and the original pagoda's two-ton bell cast in 1710 are preserved. Each day the monks rang the bell 108 times to recall Buddhism's 108 illusions of life. The bell-ringing could be heard as far as seven miles (10 km.) away.

On display on the pagoda grounds is a gray-green sedan that played a pivotal role in the Buddhist protest of President Diem's repressive policies toward Buddhists. In Saigon on June 11, 1963, the car led a procession of monks; it halted on Le Van Duyet Street. While one of the monks (Thich Quang Duc) sat in meditation, his fellow monks drenched him with gasoline. The 66-year-old monk then lit a match. The gasoline ignited instantly and the ensuing flames burned him to death. Photographs of the politically motivated suicide stunned the world and drew attention to Diem's arbitrary treatment of Buddhists. The outspoken Madame Nhu, sister-in-law of President Diem, callously referred to the monk's action as a "barbecue."

Steps from the pagoda lead to a boat landing on the river. If you are offered a boat ride, avoid the huge, noisy, smelly diesel barge that is sometimes passed off as a sampan. Instead, hire an authentic sampan with a boat person to row you quietly past the citadel walls and out into the countryside.

Poking around the area surrounding the Dong Ba market is interesting for a few hours. The surrounding streets have been disrupted since the market is currently under renovation. There are small restaurants and coffee shops on Tran Hung Dao Street which runs between the market and the citadel wall.

A restaurant specializing in good Banh Khoai can be found at the the Thuong Tu gate which is west of the market between the bridges. Just outside the Thuong Tu gate, next to the citadel wall at the foot of Dinh Bo Linh Street, is the Lac Thanh restaurant. The street leading north of the market along the citadel wall is Phan Boi Chau. A grilled rice shop and the Quoc Te restaurant once stood behind the Tao Nhan's bar, popular eating spots for US civilians formerly stationed in the area.

THE SOUTH BANK OF THE PERFUME RIVER

The foreign quarters and the Imperial Tombs, including some on the north bank, are south of the Citadel along the banks of the Perfume (Huong Giang) River.

Banh Khoai, a specialty in Hue

WALKING TOUR OF THE OLD FRENCH SECTOR—HUE'S RIGHT BANK

The numbers in parenthesis refer to the locations on the Hue map. For a leisurely walk of about three hours along the wide, straight Le Loi Street which parallels the river, begin at the **Huong Giang Hotel** (1) (where you will probably be staying). This hotel was built in 1962 as a bachelor officers' quarters for officers of the former South Vietnamese Army.

Outside the Huong Giang Hotel is Le Loi Street. To your left is the Dap Da Bridge, which leads to a typical residential section. You might explore that part of town later if you have time, but for now proceed right (west) on Le Loi Street for its historical importance. Next to the hotel, on the shore of the river, is a boat ramp and the former **Customs House** (2). After walking three short blocks you will see the large compound of buildings on the left side of the street (3) that were once military barracks for the French and later for Republic of (South) Vietnam troops. The compound is now used by the Vietnamese Army. (No photos.) Continuing along Le Loi we come to **Doc Lap Park** (4) with a monument dedicated to the Vietnamese patriot Phan Boi Chau who inspired and directed an underground independence movement in Vietnam earlier in this century. In Phan Boi Chau's later years (1923–1940), the French-controlled

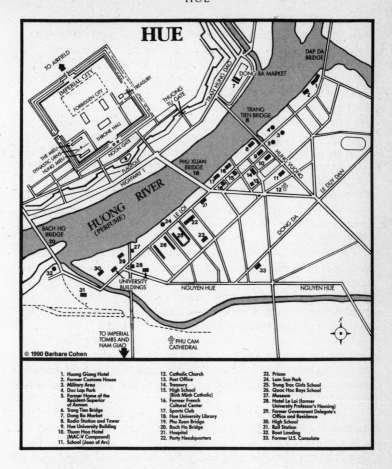

HUE

1. Huong Giang Hotel
2. Former Customs House
3. Military Area
4. Doc Lap Park
5. Former Home of the Resident-Superior of Annam
6. Trang Tien Bridge
7. Dong Ba Market
8. Radio Station and Tower
9. Hue University Building
10. Thuan Hoa Hotel (MAC-V Compound)
11. School (Joan of Arc)
12. Catholic Church
13. Post Office
14. Treasury
15. High School (Binh Minh Catholic)
16. Former French Cultural Center
17. Sports Club
18. Hue University Library
19. Phu Xuan Bridge
20. Bach Ho Bridge
21. Hospital
22. Party Headquarters
23. Prison
24. Lam Son Park
25. Trung Trac Girls School
26. Quoc Hoc Boys School
27. Museum
28. Hotel Le Loi (former University Professor's Housing)
29. Former Government Delegate's Office and Residence
30. High School
31. Rail Station
32. Boat Landing
33. Former U.S. Consulate

© 1990 Barbara Cohen

mandarins confined him in his hometown of Hue under "house arrest" to prevent him from organizing rebellions. The park has a refreshment stand that sells Hue beer and sweet soft drinks.

Opposite the park on the southeast corner of Hung Vuong Street was the living quarters of the **French Resident-Superior of Annam** (5). The older **Trang Tien Bridge** (6) (misspelled as Huong Tien in some histories) is a continuation of Hung Vuong Street. (Some older maps call it the Nguyen Huong Bridge—the street was once called Duy Tan Street.) If you are interested in exploring the wide variety of goods and produce at the colorful **Dong Ba market** (7), located on the other side of the river along the outside of the citadel walls, this bridge is the most direct route from the Huong Giang Hotel.

The **Radio Hue transmitting station** (8) was one of the first targets of the Communist Tet Offensive against the US in 1968. A bank and the Directorate of Budget of the Saigon Government once stood next to the radio station. Now the building functions as the city hall and Party headquarters. The **Hue University building,** *Su Pham Dai Hop* (9), stands on the opposite corner.

Walk on down Hung Vuong Street. Behind the university building, on the right and one block south, is the former **MACV (United States Military Assistance Command—Vietnam) compound** (10). The compound consisted of several two- and three-story buildings, including the converted French Grand Morin Hotel, now called the Thuan Hoa Hotel. The hotel once housed university professors and US personnel.

On the next block to the south is the former **Joan of Arc Catholic School** (11). Police and security offices are located on this intersection (Tran Cao Van and Hung Vuong). The **cathedral** (12), one block south, is a simple church (open for Sunday mass) with a single spire. Return to Le Loi Street by Le Dinh Dong Street, passing the **post office** (13) and former **Treasury** (14).

Once back on Le Loi Street, walk past the former **Binh Minh Catholic High School** (15) toward a lovely but fading building on the waterside at 13 Le Loi Street; this building was once the **French Information & Cultural Center** (16) and is now an official government building.

The former **Cercle Sportif,** along the waterside (17), is directly opposite the **Hue University Library** (18). This sports club and its tennis courts have endured since the French occupation. The Perfume (Huong) Hotel located in front of the sports club was once a a billet for officers serving in the Army of the Republic of Vietnam (ARVN) of the former Saigon regime.

The next bridge, **Phu Xuan** (19), is relatively new (since 1968). Prior to its construction, Highway One traffic crossed the old **Bach Ho railroad bridge** (20), visible at the western end of the street. The rail bridge had been built by the French Eiffel Company, which is currently helping to restore the country's rail system. From Hue, the highway passes around the Citadel and travels north to Hanoi.

The **City Hospital** (21) complex of 1,000 beds was built by the French. In addition to the hospital facilities, there was an associated training school in medical technology on the site. The next building on the same side of Le Loi Street is the current provincial-level **headquarters of the Binh Tri Thien Communist Party** (22) and the location of a Children's Palace in what was once the offices of the former Saigon regime's province chief. During the French regime, this building housed the offices of puppet mandarins who ruled Hue for the French. The Children's Palaces provide after-school activities and instruction in art, music, model making, sewing, and dance, similar to after-school enrichment programs in the US. The compound also contains a security office and a courtroom.

There is a **prison** (23) one block south of the river, behind Party headquarters. During the Tet offensive of 1968, Vietnamese prisoners were released and armed by the liberation forces. There is also a small park nearby on the waterside called **Lam Son** (24), after the birthplace of the historic hero, Le Loi. After World War I, a memorial was built here as a tribute to the Vietnamese who fought for France but did not return. There is a direct view from the park across the river to the flagpole of Hue's citadel, made famous by the "Viet Cong" flag that flew there for nearly a month during the 1968 Tet offensive.

The **Trung Trac High School** (25), formerly the Dong Khanh Girl's School, is named after the elder of the two Trung sisters, the national heroines who fought the Chinese invaders. The Dong Khanh student was noted for her graceful comportment, flowing *ao dais*, and shiny long black hair. Although the style of dress has changed, the girls of Hue are still lovely.

Next door to the Dong Khanh school is the counterpart school for males, the **Quoc Hoc School** (26), established in 1896 in the scholarly tradition of the Van Mieu in Hanoi. It was attended, at different times, by Ho Chi Minh, General Vo Nguyen Giap, Ngo Dinh Diem, and other influential figures from a variety of political persuasions in Vietnamese history. One story about Ho, who was admitted to the school in 1907, is particularly telling of the young radical's future. Tradition has it that when a protest by local peasants occurred the following year, Ho urged his classmates to join the peasants "as interpreters." Ho was expelled as being "rebellious."

Years later, the nationalist Phan Boi Chau, while under house arrest in Hue, was invited to lecture to the advanced students at the Quoc Hoc School. One student, Vo Nguyen Giap, must have paid close attention—Giap later became the general who led the Vietnamese Army to victory over the French, and later over the Americans. The school now conducts courses in vocational subjects such as electrical repairs and mechanics.

Just before the intersection on the river side of the street is the **Bao Tang Ho Chi Minh Museum** (27). This building once housed offices and the residence of the French-appointed government-delegate. Later, the Saigon regime also used this building for official business. Next door is the University Law School and opposite, in the triangle of the intersection of Le Loi and Nguyen Hue Streets, is the University Medical School. Just past the intersection is the university professors' housing complex that now serves as **Hotel 2 Le Loi** (28)—the site of the tragic makeshift refugee camp during the Tet offensive. A French villa-style building (29) near the river is the former **French Government Delegate's Office and Residence.**

At the very end of Le Loi street is the **Tong Hop High School** (30), formerly the Binh Linh Catholic School. Across a small bridge is the **old rail station** (31) and rail bridge. The **boat landing** (32), between the railroad station and the bridge, featured strategically in the US Marines' attempt to retake Hue during the 1968 Tet offensive. Southwest of this intersection are the Tu Dam pagoda and the Redemption Cathedral of Mother of Perpetual Help (also called Phu Cam Cathedral). In 1988, the church retained two Redemptorist priests in their 70s who were attempting to maintain the parish.

A three-block walk down Nguyen Hue Street leads to the intersection of Dong Da Street. The former **US consulate building** (33) is located on the south side of Dong Da.

IMPERIAL TOMBS

The imperial tombs are located toward the south and are not always open to the public. It is not advisable to go there without an official guide since there are no street signs and few people to help you find your way back.

Nguyen Rulers. There were 13 Nguyen rulers spanning 145 years (see list of Nguyen emperors). The tombs of six rulers are in the auspicious burial grounds to the south of the Imperial City. Some of the other kings died in exile and were buried on the Isle of Reunion, or Algiers. The gentle hills, valleys, streams, and forests of this locale make it a desirable burial ground for common people as well as the royal family.

The proper burial site of an ancestor is considered important since it can influence (positively or negatively) the lives of living descendants. The belief in geomancy (the influence of the spirits of the land on human matters) and omens remains alive in the people of Vietnam today. For centuries, grave site selection has been entrusted to geomancers, individuals who are knowledgeable concerning the favorable combination of ying and yang elements and the disposition of the five basic elements: fire, water, soil, metal, and wood.

Before President Diem's fall, his father's grave in this Hue burial ground was struck by lightning, a sign that was interpreted as an ill omen; rumors that disaster was about to befall the family spread quickly, causing a loss of confidence in Diem's leadership and perhaps contributed to his eventual assassination.

Tu Duc. Tu Duc's tomb is situated in a pine forest enclosed by a stone wall. The second son of Thieu Tri, Tu Duc had killed his older brother to gain the throne in 1847. The tomb area, a 30-acre (12-hectare), 50-monument city, which he called Eternity, was completed during his lifetime. Construction required hundreds of laborers, many of whom lost their lives from exhaustion in the process. In fact, Tu Duc mobilized the entire nation to complete the grand project. A couplet written at the time deplored the king's self-serving scheme:

"What kind of eternity is this *Eternity?*
Its walls are built of soldiers' bones.
Its moats are filled with the blood of the people."

In his lovely lakeside pavilion, Tu Duc wrote poems, drank lotus tea made from dew, and enjoyed eating meals which often consisted of 50 different dishes. In his private royal theater, one of the few private royal theaters in Asia, the obese emperor enjoyed the sensuous dances of his royal dance troupe.

The pavilion is an example of typical Vietnamese architecture. Examine the wooden roof supports done in the ancient architectural style modeled somewhat after Chinese building methods. When you visit this building, pause for a moment to enjoy the view of the lake and perhaps imagine yourself living the life of an emperor.

Opposite the lake is the terraced tomb site. The first level has gnarled trees now over 125 years old—first planted when the tomb was built. The stone stele has a biography of the emperor, and two towers symbolize his power and authority. The highest level features a huge set of copper doors designed to guard the tomb site.

After the emperor's death, his 104 concubines (he had no children) took up residence for the remainder of their lives in the little city surrounding his tomb. The emperor's body was buried somewhere on the highest terrace, but the workers who dug the grave were executed so that none could reveal the exact location. This severe protocol protected against theft of its treasures and desecration of the royal remains. Two years after Tu Duc's death, the French dug around the upper terrace in a failed attempt to find the body. In several places, the tiles around the tomb are irregular and unmatched, indicating where the French dug in their futile search; these tiles have never been replaced properly. After the reign of Tu Duc, the subsequent Hue emperors were essentially French servants. These pleasant surroundings are a popular spot for family groups, youths, and lovers who come to relax, play guitars, or simply hold hands.

Dong Khanh, the nephew and adoptive son of Tu Duc, was buried in the smallest of the Imperial tombs.

Khai Dinh. Khai Dinh was the son of Emperor Dong Khanh. His tomb is the most often photographed memorial, with its stone mandarins, horses, and life-size elephants. In the tradition of Vietnamese emperors, construction of the tomb was started before the monarch's death. Khai Dinh reportedly spent many relaxing hours at the tomb site during its construction. A flight of steps, with serpents slithering down its ramps, leads to a tableau inscribed with the emperor's virtues—both real and exaggerated.

Khai Dinh's memorial is a ferro-cement palace, the most "decorated" of all the Nguyen Dynasty tombs, encrusted from floor to ceil-

Restored emperor's residence

ing with glass and porcelain mosaics representing the four seasons. Intact vases and pottery were brought from all over the empire so that royal artists could break them into pieces of the size required for the murals. A vivid blue color, called Hue Blue, is characteristic of Hue porcelains. It is deeper than sky blue but not quite cobalt. Hue blue also adorns costumes of the Hue Royal musicians as well as the apparel worn by the imperial family. A dark green enameled tile is also characteristic of Hue ceramic workmanship. These tiles are difficult to reproduce since the old tile makers are no longer alive to share their trade secrets.

The tombs of Emperor Tu Duc and Khai Dinh represent the spectrum of Vietnamese architecture. Tu Duc's tomb was constructed in the traditional Vietnamese manner, without obvious Western influence. Khai Dinh's burial place combines aspects of both Vietnamese and French architecture, including the decorative styles of each culture.

The upper level of Khai Dinh's mausoleum presents a grand view of the countryside surrounding Mount Ngu Binh and the plain of tombs. A white statue of Quan Am, the Goddess of Mercy and Compassion, stands on a hillside to the south. In 1925, the traveler

Khai Dinh's tomb

Garstin, a spectator at Emperor Khai Dinh's funeral procession, wrote:

> At the head were two elephants hung with tassels and embroidered cloths and topped with crimson Howdahs and yellow umbrellas. Next came the palace musicians with their curious instruments and a Cinderella couch of vermillion lacquer scrawled over with golden clouds and dragons and drawn by a team of tiny white ponies. Behind them were a forest of umbrellas glowing like many-colored toadstools; forests of waving banners and oriflammes representing the five elements. Next came the Palace actors and after them red-painted booths containing the king's personal effects borne by twelve green-clad men. Next came gongs, paper lanterns, and paper vases filled with flowers. One hundred and sixty trained porters clad in black and white crouched under the red lacquer poles of the giant bier. Slips of bamboo had been placed between their teeth to keep them from chattering. Special bridges had to be built to accommodate it.

Khai Dinh's son, Bao Dai, was crowned emperor at the age of 12 and then spent nine years studying in France before assuming his father's throne. Bao Dai's rule ended in 1945 at the Noon gate entrance to the citadel when he abdicated his power by relinquishing his symbols of authority, a sword and a gold seal, to Ho Chi Minh's new government.

Duc Duc and His Predecessors. Duc Duc's tomb is the nearest to the city. He ruled for three stormy days in 1883, and was then jailed for the remainder of his life. The tombs of Gia Long and Minh Mang, Duc Duc's predecessors, are both located on the opposite side of the river. Gia Long eliminated his predecessor by having him torn apart by four elephants. Located near these tombs are the ruins of the Arena, a coliseum where emperors enjoyed watching the sport of trained elephants and tigers fighting each other to the death.

Nam Gio. About two miles (3.2 km.) directly south from the Noon gate entrance to the Imperial Palace is the Nam Gio, where the emperor performed ritual ceremonies as well as secular duties commensurate with his position as the high priest of the state. At one time, there was a royal road that crossed the Perfume River which led the emperor's procession directly to this sacred ritual site.

It is in the sandy soil of the area near the Nam Gio that hundreds of bodies (some reports estimated 3,000) were discovered after the 1968 Tet Offensive. The unearthed bodies are still a source of con-

NGUYEN DYNASTY

IMPERIAL NAME	DATES OF RULE
Gia Long	1802–1819
Minh Mang	1820–1840
Thieu Tri	1841–1847
Tu Duc	1848–1883
Duc Duc	1883 for three days
Hiep Hoa	1883 for four months
Kien Phuc	1884 for six months
Ham Nghi	1884–1885
Dong Khanh	1885–1889
Thanh Thai	1889–1907
Duy Tan	1907–1916
Khai Dinh	1916–1925
Bao Dai	1925–1945

troversy. Some investigators believe the bodies are officials of the Southern regime executed by the North Vietnamese and the National Liberation Front soldiers, who eliminated suspected enemies during the Tet attack. Others contend that the bodies may have been soldiers from both sides who died of injuries during the Tet attack and were hastily disposed of in a mass grave when the offensive failed.

QUANG TRI

The section of Highway One further north between Hue and Quang Tri has been called the "Street without Joy" because the French encountered especially tough resistance along this stretch during the Indochina War. In the US war, the Quang Tri area was also the site of many battles, with heavy losses on both sides. The old city of Quang Tri, which centers on an old citadel, sits on the bank of the Thach Ham River.

HOTEL

ACCOMMODATIONS

The two main tourist hotels in Hue for foreign visitors are on the south bank. These are the only two hotels for foreigners at this writing. You will prefer the view from the Huong Giang overlooking the river.

Huong Giang Hotel
51 Le Loi
tel. 2122

Thuan Hoa Hotel
7 Nguyen Tri Phuong
tel. 2553
This hotel seems to be reserved for East bloc advisers.

On the north bank, there are hotels for domestic use: the **Thuong Tu** at 5 Dinh Tien Hoang and the **Hang Be** at 173 Huynh Thuc Khang. The Tan May at Thuan An and the Dong Hoi in Dong Hoi are not geared for Westerners.

CUISINE

Huong Giang rice is lightly sautéed rice, seasoned with sesame seeds, herbs, dried shrimp, onions, and chilies. It has a nutty flavor.

Nem are meatballs of preserved (fermented) minced pork. The fermenting process gives the meat a bit of a sour taste. The meatballs are rolled up in a thin rice paper and then dipped in *tuong* sauce. *Tuong* sauce is a rich, nutty-flavored dipping sauce made with mung bean paste.

Com Hen is a rice with mussels. As appetizing as this dish may seem, you *must avoid* eating shellfish in Vietnam.

Banh Khoai, or happy pancake, is a crisp taco-like affair filled with meats and sprouts. It is dipped in *tuong* sauce made from bean paste and eaten with a garnish of fresh lettuce and mint.

A similar pancake-like dish of Hue is called *Banh Xeo*, which is less crisp than *Banh Khoai. Xeo* means "singing" or "sizzling" and refers to the sound the batter makes when poured into a hot pan.

Me Xung is a sweet jelly-like dessert studded with sesame.

SHOPPING

Non la, lovely conical hats made from rice husks, are a specialty of Hue. Hold one up to the light to see the design, which is hidden from view in ordinary light. Two birds or perhaps a flower or a short poem may be revealed. Let the vendor show you the variety of designs available. When you find one you like, you can compliment the workmanship by saying *"Dep Lam,"* or "very pretty."

HUE DIRECTORY

	Telephone
Binh Tri Thien Province Tourist Office, 51 Le Loi (in the Huong Giang Hotel)	2288/2355
Hue City Tourism, 18 Le Loi Street	3720/3577

Danang: Quang Nam-Danang Province

During the French occupation, the central seacoast city of Danang was called *Tourane,* a name that describes the shape of the bay of Danang which somewhat resembles a soup bowl (tureen). Danang is the capital of Quang Nam-Danang Province. Prior to the 1976 reorganization of provinces, Quang Nam-Danang was two provinces: Quang Da and Quang Nam. The area has a population of 350,000 people and one of the highest unemployment rates in the country.

HISTORY

Danang was once the center of the Indian-influenced state called Champa, formed in the second century. The Kingdom of Champa extended along the coast of present-day central Vietnam from the Hai Van pass (Annan Gate) in the north to Vung Tau in the south. In 1285, Marco Polo traveled in "Chamba" and described extensive forests of trees producing dark wood. The peripatetic Polo wrote: "The people are idolaters and pay a yearly tribute to the great Khan which consists of elephants and nothing but elephants . . . The king had 326 children."

The Chams reached a high degree of skill in architecture which can be seen in their temples of red brick still standing along the coast of central Vietnam. Among the most famous of these temple ruins is the Mi Son archaeological site outside Danang.

Incursions by the French. French missionaries, having a difficult time under the emperor's laws that outlawed proselytizing, favored a military expedition to force the emperor into permitting concessions to the French. In 1856, Napoleon III approved an expedition to pressure Emperor Tu Duc to open up Vietnam for trade. In August 1858, a man-of-war, commanded by Admiral Rigault de Genouilly, sailed into Danang's port. The admiral had planned to land at the Imperial Palace at Hue, but the estuary surrounding Hue was too shallow for the draft of his Western sailing ship. Instead, he fired at Danang's coastal defenses and landed troops to set up a fortress.

The Vietnamese General Nguyen Tri Phuong formed a resistance movement against the French, who did manage to entice some local inhabitants to collaborate with them. Danang finally fell, despite the fierce resistance put up by the courageous General Nguyen Tri Phuong. One wall (called Nguyen Tri Phuong Wall in honor of the early resistance leader) remains of an old French fort on the bank of the Thu Bon River.

The soldiers of Rigault de Genouilly were devastated by the same problems which were to harass later attempts at conquest: heat, disease, and the intense hostility of the local population. The only ground firmly held by the French after a year of fighting was the burial grounds of the hundreds of soldiers who had died of cholera and typhoid. In any case, the defeated Court of Hue, which cared for its dynastic interests, eventually yielded Tourane (Danang) to the French.

The population rose up against the French in the August Revolution in 1945, but the freedom won was short-lived. The French returned. Following the First Resistance War which ended in 1954, the country south of the 17th parallel was aided by Americans, who had taken over the anti-communist fight from the French.

The Vietnam War. On March 8, 1965, the first battalion of American Marines to arrive in Vietnam landed on the coast of Danang. Although this contingent of Marines "hit the beach" at "Red Beach" in amphibious landing craft, most marines arrived later by plane. Slated initially solely for defense of the Danang air base, which coordinated bombing missions along the Ho Chi Minh trail and north of the DMZ, the Marines soon took the offensive. During the increased American military presence that ensued, Danang became the site of the largest jet runway in South East Asia. Located west of the city, the airfield stretched almost the length of the city. The frequency of artillery fire aimed at the air base gave Danang the nickname "Rocket City." Danang's sizable American population was second only to Saigon's.

Empty hangars are all that remain of the Danang air base and the former Marine air field at the foot of Marble Mountain; the vast US military complexes, which once seemed to be cities in themselves, have all but disappeared with little to indicate that they had ever existed.

HIGHLIGHTS FOR
TRAVELERS

If you are staying at one of the hotels in the city, you can explore at your leisure. If you are fortunate enough to be on the beach, a trip or two into town will probably be enough to satisfy your curiosity.

The main waterfront street, Bach Dang, is about two miles long from the Nguyen Van Troi bridge on the south to the tip of the peninsula on the bay on the north. Danang is the birthplace of the Vietnamese commando Nguyen Van Troi after whom the bridge, built by the US Marines across the Han River, is now named.

CHAM MUSEUM

In addition to its military history, the main attraction of Danang City is the Cham Museum at the intersection of Trung Nu Vuong and the riverside street of Bach Dang. Note: There is a playground behind the Cham Museum where children can enjoy riding in miniature airplanes.

The museum contains about 300 stone art treasures. The French discovered and understood the importance of the Cham sculptural works and set up the museum under the auspices of the *École Française d'Extrême-Orient* (French Institute for Far Eastern Studies). This building, constructed in 1935, is essentially a series of open-air alcoves which affords the collection little security or protection from the elements. Much of the art heritage of Champa was transported to France during the French-colonial period. Some artifacts were shipped by personnel of the French Institute for Far Eastern Studies for study and exhibitions; other pieces were stolen and sold to wealthy international collectors.

Religious Influences. The combined philosophies and religious ideologies of Buddhism and Hinduism, as well as Islam, influenced the Cham culture. The kings of Champa adopted Indian-type names and were worshiped as god-kings. Eastern tastes also filtered their way into Cham art, which is similar the Khmer art, with some distinguishing features. The Chams carved three-dimensional sandstone figures that were displayed on pedestals so as to be visible all around; Khmer artists produced flatter, two-dimensional bas relief works of art. In addition to supporting statuary, the Cham pedestals were also used to display large phalluses of stone called *lingas*.

Cham portrayals of human features reflects their distinct racial characteristics: thick lips topped by wide mustaches, flat noses, heavily lidded eyes, and joining eyebrows. Cham stonework seems heavier, less crisply etched, earthier, and less elegant than Khmer sculpture at the Angkor ruins. While the museum does not have a gift shop, sandstone reproductions of some of these lovely pieces can be purchased at the Marble Mountain village and in shops around town.

Museum Layout. A large map in the museum's room #4 indicates existing Cham architectural sites and may be consulted for an overview before going sequentially through the rooms, each of which represents a phase in the art and history of Champa.

Room #1 contains works from the Mi Son excavation site. Most

Cham sculpture, Cham Museum

centrally placed is an altar fragment image of Skanda, the general of celestial armies and son of Shiva. He stands proudly on a peacock's back with the tail of the peacock spread out in a graceful oval behind him. A frieze, dating from the seventh century, features a wonderful depiction of a flute player. One of Champa's masterpieces, the eight-century female figure of a goddess, probably Shiva's wife, Uma, is also on display. Other treasures include Ganesha, the elephant-god; Garuda, the mythical bird-god with his eagle's beak, wings, and feathers; and Nandin, the white bull.

The next room exhibits works from Tra Kieu, once the capital of Champa, located near Mi Son on the banks of the upper reaches of the Thu Bon River. (Chinese records describe a battle between

Cham statue, Cham Museum

the Chinese Sui Dynasty Army and the Chams which took place at Tra Kieu in 605. The Chinese took home booty that included a library of 1,350 works, trained elephants, an orchestra, and 18 golden tablets.) Several of the statues from Tra Kieu honor the Hindu deities Shiva and Uma. The feminine figures are sensuous in both their voluptuous figures and their graceful poses. Durga, the wife of Shiva in her aggressive form, holds in her four hands a discus, a mace, a conch shell, and a lotus.

Works from the Dong Duong archaeological find, the Buddhist center of Champa in the tenth century, are in the third room. The first Cham statues of Buddha were unique to this period. The ornamentation style of the time exudes a wild energy expressed with complicated worm-like patterns.

The last room contains artifacts from the Thap Nam and Binh Dinh period of the tenth to 14th Centuries. When the Viets sacked the Cham capital of Indrapura, the Chams regrouped to the south at Binh Dinh where they made their new capital. The glory of Champa, however, was in its decline. The graceful style of the earlier period gave way to a style that depicted crude, barbarous strength. Terrified of external dangers from the Khmers and Vietnamese, the Chams invented fantastic animals to protect themselves.

An American, John White, traveled to Vietnam in 1819 (see section on Saigon) and spent some time at Danang. Upon his return to America, he published his experiences in A *History of a Voyage to the China Sea,* in which he wrote of the indigenous artwork: ". . . rude sculptures and paintings of monstrous animals, and incongruous shapes the hideous productions of a fantastic and vulgar imagination."

By the end of the 14th or early in the 15th century, Champa had been absorbed by the Vietnamese. Today, Cham descendants live along the seacoast where they maintain their language, style of dress (men and women wear sarongs), music, and distinct rituals concerning the dead.

WALKING TOUR STARTING AT
THE DOWNTOWN HOTELS

Numbers in parentheses refer to locations on the map of downtown Danang. A walking tour oriented from the downtown area follows:

There are state-run shops and cafés in the vicinity of the two major downtown hotels: the **Eastern** or **Oriental (Phuong Dong)**

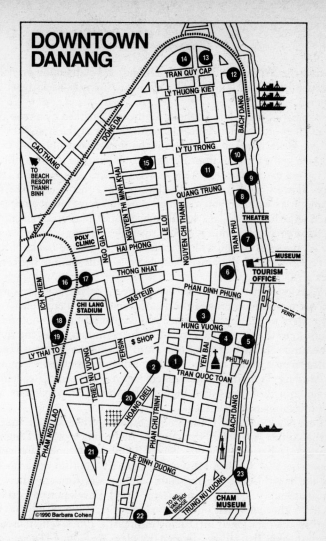

DOWNTOWN DANANG

TRAN QUY CAP
LY THUONG KIET
DONG DA
CAO THANG
TO BEACH RESORT THANH BINH
BACH DANG
LY TU TRONG
QUANG TRUNG
NGUYEN THI MINH KHAI
LE LOI
HAI PHONG
POLY CLINIC
NGO GIA TU
THONG NHAT
ICH KHIEM
PASTEUR
CHI LANG STADIUM
NGUYEN CHI THANH
PHAN DINH PHUNG
TRAN PHU
THEATER
MUSEUM
TOURISM OFFICE
FERRY
HUNG VUONG
YEN BAI
PHU THU
YERSIN
$ SHOP
LY THAI TO
TRIEU NU VUONG
TRAN QUOC TOAN
HOANG DIEU
PHAM NGU LAO
PHAN CHU TRINH
LE DINH DUONG
TRUNG NU VUONG
BACH DANG
TO NG VAN TIEU BRIDGE
CHAM MUSEUM

©1990 Barbara Cohen

Note: Information in parentheses refers to former name.

1. Hotel Phuong Dong
2. Hotel Thai Binh Duong
3. Theatre/Assembly Hall
4. Department store
5. Hon Produce Market
6. Bank
7. Post Office
8. Danang Party headquarters (Former French City Hall)
9. Seaman's Club
10. Former French Court House
11. School
12. Former US Consulate (now Workers' Club)
13. Hotel Danang
14. Hotel Dang Do
15. "Alamo"
16. Cao Dai Pagoda
17. Protestant Church
18. Trade and Handicraft Exhibition Hall
19. Con Market
20. Market
21. Pha Da Pagoda
22. Tam Bao Pagoda (Tinh Hoi)
23. Former US Press Center

(1) and the **Western (Thai Binh Duong)** (2). Charming French-style buildings, fading but basically intact, line the backstreets in this area.

The two-spired white **Catholic Cathedral** (marked by a cross on the map) is on Phu Thu Street, one block east of the hotels.

One block north of the hotels is the **theater/assembly hall** (3). A bike parking lot is in front of the theater. Instead of bikes filling the lot on the Lunar New Year (Tet), the area is filled with balloons, flowers, and goldfish. Walking toward the river on Hung Vuong Street will lead you to a small state-run **department store** (4) which sells, for US dollars, locally made handicrafts and souvenirs. The **Hon produce market** is on the riverside at **Hung Vuong Street** (5). At the market, you will be walking across the rail tracks of the riverside rail system that once extended to a point south of the Ferry Dock.

Walking north along the riverside street (Bach Dang), you will pass the ferry which crosses the Han River to the Peninsula. You may wish to mingle with the locals while traveling on the short ferry excursion to the Peninsula. Note: On the peninsula across the river is the former headquarters of the Third Marine Amphibious Force (called "Three MAF" by the US Marines) which is now a Vietnamese Military Training Center called Nguyen Ai Quoc Academy, after one of the names used by Ho Chi Minh (See Appendix for brief biography of Uncle Ho).

One block north of Hung Vuong Street on the riverside street, on the corner of Thong Nhat Street, is the office of the **Danang Tourism Department;** inside you will find a gift and handicraft shop. The **War Crimes Museum** is near the tourism department and the Ferry Dock; the museum building was formerly the US Consulate and Civil Operations and Rural Development Service (CORDS) headquarters, once nicknamed the "White Elephant" by US personnel stationed in Danang during the 1960s. The museum has a theater that shows foreign movies, including *Platoon,* an American-made feature film about the Vietnam war.

On Thong Nhat Street, one block inland from the river, is the old **French bank building** (6). Back on the riverside street, you will pass the **post office** (7) at the corner of Thong Nhat Street. Further north on Bach Dang is the former city hall, a French-style villa that is now the **Provincial Party Headquarters** (8).

On the dockside, across Quang Trung Street, is the former US Navy club which is still a club, now called the **Seaman's Institute** (9).

DANANG

The old **Café Select** on the riverfront at 42 Bach Dang is now
a canteen *(cang tien)*. Frequented at one time by US military personnel, the cafe still has grenade screens intact over its windows. To
thwart grenade attacks by the "Viet Cong," gratings had been
placed over windows of restaurants patronized by Americans.

On Tran Phu Street, one block west, is the **French elementary
school** (11), now a high school. The former **French Court House**
(10) was located at the corner of Tranh Phu and Ly Tu Trong
Streets. Along the waterfront on the north end of the city is the
former the **US Consulate Building,** now a workers' club (12).

Two **hotels** (13 and 14) on the tip of the peninsula were once
US military and civilian billets. A villa nearby that housed Americans during the war was nicknamed the **Alamo** (15).

Walk southwest past the Polyclinic Hospital (also called Hospital "C"), past the **Protestant church** (17) and the **Cao Dai pagoda**
(16) to the huge **Trade and Handicraft Exhibition Hall** (18) next
to the **Chi Lang Sports Stadium.** The Exhibition Hall displays industrial and handicraft products from Quang Nam-Danang province. The **Con Market** (19), which sells a variety of poor-quality
merchandise, is located in front of the Exhibition Hall. You could
end your walking tour at the Exhibition Hall and return to your
hotel. If you would like to spend another hour or so people-watch-
ing, you can continue on Ly Thai another 3/4 of a mile (1.2 km.)
or hail a passing cyclo (a three-wheeled pedal-driven vehicle) to
visit the lakeside "March 29 Park"—the date refers to the takeover
of Danang by the People's Liberation Army in 1975.

Just south of the **Hotel Phuong Dong** (Eastern or Oriental Ho-
tel) is a small **market** (20). The **Pha Da pagoda** (21) is between Ich
Khiem Street and Trieu Nu Vuong Street. A larger pagoda, the
Tam Bao (22), is located a few blocks west of the Cham Museum.

The Tam Bao pagoda, also called Tinh Hoi, made television
news around the world when, in May 1966, local Vietnamese military forces rebelled against Marshall Ky's forces, trapped 40 Western
reporters inside the pagoda as "witness hostages," and opened fire
upon them when they tried to leave. The intensity of the drama
escalated when, at the same time, Tran Quoc Toan Street, which
runs past the cathedral, filled with hundreds of Buddhist monks and
nuns who blocked traffic in a protest-hunger strike against the Saigon government's war machinery.

Just across the street from the Cham Museum is the former **US
Press Center** (23) building that overlooks the riverfront; according
to guides, the building now harbors a shrimp cannery.

HOI AN

Once a busy international trading port of the Cham empire, Hoi An is situated at the estuary of the Thu Bon River, just 13 miles (20.8 km.) south of present-day Danang.

History. During the 16th century, the Nguyen lords fostered international trade in the Danang area. The port of Hoi An welcomed Japanese, Indian, and Chinese traders traveling between China and India. In the spring, trading ships from the north followed the northeast monsoon south to Hoi An, where they remained until the next summer when favorable southwest winds took their sailing ships home. For the intervening four months, visiting merchant-sailors traded, and the Vietnamese port-of-call bustled with activity.

Portuguese tradesmen settled at Hoi An and in 1614 Portuguese missionaries founded a Catholic mission there. Later, Jesuits, who had been expelled from Japan in an anti-Western purge, found new hope for converts at Hoi An. The Jesuit linguist, Alexander de

Japanese bridge in Hoi An

Rhodes, was assigned to the mission at Hoi An (also called Fai Fo) in 1625. The Dutch established shops in the port city between 1636 and 1641 but left after their sponsors, the Trinh clan, lost power.

When the Chinese Ming dynasty was overthrown by the Manchus, many Ming mandarins from the coastal cities of southern China sought refuge in Hoi An. Citizens from various cities of China settled down together in localities called Minh Huong communes. Each commune erected its own temple to the protector gods of the sea; 20 or so of these distinct Chinese temples still remain.

Masts of exotic ships bobbed at anchor offshore as smaller cargo boats carried merchandise from the larger ships to the merchants' wharfside shops. Goods were unloaded through the back door into the shops. The main street of Hoi An, called China Street, lined with an unbroken row of shops four miles long, ends at the Japanese Bridge, called Lai Vien Kieu.

Japanese and Chinese refugees (and opportunists) had arrived in Hoi An at roughly the same time. Each maintained their own governor, legal codes, and traditional ways. A quaint wooden covered bridge connects the Japanese (Cam Pho) district with the Chinese Minh Huong villages. The bridge was built between the years 1593, the year of the monkey, and 1596, the year of the dog. To commemorate these dates, the builders placed two stone monkeys, with their hands piously folded, at one end of the bridge and two stone dogs at the other end. A center way allowed carts and vehicles to cross the river and the narrow sidewalk must have been jammed with pedestrians carrying bundles of merchandise on shoulder poles. A small pagoda on the center of the bridge was dedicated to the "monster that trembles in the earth"—a reference that the Japanese had transported their fear of earthquakes across the sea to their new home.

In 1637 the Japanese government shut its doors to foreign trade. As a result, the Japanese population of Hoi An soon dropped to a mere half a dozen families. The Chinese, however, remained and prospered filling in the trade gaps left by the departing Japanese.

Architectural Heritage. Because the Thu Bon estuary has filled with silt over the years, the area's sea commerce gradually shifted north to the deeper waters found in the Bay of Danang, at the mouth of the Han River. Today, Hoi An is remarkable for its preservation of original Chinese temples and the glorious homes of wealthy merchants from the past. Some of these grand residences are opened for visitors to study the architecture while pondering

Typical traditional roof structure in Hoi An

what life was once like in these communities. Note the detail work such as curved ornamental tile roofs, a set of eyes carved over a doorway, intricate door panels, carved wooden fish whose tails support roof beams, and the excellent quality of the wood on the homes at 37 Tran Phu Street and 77 Bach Dang Street.

Hoi An is near Kim Bong, a village of woodworking families who have been carving statues and furniture since ancient times. The woodworkers of Kim Bong frequently incorporate marble from nearby Marble Mountain into their furniture designs. Hoi An also specializes in the craft of carpet weaving.

MARBLE MOUNTAIN (NGU HANH SON)

Six miles from downtown Danang, five jagged crests jut above sand dunes on the edge of the sea. There is a legend about these rocks: A young man was lost in a storm at sea. His boat was wrecked and he clung desperately to a log. Just as his strength was about to give out, he was saved by a giant turtle. The youth asked how he could return the good deed. The turtle gave the youth a large egg to care for. The grateful boy handled it carefully, covered it with warm

Security guards at Marble Mountain

sand, and protected it from predators. One day the egg, huge by now, cracked open into five pieces; to the surprise of the lonely youth, a beautiful maiden emerged. She said "I am the spirit of the turtle. Thank you for caring for me." They were happily married but both knew that some day the girl would have to return to the sea. One day she turned into a turtle and crawled back into the sea. The five pieces of her cracked eggshell remain as marble hills on the beach, a testimony to the truth of this tale.

Water Mountain. Each of the rocks is dedicated to one of the basic elements: water, fire, metal, earth, and wood. The rocks are honeycombed with cave-shrines. Water Mountain (Mt. Thuy Son) is the largest and its most beautiful cave is the Huyen Khong Grotto. Climb its 157 steep steps of gray and orange marble and stop for a breather at the active monastery at the Trang Thiem Pagoda. On the left, behind the small temple and through a gate, a walkway leads to a natural opening in the face of the mountain that brings one into an awesome 80-foot-high cavern. Eerie sunlight enters and tangles of vines protrude through the natural openings in the rock ceiling. Statues of spirit guards and lesser mortals in vivid primary colors stand in silent vigil. Twenty-foot-tall statues of Buddha have been carved in the marble. The walls are etched with graffiti, some ancient and pious, and still others neither ancient nor pious.

Water Mountain was sacred to the Hindu Chams, but the small Hindu statues and Sanskrit writings that once filled the niches of the walls of this cave are no longer visible. At one time, the cave featured stalactites and stalagmites which rang when struck. These formations have since been broken off. In the rainy season, water drips continuously, moss grows on the walls, and the sweet scent of 1,000 years of incense burning lingers in the air.

A simple plaque is dedicated to the men of the People's Liberation Army who fired mortars and rockets from these caves to destroy 18 American aircraft at the US airfields below. This cave also hosted local groups who performed anti-feudalist operettas in the old days and anti-American operettas during the time of the American presence. After exploring the nooks and crannies of this cave-shrine, take the path to the right of the monastery into an open terrace. At the right is a large urn and, behind it, another cave.

Lookout points give panoramic views of the sea and a white sandy beach. The island visible 15 miles to the east is Cham Island. The water is wonderfully warm all year round. If you plan to be near this area, remember to bring along a swimsuit for a refreshing swim. Through a natural arc, narrow steps lead down to another temple and gardens ritually maintained by the community of monks.

At the foot of the mountain at Ngu Hanh Son, the local marble cutters fashion art objects from white and gray stone. Some of these objects, such as the inexpensive simple marble bracelets, are small enough to carry home easily and make unique gifts.

"China Beach" was once an in-country rest and recreation center for the US military. The US Army also ran the 95th Evacuation Hospital north of China Beach. The women who were stationed at the hospital, nurses, USO, Red Cross, and Special Services, are featured as the subject of a current US television series named "China Beach." The beach is now called My Khe and is not frequented by Western tourists.

MI SON

If special arrangements have been made, a visitor might be able to visit the archaeologic site at Mi Son. This center of Cham culture, 45 miles (72 km.) from Danang, was founded in a sacred hollow encircled by rugged mountain terrain. During the American presence, the area was declared a "free-fire zone" and Mi Son was damaged by bombardments. An arduous and hot six-mile hike (go early, bring water) uphill through the jungle is rewarded with a glimpse of a culture that reached its prime before the discovery of America. The Mi Son site is in the process of restoration with the help of Polish art historians.

HO CHI MINH TRAIL

At times visitors are offered a side trip from Danang to the Ho Chi Minh trail which weaves through this mountainous area. This ancient network of paths was used by silk and opium traders. One pilot described this elaborate network of interweaving trails (through which supplies traveled from Hanoi to the guerrillas in the south) as ". . . not so much a straight road, but a plate of spaghetti." Present-day travelers are shocked and impressed at the harsh conditions endured by the People's Liberation Army and the North Vietnamese Army in transporting supplies and personnel. Caravans of modified bicycles called "Steel Horses," carrying up to 100 pounds (220 kg.) each, plodded along in ankle-deep mud. Spaced at a distance of one's day walk were rest stops and communication centers. Now large trucks traverse a paved road called Ho Chi Minh Boulevard.

HAI VAN PASS

Visible on the roadside on the way out of Danang city, there is a large white statue of Buddha that had been erected by refugees from Hue in thanks for their survival after the 1968 Tet offensive. "Welcome Travelers" is inscribed at the base of the statue.

Next, on Highway One between Danang and Hue, there is a spectacular stretch of scenery where the mountains seem to fall into the sea at the Hai Van Pass, or "Pass of the Clouds." In addition to its aesthetic appeal, Hai Van Pass is the site of a historic seesaw struggle between several nations. For centuries this natural wall kept the northern Viets from conquering Champa. Hai Van Pass was the dividing line between the north and the south in both geographic and political terms in the past. The area is a virtual museum of

Vietnam's past wars: a large brick tower which was part of a wall fortification built in the Nguyen dynasty still stands; Japanese pill-boxes are scattered about; at the top of the hill, there is a French fort built in 1945 that is black, sinister, and solid in the mist. Look carefully among the weeds and you will discover French guns and unexploded ordinance. Don't touch: this site must not be disturbed since some of the shells are still live! Stay on the path as there may be old land mines as well. If you have the energy and the time to hike up the hill, you will see the remains of American gun emplacements and a helicopter pad.

The charming fishing village of Phu Loc beckons for a photo stop further along on the road to Hue.

The section of Highway One further north between Hue and Quang Tri has been called the "street without joy" because the French encountered especially stubborn resistance along this stretch during the Indochina War. This area was the site of many battles and heavy losses on both sides.

A section of the Reunification Railroad linking Hanoi to Ho Chi Minh City runs close to Highway One between Hue and Danang. The restoration of the rail system between the north and the south symbolizes Ho Chi Minh's concept that "The country is one and cannot be divided." The Hanoi-Vinh line, despite being heavily bombed in the 1960s, was constantly repaired and kept in operation to supply the south. The rail system essentially stopped running in 1961 because of frequent sabotage in the south. Recently, the Soviet Union has supplied equipment and the French Eiffel Company has helped in the reconstruction of a section from Danang south to Phu Cat in the southern part of Nghia Binh province.

HOTEL
ACCOMMODATIONS

There are two main hotels for foreigners in downtown Danang that are in close proximity to each other:

Thai Binh Duong (Pacific)
80 Phan Chu Trinh
tel. 22137/622921
Rooms are small and it is not as well maintained as the Phuong Dong.

Phuong Dong (Eastern)
93 Phan Chau Trinh
tel. 22654/21266

The rooms have air-conditioning. From the rooftop restaurant of
the Phuong Dong, there is a view of the surrounding mountains,
the tall lights of the soccer stadium to the northwest, and the spires
of the Catholic cathedral where masses are held on Sundays. To the
north is Monkey Mountain (named by American servicemen), the
peak of Tien Sa Mountain (Son Tra on present-day maps), which
projects onto one tip of the beautiful bay. While the US was there,
a large radar dish adorned the peak to guide bombing flights heading
north.

There are other hotels in the north end of the city which are
not usually assigned to Western travelers: the Dong Da and the
Danang.

Huu Nghi Hotel
10 Ly Thuong Kiet
tel. 21101

The Huu Nghi is reserved for domestic travelers, but has a souvenir and art shop as well as dancing to live music.

Non Nuoc Hotel (8.7 miles [13 km.] from downtown)
tel. 21470/22137

This hotel is on the peninsula on the beach of the South China
Sea. Groves of graceful filao trees secure the sand with their roots
to prevent erosion. The resort has a "summer camp" atmosphere.
At night you can watch the moon rise over the South China Sea
and, at certain times of the year, a sparkling phosphorescence of
bioluminescent organisms is stirred up by the waves.

CUISINE

Tu Du on Tran Phu Street near the Eastern (Phuong Dong) Hotel
serves some tasty dishes. One dish, called "Sea Slug" soup, actually
consists of fine slices of eel that have the appearance and texture of
mushrooms. Two other restaurants in this area are Kim Do and Binh
Da.

DANANG DIRECTORY

	Telephone
Bank for Foreign Trade	22110
Quang Nam-Danang Tourism, 48 Bach Dang, Danang	21423/22213/22212
Telex: 8216 DNTC	
Air Vietnam Office	21130

Nhatrang:
Phu Khanh Province

Nhatrang, capital of Phu Khanh Province, is located on the coast of South China Sea, 30 miles (50 km.) north of Cam Ranh Bay. Known as Khanh Hoa province under Emperor Minh Mang, the province was renamed Phu Khanh in 1976. Dai Lanh beach, called Cape Varcella during the French occupation, lies 50 miles (83 km.) north of Nhatrang and is the eastern-most point of Vietnam's mainland.

Nhatrang, in addition to its allure as a site of the ancient Cham culture, has one of the most beautiful beaches in the country. Set against a backdrop of mountains, Nhatrang is located on a three-mile (5 km.) long crescent-shaped beach of fine, smooth white sand. The beach is sheltered from winds by hills and the temperature never reaches intolerable levels. The port of Cau Da is on the southern tip of the city; the northern border is marked by the River Cai.

The romantic ambience of this area is enhanced by the delicate perfume of cinnamon that drifts down from Mt. Thien Thai and the incense trees of Van Gia forest. Ornamental plants and coconut trees add to the charm of local houses and French-style beach villas. At night, soft lights of fishing boats bob up and down to the rhythm of the gentle tides. A popular song, *Nhatrang Ngay Ve,* reflects this feeling:

White sand at night.
Holding your lover in your arms.
Listening to the whispering of the waves . . .

HIGHLIGHTS
FOR TRAVELERS

DIEN KHANH WALL

Several miles west of town is an earthen defensive structure called the Dien Khanh wall. The fortification, which has four gates, was constructed in 1793 by Prince Nguyen Phuc Anh, who later reigned as Emperor Gia Long.

PO-NAGAR

The Cham ruins of Po-Nagar (a complex of three brick buildings) dates from the seventh century and overlooks the sea near the Xom Bong Bridge (see the discussion of Cham civilization in the section on Danang). Considered sacred and a source of miraculous cures, the site is a Mecca for the sick and infirm who come here seeking alms, or a change of fate.

Thap Ba. Thap Ba (Lady or Mother of the Land and Water) tower has existed for nine centuries. Legend has it that the immortal princess Thien Ya Na teaches and guides farmers from her lofty domain. Made of baked bricks, once covered with stucco, the tower walls are decorated with carved figures of heavenly dancers, *Nandin* (sacred bulls), and *Hamsa* (sacred geese). Prince Bac Hai is worshipped in the second tower, located in the center. The third tower represents a woodcutter, the foster father of the Princess.

Chong Rock. In the area surrounding the ruins, hundreds of boulders are stockpiled on top of each other. On one very large boulder, the Chong (husband) rock, there is an impression believed to be the imprint of a large palm. Some say this impression is the imprint of Buddha's own hand. Others have a more fanciful explanation for the strange phenomenon: Just after the creation of the earth, the area was cooled and watered by streams. Each summer, fairies from heaven came down to bathe in a nearby stream, named Fairy Stream by the local people. One summer, a giant came upon the bathing fairies and, distracted by his infatuation with the lovely creatures, he stumbled and left a huge footprint. The palm print was made when he tried to grasp another rock to regain his balance.

The giant of legend must have been extremely large since Fairy Stream is 6 miles (10 km.) from Chong rock. Other local natural phenomena related to this legend include a fairy grotto, a fairy chessboard, and the belt of the lovesick giant.

TRUNG NGHIA PAGODA

One of Nhatrang's landmarks is the Trung Nghia Pagoda, also known as the Temple of the Flying Dragon. Located on top of a hill to the north of the city, the pagoda was built in the time of Emperor Gia Long to honor the mandarins and soldiers who had aided the reunification of the country.

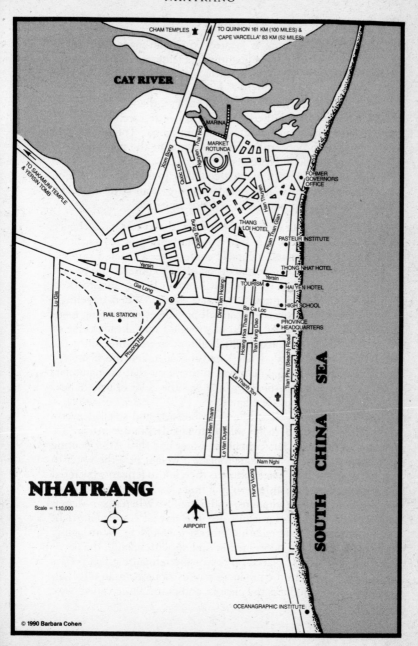

CHAM TEMPLES

TO QUINHON 161 KM (100 MILES) &
"CAPE VARCELLA" 83 KM (52 MILES)

CAY RIVER

MARINA

MARKET
ROTUNDA

Xom Bong

Quoc Lo 1

Nguyen Thai Noc

TO SAKAMUNI TEMPLE
& YERSIN TOMB

FORMER
GOVERNORS
OFFICE

Quang Trung

THANG
LOI HOTEL

Han Thuyen

Phan Thon Gian

PASTEUR INSTITUTE

Yersin

THONG NHAT HOTEL

Gia Long

Yersin

TOURISM

HAI YEN HOTEL

Dinh Tien Hoang

Ba Ca Loc

HIGH SCHOOL

Lu Gia

RAIL STATION

Hoang Hoa Tham

Tran Hung Dao

PROVINCE
HEADQUARTERS

Phuong Hiep

Le Thanh Ton

Tran Phu (Beach) Road

SOUTH CHINA SEA

To Hien Thanh

Le Van Duyet

Nam Nghi

Hung Vuong

NHATRANG

Scale: 1:10,000

N

AIRPORT

OCEANAGRAPHIC INSTITUTE

© 1990 Barbara Cohen

FISHERIES

The Tri Nguyen Institute is located on a man-made lake to the south of town. The fish-breeding institute features a natural aquarium and museum associated with the facility's shrimp and fish hatcheries.

In addition to the new Tri Nguyen Fishery, there is the Institute of Oceanography and Fisheries at Cau Da, a research center that classifies and catalogues marine flora and fauna. The center also conducts research concerning improvements in the preparation of fish flour and extracting fish fats and oil.

At one time, day trips by boat could be arranged from the Cau Da pier for picnics to nearby islands. Glass-bottom boats allowed a view of the coral reef like a vast outdoor aquarium.

Nuoc Mam Preparation. At Nhatrang, the visitor has a chance to observe experiments at a fishery or harvesting of sea swallows' nests, and perhaps attend a coracle contest (see Coracle Contests, below). Nhatrang is an especially good place to observe the process of preparing Nuoc Mam (fish sauce). Norman Lewis, an American journalist with a keen interest in Asia, wrote: "When traveling I make an effort to throw overboard all prejudices concerning food. Consequently after a brief period of struggle I had already come to terms with Nuoc Mam about which almost every writer since the first Jesuit has grumbled. I felt I had indeed taken the first steps towards connoisseurship, and it was in this spirit that I congratulated the governor on his supply, which was the color of pale honey, thickish and of obvious excellence."

Large clay jars of Nuoc Mam can be seen and smelled everywhere. Fish too small to be sold individually on the market are placed in clay vats or jars containing water and salt. After pouring boiling water into the jar, women place a weight into the water to rest on top of the fish. The mixture is then left to ferment. Bacterial action decomposes the fish, resulting in a clear, amber-brown juice that is rich in protein, vitamins, and minerals. When Nuoc Mam is made in small amounts for family use, the clay jar is sealed air-tight and buried until the fermenting process is complete. With aging, the fierce ammoniacal odors mellow and, as with brandy, the flavor improves. The weight placed on top of the fermenting fish presses out the extract. As in the production of extra pure virgin olive oil, the first pressing produces the clearest and purest sauce called Nuoc Mam Nhi or "Prime."

SEA SWALLOWS' NESTS

The rocky islands off the coast of Nhatrang are a breeding area for sea swallows. Sea swallows' nest soup is a valued delicacy as well as a medicinal tonic. The sea swallow does not walk but clutches at crags in the cliffs with its short feet. In the spring, the birds build their nests in the crevices and caves along the coast of Vietnam and on offshore islands. Both the male and the female bird extrude a thread of gel-like substance to help them create a nest. Nests are commonly white, but the more valuable ones are pink or red. The inside of the nest is soft and the rim smooth. Parent birds become thin in their obsession with nest building; the female barely has enough energy to lay the two white- and-blue speckled eggs.

Getting the nests is a precarious business. Nest harvesters carry bags for the nests and ropes for climbing down the sides of the cliffs. In addition to lowering themselves down a cliff, harvesters must avoid the poisonous snakes which feed on the swallows' eggs and hide in the cracks and crevices of the caves on the rock face. A single cave may contain as many as a thousand nests. Many are harvested, although enough nests are left to ensure survival of the swallow population (swallows make new nests in 45 days).

CORACLE CONTESTS

A coracle is a round waterproof boat made of a wicker or wooden frame. The boat is waterproofed by an ancient process that utilizes lacquering. Coracle contests occur in autumn on the beach at Nhatrang, and winning the contest is based on the capacity of a boatman to shake the vessel from side to side in a manner that propels him forward without the use of oars.

DOWNTOWN NHATRANG

The modern market rotunda is at the northwest edge of town near the Xom Bong fishing pier. Nguyen Hoang and Doc Lap Streets are the main shopping areas. Souvenirs include locally crafted shell and coral.

At the northernmost tip of the city on the beach is the former French governor's house, which is now a government building.

The Pasteur Institute is located on the waterfront at the intersection of Tran Phu and Pasteur Streets near the Thong Nhat Hotel. It was one of the several similar institutes started by Dr. Alexander John Emile Yersin. A museum is now housed in the building. Yersin's gravesite is located outside of Nhatrang on lands that once belonged to the Institute.

Francois' Restaurant on the dock was popular with Americans for its sweet lobster; it was said that the Americans had to leave by ten o'clock so the "Viet Cong" could have *their* lobster. Restaurants along the beach still offer tasty seafood and coconut juice, a specialty of Nhatrang. The Seaman's Club is a large outdoor cafe on the beach that is open to the public.

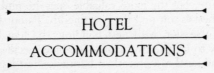

HOTEL ACCOMMODATIONS

Thang Loi Hotel
4 Pasteur Rd.
tel. 22226/22241
The best.

Hai Yen Hotel
40 Tran Phu Rd.
tel. 22974
Adequate. This hotel faces the sea and has a souvenir shop and dancing.

Thong Nhat Hotel
18 Tran Phu Rd.
tel. 22966
Has souvenir and art shop.

NHATRANG DIRECTORY

	Telephone
Phu Khanh Tourism, 1 Tran Hung Dao	22753/22754/22721

COMMERCIAL ENTERPRISES
Cotimex Phu Khanh (Phu Khanh Joint Export Import Co), 40
    Thai Nguyen
Centrimex (South Central Export-Import Corp), 48 Tran Phu
    Imports and exports products and produce for the five provinces
    of the south-central region of Vietnam.

Quinhon: Nghia Binh Province

Straddling Route 19 and Route One in Nghia Binh Province is the coastal seaport of Quinhon. Quinhon was once the center of the Cham kingdom after the Champa had been pushed southward from their northern capital by the Viets (Vietnamese of the North) in the 16th century.

HISTORY

In 1772, the Tay Son Revolt against the repressive Nguyen rulers centered around Quinhon. Led by three brothers, one of whom was Nguyen Hue, the rebellion quickly gained popular support. After Nguyen Hue's army routed the Nguyen clan, they smashed the invading Chinese forces. Nguyen Hue's success enabled him, as Emperor Quang Trung, to lead his troops north to Hanoi to reunify the country. In 1799, however, his forces were defeated at Quinhon by the French-backed Nguyen Anh, who became Emperor Gia Long. A museum in Nghia Binh Province honors the hero Nguyen Hue (Quang Trung).

During the American war in Vietnam, Quinhon was one of four US deep-water harbors in the south. The other ports were at Cam Ranh Bay, Saigon, and Danang. The US Seventh Marines, an Army transportation company, and the flying cavalry of the airmobile division came ashore at Quinhon.

In 1965, the "Flaming Dart" bombing operation was conducted by the US in response to an attack on Pleiku. The operation involved the bombing of guerrilla training centers above the DMZ. The National Liberation Front responded to this US operation on February 10, 1965, when it bombed the Quinhon US servicemen's hotel known as Viet Cuong ("The Country's Strength"), killing 21 soldiers and wounding 22 more. The hotel housed over 100 men attached to an aircraft maintenance unit.

HIGHLIGHTS
FOR TRAVELERS

The area contains many Cham temple ruins for the visitor to explore. In addition, two of Vietnam's 83 national parks are in Nghia Binh Province: Kon Cha and Kon Ka Kinh reserves are known for their limestone mountains and five-tiered tropical forest vegetation.

HOI VAN HOT SPRINGS

Not far from Quinhon are the hot springs at Hoi Van. The hot water reaches a temperature of 87° C (188° F) and is used as an aid in shredding copra, a dried coconut meat that yields coconut oil.

MI LAI

Son Mai village is a group of four hamlets located six miles (10 km.) northeast of Quang Ngai, the capital of Nghia Binh Province. Mi Lai-4 was a subdivision of Son Mai village. On March 16, 1968, a US military operation took the lives of 347 non-combatants in this village. Today a huge monument has been erected on the site in the social-realist style of a woman holding children. Stones mark the place where each person was killed, except in the nearby irrigation ditch where many died huddled together. A moving stillness pervades the clearing.

HOTEL
ACCOMMODATIONS

Quinhon Hotel
12 Nguyen Hue
Quinhon
tel. 2401

QUINHON DIRECTORY

	Telephone
Nghia Binh Tourism Office, 4 Nguyen Hue, Quinhon	2524/2206

THUAN HAI PROVINCE

Located south of Phu Khanh Province is Thuan Hai Province. Phan Thiet, on the southern coast of this dry and barren province, is the capital city. Another important city is Phanrang, which contains Cham ruins.

HOTEL
ACCOMMODATIONS

Phan Thiet Hotel
40 Tran Hung Dao
Phan Thiet
tel. 2901/2573

Thong Nhat Hotel
Thong Nhat
Phanrang
tel. 74

THUAN HAI PROVINCE DIRECTORY

	Telephone
Thuan Hai Tourist Office, 82 Trung Trac, Phan Thiet	2474/2475

CENTRAL HIGHLANDS

CAO NGUYEN PLATEAU

The central highlands contain a plateau area called the Cao Nguyen Plateau, located in southern Vietnam and northeast of Ho Chi Minh City. More specifically, it is located between the narrow coastal strip and the Annamite Mountains. The plateau is sparsely populated by unrelated groups of semi-nomadic ethnic minorities, such as the Ede (Rhade), Bahnar, Gia Rai, and the Jarai. It has enormous untapped resources: a forest area of 2.5 million hectares (6 million acres), which produces lumber, excellent soil, and good climate for coffee, tea, and rubber plantations and minerals, such as bauxite and tin, have been extracted. The Cao Nguyen Plateau is an area currently under development by "New Economic Zones" in which unemployed citizens from the country's large cities are encouraged to settle and work at agricultural and reforestation projects.

Three provinces situated in this plateau are Gialai-Kontum, Dac Lac, and Lam Dong. Gialai-Kontum is one of the most sparsely populated provinces in Vietnam. It borders both Laos and Cambodia. The capital is Pleiku. Buon Ma Thuot is the capital of Dac Lac, and Dalat is the capital of Lam Dong.

VUNG TAU—CON DAO SPECIAL ZONE

Nestled between rocky mountains that reach the sea, Vung Tau, a one-and-a-half hour drive from Ho Chi Minh City, is a renowned seaside resort with sunshine all year round. From Vung Tau, a visitor can reach the Con Dao islands in 50 minutes by plane or 12 hours by boat. Formerly an exile colony, Con Dao (France's Devil Island) remains a symbol of the unwavering patriotism of Vietnamese revolutionaries.

Vung Tau was (formerly Cape St. Jacques) once the customs and immigration center for Saigon, and ships were required to stop there for proper clearance before sailing up the Saigon River. From Saigon to Vung Tau, today's travelers pass the Tri An Falls (the site of a new dam) on the Dong Nai River.

On one of the hills that forms the peninsula there's a lighthouse, and on another hill, a statue of the Virgin with arms outstretched to the sea.

The impressive Pagoda of the Sleeping Buddha (a 30-foot [9-m.] reclining Buddha) sits on a hillside to the west and above the harbor. A famous statue of Buddha fashioned of precious stone dignifies the Linh Son Pagoda in the Thang Tam section on the northern side of town.

The beach on the east side of the peninsula, called "back beach," once served as a rest center for French officers and, later, for Americans and Australian soldiers. Vung Tau now accommodates government workers on holiday.

In the early morning, the marina bustles with fishing boats—colorful eyes painted on their prows—casting off for the catch of the day. Offshore islands feature several Buddhist shrines, old Japanese

Panoramic view of Vung Tau

artillery sites, and oil rigs. A petrochemical complex is under construction close to the city.

At one time, favorite restaurants among Americans were Irene's and Cyrano's, which had a good view of the fishing boats from the patio. Good restaurants still occupy these locations.

HOTEL
ACCOMMODATIONS

Hoa Binh Hotel (formerly called Palace Hotel)
11 Nguyen Trai, Chau Thanh Ward
Vung Tau
tel. 2265/2411
150 rooms with air-conditioning.

Thang Muoi
5 Thuy Van
Tam Thang Ward
tel. 2665

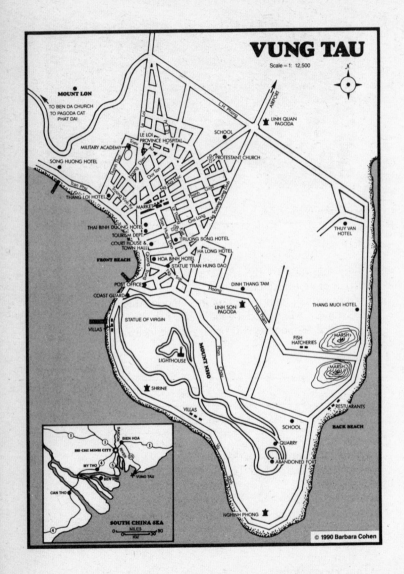

VUNG TAU

Scale = 1: 12,500

MOUNT LON

TO BEN DA CHURCH
TO PAGODA CAT
PHAT DAI

LH Phong
AIRPORT

LINH QUAN
PAGODA

SCHOOL

LE LOI
PROVINCE HOSPITAL

MILITARY ACADEMY

PROTESTANT CHURCH

SONG HUONG HOTEL

Tran Phu

THANG LOI HOTEL

MARKET

THUY VAN
HOTEL

THAI BINH DUONG HOTEL
TOURISM DEPT.
COURT HOUSE &
TOWN HALL

Gia Long

TRUONG SONG HOTEL

HA LONG HOTEL

FRONT BEACH

HOA BINH HOTEL
STATUE TRAN HUNG DAO

POST OFFICE

DINH THANG TAM

Hoang

COAST GUARD

LINH SON
PAGODA

THANG MUOI HOTEL

STATUE OF VIRGIN

VILLAS

MOUNT NHO

FISH
HATCHERIES

MARSH

LIGHTHOUSE

MARSH

SHRINE

VILLAS

RESTUARANTS

SCHOOL

BACK BEACH

QUARRY

ABANDONED FORT

BIEN HOA

HO CHI MINH CITY

MY THO

BEN TRE

VUNG TAU

CAN THO

NGHINH PHONG

SOUTH CHINA SEA

MILES
KM

© 1990 Barbara Cohen

Thang Loi
1 Duy Tan
Chau Thanhward
tel. 2135

Thai Binh Duong
6 Le Loi, Chau Thanh Ward
Vung Tau
tel. 2279
A very good hotel, once frequented by Americans, but now used exclusivley by government officials.

VUNG TAU DIRECTORY

	Telephone
Vung Tau Tourism Office (and Oil Service Company), 2 Le Loi, telex 370 VUNG TAU—originally set up to service oil specialists from Western countries exploring for offshore oil; an entire residential section of Vung Tau, called Lam Son, has been upgraded for Soviet and East bloc oil specialists	90195/2603

Dalat: Lam Dong Province

CENTRAL REGION

Dalat (the City of Love) is the picturesque capital city of Lam Dong Province, which unites the two former provinces of Lam Dong and Tuyen Duc. With a population of almost 600,000, Dalat is 215 miles (344 km.) from Ho Chi Minh City (145 miles (232 km.) by air with flights running twice weekly from Ho Chi Minh City). An important industry is the mining of bauxite ore from deposits in the laterite basaltic formations found in the area.

More than 4,000 feet (1,220 m.) above sea level, the highland city of Dalat in the Cao Nguyen plateau basks in a region of magnificent lakes, waterfalls, and a 7,000-foot (2,135 m.) mountain peak to the north. Once called the "summer capital," Dalat has a mild climate year round (16°C [61°F]) and is reminiscent of the alpine areas of Europe with its pine forests, rolling hills, and small lakes. The sky in the high plateau is a deep blue. Some of the many lakes in the area are Xuan Huong, Than Tho (Sorrowful Sighs), Me Linh, Van Kiep, and Suoi Vang (Golden Brook).

HISTORY

Dalat was founded around 1920 by French physician, Alexander Yersin,* who felt the cool climate would make an ideal therapeutic

---

*Alexander Yersin (1863-1943) studied medicine in Paris where he worked under the famous French bacteriologist, Louis Pasteur. After receiving his medical degree, Yersin joined the Messageries Maritimes Company as a medical officer and set out for Indochina. He fell in love with the mountainous region of the central part of Vietnam—what is now Dalat. His proposals to the French administrators that a town for therapeutic vacations be founded there were implemented. Yersin went on to study a devastating plague in Hong Kong and discovered that rats carried the bacteria that caused the devastating disease. In 1885, Yersin founded the Pasteur Institute in Nhatrang, and he was instrumental in founding the College of Medicine in Hanoi. He was later made inspector general of all the Pasteur Institutes in French Indochina. Although his main interest was infectious diseases, he was also a horticulturist who introduced the first rubber and quinine trees to Vietnam. Yersin, the humanitarian, led a simple life and was well loved for his concern for bettering human life. The Yersin Lycée in Dalat was founded in his honor. His grave is located outside Nhatrang.

retreat for his European patients who suffered from the debilitating effects of the tropical climate. The area was originally inhabited only by highland ethnic minorities, called Montagnards (mountaineers) by the French. Lowlander Vietnamese, however, did not enjoy living year-round in the highlands. They considered the "climate" to be unhealthy because of uncharted jungle, savage tribes, and dan-

Memorial over Dr. Yersin's gravesite, outside Nhatrang

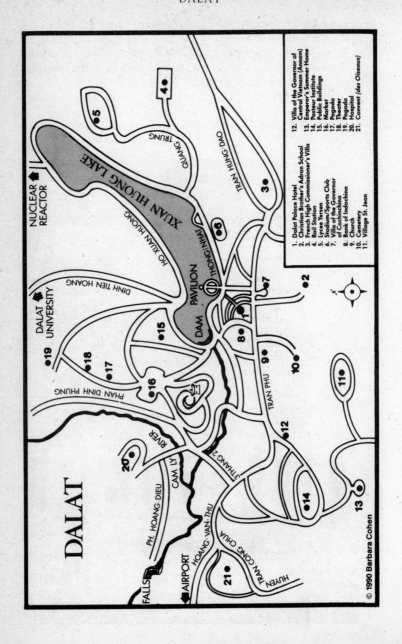

DALAT

XUAN HUONG LAKE

NUCLEAR REACTOR

DALAT UNIVERSITY

DINH TIEN HOANG

HO XUAN HUONG

QUANG TRUNG

TRAN HUNG DAO

THONG NHAT

DAM PAVILION

PHAN DINH PHUNG

TRAN PHU

3 THANG 2

CAM LY RIVER

PH. HOANG DIEU

HOANG VAN THU

HUYEN TRAN CONG CHUA

AIRPORT

FALLS

1. Dalat Palace Hotel
2. Christian Brother's Adran School
3. French High Commissioner's Villa
4. Rail Station
5. Lycée Yersen
6. Stadium/Sports Club
7. Villa of the Governor of Cochinchina
8. Bank of Indochina
9. Church
10. Cemetery
11. Village St. Jean
12. Villa of the Governor of Central Vietnam (Annam)
13. Emperor's Summer Home
14. Pasteur Institute
15. Public Buildings
16. Market
17. Pagoda
18. Theater
19. Pagoda
20. Hospital
21. Convent (des Oiseaux)

© 1990 Barbara Cohen

gerous wild animals (former US president Theodore Roosevelt maintained a hunting lodge in Dalat). The French government was interested in developing the resources of this area, particularly in cultivating vegetables, tea, coffee, and especially rubber. Large land grants were made available to Frenchmen, Chinese, and favored Vietnamese on the agreement that they make immediate improvements such as land clearing and irrigation.

As the French began settling these areas, they brought in Vietnamese as servants, merchants, transporters, and laborers. The French built homes reminiscent of alpine cottages and initiated experimental agriculture programs for growing rubber, coffee, and European vegetables. After 1954, many Vietnamese Catholics, who left the North when the Viet Minh came to power, settled in the Dalat area and established more experimental farms. The Vietnamese population in the area gradually increased.

During the Vietnam War, Dalat grew rapidly as a farming area as it provided tons of fresh vegetables for the Saigon market and the US Army.

In addition to its agricultural importance, the natural beauty of Dalat soon made it the honeymoon capital of the country. Even now, newlyweds enjoy walking among the gently rolling hills and having picnics on the rocks near the falls or beside the romantic lakes. Strolling or riding horseback around the lake is an invigorating experience.

RELIGIOUS INSTITUTIONS

At one time, the town had three churches, a convent, and a seminary. The Notre Dame de Long Bien Catholic Church and the Convent des Oiseaux, formerly a girl's school, attest to the strong French influence and the subsequent large numbers of northern Catholics who arrived in 1954. Notre Dame is a European-style church. Nearby, at the Convent des Oiseaux, the nuns wore traditional black habits. Dalat was once the home of the Eau de Vie, a religious order composed of former French prostitutes who worked to rehabilitate other prostitutes in countries around the world. These women once ran a charming restaurant in Dalat to support themselves and their cause. Dalat has a Protestant church; Linh Son is one of the more prominent pagodas in the area.

ETHNIC MINORITIES

Although few ethnic minority groups live in town, you may see them around the market or walking along the road bearing their

Cham woman

distinctive back baskets. The present government discourages slash-
and-burn agriculture, which is ecologically destructive, and promotes (through education and specific projects such as irrigation)
settlement in villages to cultivate paddy rice, or grow commercial
crops such as tea, coffee, or medicinal plants. Traditional houses of
bamboo and thatch are also discouraged in favor of more substantial

wood houses with tin or tile roofs. It would be well worth the effort to arrange a trip out to the countryside to visit a highland village and observe how the Montagnards live, work, and make handicrafts. Since major changes are taking place in the highlands, now is a good time to visit before too many influences change the nature of the highlanders' way of life.

HIGHLIGHTS
FOR TRAVELERS

The Dalat area, including the town of Dalat, has grown rapidly in population in recent years due to the government's policy of encouraging the relocation of people from overcrowded areas, especially the Red River delta, to New Economic Zones in the less populated highlands. Despite the influx of new citizens, the town still retains its distinctive flavor as a resort, famous for its scenery and flowers. The center of the town sits on the end of Xuan Huong Lake called Sighing Lake because of the soft whispering of the pine trees.

WILDLIFE

The Dalat to Ho Chi Minh City road passes through some of the most beautiful scenery in Vietnam: the breathtaking Prenn mountain pass and the Da Tan La falls. Prenn is the site of the zoo which was once the base camp for hunters of tiger, deer, and elephant. Emperor Bao Dai hunted here using hunting boxes, camouflaged treetop enclosures where he and his party would sit to watch for game to appear. Meanwhile, spread out in a circle around the treetop "boxes," hired local tribesmen would beat drums while walking closer toward the center of the circle. Animals, caught in the circle of noise, would come closer and closer to the waiting hunters.

Although much wildlife was frightened away or killed during the American war in Vietnam, wild game managed to survive in the area. In addition to better known jungle mammals, there are the now-endangered kouprey, a small forest cow; the gaur, another wild ox; and the gayal, its smaller cousin. Colorful wild birds, such as parrots and tragopan, also populate the forests. The resumption of hunting is planned by the current government, beginning with waterfowl.

The Cat Tien Preserve protects rhinoceroses and wild cranes. In addition to endangered animals, the preserve is a haven for two rare species of pine. One is called "Dalat five needle" pine, of which there are only ten trees left, one of them 1,500 years old. The other rare pine species is the "two flat needle" pine, named after the flat shape of its paired needles.

THE MARKETPLACE

The town center has a two-story market, which US aid helped to build, and many small grill-front shops. The lower level of the marketplace is alive with flowers of all colors and delicious fruits such as plums, peaches, and pears. The upper level sells varieties of household goods, clothing fabric, gifts and crafts. In the early morning, native Montagnards come to town to trade firewood, mushrooms, and crafts for staple supplies. Women of ethnic minorities dressed in colorful costumes come down from their mountain villages to buy such necessities as embroidery thread and pots. Some traders arrive on horseback and in wagons drawn by tiny ponies that are typical of the highland area.

VILLAS

Driving around town to see the many French-style villas is a worthwhile outing. Emperor Bao Dai in the early 1950s conducted the affairs of state from an office-villa in Dalat. On the hill along Ly Thai To Avenue, villas are spread out, set amongst the pines and delicate mauve flowers of the mimosa shrub. There are also gardens of gladiolus, roses, mimosa, bougainvillea, hibiscus, and tree-size poinsettia. Peach, plum, and pear trees bloom colorfully in the spring on the rich red volcanic soil. Nearby, there's the cemetery of war dead and the Pagoda Linh Son. A golf course, built by Americans in the 1960s, was once situated on the north side of the lake.

INSTITUTIONS

While the US was in Vietnam, the Armed Forces Staff College (the Vietnamese "West Point" that had been established by the French) was an active military school. The Geographic Institute was located in this town as well as the only private Catholic university in Vietnam, Dalat University, which is now part of the national university system.

NUCLEAR REACTOR

A nuclear reactor was constructed in the Dalat area by the American Atoms for Peace program in 1963. Four days before his assassination, Diem performed the building's opening ceremonies. The 57

"Cowgirls" and "cowboys" outside cafe, Dalat

radioactive fuel rods, each in its own lead-lined barrel, were removed from the Triga Mark 2 reactor just days before the departure of Americans in 1975. The reactor has since been repaired with Soviet aid and is used for experimental work.

DA NHIM DAM

The nearby Da Nhim dam, financed by the Japanese as a war reparations project, currently provides power for Ho Chi Minh City.

OUTSIDE OF TOWN

If you continue to drive out of town you will pass a series of small villages. Leave early to see the vegetable growers in Sao Nam hamlet working in the morning mist. Small souvenir shops in the upper part of town offer authentic handicrafts such as baskets, musical instruments, and pipes, made by the indigenous minorities. The sale and availability of local handicrafts depends on the time of year: planting season, New Year. Because of the cool climate, the native girls are known for their rosy cheeks.

The Cam Ly Falls are near the site of the former US military airfield. There are also falls at Pongour, Uyen Uong, and Gougal.

HOTEL

ACCOMMODATIONS

The Dalat Palace Hotel
2 Tran Phu
tel. 2203
Located near the center of town, with an imposing view of the Xuan Huong Lake, the Dalat Palace Hotel is the oldest and most elegant hotel in town. This 52-room hotel was once a hunting lodge (built in 1923) and the wood paneling conveys a somewhat masculine character. Suites feature massive teak beds; pewterware and china from former days still adorn the shelves.

The Dalat Hotel
7 Tran Phu
tel. 2363
Another major vintage hotel. Many lovely old villas have been renovated for domestic tourists. Additional hotel space is being built and a recreation center is under construction on Duc Trong and Quang Trung lakes.

Hotel Ngoc Lan
54 Nguyen Tri Phuong
tel. 2136

CUISINE

Some of the local restaurants include the Thuy Ta, Thanh Thuy, Xuan Huong, Duc Trong, and the Bao Loc. French-style croissants baked on the premises are delicious, and a hot sweet pudding (Che Ba Ba or Che Khoai) will warm you on a cool day.

A lovely cafe below the Dalat Palace Hotel on the edge of the Xuan Huong Lake is an enjoyable place to sit and sip coffee, or to drink the famous Lam Dai Dong tea of the region while watching couples in paddle boats skim past.

DALAT DIRECTORY

	Telephone
Lam Dong Tourism, 12 Tran Phu	2021/2034

Ho Chi Minh Municipality

Ho Chi Minh Municipality, with a population of nearly four million, is the largest city in Vietnam and one of three self-administering municipalities in the country (the others are Hanoi and Haiphong). Ho Chi Minh Municipality encompasses the former separate districts of Saigon, Cholon, Gia Dinh, and Cu Chi. Ho Chi Minh City lies 1,159 miles (1,738 km.) south of Hanoi by overland roads. The municipality is commonly called Ho Chi Minh City (formerly Saigon); many of its citizens, even officials, still refer to the downtown area as "Saigon." The breakdown of municipality to city to downtown is analogous to, say, the metropolitan New York, New Jersey, Connecticut area as the municipality, Manhattan as the city, and the 42nd Street area as downtown. Ho Chi Minh Municipality is surrounded by four provinces: Song Be, noted for its lacquerware and the site of a historic bronze casting base; Tay Ninh, noted for the Cao Dai Pagoda; Dong Nai, which contains the important city of Bien Hoa; and Long An, which marks the beginning of the fertile agricultural lands of the Mekong Delta.

HISTORY

The Ho Chi Minh City area was occupied from the second to the seventh century by the citizens of the kingdom of Funan; the region was part of the Khmer kingdom of Chenla in the sixth to eighth centuries. In the 11th and 12th centuries, Saigon was a seaport of the kingdom of Angkor, which had its seat of government based near the great natural reservoir of Tonle Sap in Cambodia.

Settlements in the southern part of Vietnam occurred horizontally along natural waterways and man-made canals, whereas the North was settled in population clusters spread out in the agricultural plains. By the 16th century, the northern Viets had pushed their way south into Cham and Khmer territory. Early in the 17th century, Viet pioneers and Chinese merchants settled in the eastern region of the Mekong. Prior to the French colonial era, Saigon was known as Gia Dinh Thanh, a vice-royalty governed by a mandarin-governor from the capital at Hue.

Ho Chi Minh Municipality consists of ten administrative wards (Quan).

HIGHLIGHTS
FOR TRAVELERS

SAIGON SECTOR

Under the French, this section was called the "Pearl of the Orient." During the 1960s, downtown Saigon was alive with American military personnel, journalists, and civilian contract workers. Bars and nightclubs lit up the streets in the evenings while pretty hostesses sat with lonely GIs and drank watered-down drinks called "Saigon Tea." Small blue-and-white Renault taxis and motorized three-wheeled "cyclos" dashed madly through the streets. Today, the taxis are gone, the pedicabs are powered by human energy, and bicycles dominate the streets.

WALKING TOUR OF DOWNTOWN SAIGON

The numbers in parentheses refer to the locations on the Downtown Saigon map. At a brisk pace, this walk takes about one and a half hours. If you linger to have a bowl of soup (*pho*), purchase souvenirs, or chat with Amerasian youths, your foot tour may take up to four hours.

Start at the circle at the foot of Hai Ba Trung Street and the waterfront of the Saigon River. Hai Ba Trung is the main artery carrying traffic from the dock on the Saigon River across town to Tan Son Nhut Airport. Ton Duc Thang is the waterfront street.

At the **circle** (1) there was once a statue of Admiral Rigault de Genouilly, the French naval commander and the French naval headquarters was nearby to the north. In the 1950s, Madame Nhu, sister-in-law of President Diem, erected a statue honoring the heroic Trung Sisters who led attacks on the Chinese near Hanoi. Some say the face of the statue of Queen Trung Trac resembled Madame Nhu herself. After the assassination of Diem, the look-alike statue of his sister-in-law was torn down and replaced by a statue of Tran Hung Dao (who fought the Mongols of Kublai Khan in the 13th century) that overlooks the action on the docks.

The ferry which crosses the Saigon River docks here, and the My Canh floating restaurant (bombed in 1968) still serves dinners.

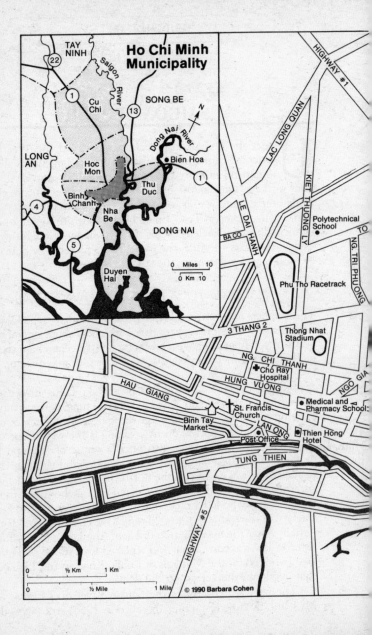

Ho Chi Minh
Municipality

TAY
NINH

22

Saigon River

1

Cu
Chi

SONG BE

13

N

LONG
AN

Dong Nai River

Bien Hoa

1

Hoc
Mon

Thu
Duc

Binh
Chanh

Nha
Be

DONG NAI

4

5

0   Miles   10

0   Km   10

Duyen
Hai

HIGHWAY #1

LAC LONG QUAN

KIET THUONG LY

Polytechnical
School

NG. TRI PHUONG

TO

LE DAI HANH

BA CO

Phu Tho Racetrack

3 THANG 2

Thong Nhat
Stadium

NG.   CHI   THANH

NGO GIA

Cho Ray
Hospital

HUNG
VUONG

HAU   GIANG

Medical and
Pharmacy School

St. Francis
Church

Binh Tay
Market

LAN ONG

Thien Hong
Hotel

Post Office

TUNG   THIEN

HIGHWAY #5

0   ½ Km   1 Km

0   ½ Mile   1 Mile

© 1990 Barbara Cohen

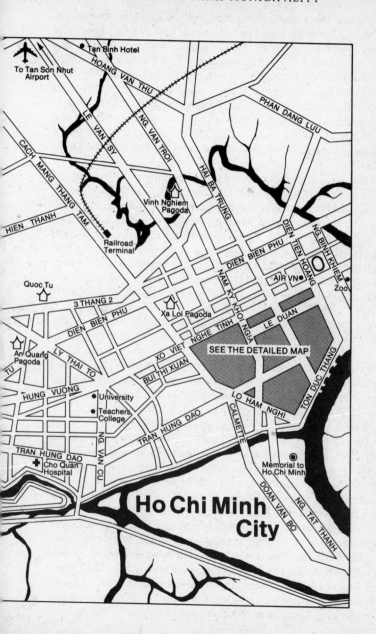

Walk one block south along the river to Dong Khoi Street (Simultaneous Uprising). Lined by large shade trees, Dong Khoi Street has had many incarnations and changing fortunes. During the French era, Dong Khoi Street was called Rue Catinat, considered the Fifth Avenue of Saigon: its fashionable and expensive shops featured antiques, jewelry, perfumes, and fashions from Paris. On the sidewalk, further up the street, mosaic tiles imbedded in cement still form the words *Rue Catinat*. Many older citizens still call the avenue Catinat. At the south end of Dong Khoi and the river stands the former Majestic Hotel, now called the **Cuu Long (Nine Dragons)** (2).

At the north end of Dong Khoi is the Catholic cathedral and the post office. On a Sunday or Holy Day after mass, Catholic citizens at one time could be seen promenading from the cathedral to the quay, stopping to examine displays in shop windows, or to snack on grilled squid with peppers. After World War II, Catinat became Tu Do Street (Freedom). The street lost some of its elegance in the late 1960s when flashy bars and nightclubs popped up to serve the needs of American military personnel. Earlier, the French had solved the problem of lonely soldiers by establishing bordellos on the outskirts of town.

The Cuu Long Hotel was a barracks for Japanese soldiers during World War II when the Japanese controlled Indochina through the French Vichy government. From the hotel's riverside Patio Cafe, one can watch ships entering the port to the north. The rooftop restaurant has a view of the graceful curve in the Saigon River and of the Newport shipyards, built originally by the French and later utilized by American military and civilian contractors. One block south of the Cuu Long Hotel is Nguyen Hue Street, the flower street of Saigon (which we will explore later). (While it may be pleasant to walk along the waterfront at night, beware of attractively made-up, aggressive transvestites, and other thieves who can steal your wallet in a flash, or pull off your watch or neck chain.)

Walking up Dong Khoi Street one passes the movie theater next to the Cuu Long Hotel. Further along are the buildings that once housed bars, strip joints, and night clubs. During the American war in Vietnam, some of the bars on this street of flashing neon lights were: the **Melody, San Francisco, Rainbow, Bluebird, Rose, Mimi's, Papillion, Tu Do, Wild West,** and **Playboy** (3). The Sporting Bar was at 61. There were also some good restaurants, such as Le Castel and Maxime's—considered one of the more fashionable clubs in the city. Soon after the liberation of Saigon by the North-

Downtown
Ho Chi Minh City
(Saigon)

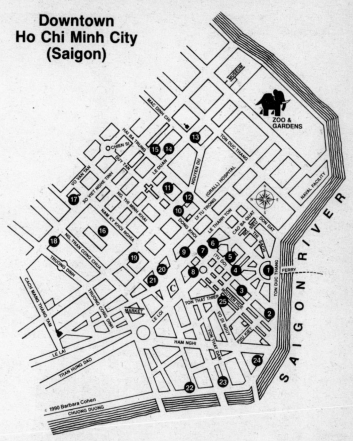

Note: Information in parentheses refers to former name.

1. Trang Hung Dao Circle
2. Cuu Long Hotel (Majestic Hotel)
3. Maxime's
4. Huong Sen Hotel (Astor Hotel)
5. Doc Lap Hotel (Caravelle Hotel)
6. Dong Khoi Hotel (Continental Hotel)
7. Bong Sen Hotel (Eden Building)
8. Ben Thanh Hotel (Rex Hotel)
9. Ho Chi Minh City People's Committee Headquarters (City Hall)
10. Control Bureau (French Sûreté Headquarters)
11. Central Post Office
12. School (Taberd Institute-Christian Brothers' Boys School)
13. British Consulate (British Embassy)
14. State Petroleum Authority (US Embassy)
15. French Consulate (French Embassy)
16. Reunification Hall (Presidential Palace)
17. School (Lycée Chasseloup Laubat)
18. Workers' Sports Club (Cercle Sportif)
19. Court House and Ministry of Justice
20. War Museum (Gia Long Palace)
21. Scientific Library (National Library)
22. Dien Hong Conference Hall (Senate Building)
23. State Bank (Bank of Indochina)
24. Proposed site for Hyatt Regency Hotel (Club Nautique)
25. Huu Nghi Hotel (Saigon Palace)
C. Casino

Catholic cathedral

ern Communists, Maxime's became a check-in point for former Saigon soldiers. Today, it is once again a restaurant.

The nine-story Catinat Hotel at 69 had the Pink Nightclub on the first floor and also boasted the only hotel swimming pool in Saigon. The 50-room Astor Hotel was on the right at 70 (now the **Huong Sen Hotel) (4)** and the French restaurant Cintra was at 104. The Girvral Café, the action center of the city, was located at the angle where Le Loi Street meets Dong Khoi. The café is still open— facing the theater plaza opposite the Caravelle Hotel. The Girvral was a place for Catholic citizens to enjoy an ice cream or brunch after mass at the cathedral. In the 1960s, the cafe's yellow plastic tables were a meeting place for the foreign press corps. This zone became a center for word-of-mouth news: Radio Catinat" or the "Girvral Grapevine." The statue of crouching South Vietnamese marines that once stood in the plaza in front of the former National Assembly was torn down in 1975.

At 165 was the Bao Chu shop, one of the town's most exclusive jewelers. After the liberation in 1975, the owners of the once elegant shop began selling soup on the sidewalk outside.

Tourists interested in wonderful embroidery and needlework should visit the Theu Tay shop at 211-C.

When the Japanese surrendered in August 1945, a huge crowd gathered and raised the Viet Minh flag over the lovely French Municipal Theater that, after 1956, housed the lower division of the Republic of Vietnam National Assembly. The building now houses an active theater.

A wide center divider and promenade in front of the theater is Lam Son square. Le Loi Street begins here. Lam Son in North Vietnam was the birthplace of the national Vietnamese hero Le Loi.

Changing politics have not altered everything. There are still book stalls on Le Loi Street as there were under the French colonial regime and, in the spring, the tall trees still drop lovely yellow confetti-like blossoms onto the ground. Looking away from the theater down Le Loi Street, you have a straight-ahead view of the market. As you face the theater, on your right is the former Caravelle Hotel, renamed **Doc Lap (5)** and, on the left at 132 Dong Khoi Street, the Continental, renamed **Dong Khoi,** has completed its renovation (6).

The Societé des Grands Hotels Indochinois built the Continental Palace back in the Belle Epoque days of 1885. The Continental became part of its chain of elegant hotels which included the Hotel Royal in Phnom Penh and others in Vung Tau, Hue, and Hanoi. In 1925, one could linger after dinner to listen to a band play Viennese waltzes. The little tables of the veranda café, situated under slowly rotating fans, were adorned with pink lamp-shades. In 1926, this is what Somerset Maugham, the British author, wrote about Saigon and the Continental Hotel in *The Gentleman of the Parlour*:

Saigon has all the air of a little provincial town in the South of France. It is laid out with broad streets, shaded with handsome trees, and there is a bustle in them that is quite unlike the bustle of an Eastern town in an English colony. It is a blithe and smiling place. It has an opera house, white and shining, built in the flamboyant style of the Third Republic and a Hotel de Ville which is very grand, new and ornate. Outside the hotel are terraces, and at the hour of the aperitif, they are crowded with bearded, gesticulating Frenchmen drinking the sweet and sickly beverages . . . which they drink in France and they talk nineteen to the dozen in the rolling accent of the Midi. Gay little ladies who have something to do with the local theater are dressed in smart clothes and with their penciled eyebrows and rouged cheeks bring a cheerful air of sophistication . . . It is very agreeable to sit under the awning on the terrace of the Hotel Continental, and with an innocent drink before you, read in the local newspaper heated controversies upon the affairs of the colony.

During the colonial war, only officers, not enlisted soldiers, were allowed on the Continental terrace. In 1945 and 1946, the Viet Minh led anti-French demonstrations on the streets outside the hotel, but never actually entered the building. When the Vietnamese staff of the Continental went on strike in sympathy with the demonstrators, the French guests ran the hotel themselves.

Graham Greene, the British author, once lived in the hotel annex across the street. The terraced cafe of the Continental Hotel featured in Green's *The Quiet American* as the meeting place of the British journalist, Fowler, and the idealistic but naive American, Pyle. In the restaurant and art gallery (called "La Dolce Vita") next door to the Continental, young Saigon painters displayed their works.

Next door to the Continental Hotel, north behind the theater, was the taller former Brink Hotel. General Francis Brink was a US Army general stationed in Saigon in 1950 as part of the US Military Advisory and Assistance Group. The Brink building housed US officers and, after the Paris Accords in 1972, hosted the Defense Attaché Office and embassy personnel. Behind the theater on the same side as the Doc Lap Hotel (Caravelle) stood the Ambassador Hotel that had a US Navy exchange.

A French opium factory was located at 74 Hai Ba Trung Street. The processing plants of the French opium monopoly were identified by a sign over the entrance announcing "Manufacture d'Opium." The raw, gummy opium, in coconut-size balls wrapped in poppy leaves, was packed in bales when it arrived at the lab for processing. The raw product was refined and boxed into 100, 40, 20, and 5 gram boxes. It was said by some that if the government did not regulate the price of opium, the colonists who found pleasure in the poppy would be cheated outrageously by the Chinese who acted as middlemen in marketing the product.

The Doc Lap Hotel (Caravelle) at 19-23 Lam Son Square, on the right side of the theater, was the US press corps headquarters. The glass doors feature a stylish art deco design, and the famous view from the roof is still as fascinating as it was in the 1960s and 1970s when journalists reported they could safely and comfortably observe the guerrilla war being waged just across the river without having to leave their drinks. In April 1960, 18 prominent Vietnamese politicians met in the hotel dining room to draft a letter to President Diem. The letter became known as the Caravelle Manifesto and proposed reforms such as liberalizing civil rights. Diem's police rounded up and jailed the signers.

The **Eden Building** (7) housed the offices of representatives of the international press and wire services. Ramuntcho's Restaurant and lovely shops graced its ground floor arcade and passageways. Although it is now the Bong Sen Hotel, one can still make out the letters "Sanyo" on the front of the building over where the news offices once dispatched news of the war.

The former **Saigon City Hall** (9), now the headquarters of the People's City Committee, was built at the turn of the century. After World War II, the defeat of the occupying Japanese left Saigon in political chaos. While the French regrouped to win back power, the Viet Minh set up a ruling committee. With British support, however, the French regained control of Vietnam. French troops who had been imprisoned by the Japanese were let loose against the Viet Minh. The freed French soldiers ran wild through the streets to the City Hall where the Viet Minh had set up a provisional executive government. Unable to contain the released French prisoners, the Viet Minh fell back to hiding places in the suburbs where they began their guerrilla activities. This retreat was the start of the first Indochina war.

Saigon Street Scene

Diagonally across Lam Son Square from the old City Hall is the **Rex** or **Ben Thanh Hotel,** the former US Bachelor's Officers Quarters and PX (8). The hotel also contained the offices of JUSPAO (the Joint United States Public Affairs Office) from which correspondents could call their newspapers and magazines in the United States.

Remodeled in 1985, the lobby features an ornate molded ceiling, a marble floor, and a graceful wooden reception desk. The outdoor bar atop the Rex has a wonderful view of the city; its plantings and topiary shrubs make this a refreshing stop during sightseeing and shopping. In the second floor bar, there's dancing several nights a week by both Western and Vietnamese dancing fans. The dance floor features flashing lights and a live disco band with both male and female singers performing on different nights. Corners of the darkened disco room are discreet havens for lovers preferring to sit out the dances in each others' arms. There is a cover charge.

After a break on the Rex rooftop, continue on Dong Khoi Street to the Cathedral. One block up on the left, you will pass the site of the former La Pagoda Café. Just before you reach the post office and cathedral, you will pass (on your right) the building used by the French Sûreté as both a **prison** and **police headquarters** (10).

The active Cathedral of the Virgin Mary (many young people attend services) is located in what was once called Place Pigneau de Béhaine and later, John F. Kennedy Square. The church is built in

Ben Thanh (formerly Rex) Hotel

the Western style of red brick, with a spire above each side of the central doors. Masses are held early each weekday morning, and on Saturday evening and Sunday at 4, 5 and 6 PM. Outside the church gates vendors sell rosary beads, religious medals, and holy pictures. Situated in the park between the cathedral and the Reunification Palace are tall tamarind trees with distinctive reddish bark. The **Central Post Office** (11), completed at the same time as the church in 1883, is to the left of the cathedral.

When you have finished visiting the church and mailing your letters, return to Nguyen Du Street (formerly Rue Taberd). Next to the former Sûreté headquarters is a compound enclosed by a high stone wall which once housed the **Taberd Institute** (12)—the former Catholic Christian Brothers Boys High School, established in 1874. Many students were the children of alliances between French men and Vietnamese women. In contrast to the lycée-type school, where the language of instruction was French, instruction at this school was conducted in Vietnamese. During the time of the Japanese occupation, the school served as a hospital.

Cross Hai Ba Trung Street and walk on Nguyen Du two blocks northeast past the Grall Hospital Complex onto Le Duan Street, formerly Thong Nhat Street. Le Duan Street is listed on older down-town maps as 30 Thang 4 Street—its name was changed to honor Le Duan, Lao Dong (Workers) Party Secretary, after his death in July 1986. *30 Thang 4* means April 30, and commemorated the Communist takeover of Saigon on April 30, 1975. The former seats of foreign power resided on this street: the American, French, and British embassies, the Saigon government's prime minister's office, and the presidential palace.

The former **British Embassy building** (13) is at the corner of Mac Dinh Chi and Le Duan. In 1942 this building was taken over from the British consulate-general for use by the Japanese military police. From here, a look down Le Duan Street affords a glimpse of greenery in the botanical gardens and zoo compound—you might want to save an entire morning for a leisurely visit there. During the years of the foreign-supported Saigon government, the prime minister's office was a French-style mansion located two hundred yards beyond the American Embassy on the other side of Le Duan Street, halfway between the embassy and the zoo.

One-half block back on Le Duan is the former **American Embas-sy** (14), a large, white, rectangular building on the north side of the street. Before this large complex was built, the previous American embassy building (which was blown up by a car rigged with a 250-pound bomb in 1965) had been located closer to the waterfront on Ham Nghi Street. The embassy building, designed by the American architect Edward Durrell Stone (1902–1978), was completed in 1967. Stone also designed the United States Embassy in New Delhi, the United States Pavilion for the Brussels World's Fair, and the John F. Kennedy Center in Washington, D.C.

The former embassy building now contains offices of Vietnam's State Petroleum Authority. During the last days of the American presence before Saigon fell to the Communists, oil was discovered from exploratory offshore wells drilled by American companies. Al-though the Vietsovpetro Company is currently working to develop the natural gas and oil offshore sites, minimal amounts of the stored energy are being processed.

In January 1968, during the nationwide Tet attacks on major cities, the grounds of the American Embassy were attacked by a seventeen-man Communist commando unit wearing uniforms of the South Vietnamese Army. A memorial plaque at the entrance gate commemorates the death squad, including two embassy drivers. Five American Marines and MPs were also killed in the attack.

From the roof of the embassy complex, the last US helicopter dramatically left Saigon on April 30, 1975.

South of the American Embassy, and separated by a wall, is the **French Embassy** (15). The French Consulate is still located on the same street at 27 Xo Viet Nghe Tinh (the embassy is now in Hanoi). Across the street from the Petroleum Authority is a smaller building, formerly the New Zealand Embassy.

The current Soviet Union Consulate is now located in the building of the former US ambassador's residence on Dien Bien Phu Street.

Return along Le Duan in the direction of the church toward **Reunification Hall** (Thong Nhat Palace) (16). The Reunification Palace, a large rectangular building inside a grassy park southwest of the cathedral, is on the site of the former residence of the French Governor-General of all Indochina. The French Indochinese Union included the colony of Cochinchina and the protectorates of Ton-

Downtown Ho Chi Minh City from the Ben Thanh Hotel rooftop cafe

kin and Annam (in the north). The offices of the governor of Co-chinchina were in the Gia Long Palace (see below).

Called the Norodom Palace, the original Reunification Palace was built in 1868. The governor-general spent little time here since his principal seat of power was in Hanoi. On September 7, 1955, the palace was turned over by the French to Diem's government. Diem made his official residence here and the building acquired the name "Presidential Palace." In February 1962, a pilot of the South Vietnamese Air Force defected and flew his AD-6 airplane over the palace, bombing and partially destroying the building. A new presidential palace was designed and built on the same site between 1963 and 1966 under the supervision of Ngo Viet Thu, a Vietnamese architect trained in Rome. Advice was sought from a geomancer (one who consults the spirits of land formations for the most auspicious site) about the best shape and position for the new four-story presidential palace. Construction had not quite been completed when a coup unceremoniously removed Diem from power in November 1963.

The wrought-iron gates in front of the palace became famous when, on April 30, 1975, a Soviet-built tank (number 844) of the NVA tank brigade crashed through the gates, completing the take-over of Saigon by Communist forces. General Duong Van Minh surrendered on the front steps. After the previous president, General Thieu, fled, Minh had taken over as president in an effort to negotiate with and accommodate the Communists whose tanks were already on the edge of the city.

The building is light and airy, with cool walkways and large meeting halls. Wide glass doors can be opened to the breezes or closed for private discussions. The conference hall is now used for meetings of representatives of mass organizations (women's groups, students, etc.) and to welcome delegations from abroad. The palatial grounds are used for rallies and parades.

Guided tours of the inside of Reunification Palace are available. Thieu had a bombproof basement shelter from which he conducted the government affairs during the last days of April 1975—it's worth inquiring about if you can view the bunker.

On the northwest corner of Reunification Park grounds, at Nam Ky Khoi Nghia and Xo Viet Nghe Tinh (called Rue Chasseloup Laubat during the French occupation), is the **Lycée Chasseloup Laubat (17)**, named after the French naval and colonies minister who, in 1860, encouraged Napoleon III to become militarily involved in Vietnam. The lycée was a type of school similar to those in France, with classes taught in French. History was the same as taught in France, starting with, "Our ancestors, the Gauls . . . " The Lycée Chasseloup Laubat was called College Indigène. Children from primary schools in each administrative district of the colony competed for the 100 tuition-free places.

To the northwest of the cathedral was the elegant residential section of Saigon. Harry Hervey, an American writer traveling in Indochina during the early part of this century, wrote: "To live 'beyond the cathedral,' while not actually a privilege, is at least an advantage, in as much as one's neighbors are sure to be the very best colonials."

The house at 3 Vo Van Tan became "Big Minh's" (Duong Van Minh) villa. "Big Minh" was the last Prime Minister of the Saigon Government, having taken office just a few days prior to the April 30 Communist takeover.

From their clandestine radio station at 7 Xo Viet Nghe Tinh, the CIA transmitted programs at a frequency close to that of the national liberation radio.

The **Worker's Sport Club** (18), a youth recreation club on Xo Viet Nghe Tinh, was once an exclusive recreation club (called Cercle Sportif) for the French of Saigon; there was a separate sports club for "Annamites" (Vietnamese).

Lawyers' offices once lined the Rue Taberd, now Nguyen Du, near the Court building. Nearby on Nguyen Du stood the **Supreme Court** and **Ministry of Justice** (19).

The former **Gia Long Palace** (20), a lovely white building with beautiful grounds, is just off Nam Ky Khoi Nghia on Ly Tu Truong (formerly Gia Long Street). Sometimes mistaken for the Reunification Palace where the governor-general of Indochina resided, the Gia Long Palace was home to the governor-residence of the French colony of Cochinchina. Gia Long Palace now contains the Museum of War Crimes—displays of gory anti-American propaganda such as wrenching photographs of trenches filled with mutilated corpses and a "guillotine" allegedly used by American soldiers to remove the heads of Vietnamese. The squeamish are advised to avoid this exhibit and remain outside in the quiet garden.

Of the three divisions of Vietnam under the French, only Cochinchina was technically a colony administered directly by a French-staffed civil service under its own governor. The colony sent a deputy, elected by the French citizens of the colony, to the French legislature and the colony was left to administer justice under the French judicial system. Tonkin and Annam retained a harsh tradi-

War Museum (formerly Gia Long Palace)

tional system of justice applied by the mandarins. In Tonkin, although the mandarinate was retained, important decisions were made by the French senior-resident in Hanoi. In Annam, also a protectorate, the emperor maintained symbolic status and here, too, the French senior-resident ruled euphemistically as "advisor" to the mandarinate.

One block south of the Court is a prison and the **City General Scientific and Technical Library** (former National Library) (21). In 1966, the library had 600,000 volumes, including classic literary works. Many rare volumes were destroyed by the Communists after 1975 in an effort to rid the country of "decadent" reading materials.

Cross the shoemakers street, Ly Thanh Ton, on the way back to the waterfront. Craftsmen and women on this street fashion Western-style shoes to order. The Casino club (C) is located at Le Loi and Nguyen Thi Minh Khai.

The white building with pillars on the quay at the corner of Nam Ky Khoi Nghai (Cong Ly) is the former Vietnamese Senate building, or **Dien Hong Conference Hall** (22). This building was the headquarters of the Japanese Army during their occupation of Vietnam in World War II.

Before it moved uptown to the site on Le Duan Street, the American Embassy was at 4 Vo Di Nguy. Dozens of banks had their headquarters on Ham Nghi Street and on Vo Di Nguy Street—Ham Nghi Street is still the financial center of the city. The next block was taken up entirely by the Bank of Indochina, which became the National Bank in the late 1950s and 1960s, and is currently the **State Bank** (23). You might want to wander up Ton That Dam Street to the so-called "thieves' market," where a variety of goods, including sophisticated electronics, are sold in outdoor stalls.

Across the Bach Ben Nghe Bridge, there is a building on the dock that commemorates Ho Chi Minh's departure from Vietnam as a humble mess-boy on an ocean liner in 1911. As an expatriate, Ho travelled for many years before finally returning to his homeland in 1941.

The French sailing club **(Club Nautique)** (24) was once located at the riverside and Ham Nghi. This location was also the site of a proposed (in 1973) Hyatt Regency Saigon Resort complex, a four-restaurant, 22-story, 550-room convention and conference center. Hilton and Sheraton had already broken ground in 1973 for new hotels in Saigon. Construction plans were thwarted when in April 1975 the North Vietnamese Army and the National Liberation Front took over the country, forcing Americans (including the US ambassador) and Vietnamese who worked with them to flee.

Return to Nguyen Hue Street (formerly Boulevard Charner). Around February, during Tet, this street explodes with color: flowers, animal-shaped balloons, fireworks, and citizens dressed up in their finest. The Communist government, however, encourages its citizens to spend less on fireworks and candies and to remember the New Year by visiting orphanages and wounded veterans. Extravagance and showing off of finery are discouraged. Even so, during Tet, flower stalls sell brilliant gladiolus, mums, and potted miniature orange plants.

At 56-64 is the high-rise **Huu Nghi Hotel** (25), formerly the Central (or Saigon) Palace. The Carolina Bar, at 62, was later called the Pink Nightclub; there is still a nightclub in the Huu Nghi Hotel. The disco on the first floor plays recorded music for a lively young crowd while a nightclub on the rooftop offers live music for mature, formal couples.

The Grand Hotel des Nations was once at 70 and the Le Triomphe, a restaurant and tea room, occupied 104. The former Korean Embassy was at 109; 119 was the former Saigon USO, while 143 formerly housed the Abraham Lincoln Library of the USIS (United States Information Services).

You are now back at the center of town; this is a good time and location to decide whether to explore the city in more detail.

BOTANICAL GARDENS AND ZOO

The Botanical Gardens and Zoo, in the northeast section of the downtown area, is an agreeable place to join relaxed and friendly Vietnamese families who are enjoying their free time. A collection of mature equatorial plants are exhibited in the botanical gardens. The National Museum on the grounds displays art works from each phase of Vietnam's history and authentic costumes of the ethnic minorities. Located opposite the museum is a monument once dedicated to the "Annamite" soldiers who died fighting for France in World War I. The memorial, built in typical Vietnamese-style architecture, is currently a memorial to Confucius. It was rumored that former presidents Diem and Thieu maintained a secret prison beneath the zoo.

XA LOI TEMPLE

Several blocks to the northwest of the Reunification Palace on Dien Bien Phu Street is the Xa Loi Temple, a modern concrete structure with an exquisite five-story bell tower that housed outspoken monks who, in the summer of 1963, protested President Diem's repressive policies against the Buddhists. In August 1963, Diem's brother, Ngo Dinh Nhu, attacked the pagoda and arrested 400 monks and nuns. Nhu used secret police and intelligence agents dressed in army uniforms, hoping the vicious attack would be attributed to the army generals and that the resulting publicity would weaken a military coup about to take place against his brother.

CHO BEN THANH MARKET

Eight streets converge on the Cho Ben Thanh market, near the former railroad station. One could fill a fascinating morning here, especially around Tet when it's jammed in a delightful manner. Every type of product and service is available, from books to sausages, including restaurants and beauty shops. The market facade has been repainted; the clock in the tower of the central entrance, stopped for many years, has been repaired to once again keep pace with the

Cho Ben Thanh market

times. The circle, once called Place Eugene Cuniac, across the street has a statue with a plaque (that reads Tran Nguyen Han) honoring Tran Hung Dao, a hero of the conquest against the Chinese invaders.

CHIEN SI CIRCLE

Chien Si means fighter or soldier. Located at 4 Duy Tan Street is the Cultural Youth House, a sports club that hosts singing and dancing events. A police station is situated at the northwest corner. The Department of Waterworks was also on this circle under the French occupation. In the 1930s, an American Consulate was on the eastern side of the circle (the American Embassy was in Hanoi at that time). The Ecole Maternelle (later the Law School and the Faculty of Letters of Saigon University) was located on this circle, where today one finds the School of Economics and Architecture at 17 Duy Tan Street.

American civilians once lived in the apartments around this circle. Colonel Landsdale, the American psychological warfare expert and advisor to President Diem in the first years of his presidency, lived in a house at the north corner of this square. In the early 1970s, US intelligence analysts lived at 6 Chien Si.

CHOLON DISTRICT

Gontran de Poncins, a French adventurer who visited Cholon in the 1950s, wrote: "Cholon is a night city with electric signs in Chinese characters that gleam like rubies and taxi girls whose shapely bodies stir the customer, who will go off empty handed, though the attraction retains its compelling force. Cholon is the gambling city . . . the city of opium dives where for a few piasters you can have a flap board bed, a nugget of opium, a boy to prepare your pipes . . . Cholon is open to all desires."

The name Cholon means "Great Market" (*Cho* means market; *Lon* means large). Chinese buyers and millers of rice, importers, traders, and manufacturers did their business in Cholon. In the 1960s, Chinese merchants controlled more than 50% of South Vietnam's imports, and nearly all of the nation's foreign exchange and textile factories. The socialist government frowned upon the large profits retained by the Chinese capitalist merchant class. In 1978, Chinese-owned firms were nationalized. As tensions between Vietnam and China reached a peak in the spring of 1979, thousands of Chinese-Vietnamese (essentially the middle-class of the country), called Hoa, left Vietnam.

Cholon has many superb restaurants, temples, markets, orphanages, specialty hospitals, and the Redemptarist Cathedral. Near the

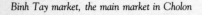

Binh Tay market, the main market in Cholon

Binh Tay market in western Cholon stands the St. Francis Catholic Church where Diem and his brother fled in November 1963 to escape the military coup. The brothers were discovered hiding here and assassinated. Off Ngo Gia Tu Street, one can still find the An Quang Pagoda, an active Buddhist center. The Phu Tho race track is also in this section.

HO CHI MINH CITY UNIVERSITY

The University of Ho Chi Minh City at 227 Nguyen Van Cu Street is the largest institution of higher learning in Vietnam. The University has a faculty of literature, philosophy, history, and law, as well as advanced schools of engineering and education. Consisting of three interconnecting four-story buildings, the College of Medicine and Pharmacy, built in 1967, is at 217 Nguyen Bang Hong Street.

Traveling on Tran Hung Dao, one passes the huge Grande Monde Casino. During the 1950s, the USMAAG (US Military Assistance and Advisory Group which controlled US aid to French forces during their war with Viet Minh) headquarters was located in a lovely building on an extension of Tran Hung Dao Street called Dong Khanh Street.

GIA DINH DISTRICT

This section encompasses the Tan Son Nhut airport, once Asia's busiest airport. Steel and concrete honeycomb revetments, which once protected US jets and bombers, are still in place on the airfield. On the road from the airport to town, a faded but still legible sign reads: MACV-HQ—referring to the headquarters of the Military Assistance Command for Vietnam, called "Pentagon East." After the American military withdrew in 1973, this vast compound became the Defense Attaché Office (DAO) and, in April 1975, it was used as a processing center for evacuating Americans and KIP (key indigenous personnel). The complex contained a post exchange, a gym, a bowling alley, a swimming pool and tennis courts, as well as barracks and headquarters of many military units. Many other US military facilities, such as the Third Field Hospital and the Dodge City BOQ (bachelor officers' quarters) were also on the site. The Tan Binh Hotel (formerly called the First Hotel), with a pool and tennis courts, is also located in this section.

TEMPLE OF MARSHAL LE VAN DUYET

Le Van Duyet, a eunuch and military leader under the first Nguyen emperor, Gia Long, controlled the southern portion of the newly consolidated country. The succeeding Emperor, Minh Mang, prohibited eunuchs from becoming mandarins and destroyed the temple to Le Van Duyet in an effort to eliminate the powerful eunuch system of service within the mandarin hierarchy. Although the tomb was rebuilt by his successor, Thieu Tri, the eunuch system of mandarin rank did not survive.

TOMB OF THE BISHOP OF ADRAN

The tomb of the Bishop, a Franciscan named Pigneau de Béhaine, was once located in the Gia Dinh area. The Bishop arrived in Vietnam at the end of the 18th century when the country was in the midst of political chaos. The Nguyen Dynasty was beset by dissension over royal succession involving the Mac and the Trinh families, further compounded by insurrections led by peasant rebels. Revolts and the Mac-Trinh-Nguyen struggle nearly extinguished the Nguyen clan. Nguyen Anh, the last survivor, secured the support of the bishop and obtained weapons to save the family line. The bishop's military actions spearheaded France's conquest of Vietnam. Descriptions of the bishop's tomb say it was surrounded by masonry screens, one of which had a bas-relief of a flying dragon with a Bible and a sword strapped to its back. The inscription praised the close bonds between the bishop and Nguyen Anh, who became Emperor Gia Long.

CU CHI DISTRICT

The Cu Chi district is adjacent to the northwest of Ho Chi Minh City. Cu Chi is a must on the travel list of anyone interested in understanding a vital aspect of the guerrilla war fought by the Vietnamese; its tunnel complex is of interest to American veterans and war buffs of all nationalities.

The ride northwest along Highway 22, from Saigon to the tunnel complex, is a tapestry of busy local color. You will pass through the agricultural Hoc Mon area of Ho Chi Minh Municipality where the scenery is rural: jackfruit trees, fields of peanuts, flocks of geese, wood carriers, wagons pulled by small ponies, and mothers and babies napping in string hammocks. The present population of Cu

Chi is 200,000, up from 80,000 during the war. During the French colonial period, the area around Cu Chi was the site of the huge Michelin rubber plantation.

CU CHI TUNNEL COMPLEX

Although most tunnels have been collapsed for safety reasons, one demonstration section of a tunnel has been preserved for visitors. A nearby visitors' center has charts illustrating the impressive extent of the tunnel system.

The crisscrossing tunnels were begun in the late 1940s by local resistance fighters looking for a place to hide their weapons from the French. In August 1945, a Viet Minh resistance group headquartered in this area (then called Maquis D) seized power from the French for 30 days. This short-lived Viet Minh victory is commemorated by the Saigon street: *Cach Mang Thang Tam,* or "August Revolution." In 1954, after the French left, the United States became increasingly involved in Vietnam through advisors and, in 1964, direct military action. The US 25th "Tropic Lightning" Division moved into the area (because the water level was low there) and unknowingly located their headquarters directly over the tunnels. At its most extensive stage, the tunnel system spread out for 210 miles (340 km.). The US military knew about the tunnels and aimed to destroy them. There was a saying among them at the time: "If Cu Chi goes, Saigon will be lost."

The Strategic Hamlet Program, started by the US in March 1962 and dubbed "Operation Sunrise," was based on British counterinsurgency programs against the Chinese Communists in Malaya. The plan was simple: relocated Vietnamese citizens were armed and trained to defend themselves against the "Viet Cong" (the Communists). Promised a new and better life, citizens of Cu Chi were moved from their villages into 180 relocation villages. "Find and Clear" (to clear the enemy from the tunnels) operations and psychological campaigns were conducted.

Once the citizens had been removed, Cu Chi became a free-fire zone. In one day, 80 tons of B-52 ordinance fell on the area. After the zone was denuded by defoliation, seeds of quick-growing grass were sown to supress the regrowth of indigenous plants. The "American grasses," as the new grass was called by the locals, dried up rapidly during the dry season. As a result, a spark from an exploding bomb would easily ignite the grass, instantly removing any enemy ground cover and hiding places. Food crops in the area were also lost in the process.

Motivated by anger, some citizens returned to their endangered

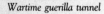

Wartime guerilla tunnel

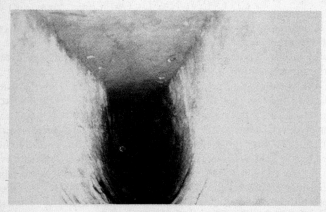

homes, where they joined the guerrillas, protecting themselves by widening and deepening the existing tunnels. Soon all activities of daily life were carried out underground. The tunnels allowed the guerrillas to travel undetected below patrolled roads and from one village to another. The local inhabitants followed the slogan: "Learn to walk without footprints, talk without sound, cook without smoke, and become invisible during all activities. That is the way to survive."

The tunnels under Cu Chi were at different levels, some up to 23 feet (7 m.) deep. First, two air holes were dug about 33 to 66 feet (10–20 m.) apart. The freshly removed dirt had to be carefully hidden since signs of recent digging would alert the Army of the Republic of Vietnam (Saigon troops) and US patrols. Recent bomb craters made an inconspicuous place to hide the dirt since the soil was already disrupted. Soon, a subterranean world evolved, with meeting halls and kitchens built underground. Water holes were dug for fresh drinking water and air holes were protected by booby traps. Entrance openings were expertly camouflaged as tree stumps, under cooking pots, in barns, and with plugs of live vegetation.

General William Westmoreland, Commander of US forces in Vietnam, learned of the existence of the tunnels and had a diagram drawn from intelligence of the system, a copy of which hangs in the visitor's center of the tunnels. In Westmoreland's version, the inhabitants of the tunnels were standing upright and wearing conical hats. His information also led him to believe the tunnels extended under the local branch of the Saigon River. Actually, there was one opening to a tunnel (650 feet [200m.] from the demonstration tunnel) that was dug below the water line at the river bank. Those using this entry point had to swim underwater into the tunnel. The South Vietnamese and US Navy patrol boats never found this tunnel opening.

Soldiers of the Big Red One chemical platoon were assigned to enter the narrow tunnels to rid them of the enemy. Members of the chemical platoon, chosen for their slim build, courage, and lack of claustrophobia, were volunteers called "Tunnel Rats." Hunting dogs also were used to assist in locating the enemy. Since units of dogs would sniff out the Viet Cong, local guerrilla militia used hot pepper to chase the dogs off the scent. This tactic, however, was not successful. When the dog handlers realized the enemy was using hot peppers to discourage the dogs from proceeding, they were encouraged to investigate more carefully. The tunnel dwellers changed many of their camouflage methods, including the use of American articles of clothing, soap, tobacco, and shaving cream to confuse the dogs.

After a search operation, people came out of the tunnels and resumed normal life above ground. Only a direct hit by a B-52 could destroy the tunnel system and many lives were lost in the terrifying bombings that attempted to do so. The Cu Chi district was also the headquarters for the coordination of the 1968 Tet Offensive on Saigon.

Visitors can experience a bit of tunnel life by entering a 165-foot (50 m.) stretch of tunnel that has been preserved and widened for Western physiques. While the tunnel is now somewhat broader, the crawl requires one to move along the hot and dark underground shaft on hands and knees. The minimal discomfort can only hint at the grueling experiences that took place in these tunnels during wartime.

Newly planted eucalyptus trees cover the once barren area over Cu Chi, with an occasional bomb crater scarring the land. The wreckage of a rusting B-41 tank hit by a B-40 hand-held anti-tank rocket remains a grim reminder of the US war in Vietnam.

HOTEL
ACCOMMODATIONS

Although unconfirmed by the Holiday Inn chain at this writing, the Vietnam News Agency (VNA) reported (April 1989) that Holiday Inn had agreed to construct a 500-room hotel as a joint venture with the Crystal Center Properties International of Hong Kong and the Tourist Bureau of Ho Chi Minh City. The hotel is expected to be commissioned in 1990. In addition, according to the VNA, the Sheraton chain has expressed interest in building tourist hotels in Ho Chi Minh City, Hanoi, and central Vietnam. An Australian company has towed a 200-room floating hotel from Australia's Great Barrier Reef to the Saigon River for use by tourists and business visitors.

Cuu Long (Majestic) Hotel
1 Dong Khoi Rd.
tel. 95515 and 95517
Telex 275 SG
Restaurant, international conference hall, cafeteria, souvenir and art shop. Laundry.

Ben Thanh (Rex) Hotel
141 Nguyen Hue
tel. 92185/93115
Telex 8201 HO BT-HCM
Restaurant, variety shows, conference hall, swimming pool, terraced bar, art shop, tailor, haircuts, laundry, sauna, cinema, post office.

Huu Nghi (Palace) Hotel
56–64 Nguyen Hue
tel. 97284
Telex 8208 HU HN-HCM
Swimming pool, dancing, restaurant, souvenir art shop.

Doc Lap (Caravelle) Hotel
19–23 Lam Som Square
tel. 93704/93706
Telex 8259 HO DL-HCM
Restaurant, laundry.

Huong Duong Hotel
150 Nguyen Thi Minh Khai
tel. 92404
Tennis courts, souvenir shop. This hotel hosts mostly Eastern European guests.

Bong Sen Hotel
117–119 Dong Khoi Rd.
tel. 99127/91516/20545

The following Saigon hotels are reserved for domestic travelers: **Thien Hong,** 52-56 Tan Da; **Thang Long,** 68A Nguyen Hue; **Vinh Loi,** 129-133 Ham Nghi; and **Hai Au,** 132 Dong Khoi.

Tan Binh Hotel
201 Hoang Van Thu
tel. 44282/44026/44027
Swimming pool, tennis courts, sauna. This hotel is near the airport and a few miles from downtown. Occasionally, there is dancing.

CUISINE

Restaurants in Saigon, such as the Tai Nam, open up and close down regularly. Heavy taxes levied on private businesses by the Communist government, especially those enterprises becoming too successful, can place the owner in a 95% tax bracket.

The Two Palms Restaurant on Le Lai Street, along the rail tracks and off the market circle, is operated by a program to aid orphan children. The Vietnamese name for this restaurant is *Nha Tinh Thuong,* or "House of Love." One can enjoy a feast here for very little: giant crispy fried fish and Oriental chicken salad.

Pho Binh, at 7 Ly Chinh Thang in Ward 3, serves "Hanoi soup." The restaurant was a liaison office and shelter for Commando group S-100 on the night it attacked the US Embassy during the Tet Offensive of 1968.

Madame Dai's Bibliotheque is located at 84A Nguyen Du Street. Find the current phone number of Madame Dai's restaurant, and call ahead. Madame Dai, a lawyer trained in Paris after World War II, is elegant and fluent in many languages. She was a dissident member of Thieu's National Assembly. In 1976, when the need for the private practice of law was no longer necessary under the Communist regime, she began to serve dinners in the library of her former law office. The restaurant was situated on a street near the courthouse where many lawyers had their practices, one block from the cathedral. Several nights a week, a few foreign guests dine on continental meals amid shelves of law books. The restaurant features a collection of live cats and antique ceramics. Madame Dai also has a storefront antique shop at 30 Ngo Duc Ke, one block from the Cuu Long Hotel.

The Café Hoan Kiem is at 27 Ngo Duc Ke.

My Canh is a floating restaurant on the Saigon River near the ferry dock. Finally, Van Canh Restaurant is located on 184 Rue Calmette. The telephone number is 94963.

In the Cholon section is the Arc-en-Ciel Hotel and Restaurant on 55 Tan Da Street (tel. 56924). This restaurant is known for its "Beef Seven Ways"—seven courses of beef are offered, starting with beef soup.

HO CHI MINH MUNICIPALITY DIRECTORY

	Telephone
VietnamTourism (Saigon Office of National Tourism Department), 71 Nguyen Hue, telex 295 DULIVINA SG	90772/ 90775/ 90776
Tourism Department of Ho Chi Minh City, 1 Dong Khoi, telex 275 SG and 276 SG	95515/95517
Air Vietnam Office, 27B Nguyen Dinh Chieu	99980/99910
Air France Office, Doc Lap Hotel, Lam Son Square	41278

COMMERCIAL ENTERPRISES	Telephone
Petechim (Vietnam Oil and Gas Corporation), 72 Xo Viet Nghe Tinh	52526
Rubexim (Vietnam National Rubber Export-Import Corporation), 64 Truong Dinh	90409
Viettronimex (Vietnam Electronics Import-Export Company), 74-76 Nguyen Hue	98200
Vimedex (Vietnam Medical Products Export-Import Corp), 34 Nguyen Hue and 246 Cong Quynh	25953
Vinafood (Vietnam National Food Import-Export), 24 Vo Van Tan	97676
Imexco, 8 Nguyen Hue—This firm imports and exports products of the municipality of Ho Chi Minh City	95938

SCHOOLS/EDUCATIONAL INSTITUTIONS

College of Economics, 17 Duy Tan
The University of Ho Chi Minh City, 227 Nguyen Van Cu Street
The College of Medicine and Pharmacy, 217 Nguyen Bang Hong
   Street
Children's Pioneer House, 4 Tu Xuong
Library of Ho Chi Minh City, 69 Ly Tu Trong
Library of Social Studies, 34 Ly Tu Trong
Conservatory of Music, 112 Nguyen Du

DAY TRIPS OUTSIDE OF
HO CHI MINH CITY

The visitor can hire a car or van plus a guide from downtown Saigon Tourism to travel to outlying areas. One or more side trips might be included on preplanned group tours. Trips may be planned to Ho Chi Minh Municipality (Saigon, Cholon, Gia Dinh, and Cu Chi districts) and/or the areas listed below.

MEKONG DELTA

The Mekong delta begins at Tan An on Highway 4, 25 miles (40 km.) southwest of Saigon. Nine provinces (from north to south) make up the Mekong delta: Long An, Tien Giang, Dong Thap, Ben Tre, An Giang, Cuu Long, Kien Giang, Hau Giang, and Minh Hai. Several branches of the Mekong River, the Tien Giang and the larger Hau Giang (Bassac), flow through the 9.25 million acres (3,723,189 hectares) of the delta. By the time these waterways reach the sea, they have branched off into nine tributaries—which accounts for the Mekong's historic name of Cuu Long (Nine Dragons).

One hundred years ago the upper course of the Mekong River was unknown to Westerners. In 1866, six Frenchmen led by Francis Garnier formed an expedition to explore the course of the Mekong River, hoping to find a river route to the heart of China. Although the river did not lead them to their goal, they were able to map over 4,000 miles (6500 km.) of previously uncharted terrain (250 miles [400 km.] of the river are in Vietnam).

Agriculture in the Delta. Because of the area's great natural reservoir, Cambodia's Tonle Sap, the Mekong plain never gets as dry as the Red River delta and the ebb and flow of the water levels are moderate year round. Since dikes (the main form of water control in the North) are unknown in the South, water on the delta has been controlled, since ancient times, by a network of canals. Fish, especially the *tai tuong* or "elephant ear" variety capable of thriving in brackish water, are raised in family ponds by almost all families of the province.

Pineapples were introduced into Vietnam in the last century. Today, there are large state-operated pineapple farms at Phan Van Hai and Le Minh Xuan on the outskirts of Ho Chi Minh City, and in the provinces of Tien Giang and Lam Dong. Pineapples require strong sunlight, high humidity, and a planting-to-harvesting season of 12 to 18 months. Although collectivization of farmlands is encouraged by the government, growers in the South are independent and stubbornly resist giving up their land to a commune. In late 1986, the government, recognizing and accepting this resistance, instituted economic reforms to encourage private production, such as the production contract system that permits some free enterprise.

Bananas are also cultivated in the delta. The growth process is started by cutting an underground shoot from a mature plant. After 10 months a bud with many small purple leaves appears at the tip of the stem. The leaves roll back to reveal clusters of small flowers which eventually develop into clusters of bananas called hands.

Long An Province. Long An Province is southeast of Ho Chi Minh Municipality and borders the "Parrot's Beak" section of Cambodia. Tan An is the province's capital. Long An begins the fertile agricultural lands of the Mekong delta. Its unique geographic feature is the Plain of Reeds. A floating, salt-resistant rice thrives in this swampy area. The seeds are distributed on the muddy fields at the very start of the rainy season. When the heavy rains fall, the seedlings have already sprouted just above the water line. At this stage, the rice plant continues growing as the water level rises. As the waters eventually recede, the tall rice plants, now heavy with rice kernals and having no water to keep them upright, flop back into the low water—from this position, the plants send down runners to form new roots to complete a self-perpetuating cycle.

My Tho: Tien Giang Province. My Tho is a fifty-minute ride south from Saigon, and is the capital of Tien Giang Province. Upon arrival, a visitor might arrange a boat trip to the nearby Thoi Son agriculture and fishing collective. After the boat excursion on the Tien River and a hike through a banana plantation situated along narrow dikes and across pole bridges, the visitor stops at a large, well-constructed "typical farmer's home." Examine the back rooms for a glimpse of the kitchen and sleeping areas characteristic of rural life in this part of Vietnam.

At the mouth of the Mekong near My Tho is Con Phung Island, the former home of the Cao Dai community once headed by a monk called the "Coconut Monk." Although he did not speak, the monk was "outspoken" and anti-war, making his island a sanctuary for deserters and refugees. He wrote down communications for his disci-

My Tho city

ples. Some say that the monk, educated in France, had been an engineer while others say he entered a Buddhist monastery at a young age. Whatever the truth of his background, in 1964 he began a community on Con Phung Island that advocated a united Vietnam. To emphasize the idea of reunification, the dock at the entrance to his island was formed in the shape of a large map of North and South Vietnam. He also built one 60-foot (18 m.) tall tower in the likeness of Jesus Christ and another tower to honor Buddha. He was jailed several times for protesting Diem's policies. The "Coconut Monk" even nominated himself as a candidate for president against the American-backed General Thieu. After the Communists came to power in 1975, his community dissolved.

Outside My Tho is a snake farm that breeds snakes for medicinal purposes. The venom is used to make anti-snake bite serum, anesthetics, and cough suppressants. The flesh, blood, and gall bladder of marine snakes and cobras are used to treat skeletal aches. The Vinh Trang Pagoda is also in My Tho city.

Dong Thap Province. Formed from the 1976 merger of Sa Dec and Kien Phong provinces, Dong Thap Province was part of Cambodia until it was ceded to Vietnam's Emperor Nguyen Phuc Khoat (who reigned from 1738 to 1765). The province was transferred because the Cambodian King, Nac Ton, was grateful for the Vietnamese help in quelling a rebellion in Cambodia. Dong Thap Province's products include shrimp chips (*banh phong tom*) and coconuts.

Ben Tre Province. Ben Tre, just south of My Tho, is composed of many islands. It is noted for its revolutionary spirit and as the hometown of the woman Deputy Commander of the Liberation Army, General Nguyen Thi Dinh. During the 1960s and early 1970s, General Dinh organized and trained women to fight a guerrilla war. Then, in 1979, she became president of Vietnam's Women's Association, a mass organization that recommends national policy on women's issues and encourages women to fulfill socialist ideals.

Coconuts are a specialty of Ben Tre. During the recent war with the US, coconut trees replaced bananas and sugarcane since both provided better ground cover for guerrillas and required less care. Women standing behind heaps of coconuts will beckon to you at Tam Quan. Stop there for a treat. The vendor will whack off the top of the coconut with a huge cleaver, pierce the white skin, and stick in a straw with which to drink the fresh juice. During the war, since kerosene was scarce, coconut oil was also used for lighting. A special honey with a distinctive taste is produced by bees that extract necter from the coconut flowers.

An Giang Province. An Giang is a rich agricultural province, known as the center of the Hoa Hao religion. In addition to a variety of fish, soy and mung beans, An Giang produces corn, sweet potatoes, tobacco, and floating rice.

Cuu Long Province. Cuu Long Province is made up of the two former provinces of Vinh Long and Tra Vinh. Vinh Long is the main city of the province. A trip on route 7A east through the Long Vinh countryside flows through quiet rice fields that appear untouched by the modern world. Route 7A crosses the Mang Thi River Canal which cuts across the province to connect the Bassac and Mekong rivers. Tra Vinh is 42 miles (68 km.) from Vinh Long. A four-mile drive on a dirt road from Tra Vinh leads to a site truly forgotten by time. Surrounding a man-made lake, called Ba Om, are centuries-old brick temples, still cared for by the local monks.

The timeless beauty of the ancient Khmer-influenced religious complex is heightened by the protective shade of tropical trees. You may wish that there were a hotel nearby so that you could spend time contemplating the serene atmosphere and significance of the temples.

(For the war-time history of Vinh Long see Bibliography: Harvey Meyerson's *Vinh Long.*)

Oc Eo: Kien Giang Province. On the Hau River, vestiges of the ancient culture of Oc Eo have been discovered between the Plain of Reeds and Cape Ca Mau. The origins and nature of the culture that flourished at this site are still vague. Excavations and C-14 (carbon) dating of the archaeologic finds there continue to contribute a clearer understanding of the Oc Eo. French scholars found evidence that Oc Eo had been a port city of Funan, a kingdom that preceded Champa. The city at Oc Eo, which flourished from the second to the seventh centuries, contained large temples and palaces on granite foundations. These structures differed from those of the Khmer or the Cham cultures.

There is evidence of active trading and cultural exchanges between the port of Oc Eo with India and Central Asia. In addition, Roman coin-like medals found at Oc Eo support the theory of trade with the Mediterranean area in the second century. Funan culture was based on wet rice cultivation; its canals and waterways (still used today) crossed the country. Fine examples of worked bronze, jade, silver, and gold attest to the Funan's knowledge of metalworking. Ceramic vessels of Oc Eo had ring-footed bottoms, narrow necks and mouths; pots featured a spout with zig-zag, cross-hatched patterns.

Can Tho: Hau Giang Province. Situated 112 miles (169 km.) southwest of Ho Chi Minh City in Hau Giang Province, Can Tho is the main rice-producing area of the country. Rice planting takes place in July; the rice seedlings are transplanted a month later.

Lying by the Hau Giang River, Can Tho is a junction of communication. It is a thriving commercial center, with a busy shipping industry.

Visitors can take a boat ride along the Hau River and observe the changing landscapes while observing life on the river. Also of interest in Can Tho are tours of the Song Hau State Farm and Fruit Plantation, the Orchid Gardens, the Can Tho University, Medical School and hospital, and the Museum of the Ninth Military Zone.

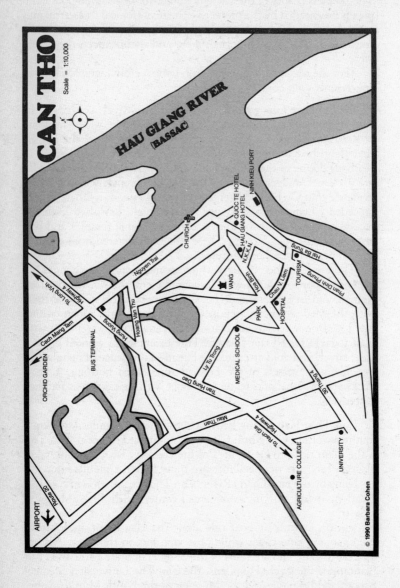

CAN THO

Scale = 1:10,000

HAU GIANG RIVER
(BASSAC)

CHURCH

NGUYEN TRAI

QUOC TE HOTEL

HAU GIANG HOTEL

NINH KIEU PORT

N.K.K.N.

HOA BINH

VANG

CHAU V. LIEM

HAI BA TRUNG

PHAN DINH PHUNG

TOURISM

PARK

HOSPITAL

HOANG VAN THU

HUNG VUONG

LY TU TRONG

MEDICAL SCHOOL

TRAN HUNG DAO

30 THANG 4

MAU THAN

Highway 4

To Rach Gia

AGRICULTURE COLLEGE

UNIVERSITY

Cach Mang Tam

To Long Vinh

Highway 4

BUS TERMINAL

ORCHID GARDEN

Route 20

AIRPORT

© 1990 Barbara Cohen

Minh Hai Province. The southernmost tip of Vietnam, called Ca Mau, is in Minh Hai province. There, you will find the U Minh forest, a low-lying area of mud flats and mangrove swamps, that stretches to the Gulf of Thailand on the western coast. In addition to its unique geography, the U Minh forest is economically significant for its shrimp fishing and mangroves. Mangrove is a light, strong wood used to make oars and mangrove coal.

TAY NINH PROVINCE

Tay Ninh province is the home of the large, colorful Cao Dai Temple (see section on religion for more about Cao Dai). In the center of the province is a mountain called the Black Virgin (Ba Den). A pagoda to the goddess is located near the top of the mountain.

BIEN HOA: DONG NAI PROVINCE

Bien Hoa, which specializes in pottery and bronze work, is located about 20 miles (32 km.) from Ho Chi Minh City on the banks of the Dong Nai River in Dong Nai Province.

The Soldiers' Cemetery—Army of the Republic of Vietnam (Saigon government) military personnel—was on the Bien Hoa highway (from Saigon to Thu Duc). A statue of a human figure called "Sorrow" graced the entrance to the cemetery. The stone figure depicted mourning so vividly that some people believed they could hear it weeping at night. The Soldiers' Cemetery has since been bulldozed and is now the site of a radar station.

Bien Hoa was the site of a large military air base during the Vietnam conflict. From this installation, Australian airmen of the Royal Australian Air Force (RAAF), who arrived in August 1964, flew de Havilland C-7A transports called Caribous. The RAAF also had English Canberry B-57 bombers based at Phang Rang on the coast. Between April 1967 and May 1971, the RAAF flew nearly 12,000 bombing sorties over the Ho Chi Minh Trail supply routes. In June 1965, the first battalion of the Royal Australian Regiment arrived in Vietnam. Later, squadrons of Iroquois helicopters arrived by RAAF Hercules air transport. By 1969, the combined forces of Australian and New Zealand forces in Vietnam reached a peak of over 8,000 men.

Buu-Son Temple. Hidden for centuries by the roots of a large tree, a 15th-century stone Cham statue can now be viewed in the

Buu-Son Temple. The land of former hunting grounds can be found on the nearby Lagna Plain. Theodore Roosevelt, Jr., son of the American president, and his brother, Kermit, hunted here to collect large animal specimens for the Museum of Chicago. In 1933, the Roosevelt brothers wrote about their adventures on this hunting expedition in the *Three Kingdoms of Indochina*.

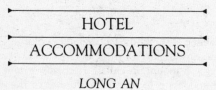

HOTEL
ACCOMMODATIONS

LONG AN

Bong Sen Hotel
7 Provincial Route 3
Tan An
tel. 439

Huong Tram Hotel
60 Nguyen Trung Truc
Tan An
tel. 388

TIEN GIANG

The Ap Bac Hotel. Located on My Tho waterfront street, the Ap Bac serves local specialties as well as fresh seafood and crab dishes. In addition to seafood, the specialty of My Tho is *Canh bap cai goi thit*, a soup with tiny packets of meat wrapped neatly in cabbage leaves. *Huu Tieu My Tho* is a hearty rice noodle soup.

The Ap Bac Hotel is named after the battle of Ap Bac (the first large-scale battle using helicopters), which took place in the delta during January 1963. The National Liberation Front soldiers (Viet Cong), forewarned of the assault, were able to ambush the Saigon troops that had been airlifted into the area by American helicopters. Five choppers were downed and three American advisers were killed. At that time, in 1963, American advisers only accompanied South Vietnamese troops into battle. In March 1965, US ground troops arrived in Vietnam to engage in combat.

DONG THAP

Sadec Hotel
108/5A Hung Vuong
Sadec
tel. 2498

Cao Lanh Hotel
Doc Binh Kieu
Cao Lanh
tel. 234

BEN TRE

Ben Tre Hotel
16 Hai Ba Trung
Ben Tre
tel. 2240

AN GIANG

Thai Binh
12 Nguyen Hue
Long Xuyen
tel. 7253

Long Xuyen
17 Van Cung
Long Xuyen
tel. 6555

Chau Doc
17 Doc Phu Thu
Chau Doc
tel. 2084

CUU LONG

Cuu Long Hotel
1 May First Street
Vinh Long
tel. 2494/2529/2357

KIEN GIANG

May First Hotel
38 Hung Son
Rach Gia
tel. 314

To Chau Hotel
4F Ho Chi Minh Street
Rach Gia

HAU GIANG

Quoc Te Hotel
12 Hai Ba Trung
Can Tho
tel. 35793/20794

Hau Giang Hotel
34 Nam Ky Khoi Nghia
Can Tho
tel. 35537/35181

MINH HAI

Minh Hai Hotel
14 Hoang Van Thu
Minh Hai
tel. 621

Ca Mau Hotel
20 Phan Ngoc Hien
tel. 165

DIRECTORY

	Telephone
TAY NINH	
Tay Ninh Tourism, 4/3A Trung Nu Vuong, Tay Ninh	2376
DONG NAI	
Dong Nai Tourism, 105 Highway One, Bien Hoa	2367
LONG AN PROVINCE	
Long An Tourism, 7 Provincial Route 3, Tan An	227/425

	Telephone
TIEN GIANG	
Tien Giang Tourist Office, 66 Hung Vuong, My Tho	
DONG THAP	**Telephone**
Dong Thap Tourist Office, 108/5 A Hung Vuong, Sadec	2204
BEN TRE	**Telephone**
Ben Tre Tourism, 65 Dong Khoi, Ben Tre	2197–706
AN GIANG	**Telephone**
An Giang Tourism Office, 17 Nguyen Van Cung, Long Xuyen	6544 or 6367
CUU LONG	**Telephone**
Cuu Long Tourist Office, 1 May First Street, Vinh Long	2494/2529/2357
KIEN GIANG	**Telephone**
Kien Giang Tourist Office, 12 Ly Tu Trong, Rach Gia	2081
HAU GIANG	**Telephone**
Hau Giang Tourism, 27 Chau Van Liem, Can Tho	20147/35275
MINH HAI	**Telephone**
Minh Hai Tourist Office, 14 Hoang Van Thu, Minh Hai	369/560/621

CAMBODIA:

Angkor

Visitors to Vietnam should consider making the short flight to Cambodia to see Angkor, unquestionably one of the wonders of the ancient world. Center of a once mighty empire, Angkor (*Angkor* means city in the Khmer language) is one of the most fascinating tourist meccas in the world. At the height of its glory, the Kingdom of Angkor covered more area than modern Cambodia and extended from the South China Sea to the Indian Ocean. The Khmer realm included all of the plain and the delta of the Mekong River, the south of present-day Laos, and the Menam River plain in southeast Thailand. Angkor today represents the ruins of new cities built over old ones during five centuries (from the 10th to 15th) of growth under the rule of over 30 monarchs. The 70-plus archaeological sites of Angkor, which constituted the capital of the vast kingdom, covers an area of nearly 75-square miles (195 sq. km.) and extends from the shore of the Great Lake to Mount Kulen to the north.

Although European missionaries in the 16th and 17th centuries had reported the presence of a lost city overgrown by the jungle in northeastern Cambodia not far from the great lake of Tonle Sap, no systematic exploration occurred until 1860 when the French naturalist, Henri Mouhot, visited the site and described his find to the Western world: "Grander than anything left to us by Greece or Rome." Because of the dense jungle cover, even Mouhot did not realize the vastness of the ancient city. His writings about Angkor and premature death in Laos encouraged archaeologists of the École Française d'Extrême-Orient (The French School of Far Eastern Studies) to painstakingly reclaim the ruins from the jungle. In 1923, after seeing the lost city revealed, Somerset Maugham wrote: "I have never seen anything in the world more beautiful than the temples of Angkor, but I do not know how on earth I am going to set down in black and white such an account of them as will give even the most sensitive reader more than a confused and shadowy impression of their grandeur."

In 1970, the area of Angkor Wat was in the hands of the North Vietnamese Army and local guerrillas sympathetic to their cause against the American-backed government. A 60-square mile (156-sq.-km.) zone around Angkor was declared "liberated" and included a guerrilla base where anti-aircraft units were set up alongside ar-

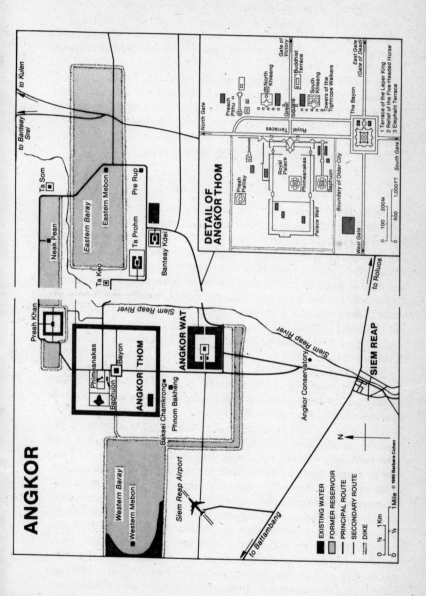

ANGKOR

DETAIL OF ANGKOR THOM

to Kulen
to Banteay Srei

Ta Som
Neak Pean
Ta Keo
Eastern Mebon
Eastern Baray
Ta Prohm
Pre Rup
Banteay Kdei

Preah Khan
Siem Reap River
Phimeanakas
Bayon
Baphuon
ANGKOR THOM
ANGKOR WAT
Baksei Chamkrong
Phnom Bakheng

Western Baray
Western Mebon
Siem Reap Airport

Angkor Conservatory
Siem Reap River
SIEM REAP

to Battambang
to Roluos

N

EXISTING WATER
FORMER RESERVOIR
PRINCIPAL ROUTE
SECONDARY ROUTE
DIKE

0   ½   1 Km
0   ½   1 Mile   © 1990 Barbara Cohen

North Gate
Preah Pithu
North Khleang
Buddhist Terrace
South Khleang
Towers of the Tightrope Walkers
Green Square
Royal Terraces
Preah Palilay
Royal Palace
Phimeanakas
Baphuon
Palace Wall
West Gate
Boundary of Older City
South Gate
East Gate (Gate of Dead)
Gate of Victory
The Bayon
1 Terrace of the Leper King
2 Relief of the Five-Headed Horse
3 Elephant Terrace

0   100   200 M
0   500   1,000 FT

chaeological treasures. Hoping to save the ruins from weapons fire, the Cambodian government refrained from attacking North Vietnamese units. In 1979, Vietnamese troops entered Cambodia once again, this time to drive out the Khmer Rouge, the fanatic Communist regime under Pol Pot.

For the past ten years Cambodia has been ruled by a Vietnamese-backed government. During the past two decades of Cambodian civil war, the treasures of Angkor have been off-limits to tourism. In early 1990, rival Cambodian groups were seriously negotiating a ceasefire. As a result, the sporadic skirmishes around the Angkor site have been checked and visitors are returning.

GETTING THERE

In mid-1989, US travel agencies were still prohibited from engaging in any form of tourist business in Cambodia as well as Vietnam. Until this travel embargo is lifted, US citizens must make their travel arrangements to Cambodia through agencies based in Bangkok, Australia, France, Canada, or elsewhere. Itineraries can also be made through a travel agency familiar with Southeast Asia such as those listed in the section on Making Travel Arrangements to Vietnam. Thai Airways is planning one day trips from Bangkok. Visitors to Hanoi have been able to acquire visas for traveling in Cambodia by applying to the Cambodian embassy in Hanoi at 71 Tran Hung Dao Street, tel. 57902.

The hotels at Siem Reap where visitors to Angkor once stayed have recently reopened for overnight guests. The new Air France hotel had just been completed when the country was plunged into the nightmare bloodbath of Pol Pot.

Since hotels near Angkor are closed, a visit to the ruins, at this writing, is basically a day trip. The excursion begins with a brief flight (under an hour) via Cambodian Airlines from Phnom Penh to the nearby town of Siem Reap for the day's outing in Angkor. Visitors must follow a schedule that flies them out of the Angkor Wat area by the end of the day. Although experts recommend three days as the minimum time required to explore the ruins adequately, anyone having the opportunity to spend even a few hours there may consider themselves fortunate. If you are going to Angkor, make the most of your time at the ruins by first reading one of the many guidebooks on the history and archaeology of Angkor. Although Cambodian guides are knowledgeable and informative, time constraints limit them to summarizing a vast amount of information.

EARLY HISTORY

The metropolis of Angkor was heir to the ancient kingdoms of Funan and Chenla. Funan was an India-influenced maritime center located on the Gulf of Thailand with its capital located at Oc Eo on the southernmost tip of present-day Vietnam. Founded in the first century AD, Funan reached its peak at the end of the fifth century AD. By AD 550, Funan had been engulfed by a kingdom of rice-cultivators to its north called Chenla by Chinese envoys. Kambu Svayambhuva was the king of Chenla. Under his reign the people began to call themselves Kambujadesa, children of Kambu, and their country, Kambuja.

The absorption of the Funan kingdom represented the Pre-Angkor period of the Khmer Empire which lasted until AD 802. During this time the Khmers were briefly under the influence of Java. In the ninth century, Chenla, in turn, was "liberated" from the Javanese by King Jayavarman II who united its scattered settlements under his rule. The origin of Jayavarman II is a mystery. Some legends tell that he was raised as a child in the Sailendra Court (Sailendra included Sumatra, Java, and much of Malay) and was sent to establish a Javanese colony on the mainland.

The Khmers under Jayavarman II went on to subdue the Mon people who lived in the valley of the Menam river basin on their western flank. In addition to expanding the fledgling empire, Jayavarman II secured for himself, as well as his successors, supreme authority within the society by setting up the cult of devaraja, the worship of the king as a god.

EVOLUTION OF ARCHITECTURAL STYLE

Although the magnificent history of the Khmer Empire cannot be grasped through a recital of successive styles of architecture and sculpture, all that remains for evaluating its greatness are the eloquent stone skeletons. Unfortunately, most of the smaller monuments and buildings of the Khmer empire had been constructed in wood, which the jungle climate has long since destroyed. The remarkable stoneworks built by hordes of slaves and prisoners-of-war remain, however. An outline of Khmer history and brief descriptions of temples representing periods in the kingdom's history follows:

In the Pre-Angkorian period, Khmer buildings were constructed with large bricks set in place without mortar. Bricks, along with stone, laterite, and sandstone, were used until the end of the Angkor period. Sandstone was quarried in Phnom Kulen, a mountain of sandstone north of Angkor, and shipped to the construction sites along the kingdom's broad canals. Sand-filled trenches were used as foundations for building walls. Next, slabs of laterite, a red clay that hardens after it is extracted from the ground, were placed over the sand-filled trenches. Walls were then positioned to rest on the laterite slabs. Since the builders had used sand-filled trenches as foundations for their walls, water from the rains and nearby streams that has seeped in over the years has shifted the sand, causing the walls to move and eventually crack.

Buildings in the Angkor area evolved from brick to sandstone, from single-tower to multiple-tower temples, and from ground-level shrines to those raised to the heights of elevated pyramids. The layout of each temple complex was centralized, symmetrical, rectangular, and remained consistent throughout the years. Each temple had a terrace, a tower with a tiny room, and a vaulted gallery running around one level of the building. All temple towers were capped with stone pillars in the shape of lotuses, encrusted in gold leaf.

Angkor Wat

Khmer architects never discovered the advantages of the key-stone arch which would have allowed them to build round archways. The keystone is a wedge-shaped stone placed at the center of an arch which locks the other stones of the arch in place. Khmer construction involved placing one flat stone upon another in balanced tiers. Because this method, called *corbel* construction, could not be used for the ceilings of large audience halls, sturdy beams of wood were used to support the roofs. Many roofs at the ruins have collapsed as the wooden beams have succumbed to the effects of time.

The stone towers did not need to be large as they were designed to shelter the image of the god-priest-king, while worshippers crowded outside in the courtyards. In the center of the temple, the exclusive domain of the priests, sat an image of the god, or a large *linga* (i.e., a stone phallus thought to contain the soul or essence of the king-god). Each temple is enclosed within a series of concentric walls; to gain access to the center, visitors must pass through many gateways and doors.

There are two general phases of Angkor styles. The first, from the 9th century to the 11th century, includes Kulen, Prah Ko, Bakheng, Koh Ker, and Banteay Srei. The second phase, from the 11th to the 15th century, includes the Baphuon, the Angkor Wat, and the Bayon styles.

First Phase of Angkor Construction: 9th Century. The Khmer kings, after gaining independence from Java's influence in the ninth century, built several cities on the northern shore of the Great Lake, in the area of Siem Reap.

The main shrine of King Jayavarman II at Kulen (Lychee mountain), of which little remains, was 25 miles (40 km.) northwest of Angkor Thom. Overseeing a religious ceremony from this mountain, the king proclaimed the country's freedom from Java. Waters from the Siem Reap River, which runs through Angkor, are considered holy because the river originates on this sacred mountain (Mount of Kulen) before descending to lower elevations in water-rapids and falls. Since the waters flow over sacred images carved on the stones of the riverbed over 1,000 years ago, it is believed the waters are further sanctified and imbued with the stones' sacred qualities.

Prah Ko temple was dedicated at Roluos (southeast of present-day Siem Reap) by Indravarman, a successor of Jayavarman II, to the funerary cult of the king's ancestors. Indravarman expanded the irrigation systems with remarkable vitalizing economic effects on the kingdom's food production. Some original pieces of external plaster remain on the wall of Prah Ko.

Bakong, near Roluos, is the most important monument of Indravarman's reign because it housed the royal *linga.* The temple is located on a man-made hill and follows a uniformity of construction upon which later buildings were modeled—that is, a steep pyramid with central tower. Examples of bas-relief,* an advance over previous flatter styles, can be seen in the figures that stand out somewhat from the walls at Bakong. The central shrine of Bakong was rebuilt in the 12th century.

Bakheng, erected in 893 by Yasovarman (the son of Indravarman), was the first temple of Angkor proper. Located just outside and south of Angkor Thom, Bakheng later became the home of Yasovarman's *linga* and his tomb after death. Bakheng is the first Khmer building constructed entirely of sandstone and the first to depict a map of the mythical heavens. The temple has seven levels, like its celestial model, Mount Meru.

Bakheng is a complex of buildings surrounded by five shrines and incorporating 108 small towers. Situated on a steep hill, the buildings are approached by a stairway guarded by stone lions. The 13th-century Chinese envoy, Chou Ta-kuan, described these lions as "golden." The main pyramid-shaped structure rises in five many-tiered towers to the top platform where, surrounded by the smaller towers, a central obelisk thrusts upward into the air, heralding the power of the king. A great Buddha statue once stood inside the base of the great obelisk. In the rear of the tower on a stone altar was a *linga.* The extent of this temple complex was larger than Angkor Thom, which was built later.

Baksei Chamkrong, built in the beginning of the tenth century and located at the south gate of Angkor Thom, represents a transition between the previous (Bakheng) architectural style and that of the Koh Ker Temple; subsequent temples project a distinct pyramidal silhouette. Baksei Chamkrong was the first Khmer temple built entirely of durable stone and brick. A masterpiece of balance and proportion, a single brick tower 45-1/2 feet (13 m.) still stands on a laterite base.

---

*Rubbings of the stone bas-relief figures used to be made by shaping wet paper around the bas-relief figures and then rubbing charcoal over the paper. The charcoal captured the image beneath the paper and, in the process, eroded the delicate stone features of the reliefs. To preserve the artifacts, stone rubbings are no longer permitted.

Koh Ker is a massive ceremonial complex northeast of Angkor. The Chams ruled Angkor for two decades and made Koh Ker the capital of its colony. Angkor once again became the Khmer capital after AD 944. The temple, now sadly in ruins, once housed an awe-inspiring *linga* more then 100 feet (30 m.) high.

Banteay Srei, an architectural jewel 15-1/2 miles (25 km.) north of Angkor Thom, was built in AD 967 and rediscovered in 1914. It is called the "citadel of women" because it has a low, rather than upthrusting, shape and it is decorated with fine feminine carvings on pink sandstone instead of the plaster-coated carved brick found on earlier structures. The *apsaras* (heavenly female dancers) here have more voluptuous curves than appear elsewhere in Angkor. Representations of monkeys, wild cats, and parrots line the platforms in the main enclosure—images not seen in other buildings.

In the early 1920s, Andre Malraux, the French revolutionary writer, was accused of stealing sculpture from Banteay Srei and imprisoned by the French-colonial authorities. Later, Malraux published the *Royal Way* in which he captures the exotic, mystic nature of the ruins.

Phimeanakas, the "Celestial Palace," was built in the tenth century around the same time as Banteay Srei. The "Celestial Palace" was the temple-mountain that marked the center of the capital of Jayavarman V where the king spent the first watch of every night in the company of the spirit of the sacred Naga, the country's protector. The temple was in the center of a royal palace complex which no longer exists. A Malay called Suryavarman I usurped the throne from Jayavarman V.

The Second Phase of Angkor Works: 11th Century. Just south and up against the walls of the Phimeanakas, lies **Baphuon,** which was called "copper tower" by the Chinese envoy and reporter, Chou Ta-kuan, probably because its tower was once of gilded wood, or sheathed with plates of copper or gold leaf. The temple has an elevated causeway supported by round columns. The sandstone walls were reinforced by wooden beams in the middle; when the wood rotted, the walls collapsed. Once the center of a town, this temple is now covered by the later ruins of Angkor Thom. In size, the copper tower is second only to the Bayon among the monuments of Angkor Thom. Of Baphuon, Somerset Maugham said:"No building on earth seems more sure of itself." The temple was in the process of reconstruction in 1970 when guerrilla war prevented its completion.

The Classical Age: The 12th Century. Erected before AD 1150, **Angkor Wat** (Wat means temple) is the funeral temple of Surya-varaman II. Anna Leonowens, the governess, Anna, of Anna and the King of Siam (also populary known from the play *The King and I*), has called the ruins "a petrified dream of some Michelangelo of giants, more impressive in its loneliness, more elegant in its grace, than aught Greece and Rome have left us."

Covering an area of one square mile (1.6 sq. km.), Angkor Wat is one of the largest temple complexes in the world. The temple is dedicated to the god Vishnu, of whom the Emperor was considered a reincarnation. A sacred statue of Vishnu stood in the base of the central tower. By the 15th century, the Wat evolved into a Buddhist religious center. Angkor Wat was built outside the city walls and is the only building in Angkor whose entrance faces west (the direc-tion of the dead) instead of east, the direction of sunrise and life.

Basically a three-layered pyramid, Angkor Wat has towers at the corners of each story. The towers, called *prasats*, represent lotus buds about to burst into bloom. Each story is set back a bit from the direct center of the terrace below, giving an illusion of additional height. The stairs leading upward into the temple are roofed. The *naga* bal-ustrades lining the main entrance repeat the Churning of the Sea of Milk theme (see below). To the left, facing the Wat, are deities pulling in one direction; to the right are the demons pulling the serpent in the opposite direction.

The marvelous bas-relief of Angkor Wat's outer wall of the lower picture gallery depicts scenes of the *Ramayama*. The *Ramayama* is the Hindu epic of good against evil as told through the struggles of Rama and his enemy, Ravana. Since Rama was an incarnation of Vishnu (to whom Angkor Wat is dedicated) and the emperor was considered the incarnation of Vishnu, the *Ramayana* is a natural theme to be depicted on the gallery walls. The bas-relief figures also tell the story of Suryavarman II, first being crowned and then at the head of his army, riding an elephant into battle against the Chams. The panel called "Days of Judgment" portrays the 32 hells of Brahm-inism, including the hell of sharp-thorned trees, the hell of choking, and the hell of tears. Yama, the judge of the dead, rides an ox amid this hellish agony. Fortunately for posterity, these scenes have been protected by a gallery roof and are well preserved.

Inside the moat of Angkor Wat near a lotus pond among fruit trees is an active 150-year-old Buddhist monastery. Because these monks have kept the jungle from engulfing their home, the Wat here is better preserved than other structures in the area.

Angkor Wat represents the highpoint in the evolution of Khmer architecture; all subsequent monument building begins an age of excess and decadence.

The Zenith of Angkor Splendor. In 1177, the Chams sacked Angkor Thom, looting and destroying many Khmer treasures. Several years later, King Jayavarman VII drove the Chams out and restored the royal city to its former grandeur. With the Chams reduced to vassal status, the Buddhist (Mahayana) Jayavarman VII devoted his energies to massive building projects that included the temple of Bayon (dedicated to Buddha whom the Khmers worshipped as a god) and at least 102 hospitals throughout the kingdom. The royal city had libraries containing palm-leaf books, but only writings on stone survive. At its cultural height, Angkor Thom may have had one million inhabitants.

Angkor Thom (which means *great city*), the royal city itself, covers an area of four square miles (10.4 sq. km.). The total length of the wall surrounding the city is 7-1/2 miles (12 km.); incorporated into the wall are a number of earlier buildings: Baphuon and Phimeanakas. The city is dominated by a mania for colossal size, punctuated with enormous numbers of towers and reliefs.

Great gates were decorated with representations of the face of Lokesvara, the compassionate holy one who postponed going to heaven to remain on earth and accomplish good deeds. The faces reportedly bear a resemblance to Jayavarman himself. Gigantic three-headed stone elephants flank these enormous gates that once allowed elephants to parade through. Past the gates, one gained access to the city over *naga*-decorated bridges.

Four roads led from four gates to converge in the geometric center of the city (the temple of Bayon). A broad causeway leads to the opening called the Gate of Victory, which connects the eastern reservoir to the temple of Bayon. The gate leads from the outer walls to the large square, which has an access gate to the north. The southern approach to the city is on a causeway lined with 54 statues of giants struggling with Naga, enacting the *Churning of the Sea* Creation myth.

In the center is a great square, bounded on the west by the walls of the Royal Palace and Baphuon, on the south by Bayon, and on the east by the royal terrace and a stand of the restored oblong buildings called the Towers of Tightrope Walkers—a misnomer since most authorities believe the towers were used to confine prisoners of the state. The Chinese envoy to Angkor, Chou Ta-kuan, reported that innocent people confined to the towers suffered no ill-effects, while the guilty would break out into a fever and develop a fatal disease within five days of their incarceration. Given the prison context of the complex as described by Chou Ta-kuan, the Towers of Tightrope Walkers could be subtly interpreted as referring to the accused offenders who walked a fine line between life and death.

Within the city itself is the elephant terrace with its frieze of life-size marching elephants that run along the Royal Plaza for 1,500 feet (427 m.). On top of the stone elephant terrace stood wooden pavilions decorated with gold that shaded the king when he viewed games and processions or held court.

Slightly to the north and as an extension of the terrace of elephants is the terrace of the Leper King, named after a statue found in the area. Although French art historians deny that the statue portrays a leper, Cambodian legend does describe a leader who was afflicted with the disease. The statue in question is on display in the National Musuem in Phnom Penh.

Bayon, the temple of Angkor Thom, is located in the city's geographic center. The 50-tower temple is an awesome sight. At first glance, the complex seems a shapeless mass of stone. Suddenly, further scrutiny reveals a face, enigmatic and silent, watching with half-closed eyes. Soon, another face is made out, and another, and still yet another, until they are all around—silent, heavy, and impressive, staring from a primitive and remote time.

Each tower of Bayon features Lokesvara's four faces that are associated with the compassionate attitude of "looking everyway at once." The expressions on the stone faces seem to glisten and then pass slowly into shadow, as the bright Cambodian sun moves across the sky. The art conservator Henri Parmentier found the enigmatic faces "profoundly affecting." On a moonlit night, the faces of Bayon can be unnerving, enlightening, or exquisitely romantic, depending upon the frame of mind one brings to the experience.

Bas-reliefs of the Bayon are a mixture of Hindu mythology and a humanist feeling introduced by the Buddhism of Jayavarman VII. Scenes show common folk activities, many of which duplicate the activities of today's Cambodian citizens, such as the preparation of rice, a visit to a healer, selling, and buying. Amusements are depicted in the form of hunting and acrobatics, including sporting events such as cockfights and wild boar contests. The reliefs also portray violent scenes of battle. Bayon is noted for the decorative figures of *apsaras*, the heavenly creatures with incredibly sweet expressions, flying on the spray of ocean waves.

"Sea of Milk" myth in bas relief, Angkor

Preah Khan, a Buddhist temple built by King Jayavarman VII to honor his dead father, is located in the town where the king routed the Chams. The temple has two levels supported by round stone columns (round columns are unusual at Angkor) and a wooden stairway used to access the upper floor. Because of its unusual round columns, it is believed the temple was modeled after a wooden building long since decomposed in the jungle climate. Silken tapestries from China once hung on the inside walls. The temple contains stones with inscriptions in Sanskrit, the classic language of India. Walls surrounding the temple complex are from 2,296 to 2,625 feet (700–800 m.) in length.

Sras Srang, a wooden pavilion built during the reign of Jayavarman VII on the shore of the women's bath, is situated on a small lake. Chou Ta-kuan observed the women bathing: "They have no shame about leaving their clothes on the river bank and going into the water." Although the wooden pavilion has disappeared, the stone nagas that led from the bathhouse to the water remain.

Ta Prohm was built by Jayavarman VII as a shrine for his mother and as a monastery devoted to its upkeep. A stele referred to the temple as a monument "whose limbs are adorned with gold and resplendent with gems." The magnificent roots of a tree pushing between the huge stone blocks of the temple have been left that way intentionally, at the suggestion of French art conservators Bernard Groslier and George Coedes, who devoted years to the understanding and preservation of the treasures at Angkor. The sight of the tree's powerful embrace of the stone evokes feelings a visitor will very likely remember forever. In 1948, Sir Malcolm MacDonald, a British envoy to Southeast Asia, described the ancient roots: ". . . tendons of the roots clasp the gateway like a hundred tentacles of an octopus, clutching at its four carved human faces, blinding their eyes, crushing their noses and sealing their lips in a suffocating network of strangleholds."

Two species of tree are associated with the ruins of Angkor: the silk-cotton tree and the banyan-like fig tree.

The tree at Ta Prohm is commonly called bombax or Kapok, the silk-cotton tree. Its trunk is straight and at elevations from 20 to 40 feet (6 to 12 m.), branches flare out at right angles like the spokes of an umbrella. The bark is a creamy beige with indentations; sunlight gives the bark a satin glow. Gnarled, muscular roots have wedged and forced their way up into the crevices, loosening and dislodging the great stones.

The other type of tree seen at the Angkor ruins is that at Ta

Giants pulling serpent, Angkor Thom

Som. The tree at Ta Som is a banyan-like fig whose trunk is made up of seemingly separate trees with giant coil-like roots that have the appearance of great reptiles.

Although the integrity of the empire lasted two centuries after the death of Jayavarman VII, the end of his reign marked the beginning of cultural decay. Foreign possessions were lost in wars; attacks of the Mongols from the north drove the Thais south into Khmer land; invasions by the Thais from Ayuthya eroded more and more of the Khmer Empire and repeated raids led to moving the capital further southward to Phnom Penh in 1434.

Since huge blocks of cut stone remain in the quarry, ready to be placed in yet another temple, Angkor must have been abandoned in great haste. Crosbie Garstin, a British writer who traveled to Angkor in the 1920s and author of *The Dragon and the Lotus,* imagined the end of the empire:

> Then came the terrible news: the terrible armies of the Siamese had swept upon the surrounding villages and were nearer to Angkor. The king was aroused in his golden tower. Tall fires blazed in the streets. In the houses, mail and chain rattled as warriors prepared . . . and then the dawn . . . the first stage of the great battle, perhaps beyond Preh Khan, or if the enemy approached from the south, around Angkor Wat. Can you see the bodies, the war chariots grinding to death those who lay wounded? And hear the sounds? The trumpeting of angry beasts; the cries and all the crashing noises. It must have lasted for days, that battle and then perhaps the slaves, given courage by the failing strength of their masters, rose in rebellion. Fighting within and without. A last time the drums beat on the walls. After that, silence . . . and the forest growing, growing. . . .

Angkor was abandoned 200 years after the death of Jayavarman VII and, by the 15th century, the Khmer civilization had fallen into obscurity. The proud Khmer race, however, survives.

GEOGRAPHY

Built between the sandstone mountains of Dangrek and the shore of the great Lake, Tonle Sap, Angkor was once much more accessible by sea, since the lake is the vestige of a wide inlet of the South China Sea that formerly covered the south central portion of the Cambodian lowlands. Due to the deposition of silt on its periphery, the lake continues to decrease in size. In the high-water season,

June to October, when the snows in the Himalayas are melting, water flows into the Tonle Sap, doubling and sometimes quadrupling the size of the lake, which covers roughly 1,000 square miles (2,600 sq. km.). The lake acts as a natural dam protecting the lower Mekong region from flooding. In the dry season from November through June, water from the lake drains southward into the Mekong River system to the South China Sea.

RELIGIOUS INFLUENCE

Understanding the belief system of the builders of the marvels at Angkor is the key to fully appreciating the symbolic magnificence of the ruins. Greatly influenced by India, the Khmer religion was an integral aspect of their civilization and building philosophy. The kings up to Jayavarman VII were Hindu. Subsequently, Hindus of the kingdom continued to worship Shiva in their temples while Buddhists, too, practiced their beliefs freely. In time there was a synthesis of beliefs, with citizens paying homage to both Shiva and Buddha.

Various temples which can be viewed today at Angkor are primarily mausoleums. The temple, where the kings were priests during their lifetimes, also housed the ashes and the spirits of the deceased god-kings; relatives of the king would also live in these sacred structures after the kings's death. Consequently, the temple itself was the holiest of holies, the spiritual and temporal center of the kingdom.

From a design aspect, the temples of Angkor were temporal recreations of the mythical Mount Meru—the holy mountain at the center of the cosmos that represented heaven on earth as conceptualized by the Khmers. As envisioned by the Khmers, the universe had a central "continent" where mortals lived. In the exact center of the continent, which was surrounded by a rock wall, stood the cosmic Mount Meru, home of the gods. Beyond the rock wall was an endless ocean.

The temple of Bakheng, built on the summit of a hill, is the earliest stone building known to recreate the Khmer's concept of the heavens. Like Mount Meru, Bakheng has seven levels and five peaks. The temple's wide moat symbolizes the endless ocean beyond the walls of the mythical continent. At Angkor Wat, the monumental temple of Jayavarman VII represents the height of Khmer architecture. All the elements of the "heavenly universe" myth are present in this complex. At the highest point of Mount Meru stood an image of Shiva, Vishnu, or Brahma.

The Buddhist temples of Angkor were dedicated to the Mahayana, or the Greater Vehicle sect of Buddhism. (Contemporary Cambodia practices the Buddhism of the Theravada sect.) Buddha to the Khmers was not the revered historical figure he was in India; the Khmers worshipped him as a god. Khmer art frequently depicts Buddha in a meditative state protected by a seven- or nine-headed *naga*, or serpent—this portrayal of the Buddha is called the Muchalinda Buddha.

Religious Role of the King. Religious and political hierarchy began with the king-god-priest in whom temporal and holy power were united. Worshipped as one of the many incarnations of the Hindu gods, the essence of the king's priestly and imperial power was in the *linga*, the large stone phallus which was the masculine manifestation of Shiva. The *linga*, enshrined in the precise center of a temple sanctuary, was the spiritual axis of the kingdom where the king communicated with the gods. The sanctuary is a feature of Indian religious architecture preserved in Khmer temples. Catastrophies such as wars, epidemics, or droughts were warded off by the king's daily communication with the gods who transmitted their divine powers to him.

Religion and Water Conservation. The Khmer people led lives ordered by their religious system. Rituals regulated agriculture, the caste system, and especially water conservation. Food production was based largely on water management since the plain of Angkor was dry for six months of the year. Vast plains surrounding the royal city of Angkor Thom were irrigated by an immense network of canals, rectangular reservoirs called *baray*, and dikes that conserved precious water used for farming during the dry season. The Western Baray, five miles long (8 km.) and west of Angkor Thom, is the largest reservoir.

This remarkable feat of hydraulic engineering was intimately interwoven within the Khmer Empire's religious rituals and beliefs. For example, the Hindu myth of Creation, the *Churning of the Sea of Milk*, tells of the battle-like tug of war between gods and devils struggling with a giant many-headed *naga* (serpent) to produce ambrosia, the elixir of life from the Sea of Milk. Sculptural representations of this myth can be seen in the five gates of Angkor Thom, and outside Preah Khan. Each side of the bridge leading to the temple of Angkor Thom is flanked by 54 gigantic stone generals. Each of the powerful generals is holding the serpent (called Vasuki) with both hands while pulling with all his strength as if he were engaged in a desperate tug of war. The creation myth includes Vishnu, who, in his incarnation as a tortoise, sits on the ocean floor of the Sea of Milk. His tortoise-shell back supports the base of Mount Mandara. When rotated, the mountain peak will churn the milk into the sea below. To set the mountain in motion, the stone giants pull, in a back-and-forth motion, on the serpent's body which is coiled around the mountain peak. This strenuous ritual will stir up the sea to give up lost objects, such as ambrosia—the source of immortality; the stirring action would also bring back the rains, necessary for the survival of mortals.

DAILY LIFE

Written reports (*Memoirs on the Customs of the Cambodians*) by Chou Ta-kuan, a Chinese envoy to Angkor at the end of the 13th century, describe the Khmer court, daily life of the ordinary citizen, cooking, homes, markets, and the culture in general. The Chinese envoy describes Angkor as a busy trade center and a study in opulence. Great caravans from India and China brought silk and sandlewood, gold and musk to adorn their buildings and citizens. Jewels from all over the world enriched their temples. Families that had beautiful daughters sent them to the palace where they served as attendants, bodyguards trained in deadly martial arts, palanquin carriers, dancers, and consorts. The women of the court anointed themselves with sweet oil and wore brilliant-colored skirts, shining gems, and fresh flowers in their hair.

Many birds were in the air then. White-headed kites with brown backs visited the canals of the Siem Reap River. Migrating pelicans, ibis, and egrets came in turn. Kingfishers were caught for their colorful feathers which were prized in China. The river banks were planted with lush coconut trees and banana plants. The air smelled of spices, cardamom, and pepper. Lotus flowers floated on the ponds. Temples gleamed and dazzled the city with gold.

Chou Ta-kuan reported: "Twice a day the king holds audience for affairs of government. Whoever of the officials of the people wishes to see the king sits on the ground and awaits him." The king held the Prah Kahn, a sacred sword symbolizing the lightning bolt of the god, Indra. In these session, people brought legal cases for the god-king to judge.

LANGUAGE

The script used by the Khmers was Sanskrit, the classical language of India. Samples of Khmer script still remain etched in stone at the ruins.

ROADS

The Khmer empire was connected through a network of roads that extended from its major cities to far-off provinces. Some of the old roadbeds still exist. In southern Laos around Wat Phu in Champassak, stretches of medieval road are visible by aerial observation. Wat Phu is the northernmost of the Khmer stone temples. The roads were traveled by elephants, horses, and ox carts (ox carts seen in present-day Cambodia are similar to those depicted on the bas relief at Angkor).

Angkor: Glossary of Selected Terms

Apsaras	Lovely female spirits who dance for the gods and effortlessly ride the spray of ocean waves.
Asuras	Male demons who can take the form of animals. At Angkor the asuras have round eyes and downturned mouths.
Banteay	A citadel.
Baray	A reservoir.
Bas-relief	Stone carvings in which the image projects beyond the surface of the flat rock.
Brahma	According to Hinduism, the Supreme essence of the universe or a member of the Hindu trinity of Brahma, Vishnu, and Shiva.
Champa	The India-influenced empire on the eastern seacoast of the Indochina peninsula that reached its peak of power from the sixth to the 15th century.
Corbel construction	Method of constructing doorways and arches in a tiered arrangement without the use of the keystone.
Devaraja	A cult that worships the king as god.
Deva	Male god identified by almond-eyes and determined facial features.
Devata	Sacred female spirits who serve the gods.
Garuda	Mythical animal with human body and the head of a bird. This creature was the enemy of Naga. Vishnu rode on Garuda.
Hinayana	Buddhist sect, the predominant religion of present-day Cambodia; stresses that salvation is attainable by common folk through self-discipline and leading an ascetic life.

Khmer	A race of undetermined origins living in the southern region of the Indochina peninsula.
Kulen	The hill area north of Angkor where Jayavarman II proclaimed independence from Java.
Indra	Hindu supreme god who also ruled over rain and storms. Indra used the thunderbolt and discus as weapons.
Laterite	Red clay which dries to a hard consistency when unearthed.
Linga	Stone representation of a phallus and symbol of the king.
Lokesvara	The compassionate incarnation of Buddha who postponed his entrance into heaven to remain on earth to perform good deeds.
Mahayana	(also called the Great Vehicle) One of the two major forms of Buddhism (the other is Hinayana, or Theravada) that flourished in Cambodia from the first to the 13th century. Mahayana stressed that salvation was attainable through the intercession of the gods of the Buddhist pantheon. Hinayana taught its followers that salvation was reachable through self-discipline and leading an ascetic life.
Makara	Monster fish depicted on bas-reliefs at Angkor and on dragon boats of present-day Cambodian sailors. The creature has the trunk of an elephant and the body of a reptile.
Naga	Sanskrit for snake. A common symbol in Khmer art, the *naga* usually takes the form of a giant-hooded or many-headed cobra. The Khmers believed snake deities dwelled under the earth and in waters. Naga is the enemy of Garuda.
Phnom	Khmer for hill.
Prasats	Towers representing lotus buds.
Ramayana	Hindu epic of the struggles of the hero Rama against the evil forces of Ravana.
Roluos	A complex of Khmer temples southeast of Siem Reap that predate those found at Angkor.
Sanskrit	Ancient classic language of the Hindus that retains many characteristics of the parent Indo-European language.
Shiva (also Siva)	The Hindu god of destruction and creation. A member of the Hindu trinity along with Brahma and Vishnu. In his wild and threatening aspect, he dances to announce the end of the world.

Tonle Sap	The Great Lake in Northwestern Cambodia.
Vishnu	Second god of the Hindu trinity, including Brahma and Shiva. He has ten incarnations that take either animal or human form. Two of the most well-known incarnations are Krishna and Rama. Vishnu is known as the preserver of life.
Wat	Buddhist pagoda and monastery.
Yama	Yama and his twin sister, Yami, were, according to the Khmers, the first man and woman. Yama was the first man to die and, in so doing, became the king of the dead.

The Angkor Conservancy

Headquartered in a building located between Angkor Wat and Siem Reap, the Angkor Conservancy was founded in 1908 by the French Government to preserve, interpret, and reconstruct the archaeological treasures of Angkor. Many pieces of Khmer art were brought to France and studied at the Musée Guiment and, to a lesser degree, at the Indochina Museum of the Trocadero. Some archaeologists, such as Henri Marchal, French explorer and reconstructor of Banteai Srei, were so taken with the ruins that they worked and lived most of their professional lives at Angkor.

After Cambodia gained its independence from France in 1953, the Conservancy was supported by the Royal Cambodian Government and France. Bernard Philippe Groslier of France, a world renowned art conservator and archaeologist, left the site in 1972 when anti-government guerillas took over the area. Under Groslier's leadership at the Conservancy, new foundations were added to the temples and a system of drains were installed to carry water away from sinking temples. Some staff members presently in charge of the Conservancy are former assistants of Groslier.

Preserving the ruins has taken on an international fervor. In 1986, Indian art conservators initiated a six- to eight-year project designed to chemically clean the stone at the ruins using techniques that had proved successful on Indian archaeological treasures. Cuban conservationist and engineers have aided the reconstruction process and the Soviet Union has also contributed by training Khmer personnel in archaeologic restoration.

Bibliography

Bourne, Peter (pseudonym for Bruce Jeffries). *When God Slept.* G. P. Putnam's Sons (now Putnam Publishing Group), New York, 1956.

Chou Ta-kuan, *Notes on the Customs of Cambodia.* Translated from the French version of Paul Pelliot by J. Gilman D'Arcy. Social Science Association Press, Bangkok, 1967.

Giteau, Madeline. *The Civilization of Angkor.* Rizzoli International Publications, Inc., New York, 1976.

Leonowens, Anna H. *The English Governess at the Siamese Court.* Oxford University Press, London, 1988 (reprint of 1870 book).

MacDonald, Malcolm. *Angkor and the Khmers.* Frederick A. Praeger, New York, 1959.

Malraux, Andre. *The Royal Way.* Random House, New York, 1935.

Moore, Robert W., & Fievet, Maurice. *Angkor Jewel of the Jungle.* National Geographic, Vol. 117, No. 4, April 1960.

White, Peter. *Temples of Angkor: Will They Survive?* National Geographic Magazine, Vol. 161, No. 5, May 1982.

Permentier, Henri. *Angkor.* Saigon, 1955.

Key Dates in

Khmer History

Since the exact dates for some reigns are unknown and some periods were ruled by several kings, the information in this chart is incomplete.

Note: Commonly translated as protector, the suffix *arman* is derived from the Indian title meaning protege—e.g., Indra/varman, the protege of Indra and Jaya/varman, the protege of Jaya.

KING	DATE/REIGN (AD)	COMMENT
	1-500	Southern coastal settlements of Funan
	550	Funan and Chenla (inland to the north) unite
Jayavarman I	657-681	Brief occupation by Sailendra rulers of Java
Jayavarman II	802-850	Founding of empire at Angkor, first at Kulen, then at Roluos; founding of god-king cult

KING	DATE/REIGN (AD)	COMMENT
Jayavarman III	850-877	
Indravarman I	877-889	Buildings in the style of Roluos, predating temples at Angkor
Yoshovarman I	889-900	Building style of Bakheng; irrigation projects; Eastern Baray (reservoir)
Harshavarman I	900-920	
Ishanavarman II	921	Baksei Chamkrong temple built
Jayavarman IV	921-941	Usurper who moved the capital of the empire to Koh Ker
Harshavarman II	941-944	
Rajendarvarman	944-968	(967) Banteai Srei; Angkor becomes the center of Khmer Empire
Jayavarman V	968-1001	Phimeanakas
Udayadityavarman	1001-1050	Ta Keo; Thai Kingdom conquered
Suryavarman I	1050-1065	Baphuon; West Bebon temple erected in the center of Western Baray; wars with Champa, Thai states, Vietnam
Udayadityavarman II		
Harshavarman III		
Jayavarman VI		
Dharanindarvarman I		
Suryavarman II	1113-1150	Angkor Wat
	1177	Chams invade Angkor
Dharanindarvarman II		
Yoshovarman II		
Jayavarman VII	1181-1218	Chams driven out; founding of cult devoted to Mahayana Buddhism
	1186	Ta Prohm

KING	DATE/REIGN (AD)	COMMENT
	1191	Preah Khan; Angkor Thom; Bayon
Indravarman II	1275	Thai power increasing and centralized around Chiang Mai
Jayavarman VIII	1243-1295	
	1280	Thai invasions
	1282	Mongols fought off
	1296	Chou Ta-kuan, Chinese envoy, visits Angkor
	1353	Thais (center in Ayudhya) sack Angkor
	1431	Thai army conquers Angkor; Khmers retreat and move capital further south to Vyadhapura (present-day Phnom Penh)

V. APPENDIX

An Annotated
Reading List
for Vietnam Travelers

BOOKS

Baron, Samuel. *Description of the Tonkin Kingdom.* Paris (in French), 1752.

Candee, Helen Churchill. *New Journeys in Old Asia.* Frederick A. Stokes Company, New York, 1927.

Cohen, Joan Lebold, photographs by Bela Kalman. *Angkor Monuments of the God-Kings.* Harry N. Abrams, Inc., Publishers, New York, 1975. Lovely photographs with descriptions.

Coolidge, Harold J. Jr., and Theodore Roosevelt. *Three Kingdoms of Indo-China.* Thomas Y. Crowell Company, New York, 1933.

Crosbie, Garstin. *The Dragon and the Lotus.* William Heinemann Ltd., London, 1928

de Poncins, Gontran. *From a Chinese City.* Translated from the French by Bernard Frechtman. Doubleday & Company, Inc., Garden City, New York, 1957.

Duiker, William. *Since the Fall of Saigon.* Ohio University Press, Athens, Ohio, 1980.

Durand, Maurice M., and Nguyen Tran Huan. Translated from the French by D.M. Hawke. *An Introduction to Vietnamese Literature.* Columbia University Press, New York, 1985.

Greene, Graham. *The Quiet American.* Viking, New York, 1956.

Halberstam, David. *Ho. A Biography of Ho Chi Minh.* Alfred A. Knolf, New York, 1987.

Hervey, Harry. *King Cobra. An Autobiography of Travel in French Indo-China.* King Cobra Cosmopolitan Book Corporation, New York, 1927.

Hickey, Gerald C. *Village in Vietnam.* Yale University Press, New Haven, 1964.

Huynh Sanh Thong *Nguyen Du-The Tale of Kieu.* (bilingual edition) Yale University Press, New Haven and London, 1983.

Huynh Sanh Thong. Editor and translator. *The Heritage of Vietnamese Poetry.* Yale University Press, New Haven and London, 1979.

Lacouture, Jean. Translated from the French by Peter Wiles. *Ho Chi Minh: A Political Biography*. Random House, New York, 1968.

Landsdale, Major General Edward Geary, USAF (Ret). *In the Midst of Wars—An American's Mission to Southeast Asia*. Harper & Row, Publishers, New York, 1972.

Lewis, Norman. *A Dragon Apparent. Travels in IndoChina*. Charles Scribner's Sons, New York, 1951.

Lewis, Paul and Elaine. *Peoples of the Golden Triangle: Six Tribes in Thailand*. Thames and Hudson Ltd., New York and London, 1984.

Mangold, Tom and Penycate, John. *The Tunnels of Cu Chi. The Untold Story of Vietnam*. Random House, New York, 1987.

Mangold, Tom, and Penycate, John. *The Illustrated History of Tunnel Warfare*. Bantam Books, New York, 1985.

Maugham, Somerset. *The Gentleman in the Parlour: A Record of Journey from Rangoon to Haiphong 1930*. Oxford University Press, London and New York, Reprinted 1966.

Meyerson, Harvey. *Vinh Long*. Houghton Mifflin Co, Boston, 1970.

Nguyen Long (with Harry Kendall). *After the Fall: Daily Life Under the Vietnamese Communists*. University of California Press, Berkeley, 1981.

Nguyen Ngoc Bich (translator). *A Thousand Years of Vietnamese Poetry*. Alfred A. Knopf, Inc., New York, 1974.

Osborne, Milton. *River Road to China: The Mekong River Expedition 1866–1873*. Liveright, New York, 1975.

Pike, Douglas. *History of Vietnamese Communism*. Hoover Institute Press, Stanford, California, 1978.

Pike, Douglas. *PAVN: People's Army of Vietnam*. Presidio Press Novato, California, 1986.

Pym, Christopher, editor. *Henri Mouhot's Diary: Travels in the Central Parts of Siam, Cambodia and Laos During the Years 1858–61*. Oxford in Asia: Historical Reprints, Kuala Lumpur, Oxford University Press, London and New York, 1966.

Reid, Anthony. *Southeast Asia in the Age of Commerce 1450–1680. Volume One: The Lands Below the Winds*. Yale University Press, New Haven and London, 1988.

Shaplen, Robert. *Bitter Victory*. Harper and Row Publishers, New York, 1986.

Shawcross, William. *River Journeys*. Hippocrene Books, 1985. Contains a description of a trip on the Mekong River taken by the author in 1983.

Snepp, Frank. *Decent Interval*. Random House, New York, 1977.

Stuart, Anh-Thu. *Vietnamese Cooking: Recipes My Mother Taught Me*, Angus & Robertson Publishers, Australia and London, 1986.

Taylor, Keith Weller. *The Birth of Viet Nam*. University of California Press, Berkeley, 1983.

Thompson, Virginia. *French Indochina*. Octagon Books, New York, 1968.

Theroux, Paul. *The Great Railway Bazaar*. Houghton Mifflin, Co., Boston, 1975. Chapters 24–25 on the railway of Vietnam.

White, John. *History of a Voyage to the China Sea.* Wells and Lilly, Boston, 1823.

Woodside, Alexander. *Community and Revolution in Modern Vietnam.* Houghton-Mifflin Co. Boston, 1976

MAGAZINE ARTICLES

Alexander, David with photos by John Everington. "Reviving Hue-Vietnam's Broken Heart on the River of Perfumes." Smithsonian, June 86, 44–55.

Egbert W. Pfeffer. "The Conservation of Nature in Vietnam." Environmental Conservation, Vol. II, No. 3, 1983.

Kemf, Elizabeth. "Indochina's Forest Ox." New Scientist, June 30, 1988.

Kemf, Elizabeth. "Vietnam: Rebuilding a Countryside." New Scientist, June 23, 1988.

Simons, Lewis M. with photography by Christopher Pillitz. "Incentives and Moonlighting." Smithsonian, April 1987.

Sochurek, Howard. "Slow Train Through Viet Nam's War." National Geographic, Vol. 126, No. 3, September 1964.

Sochurek, Howard. "Americans in Action in Viet Nam." National Geographic Vol. 127, No. 1, January 1965.

Westing, A.H. & Westing, C.E. "Endangered Species and Habitats of Vietnam." Environmental Conservation, Vol. 8, No. 1, 1981, 59–62.

White, Peter and Garrett, W.E. "The Mekong River of Terror and Hope." National Geographic Magazine, Vol. 134, No. 6, December 1968.

The Vietnam Forum. (A scholarly quarterly review of Vietnamese Culture.)
Yale Center for International and Area Studies
Council on Southeast Asia Studies
Box 13A Yale Station
New Haven, CT 06520

FILM

Vietnam After the Fire: Broadcast (1989) as part of the National Geographic Explorer Series. The film contains an interview with Prof. E.W. Pfeiffer, an ecologic zoologist from the University of Montana, concerning the ecological damage incurred by Vietnam during the war involving the US.

LANGUAGE AND PRONUNCIATION TIPS

The Vietnamese alphabet is composed of 12 vowels, 17 consonants and 19 double consonants which are pronounced as one. The consonants are b, c, d, đ, g, h, k, l, m, n, p, q, r, s, t, v, x. There are differences between the pronunciation of some sounds in the north of Vietnam and in the south. Word usage may vary also.

Consonant sounds are generally sounded as in English.

b	as in boy
c	as in sky
ch	as in church
đ	pronounced like the English d as in door
d	(no bar) pronounced like an English z as in zoo in the north and y as in yeah in the south
g	pronounced the same in the north and south, as in go
gi	a y sound, as in yeah, in the south and a z as in zoo in the north
h	as in hi
k	as in kite
l	as in lass
m	as in me
n	as in next
p	as in pat
qu	sounds like kw as in quiet
ph	pronounced as an f
r	sounds like z, as in zoo, in the north and r, as in rich, in the south
s and x	pronounced like the s in sit in the north (the word for Soviet is spelled either Xo and So with the same pronunciation); in the south the s is sounded more like sh, as in shoe
t and th	pronounced basically alike except for an aspirated h in the th; the same is true of double consonants ch and kh
v	as in verve in the north and as in bow or yeah in the south
z	as in six

Double Consonants. The 'nh' sound is like the spanish ñ. The 'Ng' sound in Vietnamese is one of the most difficult sounds for Westerners to pronounce. It is similar to the ng in the English word sung. Say the word "sung" several times while holding a hand to your vocal cords. Note that the sound vibrates deep in the back of the throat. Gradually drop the 's' from the word and then the 'u' and the remaining sound is the Vietnamese 'ng'. The name Nguyen can be approximated by: *Ngoo wen.*

Many consonant sounds, e.g., -b, -d, -f, -g, -l, -r, -s, -v, -z, may not occur in the final position. Even when p, t, and k do occur in the final position, they are unaspirated and, therefore, barely audible to the Western ear.

Vowels. There are 11 simple vowel sounds in the Vietnamese language. Unmodified vowel sounds are similar to the sound that the vowel makes in romance languages. Now the situation becomes complicated by the use of diacritical marks. Note that these do not indicate tones which will be discussed later.

a	pronounced like ah, as in father
ă	lips spread somewhat as in hut
â	as in ham
e	as in bat
ê	as in bay
i and y	as in bee—thus the Vietnamese word for American: Mỹ is pronounced Mee
o	aw as in straw
ô	as in low
o'	no similar sound in English; closest is uhr
u	oo as in foot; when in the final position, it sounds like boo
u'	no similar sound in English; closest is ugh

Tones. Vietnamese is a tonal language. In addition to the diacritical marks described above, vowels can have tones. The vowels sound like tones or notes on a scale. To indicate which tone a vowel takes, one of five accents, or no accent, is placed above or below the vowel. These accents indicate the rising, falling, or wavering of the voice that is essential to the meaning of the word. Northerners distinguish six tones; Southerners, softer and more fluid in their speech, distinguish five.

The six tones are:

no tone Level. Starts and ends on the same level.

·   Written below the vowel is a heavy sound. It starts low and sharply falls even lower. You feel a push in the abdominal muscles.

/   Rising. It starts above the level tone and rises to a high pitch.

\   Falling. This starts off fairly low and falls slowly to bottom of normal range.

?   Wavering.

~   Interrupted. It starts a bit below the level tone and dips suddenly. These last two tones are not differentiated in the south.

General Rules. Below is a list of rules to help you in your communications with the Vietnamese.

—Vietnamese verbs do not change form; e.g., walk and walks, walking, walked. To indicated past or future tense an additional tense marker word is added to the verb.

—There are no articles in Vietnamese; e.g., a, an, the.

—Plural endings on nouns do not occur.

—There are no prefixes or suffixes, as in unfold or greatness.

—Modifiers and classifiers follow the words they modify; e.g., I have maps large three sheets. (Sheets is a classifier for single pieces of paper.)

—Predicate adjectives do not require the use of the verb "to be"; e.g. "The dress is pretty" translates literally as "Dress pretty."

—Negative interrogative statements may be confusing to English speakers. "Don't you like it?" is answered as "Yes, I don't."

—If a question can be answered with a "yes" or "no," then the helping word, called a question particle, *khong* is added to the end of the question. "Does Ba work here?" is translated "Ba works here, yes or no?"

Vietnamese Names. Vietnamese names are made up of three elements, such as *Nguyen Thi Binh*. There are only about ten or twelve common Vietnamese family names, the most common being *Nguyen*. Fifty-four percent of families are named *Nguyen*. Some names are taken from the dynasty in power. Unlike the given name, many of which can be male or female, the middle name usually tells the sex of the person: the most common middle name for girls is *Thi* and for boys is *Van*.

First is the family or the clan name: *Nguyen*. Next is the middle name, *Thi*, and third the given name, *Binh*. To complicate things more for English speakers, Vietnamese use their third or given name after the title of respect. Thus, Dr. Nguyen Thi Binh is called Dr. Binh or Madame Binh and General Vo Nguyen Giap is properly called General Giap, even though he comes from the Vo family. His daughter, Vo Hong Anh, since she has a doctorate in Physics, is Dr. Anh. When speaking to an older or equal-aged person, use the polite form Mr. or Mrs. or Madame: *Ong* and *Ba* whether or not the surname is used, whereas in English it is acceptable to leave off the sir or madame or use the ambiguous pronoun: you. For example, one will say "Hello, madame": *Chao Ba* and "Thank you, sir": *Cam on, Ong*. "How are you?" to a married woman would be literally: "Lady fine, no?" *"Ba manh khoe, khong?"*

Language Guides. Try to take along a phrase book. Even if you never learn the difficult pronunciation, you can point to your question and allow the other person to point to the response. The following are language aides that might help:

Vietnamese Phrase Book in paperback by Nguyen Dinh Hoa, Ph.D. Charles Tuttle and Co., Inc. of Rutland, Vermont, and Tokyo, Japan 1976.

Easy Vietnamese for You. A paperback book of 186 pages by Tran Buu Duc; published in Saigon in 1963 and later reprinted. Available at:
May Hong Bookstore
115 N. Fourth Street
San Jose, CA 95112

Language/30
Educational Service Corp.
725 K Street, N. W. Suite 408
Washington, D.C. 20006
Two cassettes and a pamphlet. 1960, revised 1980.

Foreign Service Institute: Vietnamese Language Course
Department of State
Washington, DC 20520
Vietnamese language cassettes and books by Eleanor H. Jorden, and others. Expensive and extensive. For the serious student.

Vietnamese Phrases
for Travelers

GENERAL

ENGLISH	SIMILAR ENGLISH SOUND	VIETNAMESE
Madame*	*ba*	Bà
Sir*	*om*	Ông
Miss*	*co*	Cô
friend (comrade)*	*ban*	bạn
hello	*chow*	chào
please	*seen*	Xin / Làm ơn
Excuse me		Xin lỗi
Thank you very much	*Cam (rising) on nhew*	Cám ơn nhiều
How much?	*bow nhew*	Bao nhiêu?
very pretty	*deb lum*	đẹp lắm
expensive	*muck (duk)*	mắc / đắt
yes	*ya (south)*	dạ
	za (north)	
	vun	vâng (in the north)
is possible	*duk*	được
That's right/That's correct	*fi*	phải
no	*khum*	không
What's this?	*Cai ni la cai zi (zi is yi in south)*	Cái này là cái gì
I want, need . . .	*toy ken*	Tôi cần .../ Tôi muốn ...
I would like . . .	*toy muon*	Tôi muốn được ...
I like . . .	*toy tic*	Tôi thích ...
I don't like . . .	*toy kum tic*	Tôi không thích ...
Where is the toilet?		Cầu tiêu ở đâu?

NATIONALITIES

ENGLISH	VIETNAMESE
I am . . .	Tôi là ...
American (US citizen)	Người Mỹ
Australian	Người Úc
British	Người Anh
Canadian	Người Canada
French	Người Pháp
Vietnamese	Người Việt
Russian	Người Nga / Người Liên Sô

NUMBERS

one	*moat*	một
two	*hi*	hai
three	*baa*	ba
four	*bone*	bốn
five	*num*	năm
six	*saow*	sáu
seven	*buy*	bảy
eight	*tam*	tám
nine	*chin*	chín
ten	*moo i*	mười
eleven	*moo i moat*	mười một
twelve	*moo i hi*	mười hai
one hundred	*moat trum*	một trăm
two hundred	*hi trum*	hai trăm
one thousand	*moat ngin (ngan)*	một nghìn (ngàn)

FOOD

ENGLISH	VIETNAMESE
to eat	ăn
to drink	uống
restaurant	tiệm ăn
I'm hungry	tôi đói
water	nước
beer	bia
sugar	đường
boiled water	nước sôi/nước nấu
soup	súp/canh
tea	nước chè
coffee	cà phê
milk (canned sweetened condensed milk)	sữa đặc
meat	thịt
peanuts	đậu phộng
bread	bánh mì
cooked rice	cơm

FRUITS

fruits in general	trái cây
banana	chuối
orange	cam
papaya	đu đủ
mango	xoài
mamgosteen	măng cụt
pineapple	thơm
watermelon	dưa hấu
sweet	ngọt
delicious	ngon
ripe	chín
unripe (green)	sống

AT THE HOTEL

ENGLISH	VIETNAMESE
hotel	khách sạn
room	phòng
key	chìa khóa
floor	sàn nhà
laundry	quần áo giặt (thợ giặt)
toilet	cầu tiêu
bed	giường
sheets	khăn trải giường
towel	khăn lau
barber	thợ hớt tóc
beauty shop	tiệm hớt tóc
to press or iron	ủi
Can you iron this for me?	Ủi cho tôi cái này được không?
Where is . . . ?	...Ở đâu?
Where do I change my money?	Tôi đổi tiền ở đâu?
Where do I buy stamps?	Tôi mua tem ở đâu?

MEDICAL TERMS

doctor	*baat see*	bác sĩ
hospital	*Nha thoong*	Nhà thương
My . . . hurts	*. . . toy dow*	... tôi đau
head	*dow*	đầu
tooth	*zung* (in north) *rung* (in south)	răng
stomach	*boong*	bụng
chest	*nguk*	ngực
diarrhea		ỉa chảy

SIGHTSEEING

ENGLISH	VIETNAMESE
museum	bảo tàng viện
pagoda	chùa
school	trường học
church	nhà thờ
theatre	rạp hát
post office	nhà bưu điện
bank	nhà băng

SHOPPING

I want to buy . . .	Tôi muốn mua ...
this	cái này
that	cái đó
How much (money)?	Bao nhiêu (tiền or đồng (most often Bao nhiêu is sufficient)
expensive	mắc, đắt
cheap	rẻ or không đắt

MAKING FRIENDS

ENGLISH	VIETNAMESE
What is your (madam, miss, mister, child) name?	Tên (bà, cô, ông, em) · là gì?

ENGLISH	VIETNAMESE
How old are you? (to a child)	Em bao nhiêu tuổi?
Do you have children? (to a married woman)	Bà có mấy đứa con?
Where do you live? (to a young woman)	Nhà cô ở đâu?
What do you do? (to a man)	Ông làm việc gì?
May I take a picture of you (sir, madame, miss, child)?	Cho tôi chụp hình ... (ông, bà, cô, em) được không?
I would like to take a photo.	Tôi muốn chụp một hình.

*The use of the proper form of address for Sir (Ong), Madame (Ba), Miss (Co), and friend (ban) is essential.

Provinces of
Vietnam

MUNICIPALITIES (3)

NAME	AREA (sq.mi./sq.km.)	POP.	POP. DENSITY (person/sq.mi./sq.km.)
Hanoi	843/2,139	2,937,800	3,570/1,373
Ho Chi Minh City	791/2,029	3,667,600	4,700/1,808
Haiphong	586/1,503	1,420,900	2,457/945

SPECIAL ZONE (1)

NAME	AREA (sq.mi./sq.km.)	POP.	POP. DENSITY (person/sq.mi./sq.km.)
Vung Tau-Con Dao	97/249	102,100	1,066/410

PROVINCES (36)

NAME	AREA (sq.mi./sq.km.)	POP.	POP. DENSITY (person/sq.mi./sq.km.)
NORTHERN REGION			
Lai Chau	6,657/17,068	387,400	60/23
Hoang Lien Son	5,792/14,852	879,500	153/59
Ha Tuyen	5,316/13,632	905,100	172/66
Cao Bang*	3,293/8,445	546,400	169/65
Lang Son*	3,193/8,187	539,900	172/66
Bac Thai	2,533/6,494	926,300	372/143
Son La	5,643/14,468	582,100	104/40
Vinh Phu	1,804/4,626	1,702,700	957/368
Ha Bac	1,798/4,609	1,929,300	1,089/419
Quang Ninh	2,316/5,938	820,100	359/138
Ha Son Binh	2,331/5,978	1,730,200	751/289

PROVINCES OF VIETNAM

PROVINCES (36)

NAME	AREA (sq.mi./sq.km.)	POP.	POP. DENSITY (person/sq.mi./sq.km.)
Hai Hung	996/2,555	2,408,400	2,452/943
Thai Binh	583/1,495	1,642,400	2,623/1,009
Ha Nam Ninh	1,468/3,763	3,080,200	2,129/819
Thanh Hoa	4,344/11,138	2,793,500	653/251
Nghe Tinh	8,776/22,502	3,457,900	400/154

CENTRAL REGION

Binh Tri Thien	7,153/18,340	2,001,800	320/123
Quang Nam Danang	4,676/11,989	1,687,500	366/141
Nghia Binh	4,641/11,900	2,367,500	517/199
Phu Khanh	3,824/9,804	1,349,700	359/138
Thuan Hai	4,436/11,374	1,095,600	249/96
Gia Lai-Con Tum	9,960/25,536	746,200	75/29
Dac Lac	7,722/19,800	661,000	89/33

SOUTHERN REGION

Lam Dong	3,874/9,933	511,300	133/51
Song Be	3,845/9,859	790,800	208/80
Tay Ninh	1,572/4,030	772,500	499/192
Dong Nai	2,955/7,578	1,741,000	598/230
Long An	1,698/4,355	1,105,300	660/254
Dong Thap	1,322/3,391	1,335,700	1,024/394
An Giang	1,362/3,493	1,812,200	1,349/519
Tien Giang	927/2,377	1,399,100	1,531/589
Ben Tre	868/2,225	1,184,100	1,383/532
Cuu Long	1,503/3,854	1,723,600	1,162/447
Hau Giang	2,389/6,126	2,559,300	1,087/418
Kien Giang	2,480/6,358	1,150,500	470/181
Minh Hai	3,002/7,697	1,371,500	463/178

*The provinces of Cao Bang and Lang Son have been recently unified into one province called Cao Lang.

Ethnic Groups

The Socialist Republic of Vietnam is a multinational state. The Kinh, or majority people, who account for 88% of the country's population, are concentrated mainly in the delta of the Red River, the coastal plains of Central Vietnam, and the Mekong delta. Fifty-three other nationalities totaling 5-1/2 million people live mostly in the mountainous areas covering two-thirds of the country that stretch from the north to the south.

Fifty-four ethnic groups in descending order of population size:[*]

1. Kinh (Viet)
2. Tay
3. Thai
4. Ma
5. Kho Mu
6. Co
7. Hoa (Chinese)
8. Khmer
9. Muong
10. Nung
11. H'mong (Meo)
12. Zao
13. Jarai
14. Ngai
15. Ede
16. Bahnar
17. Sedang
18. San Chay (Cao Lan-San Chi)
19. Kohor
20. Cham
21. San Ziu
22. Hre
23. Mnong
24. Raglai
25. Stieng
26. Bo Ru-Van Kieu
27. Tho
28. Giay
29. Ka Tu (Co Tu)
30. Johtriong (Gie-Trieng)
31. Ta Oi
32. Cho Ro
33. Khang
34. Xinh Mun
35. Ha Nhi
36. Chu Ru
37. Lao
38. La Chi
39. La Ha
40. Phu La
41. La Hu
42. Lu
43. Lo Lo
44. Chut
45. Mang
46. Pa Thon (Pathen)
47. Co Loa
48. Coong
49. Bo Y
50. Si La
51. Pu Peo
52. Brau
53. O Du
54. RoMam

Summary of
the Life of
Ho Chi Minh

Ho Chi Minh, which means "he who enlightens," was born Nguyen Sinh Cung in Nghe Tinh Province, Vietnam, on May 19, 1890. The seed for Ho's indefatigable passion for independence was most likely sown by his father, who had been dismissed from his civil service job for anti-French activities. As a young man, Ho traveled the world as a mess boy on a French ocean liner; he also worked as a pastry chief for Escoffier in London and as a photo refinisher in Paris. Like his father, Ho objected to French colonists, as well as wealthy Vietnamese who collaborated with the French, acquiring vast tracts of rich land where they exploited the peasants who worked in unhealthy conditions for starvation wages.

In Paris, under the name Nguyen Tat Thanh, Ho joined the French Socialist Party to gain supporters to free his country from French rule. Ho later called himself Nguyen Ai Quoc, commonly translated as Nguyen the Patriot. (Taking new names is not uncommon in Asia when a change in life circumstances occurs. The term "aliases," with its pejorative implication of hiding one's true identity, does not apply to this Asian name-changing tradition.) In 1915 he visited the US.

Ho admired the philosophy of the US President Woodrow Wilson whose Fourteen Points (a set of principles proposed as a basis for ending WWI) included self-determination for all people. In 1919, at the Versailles Peace Conference (which officially ended WWI), Ho called for the application of Wilson's concept of self-determination to the people of Vietnam. His struggles led him to join the new French Communist Party. He left Paris in 1923 and continued his revolutionary training and activities with visits to China and Russia. In 1930 he founded the Indochinese Communist Party. On a mission to China he was arrested as a spy and spent 15 months as a prisoner of the Chinese.

WORLD WAR II

After many years of self-imposed exile, Ho finally returned to Vietnam in 1941 and cooperated with American intelligence officers who were attempting to erode Japanese influence in Southeast Asia.

To fight the Japanese, Ho organized the League for Independence of Vietnam, known in the West as the Viet Minh. His group, including General Vo Nguyen Giap, operated from the country's northern border area to aid downed US pilots and to gain intelligence on Japanese military movements. American flight crews under General Claire Chennault bombed Japanese occupied rail lines and port facilities. There were 214 Americans among the 4,500 allied POWs in Vietnam at the end of the war.

RELATIONS WITH FRANCE

On Sept 2, 1945, Ho officially declared the independence of Vietnam from France. In Hanoi's Ba Dinh Square he addressed half a million people with words not unlike those once written down by patriots of the American Revolution: "All men are created equal," he said. "The creator has given us certain inviolable rights: the right to Life, the right to be Free and the right to achieve happiness."

While the details of Vietnam's future relations with France were being worked out, Ho set up his government in Hanoi. In March 1946, Ho Chi Minh and the French Commissioner in Hanoi agreed to a Democratic Republic of Vietnam that would maintain ties to France. Because certain details of the agreement were left open to interpretation, the compromise fell through and the Viet Minh once again returned to their former jungle camps. Ho set up headquarters in a limestone cave at Pac Bo where he organized the Tho and other ethnic minorities, and he created a liberated zone in the seven northern provinces in northern Tonkin. The Viet Minh then fought another eight years against the reinstated French under the puppet Emperor Bao Dai.

After the French were defeated at Dien Bien Phu by the Viet Minh, the country was temporarily divided into North and South Vietnam at the 17th parallel. It was agreed that elections would be held in 1956 to vote on the eventual fate of the two halves. The South had its leadership vacuum filled by American-backed Ngo Dinh Diem. The elections to reunite the country were never held.

Resistance to Diem's government developed among anti-foreign rebels, warlords, and peasants in the countryside. Advisers and financial aid from the US flowed into South Vietnam in an effort to "stem the tide of communism in Asia." After direct military involvement of US ground troops began in 1964, Ho mobilized the efforts of the total population of the North to "liberate" the South and effect reunification under the motto that "Vietnam was one country." Men and supplies were sent south via the Ho Chi Minh

Trail to fight "American imperialism." Ho, in failing health for years with pulmonary tuberculosis, died in September 1969.

Ho, who never married, lived a simple life in a two-room house in the gardener's quarters of the former offices of the French Governor-Resident. Scholars today debate the nature of his nationalism and its ties to the international communist movement.

The Legend of
Mi Chau

An Duong was king when the Chinese invaded the kingdom of Au Lac (ancient Vietnam) around 100 BC. Although his troops fought bravely, they were outnumbered by the Chinese. Impressed by the king's love of freedom for his people, a Golden Turtle appeared to him. Urging An Duong to continue the battle, the turtle took a magic claw from its own foot and presented it to the king. When this magic claw was fitted to An Duong's crossbow, the resulting supernatural accuracy of his aim and the strength of his shot struck terror in his enemies.

The Chinese general heard of the marvelous weapon and planned to steal it by sending his son, Thung Thuy, to gain the confidence of King An Duong by serving first as one of his guards. Thung Thuy's exceptional service was rewarded by a promotion to captain, a rank that allowed him to walk about the palace freely and learn the secrets of its maze of passageways. Soon he began to seek out the magic bow. In his search, one night he came upon the private rooms of the princess, Mi Chau. Her beauty captured him and he immediately fell in love. She, in turn, was charmed by his daring and soon returned his love. An Duong happily agreed to the marriage of Thung Thuy and his daughter. Thung Thuy's father reminded him of the nature of the original military mission, calling upon filial piety and loyalty to his country to persuade his son to betray his wife's trust. Thung Thuy charmed Mi Chau into showing him where the magic claw was hidden. Then one night he stole the magic claw and substituted a useless nail.

The Chinese attacked An Duong's palace and easily made their way through the mazes based on information provided by Thung Thuy. An Duong mobilized a counterattack. When he discovered that his bow had lost its magic, he realized that he had been betrayed. The king, accompanied by his daughter, retreated on horseback to the seacoast. Mi Chau, longing for her husband, threw a few feathers from inside her down robe at each crossroad so Thung Thuy could find her. The Chinese army followed the feathers to the retreating king and eventually surrounded him.

Mi Chau felt remorse over the disaster she had brought upon her people. She begged her father to behead her. When he refused, she stabbed herself through the heart and fell into the sea. A huge oyster drank the ocean water colored by Mi Chau's blood. When the Tortoise touched the oyster, Mi Chau's blood turned into a lustrous pink pearl (Chau - Pearl). Although Mi Chau's husband survived to see his father and the Chinese army conquer King An Duong's kingdom, he did not rejoice in the victory. Thung Thuy paid a great price for his filial loyalty; he suffered and mourned for his wife whom he had truly loved.

Media in
Vietnam

PRESS

The number of press publications is, at present, 135—100 are published in Hanoi and 35 in the provinces. This number includes specialized periodicals of different economic and cultural sectors. Below is a listing of the dailies, weeklies, main periodicals, journals, and publications in foreign languages.

DAILIES

Nhan Dan (The People), organ of the Communist Party of Vietnam, 71 Hang Trong, Hanoi.

Quan Doi Nhan Dan (People's Army), organ of the People's Armed Forces, 7 Phan Dinh Phung, Hanoi.

Hanoi Moi (New Hanoi), 44 Le Thai To, Hanoi.

Saigon Giai Phong, organ of the City Committee of the Communist Party of Vietnam, 432 Xo Viet Nghe Tinh, Ho Chi Minh City.

WEEKLIES

Phu Nu (Women), organ of the Women's Union.

Lao Dong (Labor), organ of the Trade Unions Federation.

Tien Phong (Vanguard), organ of the Youth Union.

Dai Doan Ket (Great Unity), organ of the Vietnam Fatherland Front.

Van Nghe (Art and Literature), literary and artistic review.

Doc Lap (Independence), organ of the Democratic Party.

Thieu Nien Tien Phong (Vanguard Pioneers), organ of Young Pioneers.

MAIN PERIODICALS

Tap Chi Cong San (Review of Communism), monthly, organ of the Communist Party of Vietnam.

To Quoc (Fatherland), monthly, organ of the Socialist Party.
Van Hoa Nghe Thuat (Culture and Art): cultural issues.
Nghien Cuu Van Hoc (Literary Studies).
Nghien Cuu Lich Su (Historical Studies).
Khoa Hoc Thuong Thuc (Popular Science).
Tin Tuc Hoat Dong Khoa Hoc (Scientific and Technical Activities).
Tap Chi Triet Hoc (Philosophical Review).
Tap Chi Quan Doi Nhan Dan (People's Army Review).

JOURNALS

Journals of ethonology, linguistics, artistic studies, and various medical, technical, and scientific reviews.

PUBLICATIONS IN FOREIGN LANGUAGES

Vietnam Courier: Monthly, published in English and French; analyzes events in Vietnam and Indochina; 46 Tran Hung Dao, Hanoi. (Discontinued at end of 1989.)

Vietnamese Studies: Quarterly, published in English and French. Each issue focuses on a particular problem; 46 Tran Hung Dao, Hanoi.

Vietnam: Illustrated review with texts in English, French, Russian, Chinese, and Spanish; 70 Ly Thuong Kiet, Hanoi.

Vietnamese Trade Unions: Published in English, French, and Spanish by the Vietnam Federation of Trade Unions; 65 Quan Su, Hanoi.

Vietnam Youth: Published in English and French by the Vietnam Youth Federation and the Vietnam Students' Union; 64 Ba Trieu, Hanoi.

Women of Vietnam: Published in English and French by the Vietnam Women's Union; 47 Hang Chuoi, Hanoi.

Informado el Vjetnamio (News of Vietnam): organ of the Vietnam Esperanto for Peace Association.

News of Vietnam (in Russian).

RADIO

The *Voice of Vietnam* broadcasts for 22 hours a day in Vietnamese and the following foreign languages: English, French, Japanese, Korean, Spanish, Indonesian, Malay, Thai, and Chinese (Standard and Cantonese). A state organ of information, *The Voice of Vietnam,* operates under the Government Council.

TELEVISION

The Central Television Station broadcasts a daily program for foreign countries. Other regional broadcasting centers operate regularly at Tam Dao (for provinces in the Red River delta, the Midlands, and Highlands), Ho Chi Minh City, Vinh, Hue, Nha Trang, and Can Tho. The Lotus (Hoa Sen) station (headquartered at Giang Vo, Hanoi) ensures a liaison with Moscow Television and other East European member countries.

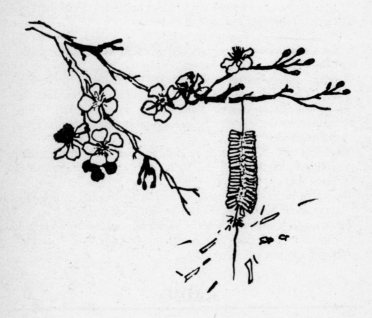

Directory

VIETNAM'S INSTITUTIONS OF HIGHER EDUCATION

HANOI

Banking College, Dong Da district
College of Architecture, Ha Dong highway, Kilometer #7
College of Agriculture #1, Trau Quy, Gia Lam district
College of Commerce, Mai Dich, Tu Liem district
College of Finance, Phuc Yen district
College of Pharmacy, 13 Le Thanh Ton
Conservatory of Hanoi, O Cho Dua
Construction College of Hanoi, Huong Canh, Vinh Phu
Economics and Planning College, Nam Bo Street
Film and Drama College, Mai Dich, Tu Liem district
Foreign Languages College, Me Tri, Dong Da district
Foreign Languages Teachers' Training College, Mai Dich, Tu Liem district
Foreign Trade College, Lang, Dong Da district
Hanoi Polytechnic, Bach Mai
International Relations and Law College, Lang Trung
Medical College, Khuong Thuong, Dong Da district
Teachers' Training College #1, Mai Dich, Tu Liem district
Teachers' Training College #2, Xuan Hoa district
Road and Rail Transport College, Cau Giay
University of Hanoi. Thuong Dinh, Dong Da district
Water Conservancy College, Dong Da district

HO CHI MINH CITY

Agriculture College #4, Thu Duc
Architecture College of Ho Chi Minh City, 196 Nguyen Thi Minh Khai Street
College of Finance of Ho Chi Minh City, 229 Dong Khoi
College of Medicine and Pharmacy, 217 Hong Bang Street
Conservatory of Ho Chi Minh City, 112 Nguyen Du Street
Ho Chi Minh City College of Economics, 17 Duy Tan
Ho Chi Minh City Polytechnic, 286 Ly Thuong Kiet Street

Technical Instructors' Training College, Thu Duc
Teachers' Training College, 222 Nguyen Van Troi Street
University of Ho Chi Minh City, 227 Nguyen Van Cu Street
Thang Long University, new private university, in Medical School,
217 Hong Bang Street

HUE

Hue Teachers' College
Medical College of Hue
University of Hue

DANANG

Danang Polytechnic, Hoa Vang district

BAC THAI

Agriculture College #3, Thai Nguyen
College of Industrial Technology, Thai Nguyen
Geology and Mining College, Pho Yen
Medical College of Viet Bac Region, Thai Nguyen
Teachers' College of Viet Bac Region, Thai Nguyen

HAIPHONG

Maritime Navigation College, Cau Dat
River Transport College, Cau Tre

PHU KHANH

Fishery and Sea Products College, Nhatrang

HA BAC

Agriculture College #4, Viet Yen district
Physical Training and Sports College, Tu Son district

HA SON BINH

Law College, Thuong Tin district
Telecommunications College, Mo, Hadong

QUANG NINH

Forestry College, Dong Trieu

CAN THO

Can Tho University, Hau Giang province

DALAT

Dalat University, Lam Dong province

QUINHON

Quinhon Teachers' College, Nghia Binh province

NGHE TINH

Vinh Teachers' College, Vinh

BUON ME THUOT

University of Tay Nguyen, Dac Lac province

BANKS OF VIETNAM

Bank for Foreign Investment and Reconstruction
10 Phan Huy Chu
Hanoi

Savings Bank for Socialism
7 Le Lai
Hanoi
   A national campaign encourages citizens to deposit a proportion of their earnings in savings accounts.

Vietbank (State Bank of Vietnam)
49 Ly Thai To
Hanoi
   Vietbank is Vietnam's currency-issuing central bank. It supervises all foreign-currency transactions and has over 500 branches throughout the country.

Vietcombank (Foreign Trade Bank)
47/49 Ly Thai To
Hanoi
   Negotiates transactions in foreign currencies. This bank has five branches in other cities.

Ho Chi Minh City Bank of Industry and Commerce
   Newly established bank in Ho Chi Minh City authorized to han-

dle joint ventures with foreigners, personal savings and loans and to invest in export companies.

Foreign banks:

Indovina. (Joint venture between Indonesia's Summa Group and Vietnam's Foreign Trade Bank). Located in building of Hong Kong Shanghai Bank's former Saigon Branch.

Banque Indosuez. Ho Chi Minh City

VIETNAM FOREIGN TRADE OFFICES

Vietcochamber (Chamber of Commerce)
33 Ba Trieu
Hanoi
Tel. 52961
Telex 4264

Provides information about and encourages the development of commercial relations between Vietnamese companies and foreign companies. It also organizes trade fairs abroad. A branch office is located in Ho Chi Minh City.

Vietcochamber oversees the work of the following located at the same address:

Foreign Trade Arbitration Committee
Marine Arbitration Committee
Vinexad (Exhibition and Public Relations Agency)

In addition, Vietcochamber is associated with:

Vinacontrol (State Inspection Company)
96 Yet Kieu
Hanoi

Controls quality and quantity of imports and exports through branches in main seaports.

IMPORT-EXPORT AGENCIES

NHATRANG

Centimex (South Central Export-Import Co.)
48 Tran Phu
Nhatrang

Controls imports and exports for the five provinces of South Central Vietnam.

HANOI

Agrexport Agricultural Products
6 Trang Tien

Animex (Livestock and Poultry)
33 Ba Trieu

Artexport Handicrafts and Art Objects
31-33 Ngo Quyen

Barotex (Bamboo and Rattan)
37 Ly Thuong Kiet

Coalimex (Coal)
47 Quang Trung

Confectimex (Foreign Trade Co. for Clothing Industry)
25 Ba Trieu

Constrexim (Construction Materials)
37 Le Dai Hanh

Intimex (Foreign Trade Enterprise)
96 Tran Hung Dao

Machinoimport (Machinery)
8 Trang Thi

Mecanimex (Mechanical Products)
54 Hai Ba Trung

Minexport Minerals
35 Hai Ba Trung

Naforimex (Forest and Produce)
19 Ba Trieu

Petrovietnam (Oil and Gas)
80 Nguyen Du

Technimex (Technology)
39 Tran Hung Dao

Techoimport (Equipment Import)
16/18 Trang Thi

Textimex (Textiles)
25 Ba Trieu

Tocontap (Sundries)
36 Ba Trieu

Vegetexco (Vegetables and Fruit)
46 Ngo Quyen

Chartering and Ship Brokerage Agency
74 Nguyen Du

Vietrans (Transporting and Warehousing Agency)
13 Ly Nam De

Vinaphim (Film Service)
73 Nguyen Trai

Vinalimex (Luxury Items, Food Products, Liqueurs, and Cigarettes)
63 Ly Thai To

Xunhasaba (Books and Periodicals)
32 Hai Ba Trung

HO CHI MINH CITY

Rubexim (Rubber)
64 Truong Dinh

Pectechim (Petroleum)
72 Xo Viet Nghe Tinh

Seaprodex (Sea Products)
2/6 Dong Khoi

Veitronimex (Electronics)
74/76 Nguyen Hue

Vimedimex (Medical Products)
34 Nguyen Hue
and 246 Cong Quynh

Vinafood (Export and Import of Food Products)
24 Vo Van Tan

SELECTED VIETNAM FRIENDSHIP ASSOCIATIONS IN WESTERN COUNTRIES

Australia-Vietnam Society, Canberra Branch
O'Connor ACT
Australia

British-Vietnam Association
Joan Yuille
52 St. John's Park
Blackheath, London SE3 7JP
Great Britain

Canadian Aid for Vietnam Civilians
Box 2543
Vancouver,
Canada V6B 3W8

AAFV
Mme. Françoise Direr
37 Rue Ballu
75009 Paris
France

Vietnam Bulletin
Maarten Van Dulleman
Postbus 715
1000 AS Amsterdam
Netherlands

US Committee for Scientific Cooperation with Vietnam
% Dr. Judith L. Ladinsky
University of Wisconsin-Madison
101 Bradley Building
1300 University Avenue
Madison, WI 53706
USA

US/VN Friendship-Aid Association of Southern California
P.O. Box 453
Murietta, CA 92362
USA

US-Vietnam Friendship Association and Newsletter
P.O. Box 5043
San Francisco, CA 94101
USA

Orderly Departure
Program

When the government of South Vietnam fell to the Communists in April 1975, 150,000 people fled the country. Over the next few years more Vietnamese left their homeland, mainly illegally and by boat. The volatile political atmosphere of Vietnam in 1978 and 1979 was marked by another massive exodus in which many people drowned, starved or were preyed upon by pirates in the open sea.

The need to establish a safe means of relocating from Vietnam became apparent to international observers. In 1979, a Memorandum of Understanding between Vietnam and the United Nations High Commission on Refugees (UNHCR) established Orderely Departure, a program through which Vietnamese seeking familiy reunion, or who were of special interest to the resettlement countries, could relocate safely and legally to more than 40 receiving countries.

Since 1979, the US Orderly Departure Program (US ODP) has brought over 60,000 people from Vietnam into America. In October 1987 a bilateral agreement was made between the US and Vietnam which has sped up the processing of Amerasians (defined below). The US ODP program is staffed by employees of the US government and the International Committee for Emigration and Migration (ICEM) with its office located at the American Embassy in Bangkok.

There are three categories of eligibility for applicants to the US ODP program:

1. Family reunification. The US accepts applications for family reunification by spouses, children, parents, and siblings of individuals residing in the US.
2. Amerasians. An Amerasian is (as defined by a 1987 US law) a person born in Vietnam after January 1962 and before January 1, 1976, and fathered by a citizen of the US. Note: By this definition the youngest Amerasian is 14 years old in January 1990. Amerasians are not required to produce documents proving this parent relationship. It is only necessary that the facts be established to the satisfaction of a consular officer of the ODP program at the face-to-face interview. Either Cauca-

ORDERLY DEPARTURE PROGRAM

sian or Black (Afro-American) features of an applicant is often regarded as enough evidence of American paternity.

One of the most important agencies that operates a registry of fathers seeking their children as well as children who have written to find their fathers is:

Pearl S. Buck Foundation, Inc.
Green Hills Farm
P.O. Box 181
Perkasie, PA 18944
tel. (215) 249-0100

3. Individuals closely associated with US policies and programs. Eligible applicants in this group include former US government direct-hire employees; employees of US firms or organizations; and former personnel of the Republic of Vietnam's government and Armed Services who received US combat awards, were trainied under US auspices, or were involved in work intimately allied with the US in Vietnam. Spouses, unmarried children and others dependent on US ODP applicants may apply to accompany them.

APPLICATION PROCESS

A relative in the US who wants to bring over a family member files an Affidavit of Relationship (AOR) plus an application for family reunification.

A non-relative sponsor can file an Immigrant Visa Petition on behalf of an applicant (form 1–130). This application is forwarded to the US ODP in Bangkok which assigns a file number to the case. The sponsor promises financial support of the applicant in the US.

Concerned individuals who are interested in assisting or sponsoring families not related to them should contact one of the voluntary agencies in the US that administers the paperwork. A number of church groups perform this function, including:

Church World Service
Immigration and Refugee Program
4475 Riverside Drive
New York, NY 10115
tel. (212)870-2078

United States Catholic Conference (USCC)
Migration and Refugee Services
920 Broadway, 8th Floor
New York, NY 10010
tel (212) 460-8077

Lutheran Immigration and Refugee Service (LIRS)
Lutheran Council in the USA
360 Park Avenue South
New York, NY 10010
tel (212) 532-6350

Persons wishing to sponsor or assist in the resettlement of Amerasians and their families should contact Interaction at the address below for the names of resettlement agencies.

Interaction
200 Park Avenue South
New York, NY 10003
tel (212) 777-8210

PRIORITIES

A refugee is defined as one who "has a well-founded fear of persecution" should they remain in the country. An immigrant is a person whose wish to relocate is based on motive other than fear of persecution. The number of immigrants accepted into the US each year is greater than the number of refugees allowed under the law. Applicants are reviewed by US ODP in Bangkok with this in mind. The US ODP program reserves the limited number of refugee spaces for those who have reason to fear political persecution.

Applications containing current Immigrant Visa Petitions, verified US employment or reeducation internment of specified durations, or evidence of American paternity are accorded top priority. In addition, special handling is given to expedite the movement of American citizens and medical emergencies. An Amerasian is a US citizen if an American father acknowledges the child as his. The US citizen father must establish a blood relationship as well as a legal relationship to the applicant. In addition to acknowledging paternity, the US father must agree to provide financial support until the child is 18 years of age.

For Amerasian youths who do not know their fathers, the face-to-face interview establishes the physical appearance of mixed racial parentage which will suffice, in many cases, to establish an American father. These Amerasian youths are not, however, processed as speedily as American citizens.

Family reunification cases are reviewed when applicants have current or near-current Immigrant Visa Petitions, and would be able to travel to the US as immigrants rather than refugees.

Further information concerning immigration may be obtained from:

US Department of State
Consular Services
Main State Building
Washington, DC 20520
tel. (202) 647-1488

LETTERS OF INTRODUCTION

The next step involves sending Letters of Introduction (LOI) by the ODP program to the Vietnamese Foreign Ministry Office. This letter indicates which applicants are eligible for further consideration through an in-country interview. LOI are presented by applicants to the Vietnamese authorities as their first step in the process. The applicant in Vietnam fills out forms with their local security office which must first approve and forward the application to the Foreign Interest Section, which, in turn, sends the application to Hanoi, Consular Section, Ministry of Foreign Affairs for final consent. Interested parties may contact the Saigon office at:

Ministry of Interior
(Foreign Interest Section)
335 Bui Thi Xuan Street
District One
Ho Chi Minh City

The Vietnamese government draws up a list of persons who are permitted to be interviewed by ODP officials. When an applicant's name appears on that list, the ODP requests that an interview be scheduled.

Sponsors and anchor relatives will be notified if further action or documentation is required from them. There is no US ODP office in Vietnam; interviews are nevertheless held in Vietnam by members of the ODP program who fly in from Bangkok for two-week stints of interviewing. The final judgement as to whether the applicant qualifies for ODP status takes place at the interview.

MEDICAL EXAM

Once the application has been approved, the individual must pass medical clearance. The results of a physical examination are reviewed by a physician on the staff of the Intergovernmental Committee for Migration. If there are no medical contraindications, the individual is placed on a roster of eligible persons; the list of names is then sent to the emigration authorities in Vietnam where travel arrangements are made for the applicant's flight to Bangkok. The Thai government requires two weeks' notice of arrival and the ODP needs the lead time to secure bookings to final destination points. At this point, Amerasians are assigned to a sponsoring voluntary agency to assist in their resettlement.

Immigrants travel directly to the US. A majority of refugees and Amerasians and their families are sent for a six-month period of cultural orientation and language classes in the Philippines before continuing to the US. Refugee travel arrangements are made by the International Organization for Migration; travel expenses are expected to be reimbursed later by refugees once they are settled. Immigrants are required to prepay their travel and visa fees.

SPEEDING UP THE PROCESS

There are many reasons why the process from application to exit takes up so much time. The primariy reason is that, although the US ODP has been processing paperwork of applications for many years, it is only since September 1987 that in-country interviews, where the final adjudication is made, have been taking place.

When attempting to speed up the processing or inquiring about the status of an application, be sure to place the ODP case number on every piece of correspondence. It might also be helpful to mail two copies of every letter, each on different days. If one letter gets lost the other will be received, and if the office gets both, the officials there will know there is someone intensely interested in the applicant's situation. Be sure to notify the ODP of changes in address and phone number.

Orderly Departure Program
Panjabhum Building
127 South Sathorn Road
Bangkok 10120
Thailand
tel. (96) 02-252-5040

UN High Commission on Refugees—Branch Office
PO Box 2-121 Rajdamnern
Bangkok 10200
Thailand

American fathers seeking information about Amerasian children should contact the ODP in Bangkok through:

Orderly Departure Program
American Embassy
Box 58
APO San Francisco
96346-0001

Note: In March 1989, Thailand, Malaysia, Singapore, Indonesia, Brunei, and the Philippines, which form the membership of the Association of Southeast Asian Nations (ASEAN), ceased offering asylum to individuals illegally leaving Vietnam. ASEAN encourages voluntary repatriation of refugees (from Vietnam, Cambodia, and Laos) already living in the make-shift border camps in Thailand, Cambodia, Malaysia, and Hong Kong.

PHOTOGRAPHIC CREDITS

Len Ackland: 209; **Terry H. Anderson:** 280; **Joe Connors:** 374, 381, 382; **John Everingham:** 304; **Fred Fulton:** 155; **Fredric M. Kaplan:** 67, 71, 74, 76, 80, 222, 224, 354; **Hal Katoaka:** 19, 24, 36, 38, 84, 91, 93, 101, 103, 115, 122, 124, 129, 186, 193, 241, 249, 322, 325, 334, 351; **Mike Miller:** 315; **Hugh Swift:** 239, 268, 269, 274, 348, 352; **Library of Congress:** 30, 106; **Vietnam Pictorial:** 262, 319; **Vietnam Pictorial—Le Kaanh Chi:** 112; **Vietnam Tourism:** 17; **Jim Watson:** 146, 223, 243, 281, 338. All other photos are those of the author.

INDEX

In this index the Vietnamese letters Ð and D are not distinguished.

India, (cont.)
   of, 192; gift of tree from, 225; rela-
   tions with Vietnam, 140; petroleum
   exploration, 130
Indian traders, 296
Indira Gandi Park, 213
Indochina Museum of Trocadero, 389
Indochina Reconcilation Project, 161
Indochina War, first, 1946–1954, 54–
   59; second, 63–86, 302
Indochinese Communist Party (ICP),
   54, 248
Indochinese Federation, 213
Indochinese Union. See French Indo-
   china Union
Indonesia, 46
Indrapura, 292
Indravarman, 375–376
Industry, 130
Infant mortality, 94
Inflation, 121
Inkslab tower, 159, 210
Insect repellent, 198, 199. See also DDT
Institute of Archaeology, 104
Institute of Folklore, 104
Institute Materia Medica, 98
Institute of Oceanography and Fisheries,
   308
Interflug (East German Airlines), 168;
   schedules 169–170
International Control Commission, 60
International Monetary Fund (IMF),
   121, 138
International Workers' Day. See May
   Day
Investment laws, 126
Iron, 130; craft, 237; tools, 248
Iroquois helicopter, 365
Irrigation, 128, 285. See also Canals;
   Dikes
Islam, 33, 45, 288
Islands, Con Dao, 38; Paracels, 38;
   Spratley, 38
Italy, Vietnamese Embassy in, 165
Itineraries of tours within Vietnam, 166,
   167, 177–182

J

Jackfruit, 195, 350
Jackson, Andrew (US President), 51
Jade Emperor, 154
Japan, 27, 128, 131, 203; Cao Dai cult
   and, 92; ceramics exported to, 115;
   defeat of Russia, 52, 142
Japanese in Vietnam, 54–56, 255, 296–
   297, 332; bridge, 297; headquarters
   of Puppet government, 215; lacquer
   artisans, 114; surrender after World
   War II, 159, 335, 337; Vietnamese
   Embassy in, 165
Jarai ethnic minority, 313
Jasmine tea, 194
Jatakas, 109
Java, 203, 373, 375
Jayavarman II, 373, 375
Jayavarman V, 377
Jayavarman VII, 379, 381, 383
Jesuits, 296
Jetlag, 152
Jewelry, customs declaration of, 177;
   shopping for, 189
Joan of Arc Catholic school, 276
Johnson administration, 73
Johnson, Lyndon Baines (US Presi-
   dent), 71; refuses reelection, 73,
   206, 249, 272
Journals published in Vietnam. See Me-
   dia in Vietnam in appendix
Judicial system, 137
Jumping elephant, 241
JUSPAO (Joint US Public Affairs Of-
   fice), 338

K

Kambuja (ancient name of Cambodia),
   373
Kampuchea, Peoples Republic of, 85,
   121, 122
Kaoupry (wild cow), 130
Karst topography, 261
Kennedy, John, F. (US President), 67,
   68; assassination of, 69
Kent State University Incident, 73

Ha Long Bay, Vietnam Photo by Jane Burrows